Data Mining Trends and Applications in Criminal Science and Investigations

Omowunmi E. Isafiade
University of Cape Town, South Africa

Antoine B. Bagula
University of the Western Cape, South Africa

A volume in the Advances in Data Mining and Database Management (ADMDM) Book Series

Information Science REFERENCE
An Imprint of IGI Global

Published in the United States of America by
Information Science Reference (an imprint of IGI Global)
701 E. Chocolate Avenue
Hershey PA 17033
Tel: 717-533-8845
Fax: 717-533-8661
E-mail: cust@igi-global.com
Web site: http://www.igi-global.com

Library of Congress Cataloging-in-Publication Data

Names: Isafiade, Omowunmi E., 1982- editor. | Bagula, Antoine B., 1960- editor.
Title: Data mining trends and applications in criminal science and investigations / Omowunmi E. Isafiade and Antoine B. Bagula, editors.
Description: Hershey : Information Science Reference, 2016. | Includes bibliographical references and index.
Identifiers: LCCN 2016010961| ISBN 9781522504634 (hardcover) | ISBN 9781522504641 (ebook)
Subjects: LCSH: Criminal investigation--Data processing. | Data mining.
Classification: LCC HV7431 .D364 2016 | DDC 363.250285/6312--dc23 LC record available at https://lccn.loc.gov/2016010961

This book is published in the IGI Global book series Advances in Data Mining and Database Management (ADMDM) (ISSN: 2327-1981; eISSN: 2327-199X)

British Cataloguing in Publication Data
A Cataloguing in Publication record for this book is available from the British Library.

Advances in Data Mining and Database Management (ADMDM) Book Series

ISSN: 2327-1981
EISSN: 2327-199X

Mission

With the large amounts of information available to organizations in today's digital world, there is a need for continual research surrounding emerging methods and tools for collecting, analyzing, and storing data.

The **Advances in Data Mining & Database Management (ADMDM)** series aims to bring together research in information retrieval, data analysis, data warehousing, and related areas in order to become an ideal resource for those working and studying in these fields. IT professionals, software engineers, academicians and upper-level students will find titles within the ADMDM book series particularly useful for staying up-to-date on emerging research, theories, and applications in the fields of data mining and database management.

Coverage

- Data warehousing
- Quantitative Structure–Activity Relationship
- Neural Networks
- Enterprise systems
- Educational Data Mining
- Database Security
- Text Mining
- Data Analysis
- Web-based information systems
- Data quality

IGI Global is currently accepting manuscripts for publication within this series. To submit a proposal for a volume in this series, please contact our Acquisition Editors at Acquisitions@igi-global.com or visit: http://www.igi-global.com/publish/.

The Advances in Data Mining and Database Management (ADMDM) Book Series (ISSN 2327-1981) is published by IGI Global, 701 E. Chocolate Avenue, Hershey, PA 17033-1240, USA, www.igi-global.com. This series is composed of titles available for purchase individually; each title is edited to be contextually exclusive from any other title within the series. For pricing and ordering information please visit http://www.igi-global.com/book-series/advances-data-mining-database-management/37146. Postmaster: Send all address changes to above address.

Titles in this Series

For a list of additional titles in this series, please visit: www.igi-global.com

Intelligent Techniques for Data Analysis in Diverse Settings
Numan Celebi (Sakarya University, Turkey)
Information Science Reference • copyright 2016 • 353pp • H/C (ISBN: 9781522500759) • US $195.00 (our price)

Managing and Processing Big Data in Cloud Computing
Rajkumar Kannan (King Faisal University, Saudi Arabia) Raihan Ur Rasool (King Faisal University, Saudi Arabia) Hai Jin (Huazhong University of Science and Technology, China) and S.R. Balasundaram (National Institute of Technology, Tiruchirappalli, India)
Information Science Reference • copyright 2016 • 307pp • H/C (ISBN: 9781466697676) • US $200.00 (our price)

Handbook of Research on Innovative Database Query Processing Techniques
Li Yan (Nanjing University of Aeronautics and Astronautics, China)
Information Science Reference • copyright 2016 • 625pp • H/C (ISBN: 9781466687677) • US $335.00 (our price)

Handbook of Research on Trends and Future Directions in Big Data and Web Intelligence
Noor Zaman (King Faisal University, Saudi Arabia) Mohamed Elhassan Seliaman (King Faisal University, Saudi Arabia) Mohd Fadzil Hassan (Universiti Teknologi PETRONAS, Malaysia) and Fausto Pedro Garcia Marquez (Campus Universitario s/n ETSII of Ciudad Real, Spain)
Information Science Reference • copyright 2015 • 500pp • H/C (ISBN: 9781466685055) • US $285.00 (our price)

Improving Knowledge Discovery through the Integration of Data Mining Techniques
Muhammad Usman (Shaheed Zulfikar Ali Bhutto Institute of Science and Technology, Pakistan)
Information Science Reference • copyright 2015 • 391pp • H/C (ISBN: 9781466685130) • US $225.00 (our price)

Modern Computational Models of Semantic Discovery in Natural Language
Jan Žižka (Mendel University in Brno, Czech Republic) and František Dařena (Mendel University in Brno, Czech Republic)
Information Science Reference • copyright 2015 • 335pp • H/C (ISBN: 9781466686908) • US $215.00 (our price)

Table of Contents

Section 4
Denial of Service, Cyber-Crime, and Intrusion Detection Management

Detailed Table of Contents

Section 1
Challenges and Existing Strategies in Public Safety and Crime Mining

Omowunmi E. Isafiade, University of Cape Town, South Africa
Antoine Bagula, University of Western Cape, South Africa
Sonia Berman, University of Cape Town, South Africa

The primary role of intelligence organisations and public safety agencies encompasses protecting the lives and property of citizens. However, the urban population growth rate tends to overshadow the available security resources. Thus, the security agencies appear to be more reactive than proactive. Public safety agencies usually have a plethora of under-utilised crime incident reports at their disposal, which if efficiently analysed could reveal some previously unknown useful information. Such information reveals insights into a range of functions in a crime investigation, which can assist in determining criminal trends and in knowledge-driven decision support. This chapter provides an overview of data mining techniques and existing applications used in this domain of interest. Features of existing applications and techniques, such as exploratory basis, model selection, algorithm advancement and result summary, are compared. Future potential of crime data mining, and open research issues, are also discussed.

The importance of data analysis across different domains is growing day by day. This is evident in the fact that crucial information is retrieved through data analysis, using different available tools. The usage of data mining as a tool to uncover the nuggets of critical and crucial information is evident in modern day scenarios. This chapter presents a discussion on the usage of data mining tools and techniques in the area of criminal science and investigations. The application of data mining techniques in criminal science help in understanding the criminal psychology and consequently provides insight into effective measures to curb crime. This chapter provides a state-of-the-art report on the research conducted in this domain of interest by using a classification scheme and providing a road map on the usage of various data mining tools and techniques. Furthermore, the challenges and opportunities in the application of data mining techniques in criminal investigation is explored and detailed in this chapter.

Today, the amount of digital data increases exponentially due to the rapid growth of the Internet, mobile, and sensory data. Crime data are arriving from multiple sources and formats. The major challenge for crime analysis is to store, manipulate, manage, and analyze data efficiently. To gain useful insight from a great amount of raw data, visual analytics techniques have been drawn attention to law enforcement agencies and researchers. The visual analytics applications do not erase the need for crime analysts' insight. To make better predictions and smarter decisions, data mining, text mining, information visualization, human-computer interaction, and analytics techniques are important to explore. This book chapter provides an overview of different types of crime data, discusses how to analyze and visualize different types of data, and explores popular visualization toolkits that have been used for crime analysis.

Given a set of crime locations, a statistically significant crime hotspot is an area where the concentration of crimes inside is significantly higher than outside. The motivation of crime hotspot detection is twofold: detecting crime hotspots to focus the deployment of police enforcement and predicting the potential residence of a serial criminal. Crime hotspot detection is computationally challenging due to the difficulty of enumerating all potential hotspot areas, selecting an interest measure to compare these with the overall crime intensity, and testing for statistical significance to reduce chance patterns. This chapter focuses on statistical significant crime hotspots. First, the foundations of spatial scan statistics and its applications (i.e. SaTScan) to circular hotspot detection are reviewed. Next, ring-shaped hotspot detection is introduced. Third, linear hotspot detection is described since most crimes occur along a road network. The chapter concludes with future research directions in crime hotspot detection.

Current generation criminal justice relies mostly on manual procedures and processes which are time-consuming and error-prone. A polygraph test consists of only "yes" or "no" questions and depends several physiological responses in subjects. It's effectiveness and accuracy have been questioned due to the possibility of swaying the examiner by individuals that are capable of controlling their physical reactions in order to defeat the lie detection exercise. The criminal justice of the future is expected to be empowered by the most modern information and communication technologies to provide various participants in the justice system with a rich set of services such as virtual court presence and hearing participation through visual sensor networks. This chapter revisits the issue of deception detection by proposing visual data mining as a non-invasive alternative to deception detection in next generation criminal justice. Image processing and machine learning techniques are used to accurately detect facial micro-expressions which have been shown to be strong indicators of deception.

Section 3
Forensics, Suspect Modeling, and Intelligence Gathering

Predictive policing (Pp) relates to identifying potentially related offences, similar criminal attributes and potential criminal activity, in order to take actionable measures in deterring crime. Similarly, Legal Decision Making Process (LDMP) considers some level of probabilistic reasoning in deriving logical evidence from crime incidents. Bayesian Networks (BN) have great potential in contributing to the area of Pp and LDMP. Being based on probabilistic reasoning, they can assess uncertainty in crime related attributes and derive useful evidence based on crime incident observations or evidential data. For example, in a particular context of crime investigation, BN based inference could help collect useful evidence about a crime scenario or incident. Such evidence promotes effective legal decision making process and can assist public safety and security agencies in allocating resources in an optimal fashion. This chapter reports on various application areas of BN in the crime domain, highlights the potential of BN and presents "thought experiments" on how offender characteristics could be modelled for decision support in legal matters. The chapter further reports on the performance of empirical analysis in the legal decision support process, in order to elucidate the practical relevance and challenges of using BN in the crime domain.

Healthcare applications are increasingly being used due to the safety and convenience brought to patients' life and healthcare professionals, respectively. Nevertheless, the use of weak authentication techniques and vulnerable communication protocols makes these applications threatened by specific classes of security attacks and e-crimes. The latter threaten the privacy, the safety and even the life of the persons using these applications, due to the fact that they handle sensitive information and implement complex and critical features. This chapter focuses on postmortem investigation of crimes on healthcare applications. After classifying crimes targeting healthcare applications, the requirements for the design of appropriate postmortem investigation system, are discussed. A literature review of proposals related to the investigation of crimes in healthcare applications together with a discussion of the advanced issues are also provided in this chapter.

This chapter provides a review about the usefulness of applying data mining techniques to detect intrusion within dynamic environments and its contribution in digital investigation. Numerous applications and models are described based on data mining analytics. The chapter addresses also different requirements that should be fulfilled to efficiently perform cyber-crime investigation based on data mining analytics. It states, at the end, future research directions related to cyber-crime investigation that could be investigated and presents new trends of data mining techniques that deal with big data to detect attacks.

Providing a safe environment for juveniles and children in online social networks is considered as one of the major factors of improving public safety. Due to the prevalence of the online conversations, mitigating the undesirable effects of child abuse in cyber space has become inevitable. Using automatic ways to combat this kind of crime is challenging and demands efficient and scalable data mining techniques. The problem can be casted as a combination of textual preprocessing in data/text mining and pattern classification in machine learning. This chapter covers different data mining methods including preprocessing, feature extraction and the

Foreword

Data mining is at the cross roads of several computer science disciplines such as database systems and machine learning. The ultimate goal is to extract meaningful information from large data sets and put this information to effective use for knowledge support. The potential applications cover all aspects of business and everyday life. An archetype is public safety. Public safety and other law enforcement agencies often seek to identify smart ways or effective strategies to deter crime. Yes, indeed data mining could play a critical role in public safety application by extracting meaningful information (smart statistics) from large data sets and putting this information to productive use in criminal science and investigation.

Criminal science and investigation deal not only with ways and means for preventing crimes but also with ways and means for proving the guilt (or innocence) of suspected criminals. Large data sets do exist today on crimes. Classical examples are the national criminal databases. However, it is challenging, tedious, error-prone and resource consuming for public safety agencies to analyse these data sets using manual or conventional approaches. Therefore, meaningful information automatically extracted from these data sets using data mining techniques is certainly a vital input to crime pattern analysis, which contributes not only to crime solving, but also to (proactive) crime prevention solutions. Accordingly, it makes sense to understand existing solutions and explore alternative or unconventional approaches to inventing solutions to deterring crime across different domains.

The collection of chapters offered by this edited book, written by internationally recognized experts, discusses selected issues in this very broad area of data mining and criminal science and investigation. All chapters were subjected to a peer-review process. The book comprises three sections and each section is made up of several chapters. The first section reviews the challenges and existing solutions in this domain. It tackles both the data mining for crime situation recognition and the frameworks for criminal science and analysis. This is followed by a section on spatial analysis, visual analytics, hotspots and visualization. The third section is devoted to forensics, suspect modelling and intelligence gathering. Denial of service, cyber-crime and intrusion detection management are discussed in the fourth and last section.

It is worth mentioning that the challenges related to public safety are magnified in developing or emerging countries such as in Africa, where crime rates are relatively high and resources for preventing them and proving guilt or innocence of suspected criminals relatively low. This makes the two co-editors (Omowunmi E. Isafiade and Antoine B. Bagula) uniquely qualified for collecting and editing the chapters of this book. They are academics in South Africa, University of Cape Town and Western Cape University (respectively) and are deeply involved in research on data mining in criminal science and investigation, research in which they factor the challenging local issues.

This book should be read by advanced public safety practitioners, crime analysts and researchers working on innovative crime prevention challenges. From a researcher's viewpoint, the book chapters provide a sound foundation to understand the scope of work in this domain of interest. The book can as well provide practitioners with a working knowledge on existing challenges and viable solutions.

Roch Glitho
Concordia University, Canada

Roch Glitho *holds a Ph.D. (Tekn.Dr.) in tele-informatics (Royal Institute of Technology, Stockholm, Sweden) and M.Sc. degrees in business economics (University of Grenoble, France), pure mathematics (University Geneva, Switzerland), and computer science (University of Geneva). He is an Associate Professor of networking and telecommunications at Concordia University Canada where he leads the telecommunication service engineering research laboratory (http://users.encs.concordia.ca/~tse/). He is also an Adjunct Professor at several other universities including Telecom Sud Paris and the University of the Western Cape– South Africa. In the past he has worked in industry for almost a quarter of a century and has held several senior technical positions at LM Ericsson in Sweden and Canada (e.g. expert, principal engineer, senior specialist). In the past he has also served as IEEE Communications Society distinguished lecturer, Editor-In-Chief of IEEE Communications Magazine and Editor- In-Chief of IEEE Communications Surveys & Tutorials.*

Preface

There is not a crime, there is not a dodge, there is not a trick, there is not a swindle, there is not a vice which does not live by secrecy. – Joseph Pulitzer

The data mining field is receiving a significant attention in today's information rich society, where data is available from different sources and formats, in large volumes, and no longer constitutes a bottleneck for knowledge acquisition. This rich information has paved the way for novel areas of research, particularly in the crime data analysis realm. Further, the potential usefulness of data mining in various domains has resulted in a holistic development of useful analytics for knowledge support in the crime data analysis domain. Data mining approaches, involving techniques at the intersection of machine learning, artificial intelligence, statistics and database systems, have proven to be valuable tools in discovering interesting, non-trivial and potentially useful information, which can assist in decision support, crime investigation, prediction and control. The importance of data mining is clearly evident in the plethora of least utilised crime incident reports archived by the law enforcement agencies and the emerging dynamics of offenders behaviour in today's world, across different domains of life. However, with the increasing nature of crime data on a daily basis, due to the high crime committing trend, historical data available on repositories and heterogeneous sources of crime information by voluntary witnesses must be efficiently and maximally utilised for knowledge discovery in combating crime. Therefore, it makes sense to explore existing and unconventional approaches to analyzing crime data across different domains in knowledge-driven decision support.

This edited book, titled *Data Mining Trends and Applications in Criminal Science and Investigation*, emerges as a result of the crucial need for improving public safety in different domains and parts of the world. It is particularly aimed at resource constrained environments such as in developing nations, where crime is increasing at an alarming rate across different domains of life and impeding economic growth. By resource constrained environments, we mean scenarios where crime intelligence experts are limited and not enough technological solutions are put in place to meet up with operational safety needs and citizens' security. For example, where the quantity of assets or population of citizens' to be protected significantly outnumbers the available public safety or security personnel, it becomes very difficult to achieve and sustain a safe society or community. However, it is profoundly liberating to discover that the use of "smart statistics" (Milgram, 2013), which can be derived through crime data mining approaches could assist in making optimal use of these limited resources and consequently counter some of the safety challenges faced in resource constrained environments. In particular, of interest is the quest to understand the nature, scope and level of impact of existing crime mining solutions across different domains and develop new paradigms for a more inclusive solution. This will provide new insights that will assist to derive interventions to tackle emerging dynamic scenarios of criminal activities. Further, this book presents emerging issues, challenges and management strategies in public safety and crime control development across different domains. These domains encompass health-care, Internet-of-things and public safety.

CHALLENGES AND OPPORTUNITIES

Crime is an anti-social behaviour which costs our society greatly in several ways. Therefore, deterring crime is a top priority for decision makers, security and public agencies, in realising a sustainable "safe and smart" city. While in recent times there have been a vast amount of techniques and solutions emerging in a bid to tackle crime, these appear to be insufficient because despite the vast resources allocated to crime, people still fall victim of crime. Moreover, offenders and crime perpetrators are devising various means to subdue existing solutions, and as such constantly inventing dynamic ways to perpetuate crime without being suspected, apprehended or convicted of any crime. In addition, these crimes are committed across different domains of life, such as in health-care, public safety, business, information and communication technology, and needs to be tackled using a more proactive (tactical and strategic) approach.

The International Association of Crime Analysts (IACA) presents various ways by which crime patterns are conceptualized for tactical and/or strategic analysis (IACA, 2011), such as crime spree, crime series, and hot-spots, to mention a few. In the field of crime data analysis, the trend in crime spree, crime series, co-location or similarity crimes, where a set of offenders repeatedly and dynamically commit related crimes is still under exploration, among others. It is important to note that while these patterns are explained individually, they sometimes interconnect as clearly expressed and/or implied by the various content of this book. More generally, crimes are committed within a space-time relation. A proper understanding of these crime patterns and criminal activities is crucial as it will help public safety and security agencies focus resources to achieve crime reduction and criminal apprehension targets. There are several advantages in using data mining techniques in criminal science and investigation and understanding crime situation using "smart statistics". Some of the advantages include the fact that:

- Deriving reliable crime-situation information, through crime data mining approaches, will assist decision makers, public safety, and security agencies in knowledge driven decision support. For example, such information will assist them in distinguishing between normal and crime prone locations, identifying patrol boundaries, better attribution of past crime, apprehension of prime suspects and determination of mitigation priorities. A direct consequence of this would be the realisation of the optimal utilization of the limited available resources, where it matters most, across different domains to achieve safety and crime reduction targets.
- Timely and accurate knowledge of crime situation creates new insights into true patterns. This will help to reduce the prevalence of criminal activities and inform effective safety policies that need to be implemented, in order to subsequently deter crime.

Therefore, crime analysts, decision makers, public safety and security agencies alike owe it to themselves to understand the nature, scope and limitations of existing crime solutions and learn new ways to confront crime challenges in support of a more proactive law enforcement, citizen security, and intelligence operation. This book provides the opportunity to understand timely and effective intervention strategies and the deep applicability of data mining techniques in criminal sciences and investigation across different domains.

ORGANIZATION OF THE BOOK

This book presents 10 chapters contributed from 30 authors and co-authors from 6 countries and region: Canada, India, Iran, South Africa, Tunisia and USA. It includes quality chapters that presents scientific concepts, framework and ideas on data mining trends and applications in criminal science and investigations across different domains, such as public safety, health-care, networking, Internet-of-things, intrusion and fraud detection. The Editorial Advisory Board and expert reviewers have confirmed the high caliber of chapters through careful refereeing of the submitted papers. For the purpose of coherence, we have organised the chapters with respect to similarity of topic addressed. The topics addressed range from crime mining issues pertaining to public safety improvements, hotspots and visual analytics, cyber-crime, intrusion detection, denial of service, juvenile abuse identification, suspect modeling and analysis of crime scenarios.

Section 1: Challenges and Existing Strategies in Public Safety and Crime Mining

Chapter 1, "On the Advancement of Using Data Mining for Crime Situation Recognition: A Comparative Review" by O. Isafiade, A. Bagula and S. Berman, presents details on existing crime data mining techniques and solutions, associated challenges and the exciting avenues that could be explored for future research. It presents the three most common strategies for exploring crime data mining, and discusses ways of integrating crime data sources for tactical crime analysis. This chapter pave the way for the discussion in Chapter 2 on the different research work that have been carried out in the field of criminal science and the kinds of knowledge support discovered from the various studies.

Chapter 2, by M. Goyal, V. Bhatnagar and A. Jain, presents a classification framework for criminal science and investigation and further presents a road map regarding the usage of various data mining tools and techniques. This chapter further elaborates on the application of data mining techniques in criminal science and investigation across different domains.

Section 2: HotSpot, Spatial, and Visual Analytics

In Chapter 3, C. Ku, A. Iriberri and G. K. Jena present a detailed information on visual analytics for crime analysis and decision support. They provide various visual representations that have been used to reveal the meaning of crime data, and visualization tools that have been used in the analysis of crime data, which allows four types of data analysis; these are statistical, textual, multimedia, and spatio-temporal. Example cases where these types of analysis have been used and the toolkits that support these analyses are also reported. Furthermore, the chapter reports on how the combination of visualization techniques with text and data mining seems to offer added benefits in crime data analysis.

E. Eftelioglu, S. Shekhar, and X. Tang present an important discussion and analysis in Chapter 4 on a computational perspective to crime hotspot analysis and detection. They focus on statistically significant hotspot detection techniques that aim to remove chance patterns, using spatial scan statistics. Three representative techniques for discovering significant crime hotspots are presented and each technique is illustrated using sample case studies on real crime datasets.

In Chapter 5, M. Ghaziasgar, N. De La Cruz, A. Bagula, and J. Connan present visual data mining as a great opportunity for criminal investigation. The chapter investigates the automatic detection of micro-expressions from a video feed using Local Binary Patterns (LBPs) as a facial feature descriptor and Support Vector Machines (SVMs) as a classifier into one of two categories, namely: "micro-expression" and "neutral expression". Facial micro-expressions have been reported to be strong indicators of deception, giving rise to the possibility of detecting deception automatically. The chapter revisits the issue of deception detection by proposing visual data mining (VDM) as a non-invasive alternative to deception detection in next generation criminal justice.

Section 3: Forensics, Suspect Modeling, and Intelligence Gathering

O. Isafiade, A. Bagula and S. Berman provide an insightful discussion and analysis in Chapter 6 on the use of Bayesian Network (BN) in Crime Suspect Modeling and Legal Decision Support. The chapter describes the value of reasoning under uncertainty in legal decision making and evidence gathering. It describes how BN based inference could help to collect useful evidence about a crime scenario in the absence of domain experts and the process of sentiment-free candidate generation and rules extraction for offenders. It further reports on the performance of empirical analysis in the legal decision support process, in order to elucidate the practical relevance and challenges of using BN in the crime domain.

In Chapter 7, N. Ellouze, S. Rekhis and N. Boudriga present the issue of Forensic Investigation of digital crimes in the healthcare domain. This domain is of particular interest due to the fact that advances in Information and Communications Technologies have led to the release of a wide set of health-care applications and these applications exhibit significant security weaknesses, which include the use of weak authentication techniques and the lack of appropriate security mechanisms. The chapter focuses on postmortem investigation of crimes on healthcare applications. After classifying crimes targeting health-care applications, the requirements for the design of an appropriate postmortem investigation system are discussed. A literature review of proposals related to the investigation of crimes in healthcare applications together with a discussion of the advanced issues in this domain then follows.

Section 4: Denial of Service, Cyber-Crime, and Intrusion Detection Management

In Chapter 8, B. Fessi, Y. Djemaiel and N. Boudriga provides a useful discussion on data mining techniques to detect intrusion within dynamic environments and its contribution in digital investigation. The chapter also presents different requirements that should be fulfilled to efficiently perform cyber-crime investigation based on data mining analytics.

M. Keyvanpour, M. Ebrahimi and N. G Nayebi, Olga Ormandjieva and Y. Suen, in Chapter 9, have capably considered improving public safety by providing a safe environment for juveniles and children in online social networks through the automatic identification of online predators. The prevalence of the online conversations have motivated the need for mitigating the undesirable effects of child abuse in cyber space. Two major on-line predator identification problems in which data mining plays an important role are:

1. Detecting predators, and
2. Visualizing and analyzing predator criminal networks.

The problem is casted as a combination of textual preprocessing in data or text mining and pattern classification in machine learning. The chapter further presents a discussion on classification algorithms in the domain of automated predator identification.

In Chapter 10, P. Machaka, A. McDonald and F. Nelwamondo have effectively perused state-of-the-art discussion on data ming techniques for distributed denial of service (DDoS) attack detection. The chapter elaborates on various techniques by which DoS attack is perpetuated and reports on the data mining techniques that are used to combat and detect these attacks, their advantages and disadvantages are explored. Furthermore, the characteristics and pervasiveness of DDoS attacks, alongside motives, mechanisms and techniques used to execute a DDoS attack, are discussed.

Omowunmi E. Isafiade
University of Cape Town, South Africa

Antoine B. Bagula
University of the Western Cape, South Africa

REFERENCES

International Association of Crime Analysts (IACA). (2011). *Crime pattern definitions for tactical analysis*. Standards, Methods, & Technology (SMT) Committee White Paper-2011-01. Retrieved from http://www.iaca.net/Publications/Whitepapers/iacawp_2011_01_crime_patterns.pdf

Milgram, A. (2013). Why smart statistics are the key to fighting crime. *TED Video*. Retrieved from https://www.ted.com/talks/anne_milgram_why_smart_statistics_are_the_key_to_fighting_crime

Acknowledgment

A special thanks to a number of people without whom we would not have been able to put the content of the book together. These include our editorial advisory board, which has been very supportive, and other expert and committed reviewers. On average, we had at least 2 reviews per chapter. We are very grateful to the many external reviewers who have assisted "in the background," and who made sure that we adhered to our schedule, provided valuable feedback, fueled our explorations, and encouraged this endeavor.

We would like to thank the large number of authors who have contributed their work to this book, for their insights, creativity, and willingness to craft their ideas in such a manner that resulted in an integrated content. While we were unable to accommodate every submission, we hope that the reviews would serve as a helpful guide to other potential contributors.

Section 1
Challenges and Existing Strategies in Public Safety and Crime Mining

Chapter 1

On the Advancement of Using Data Mining for Crime Situation Recognition: A Comparative Review

Omowunmi E. Isafiade
University of Cape Town, South Africa

Antoine Bagula
University of Western Cape, South Africa

Sonia Berman
University of Cape Town, South Africa

ABSTRACT

The primary role of intelligence organisations and public safety agencies encompasses protecting the lives and property of citizens. However, the urban population growth rate tends to overshadow the available security resources. Thus, the security agencies appear to be more reactive than proactive. Public safety agencies usually have a plethora of under-utilised crime incident reports at their disposal, which if efficiently analysed could reveal some previously unknown useful information. Such information reveals insights into a range of functions in a crime investigation, which can assist in determining criminal trends and in knowledge-driven decision support. This chapter provides an overview of data mining techniques and existing applications used in this domain of interest. Features of existing applications and techniques, such as exploratory basis, model selection, algorithm advancement and result summary, are compared. Future potential of crime data mining, and open research issues, are also discussed.

DOI: 10.4018/978-1-5225-0463-4.ch001

1. INTRODUCTION

Increased violent crime is becoming a threat all around the world, including South Africa (Republic of South Africa. South African Police Service, 2011). As a result, the central role of public safety authorities has been channelled toward eradicating or deterring such violent crime. More often than not, this is attributed to the urban population growth rate, that is rapid urbanisation. Figure 1 reveals a bar graph of the urban population growth rate in South Afric.a Furthermore, rapid urbanisation has been identified as a trend that would continue into the next decade (Chartered Financial Analyst Institute, 2013). While crime may not necessarily increase exponentially with a nation's population, the total number of crimes can be contemplated to increase as the population increases. Figure 2 presents an over-crowded community that is highly susceptible to increased criminal activity. Hence, deterring crime becomes an important top priority for realising a sustainable "safe and smart" city in any nation. Consequently, proactive measures must be put in place in anticipation of an escalation of crime activities.

A smart city is one that strategically utilizes many smart factors such as Information and Communication Technology (ICT) to increase the city's sustainable growth and strengthen city functions, while promoting citizens' happiness and wellness (Hafedh *et al*, 2012). Ensuring sustainable public safety in any country is fundamental to a "safe and smart city". Hence, efficient or tactical crime data mining or analysis, prediction, control and prevention strategies remain a current global issue.

Figure 1. Annual (%) urban population growth rate in South Africa
Republic of South Africa. Trading Economics Report, 2013.

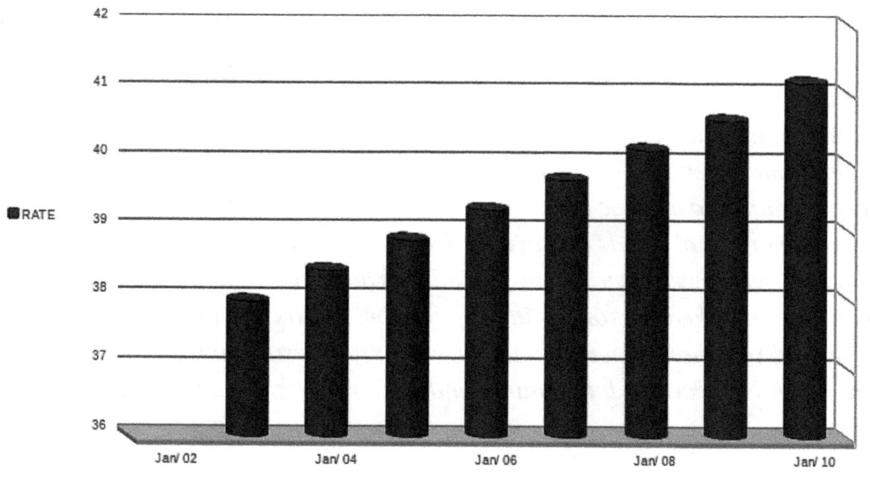

Figure 2. An overcrowded city: a crime prone population

1.1 Trends in Safety and Crime in South Africa

Crime in South Africa has dominated the public agenda (Republic of South Africa. Department of Safety and Security CSIR Pretoria, National Crime Prevention Centre, 2013). According to a victims of crime survey (Republic of South Africa. Statistics SA, 2014), crime in South Africa is increasing at an alarming rate and needs to be curbed. Figure 3 presents a summary of eight years (2004/5 to 2011/12) crime distribution across South Africa. The Government's vision is to invent new strategies for improving public safety (Republic of South Africa. Department of Safety and Security, CSIR Pretoria, National Crime Prevention Centre, 2013).

Figure 3. An eight-year distribution of crime across South Africa
Republic of South Africa. South African Police Service: Crime Statistics Overview, 2013.

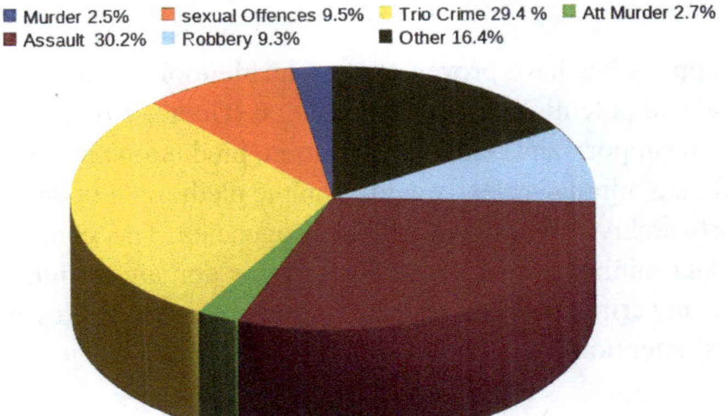

The crime trend has prompted the South African Police Service (SAPS) and policy makers into serious efforts to reduce crime in the Republic. Some of the means of crime reduction they have adopted include the following:

- Improving cooperation from communities through community policing and sector policing.
- Improving the police response period.
- Combating corruption.
- Effectively policing public disorder.

However, most of the strategies adopted by public safety authorities for combating crime, especially in developing nations, are reactive rather than proactive, and can be improved upon using data mining approaches, which entail the discovery of non-trivial, novel and useful patterns from crime data.

Data mining is receiving significant attention in today's information-rich society where data is available in large volumes and can be explored for knowledge-driven decision support. This rich information has paved the way for novel areas of research, particularly in the crime data analysis realm. Crime data mining approaches have proven useful in discovering interesting, non-trivial and potentially useful information, which can assist in decision support, and crime investigation, prediction and control. The true promise of data mining in crime investigation and public safety improvement cannot be overemphasized. With the increase in crime data on a daily basis, and the trend towards increased crime commission, historical data available in repositories and heterogeneous sources of crime information from voluntary witnesses should be explored, so that knowledge discovery can aid in combating crime. Therefore, it makes sense to explore existing and unconventional approaches to analysing crime data in knowledge-driven decision support.

1.2 Contributions and Outline

Data mining approaches have proven to be valuable tools in discovering interesting, non-trivial and potentially useful information (Gupta, 2014), which can assist in legal decision support, and crime investigation, prediction and suppression. The importance of data mining is clearly evident in the plethora of under-utilized crime incident reports archived by law enforcement agencies. This chapter provides an overview of data mining techniques applied in this domain of interest, compares features of existing crime mining applications and presents open research questions for researchers' attention.

To the best of the researchers' knowledge, there is currently no literature review of existing crime data mining applications using the approach adopted here, which compares existing application features such as exploratory basis, model selection, algorithm advancement and result summary. Furthermore, we present a high level tabular representation of the taxonomy of crime data mining tasks (Table 3). The organization of the chapter is as follows: Section 2 presents a brief review of background concepts on crime data mining. Section 3 describes existing techniques or approaches to crime data mining with a comparison of features of existing applications. In section 4, the emerging specifications for data mining tasks as well as open research issues are presented. Section 5 concludes the chapter.

2. BACKGROUND CONCEPTS: OVERVIEW OF CRIME DATA MINING

2.1 Types of Crime and Security Issues

According to Dictionary.com, crime is "an action or an instance of negligence that is deemed injurious to the public welfare or morals or to the interests of the state and that is punishable by law". Surveys and reports have identified crime as a hindrance to socio-economic development. Thus, a number of tactical and strategic mechanisms have been deployed all over the globe, to combat and prevent crime (Republic of South Africa. South African Police Service, 2011). However, the challenge of reducing or combating crime still remains and research continues in this area.

Criminal offences encompass a wide range of activities, ranging from defying a civic duty (a case in point is the refusal to pay tax) to internationally organized criminal offences (such as terrorist attacks). However, these unlawful acts have varying degrees of public influence. Furthermore, these crimes can either be serial or once-off, and can be committed by an individual or a group of individuals. Recognizing the fact that mining crime data can promote the creation and realisation of a "safe and smart" city is an important discovery and "way forward" (Milgram, 2013). Table 1 presents some incipient criminal activities, which pose serious challenges to realising a "safe and smart" city.

2.2 Integrating Crime Data Sources for Tactical Analysis

Crime pattern or situation recognition through tactical analysis of crime data is a current and relevant area of research. Crime analysts and researchers have the responsibility to mine crime data in an attempt to connect crime cases by key factors, and to present information about well-known or newly uncovered patterns to public safety and security agencies.

Table 1. Incipient crime categories at different levels

Crime Taxonomy	
Category of Crime	**Local Law Enforcement and National Security Status**
Contact Crime	Murder, sexual offences, kidnapping, attempted murder, common assault, robbery aggravating and common robbery
Contact Related Crime	Arson, malicious damage to property
Crime Detected through Police Action	Illegal possession of firearm/ammunition, driving under the influence and drug related
Property Related Crime	Residential and non-residential burglary, theft of motor vehicle/cycle, theft out of motor vehicle and stock theft
Other Serious Crime	Other theft, commercial crime and shoplifting, public violence, culpable homicide and crimen injuria

While the crime pattern recognition or identification process is reasonably standardized, there sometimes exist a misconception about what constitutes a crime pattern. Thus, the terms "crime trend", "crime hot spots" and "crime series" are regularly used interchangeably. Table 2 reveals the way crime patterns are conceptualized, according to the international association of crime analysts (IACA, 2011). It further presents a clear definition and description of the different crime patterns for tactical analysis. A proper understanding of these crime patterns is crucial, as it will help security agencies focus resources to achieve crime reduction and criminal apprehension targets. It is important to note that while these patterns are explained individually, they sometimes interconnect.

2.3 A Taxonomy of Crime Data Mining Tasks

Data mining entails the uncovering of previously unknown, useful and understandable patterns or information in a database (Khan *et al*, 2013), through the use of data analysis techniques and tools. A wide variety of patterns can be derived from the many techniques available. Crime data mining shows promise of making it convenient, easy and practical to uncover hidden information in crime databases (Chen *et al*, 2004). Such information reveals crime trends and can assist in decision making principles. Hence, research continues in this area.

According to Gupta *et al* (2013), data mining tasks are classified into five categories, which are classification, trends analysis, association, clustering and summarisation. More generally, data mining tasks can be grouped into these two categories: predictive and descriptive tasks (Deshpande & Thakare, 2010). A task is applied to specific problems or domains depending on the type of knowledge or results to be generated. It is important to note that each technique has its strengths

Table 2. Description of existing crime-patterns for tactical analysis

Crime Pattern Types			
S/N	**Pattern Classification**	**Description**	**Strategic Analysis**
1	Spree	A kind of crime series associated with a short time frame, high frequency, and almost continuous criminal act.	Focuses on analysis to include temporal properties and offender behavior.
2	Series	A set of related crimes considered to be committed by the same culprit or group of culprits.	Involves analysis to include offender behavior or profiling characteristics.
3	Hot Spot	A set of related crimes committed at locations within close vicinity of one another.	Involves analysis to include target location characteristics.
4	Hot product	A set of crimes committed by one or more criminals and targeted at a specific product or item.	Focuses analysis on types of stolen property or product.
5	Hot prey	A set of crimes committed by one or more persons on victims sharing related physical characteristics or behavior.	Involves querying data to identify common or repeated victim characteristics or behavior.
6	Hot setting	A set of related crimes committed by one or more culprits that are essentially connected by the type of location where crimes took place.	Involves spatial analysis to include attributes or characteristics of the target environment.
7	Hot place	A set of related crimes perpetrated by one or more persons at the same location.	Include spatial analysis to include location types and properties.

and weaknesses (Yahia *et al*, 2010); therefore, a careful selection of appropriate technique(s) is crucial for successful, understandable and usable mining results. Table 3 summarises existing crime data mining tasks and the techniques or approaches they use.

- **Predictive Tasks:** These estimate or infer the value of a specific target or dependent attribute that corresponds to future behavior, based on previously observed variables or attributes in training data. For example, they can predict the crime statistics that would occur in the next five years, based on past crime committing trends. These types of tasks are usually synonymous with forecasting approaches, which could be qualitative or quantitative depending on the problem to be addressed or desired results to be achieved. Predictive tasks discussed hereafter include the following:
  - **Classification/Class Identification:** A crime data mining task that is used to infer group membership for a crime object. Classification estimates category labels (ordered or unordered) for an entity class and pro-

Table 3. A taxonomy of crime data mining tasks

Field	Category	Tasks	Sample Techniques
Crime data mining	Predictive (mostly supervised approaches)	Classification	Decision-tree methods, neural networks, support vector machines, Bayesian belief networks, memory-based reasoning.
		Trend analysis	Univariate time series, multivariate time series, parametric methods, non-parametric methods, Box-Jenkins modeling.
		Regression	Ordinary least squares, linear regression and non-linear regression methods
		Probability estimation	Significance testing, maximum entropy principles, probabilistic approaches, statistical hypothesis testing
		Prediction	Extrapolation method, scenario method, Delphi survey method
	Descriptive (mostly unsupervised approaches)	Clustering	Hierarchical method: BIRCH, partitioning method: k-means, density-based method, grid-based method, soft computing method such as fuzzy clustering
		Summarization	Abstractive summarization, extractive summarization
		Association detection	Variations of Apriori techniques, association rule mining
		Sequence discovery	Sequential pattern mining approaches, sequence clustering
		Visualization	Graphical approaches for data or information summarization, icon-based techniques

duces mutually exclusive crime data sets. However, classification always requires a pre-defined classification model or scheme. Furthermore, a high level of missing data values may drastically affect crime prediction accuracy.

- **Time Series Analysis:** Uses a structured sequence of crime data points or events, typically measured at equally spaced points or uniform time intervals. Its final goal is prediction.
- **Regression:** A statistical process for the investigation of relationships among dependent and independent crime variables. It generally reveals a cause-effect relationship among crime variables or attributes.
- **Probability Estimation:** Gives a comprehensible and actionable explanation about the characteristics of a crime variable or distribution.

- **Descriptive Tasks:** These are tasks that derive correlations, trajectories and trends from crime information. They summarize the underlying association or relationship between entities in a crime data set. For example, they can identify crimes that have been committed together at a particular time or in a specific location. Descriptive tasks discussed hereafter include the following:

- **Clustering:** An iterative process of grouping a set of crime data or objects into distinct classes which are not predefined. Each class, also called a cluster, comprises objects which are very similar to each other and very dissimilar to objects of other clusters or classes. Clustering is primarily of two types: hierarchical and non-hierarchical. Where no obvious natural groupings exist, clustering algorithms can be used to find groupings. Clustering presents a high level visibility of information about the characteristics of a data set; however, once a split or merge is initiated or committed, in many clustering algorithms, this may not subsequently be reversed (Yahia *et al*, 2010).
- **Summarization:** Involves concept description, such as giving a succinct description of crime groups or classes, or the generalization or abstraction of crime data. Groups are isolated on the basis of the domain knowledge and data items. Visualization is an example of this.
- **Sequence Discovery:** An iterative process which reveals crime ordering patterns (e.g., after 3 or 4 robberies in an outdoor area, robberies in that location tend to stop (probably due to an intervention like lighting installation).
- **Association Detection/Dependency Analysis:** This can be defined as an iterative process of finding associations and relationships between crime variables, objects or entities, such as crimes committed repeatedly by an offender (e.g. crime series).

Crime data mining tasks are also categorized as supervised or unsupervised. Most predictive tasks, for example classification techniques, are supervised, while descriptive techniques are usually unsupervised.

In supervised approaches, there are two phases: training and testing. A training set of crime data is provided, which includes the pre-defined or pre-classified values of the target data or variable, in addition to the predictor variables. The provisional model then performs classification based on the structure and pattern it learned from the training set. Afterwards, the performance of the provisional mining model on a test set of data is iteratively examined and the model adjusted accordingly to reduce the error rate. Finally, the adjusted model is applied to a validation data set.

In unsupervised approaches, there is no identified target variable or value. Rather, the algorithm searches for intrinsic crime structures, relations, patterns and interconnectedness of the data, among all the existing variables or objects. Clustering is the most common unsupervised approach.

In general, a user's application and preferences determine the choice of appropriate methods or techniques to adopt in solving a crime problem. It is important to recognise that Table 3 is not all-inclusive; it provides only examples to give a high level overview of existing techniques in solving crime data mining tasks.

2.4 Classical Sequential Approach to Data Mining

Crime data mining is a powerful tool that gives predictive insight into probable crime events or activities. In order to achieve better quality results in data mining, data preprocessing activities are usually adopted (Krishnamurthy *et al*, 2012). Figure 4 presents the steps typically employed in data mining. Current data mining methodologies, such as SEMMA (Sample, Explore, Modify, Model, Assess) and CRISP-DM (Cross-Industry Standard Process for Data Mining), adopt similar steps (Ozgul, 2011).

1. **Pre-Processing Phase:** The pre-processing steps or activities include domain selection, data cleaning and selection transformation.
    a. **Domain Selection:** This involves the prioritisation and selection of one or more domains for which an analysis is to be initiated. For example, the selection of a violent crime domain. This is followed by the selection of data that are relevant to the analysis.
    b. **Data Cleaning:** The data cleaning step involves smoothing noisy data, dealing with missing values, detecting and removing outliers and resolving inconsistencies.
    c. **Selection Transformation:** This step involves the conversion of the data into an organised set, such as merging of data from multiple sources and putting the data in the correct form for a specific mining technique. Attribute selection, dimensionality reduction and data normalisation are also done at this stage.
2. **Build the Model:** Pre-processed data from the previous step is analyzed in this phase. Building the model entails the selection and utilization of one or more of the techniques highlighted in Section 2 and Table 3 to achieve specific

Figure 4. General iterative steps in data mining

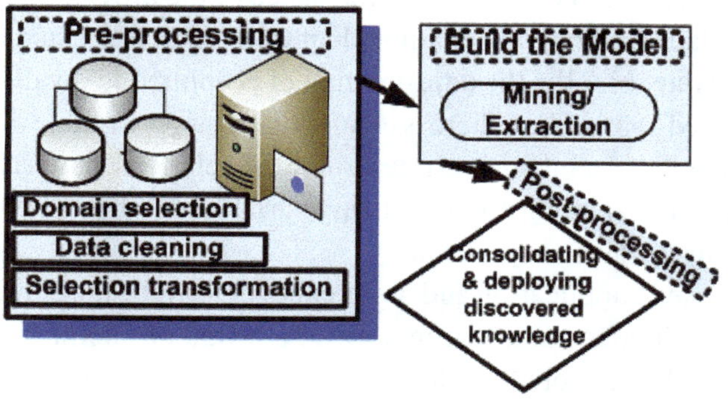

objectives. It has been pointed out that one of the major challenges in data mining is determining the technique(s) best suited to a given problem (Yahia, 2010). The choice of method selection at this stage will depend on the type of problems to be addressed and expected results to be generated, for example, whether predictive or descriptive or both.

3. **Post-Processing Phase:** The post-processing phase would involve consolidating the discovered knowledge and making it available, accessible and understandable for experts and non-experts in the public safety domain. The predictive or descriptive information obtained from the analyzed crime data is summarized at this level. This presents understandable structures, patterns or trends to decision makers.

3.0 CURRENT IMPLEMENTATION TO CRIME DATA MINING

3.1 Existing Strategies in Crime Data Mining

Crime data mining emerged as a result of different forms of knowledge that could be derived, which could assist decision makers and public safety authorities in improving their efficiency. Exploratory data analysis (EDA) is a strategy for analyzing data sets, in order to summarize their major attributes or characteristics. While much research has been conducted on spatial crime data analysis, temporal crime data analysis, and spatio-temporal crime analysis (Malathi, 2011a; Musdholifah & Hashim, 2010; Khan, 2013; Kadhim, 2011), other motivations for exploring crime data include identifying crime series or causal relationships among crime variables or attributes (Wang *et al*, 2013b). For instance, this can determine what crime types affect a particular gender group or what the age distribution for a crime type is, or identify a crime series and serial offenders. The three most common strategies for exploring crime data mining exploit:

- Spatial knowledge,
- Temporal knowledge,
- Spatio-temporal knowledge.

3.1.1 Spatial Crime Data Analysis (SCDA)

Spatial data analysis employs statistical analysis techniques that address certain problems relating to spatial characteristics of data, such as spatial heterogeneity and spatial dependency (auto-correlated patterns and structures). A relevant scenario is the identification of crime hot spots (Isafiade *et al*, 2013) or clusters of homogeneous crimes. The inherent geographical property of crime is a natural inspiration for spatial data analysis. A criminal must have come from a place and must necessarily commit or perpetrate a crime at a particular location. Thus, the emergence of sophisticated tools such as the Radio-Frequency Identification (RFID) and Geographic Information System (GIS) combined with rigorous statistical approaches have paved the way for spatial data analysis (Chainey & Ratcliffe, 2005).

GIS has the ability to integrate spatial data and information from numerous sources into one interface. This ability has triggered advanced spatial analyses that would not have been realisable or at least very difficult to achieve without the GIS. Wang *et al* (*2013a*) proposed a spatial mapping tool, coined Hotspot Optimization Tool (HOT), using a geo-spatial discriminative patterns notion. This can assist with decisions regarding the identification of safest paths for road users.

3.1.2 Temporal Crime Data Analysis (TCDA)

Crime temporal analysis methods deal with prediction or summarisation of crime temporal attributes. For example, what crime type occurs at a particular time of the day and what crime categories are committed together at a particular time. It generally leads to time dependence or temporal variations analysis, with the goal of forecasting, which is usually the end result of temporal analysis. It can be used to predict when, where and how future incidents in a crime series, trend or pattern will occur.

Temporal Association Rule (TAR), a form of incremental mining of temporal association rules, has gained much attention over the years. However, a major drawback of TAR is the requirement of multiple database re-scanning. In contrast to pioneering works on incremental mining, developed by Chang and Cheng *et al* (Chang *et al*, 2003 & Cheng *et al*, 2004), which mostly focused on reducing the frequency of database rescanning, Vincent *et al,* (Vincent *et al,* 2007) presented a time-series based analysis, *ITAR*, that uses a negative border method to address the problem of database re-scanning. Slightly different research on temporal analysis was the work of Ashby *et al* (Ashby *et al,* 2013), who detailed a comparison of methods for temporal analysis of indeterminate crimes.

3.1.3 Spatio-Temporal Crime Analysis (STCA)

Spatio-temporal analysis scenarios or methods consider both space and time in their analytic processes, e.g. PredPol technology (PredPol, 2013). This type of analysis is based on coordinates of events, such as locations of crime activities, and the time frame in which such criminal acts occurred (Ozgul *et al*, 2011 & Musdholifah *et al,* 2010). STCA attempts to answer the questions of "where" and "when" the crime occurs. The uniqueness of STCA is evident in cross- or auto-correlation between variables and parameters, where time and space variables carry much weight during crime data analysis, for example in crime hot-spots identification (Wang *et al, 2012*). Effective production of distance measures or metrics for spatial and temporal correlation is a common feature of spatio-temporal analyses. Distances between crime locations are normally not easily available for areas that are poorly planned. An easy way out is to represent such poorly planned location as clusters, so that analysis is done for each cluster. STCA can give clues as to what specific paths are safe at what period of the day, bearing in mind that shortest paths are not always the safest paths.

3.2 Existing Applications and Techniques for Crime Data Mining

Over the years, considerable effort has been put into improving the performance of existing algorithms (Malathi et al, 2011b; Khan et al, 2013; Isafiade et al, 2013; Mohammad et al, 2011; Zhang et al, 2013) and inventing new algorithms or methods for crime data mining and analysis (Li et al, 2010; Phillips et al, 2012; Wang et al, 2013, Isafiade et al, 2015). Thus, numerous projects and applications have been developed in this domain of interest. Conventional techniques for data mining such as association rule mining identify patterns in purely structured data sets (Ziauddin et al, 2012). However, contemporary approaches to data mining often identify patterns in both structured and unstructured data sets (Chen et al, 2004). Some of these techniques are discussed hereafter.

Apriori is a classic technique for learning association rules and one of the most influential techniques in exploring patterns of interest in a dataset (Buczak et al, 2010 & Ziauddin et al, 2012). It uses a bottom-up approach for expanding frequent subsets (i.e sets of items that frequently occur together), one item at a time; a step known as candidate generation. A simplified example of an association rule could be as follows:

Robbery in location $A \Rightarrow$ Murder in location A.

This could mean that a serial offender or group of offenders (gang) involved in robbery, in location *A*, end up killing their victims. However, it is very important to recognise that association rules greatly depend on the quality of the results generated from frequent crime item-set mining, e.g. FP-Growth (Han et al, 2004). FP-Growth model is a frequent pattern growth model that can be used to identify crime items (incidents) that are frequently committed together. We refer the reader to Isafiade et al, 2013 and Isafiade et al, 2015, for further details on the model.

Table 4. Support and confidence measure of an association rule

Rule	
	Support $(A \Rightarrow B) = \frac{\|B \cap A\|}{\|tuples\|}$
	Confidence $(A \Rightarrow B) = \frac{\|B \cap A\|}{\|A\|}$

Apriori has been noted for the benefit of easy parallelism and simple implementation (Ziauddin et al, 2012). However, a major drawback of this technique is that it requires repeated database scans, which is inefficient when the database cannot be memory resident. Consequently, several variants of the algorithm, such as AprioriTid and AprioriHybrid, emerged over the years to address its shortcomings (Vincent et al, 2007). AprioriHybrid combines Apriori and AprioriTid to amalgamate the strengths of both algorithms. These variants of association rule mining address inefficiencies through better pruning, refinement techniques, data structures, partitioning techniques and search strategies. Association rules present facts about the dependency or relationship between two or more items. It was initially motivated by market basket analysis, to identify items that are usually purchased together (Ziauddin et al, 2012), but can be extended to other relevant or related fields such as crime mining, to identify crimes that have been committed together or at the same location. A rule must satisfy two major factors, namely:

1. **Support:** Indicates the frequency of co-occurrence, must be sufficient.
2. **Confidence:** Indicates the correctness of the rule, must also be adequate.

The support and confidence measure is given in Table 4. Thus association rule is a two-step process; first find all the frequent itemsets, then generate strong association rules from these sets.

In addition to Apriori, other algorithms such as FP-growth and Eclat have been presented for generating association rules. The FP-growth algorithm, introduced by Han et al (Han et al, 2004) mines frequent patterns without generating candidate itemsets. First it builds a compact data structure named FP-tree, which is later traversed using a bottom-up approach, to extract frequent itemsets. The CitiSafe application (Isafiade at al., 2013) employs the FP-growth algorithm for crime data mining. An improvement made to the algorithm was the *batch-merge paradigm* adopted, which simultaneously generates all the frequent pattern trees for a particular crime itemset and ultimately merges the results, as opposed to the conventional sequential approach adopted in the FP-growth algorithm. The modelling technique successfully identified crime patterns from a fairly large number of crimes, as opposed to the limitations of current manual analysis. CitiSafe provides an effective and efficient crime incident analysis tool for law enforcement agencies and public safety organisations.

The COPLINK application (Chen et al, 2004) is one of the early large-scale projects in crime data mining. It is a project on crime database integration that was launched with the Tucson Police department and funded by the National Science Foundation and National Institute of Justice. Khan et al (Khan et al, 2013) presented four case studies to emphasize the importance and relevance of the COPLINK project. These are: automatic entity extraction from police narrative reports, using a neural network based entity extractor for deceptive criminal identity detection; identifying false witness in the database through criminal network analysis; identifying subgroups and key members in a criminal network; and authorship analysis in cybercrime.

In the area of predictive policing, PredPol has been developed in order to identify and prevent potential crime incidents (PredPol, 2013). PredPol only predicts "where" and "when" a crime incident is most likely to happen. As no personal information about individuals or demographics are utilized in making these predictions, PredPol does not predict a potential offender. Therefore, PredPol's crime prevention technology does not pose any personal privacy or profiling concerns and has proven useful in "place-based" crime deterrence in the USA.

Techniques such as clustering and fuzzy apriori approaches have been adopted in crime pattern discovery (Buczak et al, 2010 & Kadhim et al, 2011). A detailed study on the use of clustering techniques in crime data mining was presented by Krishnamurthy et al (Krishnamurthy et al, 2012). Clustering techniques sort data into specific classes based on certain features or functions, thereby minimising or maximising their intra-class similarity (Kadhim, 2011 & Devesh, 2012). K-means is a common unsupervised clustering algorithm, which partitions data items into a predefined number of clusters, based on their means (Tayal et al, 2014 & Malathi, 2011b). The algorithm aims to minimise the objective function in Equation 1 below, a squared error function.

$$J = \sum_{i=1}^{k}\sum_{j=1}^{l} l_j^{(i)} - c_j^{\ 2} \tag{1}$$

where $l_j^{(i)} - c_j^{\ 2}$ is a chosen distance function between a data point $l_j^{(i)}$ and the cluster centre c_j, a measure of the distance of the data points from their corresponding cluster centres. K-means has been identified as having a number of limitations, namely:

- High sensitivity to initialisation (choice of K items as first set of centroids).
- Problems with clusters of varying sizes.
- Problems with clusters of varying densities.

However, it remains a baseline to most clustering algorithms, and research has shown that multiple runs can help solve the initial condition (centroid) problems (Kadhim, 2011). Clustering algorithms can also be computationally expensive. Hence, several improvements on clustering techniques emerged. The K-means algorithm is a special case of the Expectation Maximisation (EM) algorithm. This special case also points to the fact that almost all aspects of K-means have been improved (Zhang et al, 2013):

- Initialization,
- Efficiency,
- Centroid and objective definitions,
- Overall process enhancements,
- Distance measures.

The work of Malathi et al (2011a) proposed a hybrid clustering model that combines the advantages of K-means and DBSCAN (Density-Based Spatial Clustering of Applications with Noise). DBSCAN uses the notion of density accessibility (closeness to the δ-neighbourhood) to define a cluster. Essentially, a point x is directly density-accessible from a point y if it is not farther away than a given distance δ. A major difference between DBSCAN and K-means is that DBSCAN does not require an initial specification of K, the number of clusters in the data, as opposed to K-means. Instead, DBSCAN requires the minimum number of points, say ξ, needed to form a dense region. Experimental results in the work of Malathi et al (2011a) indicated that DBSCAN outperforms the K-means algorithm. A similar algorithm to DBSCAN is OPTICS: (Ordering Points To Identify the Clustering Structure), which is also used for identifying density-based clusters in spatial datasets (Ankerst, 1999).

Another notable contribution is the BIRCH (Balanced Iterative Reducing and Clustering using Hierarchies) algorithm by Zhang et al (1996). BIRCH implements a scalable clustering algorithm with respect to quality of clustering and number of objects. It utilises local information in which clustering decisions are finalised without multiple data scans, and outputs a dendrogram, which encodes the clustering information of the dataset in a compact manner.

A related effort to BIRCH, with a slight modification in distance measure, was proposed by Chiu et al (2001). They proposed a probabilistic model which derives a distance measure where the distance between two clusters is equivalent to the decrease in the log-likelihood function resulting from merging. Their algorithm further implemented a procedure which allows for automatic determination of the appropriate number of clusters and the assignment of cluster membership to noisy or incomplete data.

A strategy for crime detection and criminal identification (CDCI) was proposed in the work of Tayal et al (2014). CDCI implemented data mining techniques consisting of six modules, which involve data extraction and preprocessing, clustering using K-means and classification using K-Nearest Neighbour (KNN) algorithms. KNN is a machine learning technique based on a non-parametric approach, for regression and classification (Malathi, 2011b). CDCI identifies similarities among different crimes in the feature space and organises them into predefined clusters, for classification and prediction. It was tested using crime data, between years 2000-2012, from seven different Indian cities with high crime rates and used WEKA software for verification and validation of the results from K-means. Clusters were defined based on two crime attributes: the year a crime is committed and frequency of crime. Visual aids to K-means were enhanced using Google Map Application Programming Interface, which provides an effective crime analysis visualisation tool for crime investigating agencies.

The information (sensor) fusion capabilities, extracting information from several data sources in parallel, that is inherent in the Artificial Neural Network technique has attracted the attention of several researchers. Recent research on crime mining (Jiji et al, 2013) utilised the back propagation Neural-Network (NN) classifier and compared its performance with a data association algorithm in tracking criminals automatically. The aim was to identify and extract correlations from the crime incident summaries. Empirical results from the research reveal that the back propagation network classifier outperforms the data association algorithm, in terms of identifying and tracking potential criminals and predicting future crimes.

A slightly different approach to applying NN is seen in the work of Helbich et al (2013). A related effort has been presented by Keyvanpour et al, (2010), where important entities were extracted from police narrative reports, written in plain text, and a self-organising map (SOM) clustering technique used for crime analysis and ultimately a crime matching procedure. In the former, Helbich et al (2013) applied SOM to text mining and focused on unstructured crime narrative reports. SOM is a kind of artificial neural network trained to derive a low-dimensional discretised representation of the input space, using unsupervised learning. The novelty in their research is a multi-step methodology that projects the SOM clustering output from the unstructured crime data to geographical space. Point analysis was used to explore the spatial distribution of the clusters. Their research further demonstrates that collective surveillance by individuals, through e-mails, personal interviews, written statements and telephone recordings, are powerful avenues to explore in crime analysis and prediction.

Earlier research proposed the CATCH (Computer Aided Tracking and Characterisation of Homicides) and CATCHRAPE application software (Kangas, 2001). The CATCH software uses an artificial neural network for classification of criminals in rape and murder cases and provides a means of clustering related cases that can be attributed to the same offenders. The assumption was that two different individuals with similar characteristics are capable of committing crimes with similar behaviour. SOM was used for clustering, where no initial training data was provided. SOM provided a convenient visual representation by organising the data vectors into similar data clusters on a two-dimensional map.

Bayesian belief networks (BBNs) have been employed in different ways to establish probabilistic models in criminal science and investigations. Appropriate selection of a scoring function, a structure learning algorithm and a parameter-learning algorithm are critical for the BBN to be successful. Riesen et al (2009) proposed a Bayesian network classifier to predict victimisation. The K2 and Hill Climbing algorithms were employed for prediction and optimisation respectively. In the structure learning algorithm, a local-score-based structure learning, tabu search was utilised. A major trade-off in their approach was between an increase in memory usage and a faster learning time. They concluded that only the K2 algorithm successfully built a model with more than three parent nodes. A related effort (Baumgartner et al,, 2005) addressed the challenge of space complexity by modifying the greedy search K2 algorithm through the inclusion of a-priori conditional independence relations amongst the nodes, and achieved a 15% improvement on the model.

Support Vector Machines (SVM), a set of supervised learning methods for regression and classification, have also been employed in crime mining. A recent work on cybercrime detection and prevention models to reduce data damage by malicious code, proposed a hybrid model coined *AdaSVM* (Deylami et al, 2012), which combines special features from the Adaboost algorithm with SVM (AdaSVM). AdaBoost (Ramanathan et al, 2012) is a classification technique that combines predictions from several classifiers and generates a single and robust classifier, which is very often more effective than individual classifiers. A Facebook dataset was used to evaluate the performance of the model.

Several applications and tools have been developed for spatial data mining (Chainey & Ratcliffe, 2005). A common scenario for spatial data mining is the identification of crime hotspots. Existing hotspot mapping techniques include thematic mapping, point mapping and kernel density estimation. Hot Spot Analysis (HSA) and Hotspot Optimisation Tool (HOT) are examples of existing hotspot mapping applications or tools. Wang et al (2013a) claim that the HOT application differs from other hotspot mapping tools, because HOT considers spatial crime and socio-economic related factors in addition to focusing on target crime density.

From the literature, it is clear that research in crime situation recognition, prediction and control is ongoing, as several algorithms and approaches have been implemented and even hybrid models have emerged. However, the daily increase in crime information still necessitates more effective and advanced techniques for crime analysis, for example there is little research on crime series detection (Wang et al, 2013c). The facts presented in this study confirm that there is a need to develop more hybrid models for effective strategic and tactical crime analysis.

3.3 Feature Comparison of Existing Crime Data Mining Applications and Techniques

We compare algorithm selection, content selection, exploratory basis and result summarisation of existing crime data mining techniques and applications in Table 5. While the *exploratory basis* succinctly presents the problems addressed in each article, the *model selection column* describes the major algorithm used in addressing the problem(s). *Algorithm advancement* points to any improvements that have been made on the article's chosen model and *content selection* describes the nature of data used for the experiment and/or implementation. The last column, *result summary*, gives the mode in which the results of the experiments are presented. While *qualitative* indicates analysis results presented with graphical views or visualisation, *quantitative* refers to results presented mostly in table format, specifying corresponding crime results or figures.

Table 5 presents a feature comparison of existing crime mining applications and a high level description of existing applications. Furthermore, Table 6 highlights the characteristics, strengths and weaknesses of some of the currently used techniques or models. It is evident that currently adopted techniques and models have requirements, specifications (e.g appropriate parameter selection) and characteristics that determine their degree of relevance and efficiency.

Tables 5 and 6 give an insight into the open research issues for future consideration. While there has been some effort in improving many facets of existing approaches and techniques (Malathi et al, 2011b; Khan et al, 2013; Vladimir et al, 2001), it is clear that there is room to develop more hybrid models (Deylami et al, 2012) and richer spatial and/or temporal approaches to enhance crime situation recognition and ultimately improve the productivity of public safety authorities.

Table 5. Features comparison of crime data mining applications

S/N	Features	Exploratory Basis	Model Selection/ Technique(s) Adopted	Algorithm Advancement	Content Selection	Result Summary
1	Crime-terror pattern detection (Khan et al, 2013)	Detect crime spree by the same culprit	Clustering based (K-means)	N/A	Real crime data	Visualisation (qualitative)
2	CitiSafe algorithm (Isafiade et al, 2013)	Spatial pattern & crime spree	Frequent pattern based (FP-Growth)	Batch-merge paradigm	real & synthesised data	Qualitative & quantitative
3	Predicting victimisation (Riesen et al, 2009)	Victimisation classification	Bayesian belief network (K2 & hill climbing)	N/A	Real crime data (NCVS)	Quantitative
4	Identify change in crime patterns (Malathi et al, 2011a)	Predicting irregular crime patterns	Cluster-based prediction & KNN	Distance metric & learning vector quantisation (E-KDD)	Real per capita & crime data	Visualization
5	Incremental mining for crime patterns (Vincent et al, 2007)	Spatial & temporal crime mining	Temporal Association Rule (TAR)	Incremental TAR (ITAR) with negative border method	Synthesised & real data	Visualization
6	Automatic tracking of criminals (Jiji et al, 2013)	Tracking criminals & preventing future attacks	Back propagation, NN-classifier & association algorithm	N/A	Synthesized data	Quantitative
7	Crime hotspot mapping (Wang et al, 2013a)	Spatial mapping	Hotspot mapping approaches	Hotspot Optimization Tool (HOT) with socio-economic factors	Real data set	Visualisation (qualitative) & quantitative
8	Cybercrime detection & prevention model (Deylami et al, 2012)	Reduce data damage by malicious code	Support vector machine (SVM) & Adaboost	AdaSVM (hybrid model)	Facebook dataset	Qualitative & quantitative
9	Crime & criminal detection in India (Tayal et al, 2014)	Crime detection & criminal identification	K-means clustering & KNN	N/A	Unstructured crime data	Qualitative & quantitative
10	Criminal profiling (Baumgartner et al, 2012)	Offender behavior model for criminal profiling	Bayesian Network model	Modified K2 (K2') to reduce the search space	Real crime dataset	Quantitative
11	Revised Frequent pattern model (Isafiade et al, 2015)	Spatial pattern & crime spree	Frequent pattern based (FP-Growth)	Floor-Ceil Quartile function for MST selection	Synthesised data	Qualitative & quantitative

Table 6. Features comparison of current crime data mining techniques

S/N	Features	Major Characteristics	Strength	Weakness	Choice Implication
1	Association rules e.g Apriori	A strategy for exploring patterns of interest or relationships in a dataset	Has good capability of generating candidate itemsets. Easy parallelism & implementation	May require repeated database scans. Confidence & support factors are key components	Assumes the required database can be resident in memory
2	Clustering	Involves organizing or grouping objects into groups whose members are similar in some way	Clustering presents a quick abstraction of the available data set and can be used for pattern discovery and prediction	It is quite sensitive to initial conditions during the merge or split process	Statistically isolates dataset into unique homogeneous subsets based on specified conditions or certain similarity
3	Decision trees (DT)	It is a model with a tree-like classification structure for prediction and decision support	DT is easy to understand and can be used for data exploration and predicting the outcome of new samples	Some DT approaches may use some heuristics in the classification process	DT describes data, not decisions, and may give the illusion of comprehending the target or dependent variable
4	Artificial Neural Network	A biologically inspired system that predicts an output based on the set of inputs	Very suited to classification & estimations problems	High input features may affect the results of the analysis	Complex models may lead to faulty learning process
5	Support Vector Machine (SVM)	A model that analyses a dataset and constructs separating hyperplanes for classification problems	Suited for regression & classification tasks. The kernel trick enables it to perform both linear & non-linear classification	Generalization ability of the model depends on the location of the separating hyperplane	Appropriate selection of training samples is crucial for effective analysis
6	Visualization	Effective for graphical or iconic summarization of a large dataset e.g. clusters	Presents a high level of abstraction of the available information for data exploration	It may be difficult to assimilate or understand for non-domain experts, especially when structured in a hierarchical way	Can be combined with other mining techniques and may rely on quality of the analysis or "complete" data for a good knowledge representation

4.0 RESEARCH ISSUES IN CRIME DATA MINING FOR SITUATION RECOGNITION

In this section, some research issues in crime data mining are discussed and emerging specifications for data mining approaches in this domain of interest are highlighted.

4.1 Emerging Specifications for Data Mining Approaches

Conventional approaches to data mining, as described in Section 2.4, assume that data is extracted from a database when required. However, with the concept of smart cities and the overwhelming volume of crime information that may arrive in streams, there is a need to adopt more reactive or actionable mining processes. The processing of a stream will require summarisation of some sort. One way to achieve such summarisation is to eliminate most of the undesirable elements in the stream through filtering. Another means is to consider only a fixed-length window as data arrives. However, a major challenge to processing streams is that data arrives at a very rapid rate and needs to be processed as quickly as possible in order not to lose information. Hence, there is need to develop new approaches to accommodate stream processing for actionable information, knowledge delivery and situation recognition. The concept of *big data* science, which uses parallel computing, may be relevant in this discourse. Big data science is associated with the four "*V*'s":

- **Volume:** Large volume or quantity of data.
- **Velocity:** High speed of data arrival and processing.
- **Variety:** Heterogeneous sources and types of data information.
- **Value:** Inherent value/information hidden in the available data.

An overview of current challenges in crime data mining is depicted in Figure 5. Limitations of state-of-the-art approaches include the following: some of the techniques or methods currently adopted in crime analysis do not translate into actionable strategies in the public safety operational environment. Thus, these are not practically applicable to the crime solving domain. Figure 6 presents the basic transition from data to knowledge. Understandable patterns, and effective communication of the final solution derived through tactical analysis of crime data, is crucial for operational usability of the derived knowledge.

In addition, crime data volumes are increasing on a daily basis, due to the higher crime rates. Streaming crime data which is always temporal has not received much attention. Historical data are available in repositories and there is an increase in heterogeneous sources of crime information from voluntary witnesses which need to be explored for useful crime knowledge delivery.

Figure 5. Overview of open research issues in crime data mining

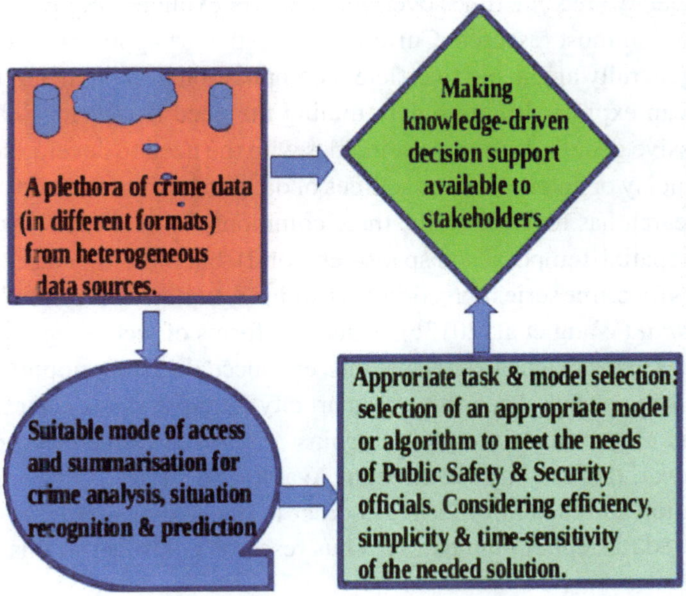

Figure 6. A basic transformation from data to knowledge

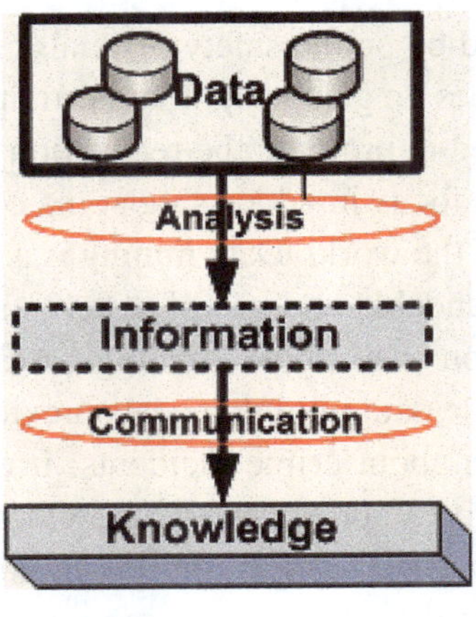

Previous approaches are limited in the volume of data they can process (Gupta, 2014). Thus, exploring large volumes of crime data is still in its infancy. One of the few studies handling large volumes of data is the work of Vladimir et al (2001). It is clear that the capabilities of current crime mining analysis approaches and techniques, for large data-set analysis, have not been fully explored.

Furthermore, performance metrics and factors such as scalability and computational efficiency are sometimes overlooked or not explicitly highlighted, defined or documented in most research. Current state-of-the-art approaches to crime data mining are generally amenable to efficient computational implementations, which researchers can explore. In crime data mining the need to develop scalable solutions for massive geographical data coincides with the need to develop solutions for incomplete, noisy or heterogeneous sources of data, for crime situation recognition.

Most research has focused on the three commonly known bases for crime data exploration (spatial, temporal and spatio-temporal), but there is paucity of research on techniques for crime series detection, for example, exploring the "how's" of crime: *modus operandi* (Wang et al, 2013c). Thus new forms of technologies, processing and techniques that can lead to new insights, enhanced decision support and process optimization are needed. According to smart city initiatives, it is clear that modern technology is a necessity for fighting against organized crime or other forms of crime. However, this may not be enough. Available data needs to be transformed into information and then knowledge, in order to reveal meaning from the trillions of bits gathered throughout the nation. Thus research continues in this domain.

5.0 SUMMARY AND CONCLUSION

Crime information archived by public safety officials can be effectively explored, using data mining approaches, to gain insight into criminal trends or patterns. Such exploration can also be used to promote the realisation of a "safe and smart" city, which is currently a global focus in addressing some of the challenges, including crime, facing most cities of the world. Data mining is a computational approach to discovering novel, understandable and useful patterns in large datasets, involving techniques at the intersection of machine learning, artificial intelligence, statistics and database systems. Crime data mining reveals previously unknown, useful and understandable information about crime incidents. It can help to channel public safety resources more effectively across geographical locations. Unlike conventional techniques of data mining such as association rule mining, which identify patterns in purely dense and structured data sets, contemporary approaches to data mining often identify patterns in both structured and unstructured data sets.

This chapter reviewed crime data mining concepts, applications and methods along with their strengths and weaknesses. Existing applications were compared, as presented in Table 5, based on five features: *exploratory basis, technique(s) adopted, algorithm advancement, content selection and result summary*. Different crime data mining approaches were explored and some research issues highlighted. Furthermore, the chapter suggests that crime-based situation recognition, through crime data mining, is an important problem to consider for enhancing the overall objective of crime situation management by decision makers in a smart city development.

It is important to know that it is impractical to adapt a unique notion or technique to all crime data mining problems. Appropriate technique(s) to solve a crime problem should be identified based on the focus or expectations of the crime analysts. Tables 2 and 3 give an insight into the likely techniques and problems that can be tackled in the crime domain. Current trends indicate that there are enormous challenges that still remain open and need to be addressed, such as developing scalable programming models, as well as efficient and effective hybrid approaches for strategic or tactical crime analysis. Such challenges involve the development of more intuitive intelligence investigation techniques for crime pattern and situation recognition, in order to foster proactive safety solutions by the public safety and law enforcement authorities. Addressing these challenges requires a paradigm shift in the minds of crime data mining researchers. Hence, research continues in this domain of interest.

ACKNOWLEDGMENT

The authors gratefully appreciate the financial support from an AIMS-DAAD Fellowship, L'oréal-UNESCO Women in Science Fellowship and resources made available by the University of Cape Town and the University of the Western Cape.

REFERENCES

Ankerst, M., Breunig, M., Kriegel, H., & Sander, J. (1999). OPTICS: Ordering Points To Identify the Clustering Structure. In *ACM International conference on Management of Data* (pp. 49-60). ACM Press.

Ashby, M., & Bowers, J. (2013). A comparison of methods for temporal analysis of aoristic crime. *Springer Open Journal of Crime Science, 2(1)*, 1–16. doi:10.1186/2193-7680-2-1

Baumgartner, K., Ferrari, S., & Salfati, C. (2005). Bayesian Network Modeling of Offender Behavior for Criminal Profiling. In *Proceedings of the 44th IEEE Conference on Decision and Control*, (pp. 2702-2709). doi:10.1109/CDC.2005.1582571

Buczak, A., & Gifford, C. (2010). Fuzzy Association Rule Mining for Community Crime Pattern Discovery. In *Proceedings of the ACM SIGKDD Workshop on Intelligence and Security Informatics*. doi:10.1145/1938606.1938608

Chainey, S., & Ratcliffe, J. (2005). *GIS and Crime Mapping. Mastering GIS: Technology, Applications and Management*. West Sussex, UK: John Wiley & Sons Ltd. doi:10.1002/9781118685181

Chartered Financial Analyst Institute. (2013). *Urban Life: open-air computers*. Retrieved from http://www.economist.com/news/special-report

Chen, H., Chung, W., Qin, Y., Chau, M., Xu, J., Wang, G., & Homa, A. et al. (2003). Crime Data Mining: An Overview and Case Studies. In *Proceedings of the Annual National Conference on Digital Government Research*.

Chen, H., Chung, W., Xu, J., Wang, G., Qin, Y., & Chau, M. (2004). Crime Data Mining: A General Framework and Some Examples. *Journal of IEEE Computer*, *37*(4), 50–56. doi:10.1109/MC.2004.1297301

Chiu, T., Fang, D., Chen, J., & Wang, Y. (2001). A Robust and Scalable Clustering Algorithm for Mixed Type Attributes in Large Database Environment. In *Proceedings of the seventh ACM SIGKDD international conference on Knowledge discovery and data mining*. . doi:10.1145/502512.502549

Deshpande, S. & Thakare, V. (2010). Data Mining System and Applications: A Review. *International Journal of Distributed and Parallel systems, 1*(1), 32-44.

Devesh, B. (2012). Emerging Trends in Utilisation of Data Mining in Criminal Investigation: An Overview. *Journal of Environmental Science, Computer Science and Engineering & Technology, 1*(2), 124-131.

Deylami, H., & Singh, Y. (2012). Adaboost and SVM based cybercrime detection and prevention model. *International Journal of Artificial Intelligence Research.*, *1*(2), 117–130.

Gupta, R. (2014). Journey from Data Mining to Web Mining to Big Data. *International Journal of Computer Trends and Technology, 10*(1), 18-20. Retrieved from www.ijcttjournal.org

Hafedh, C., Ramon, G., Theresa, A., Taewoo, N., Sehl, M., Hans, J., . . . Karine, N. (2012). Understanding Smart Cities: An Integrative Framework. In *Proceedings of the Hawaii International conference on System Sciences (HICSS)*, (pp. 2289-2297).

Han, J., Pei, J., Yin, Y., & Mao, R. (2004). *Mining Frequent Patterns without Candidate Generation. ACM International Journal of Data Mining and Knowledge Discovery, 8(1)*, 53–87.

Helbich, M., Hagenauer, J., Leitner, M., & Edwards, R. (2013). Exploration of unstructured narrative crime reports: an unsupervised neural network and point pattern analysis approach. Cartography and Geographic Information Science, 40(4).

International Association of Crime Analysts. (2011). *Crime Pattern Definitions for Tactical Analysis*. Standards, Methods, & Technology (SMT) Committee White Paper-2011-01. Retrieved from http://www.iaca.net/Publications/Whitepapers/iacawp_2011_01_crime_patterns.pdf

Isafiade, O., & Bagula, A. (2013). CitiSafe: Adaptive Spatial Pattern Knowledge Using Fp- Growth Algorithm for Crime Situation Recognition. In *Proceedings of IEEE International Conference on Ubiquitous Intelligence and Computing*. doi:10.1109/UIC-ATC.2013.72

Isafiade, O., Bagula, A., & Sonia, B. (2015). A Revised Frequent Pattern Model for Crime Situation Recognition Based on Floor-Ceil Quartile Function. In *Procedia Computer Science (PROCS5621).3rd ITQM Conference*, (*Vol. 55*, pp. 251-260). Elsevier. DOI: doi:10.1016/j.procs.2015.07.042

Jiji, G., & Anantharadha, S. (2013). Automatic Tracking of Criminals using Data Mining Techniques. Journal of the Institution of Engineers (India): Series B, 93(4), 217-221.

Kadhim, B. (2011). A Proposed Framework for Analyzing Crime Data Set Using Decision Tree and Simple K-Means clustering Algorithms. *Journal of Kufa for Mathematics and Computer.*, *1*(3), 8–24.

Kangas, L. (2001). *Artificial Neural Network System for Classification of Offenders in Murder and Rape Cases.* National Criminal Justice Reference Service (NCJRS).

Keyvanpour, M., Javideh, M., & Ebrahimi, M. (2010). Detecting and Investigating Crime by means of Data Mining: a general crime matching framework. *World Conference on Information Technology, 3*, 872-880. doi:10.1016/j.procs.2010.12.143

Khan, N. & Bhagat, V. (2013). Effective Data Mining Approach for Crime-Terror-pattern Detection using Clustering Algorithm Technique. *International Journal of Engineering Research & Technology, 2*(4), 2043-2048.

Krishnamurthy, R., & Kumar, J. (2012). Survey of Data Mining Techniques on Crime Data Analysis. *International Journal of Data Mining Techniques and Applications, 1*(2), 117-120.

Ku, C., Iriberri, A., & Leroy, G. (2008). Crime Information Extraction from Police and Witness Narrative Reports. In *Proceedings of the IEEE International Conference on Technologies for Homeland Security*. doi:10.1109/THS.2008.4534448

Li, S., Kuo, S., & Tsai, F. (2010). An Intelligent Decision-Support Model using FSOM and Rule Extraction for Crime Prevention. *International Journal of Expert Systems with Applications.*, *37*(10), 7108–7119. doi:10.1016/j.eswa.2010.03.004

Malathi, A., & Baboo, S. (2011a). Enhanced Algorithm to Identify Change in Crime Patterns. *International Journal of Combinatorial Optimization Problems and Informatics*, *2*(3), 32–38. Retrieved from http://ijcopi.org

Malathi, A., & Baboo, S. (2011b). An Enhanced Algorithm to Predict a Future Crime using Data Mining. *International Journal of Computer Applications, 21*(1), 1-6. Retrieved from http://www.ijcaonline.org/archives/volume21/number1/2478-3335

Milgram, A. (2013). Why smart statistics are the key to fighting crime. *TED-Talk video*. Retrieved from https://www.ted.com/talks/anne_milgram_why_smart_statistics_are_the_key_to_fighting_crime

Mohammad, A., Mohsen, J., Martin, E., Uwe, G., & Richard, F. (2011). Crime-Walker: A Recommendation Model for Suspect Investigation. In *Proceedings of the fifth ACM conference on Recommender systems*.

Musdholifah, A., & Hashim, S. (2010). KNN-Kernel based Clustering for Spatio-Temporal Database. In *Proceedings of IEEE International Conference on Computer and Communication Engineering (ICCCE)*. doi:10.1109/ICCCE.2010.5556805

Ozgul, F., Atzenbeck, C., Celik, A., & Erdem, Z. (2011). Incorporating Data Sources and Methodologies for Crime Data Mining. In *Proceedings of IEEE International Conference on Intelligence and Security Informatics (ISI)*. doi:10.1109/ISI.2011.5983995

Phillips, P., & Lee, I. (2012). Mining Co-distribution Patterns for Large Crime Datasets. *International Journal of Expert Systems with Applications.*, *39*(14), 11556–11563. doi:10.1016/j.eswa.2012.03.071

PredPol. (2013). *PredPol Predicts Gun Violence*. Retrieved from http://cortecs.org/wp-content/uploads/2014/10/predpol_gun-violence.pdf

Ramanathan, V., & Wechsler, H. (2012). Phishing Website Detection Using Latent Dirichlet Allocation and AdaBoost. In *Proceedings of IEEE International Conference on Intelligence and Security Informatics (ISI)*. doi:10.1109/ISI.2012.6284100

Republic of South Africa. Statistics SA. (2014). *Victims of Crime Survey: P0341.* Statistics South Africa. Private Bag X44, Pretoria 0001. Retrieved from http://beta2.statssa.gov.za/publications/P0341/P03412013.pdf

Republic of South Africa. Department of Safety and Security CSIR Pretoria, National Crime Prevention Centre. (2013). *A Manual for Community Based Crime Prevention - Making South Africa Safe*. Retrieved from http://www.causes.com/causes/

Republic of South Africa. South African Police Service. (2011). *SAPS Together Squeezing Crime to Zero: Annual Report 2010/2011.* Retrieved from www.saps.gov.za

Republic of South Africa. South African Police Service. (2013). *Crime Statistics Overview: RSA 2011/2012.* Retrieved from http://www.saps.gov.za/statistics/reports/crimestats/2012/downloads

Republic of South Africa. Trading Economics Report. (2013). *Urban population growth (annual %) in South Africa.* Retrieved from http://www.tradingeconomics.com/south-africa

Republic of South Africa. Western Cape Government Report. (2013). Retrieved from http://www.westerncape.gov.za/eng/pubs/

Riesen, M., & Serpen, G. (2009). A Bayesian Belief Network Classifier for Predicting Victimization in National Crime Victimization Survey. In *Proceedings of the International Conference on Artificial Intelligence.*

Tayal, D., & Jain, A. (2014). Crime Detection and Criminal Identification in India using Data Mining Techniques. *AI & Society: International Journal of Knowledge, Culture and Communication.*

Vincent, N., Stephen, C., Derek, L., & Cheung, Y. (2007). Incremental Mining for Temporal Association Rules for Crime Pattern Discoveries. In *Proceedings of the ACM eighteenth conference on Australasian database.*

Vladimir, E., & Ickjai, L. (2001). Data Mining Techniques for Autonomous Exploration of Large Volumes of Geo-referenced Crime Data. In *Proceedings of the 6th International Conference on Geocomputation.*

Wang, B., Dong, H., Boedihardjo, A., Lu, C., Yu, H., Chen, I., & Dai, J. (2012). An Integrated Framewrok for Spatio-Temporal-Textual Search and Mining. In *Proceedings of the ACM International Conference on Advances in Geographic Information Systems (SIGSPATIAL GIS).*

Wang, D., Ding, W., Lo, H., Stepinski, T., Salazar, J., & Morabito, M. (2013a). Crime Hotspot Mapping using the Crime Related Factors- a spatial data mining approach. *Journal of Applied Intelligence*, *39*(4), 772–781. doi:10.1007/s10489-012-0400-x

Wang, T., Rudin, C., Wagner, D., & Sevieri, R. (2013b). Learning to Detect Patterns of Crime. In Machine Learning and Knowledge Discovery in Databases (LNCS), (vol. 8190, pp. 515–530). Springer-Verlag Berlin Heidelberg. doi:10.1007/978-3-642-40994-3_33

Wang, T., Rudin, C., Wagner, D., & Sevieri, R. (2013c). *Detecting Patterns of Crime with Series Finder*. AAAI Late Breaking Track.

Yahia, M., & El-taher, M. (2010). A New Approach for Evaluation of Data Mining Techniques. *International Journal of Computer Science Issues, 7*(5), 181-186.

Zhang, C., & Fang, Z. (2013). An Improved K-means Clustering Algorithm. *Journal of Information & Computational Science.*, *10*(1), 193–199.

Zhang, T., Ramakrishnan, R., & Livny, M. (1996). BIRCH: an efficient data clustering method for very large databases. In *Proceedings of the 1996 ACM SIGMOD international conference on Management of data SIGMOD'96*. doi:10.1145/233269.233324

Ziauddin, Kammal, S., Khan, K., & Khan, M. (2012). Research on Association Rule Mining. *Journal of Advances in Computational Mathematics and its Applications, 2*(1), 226-236.

KEY TERMS AND DEFINITIONS

Crime Clustering: The grouping of crime objects such that objects in the same class have very high intra-class similarity and low inter-class similarity.

Crime Data Mining: The process of discovering interesting, non-trivial and potentially useful (actionable) crime information.

Crime Hot-Spot: locations within close proximity to one another, where crimes occur on a regular basis.

Crime Pattern: A recurring trend of crime attributes or characteristics.

Crime Situation Recognition: The act of recognition of instances of recurring or prevalent crime situations or scenarios.

Crime Tactical Analysis: A crime analysis that is strategically planned in order to combat a specific crime.

Crime Taxonomy: A classification of crime according to certain elements or operating characteristics of occurrence.

APPENDIX: LIST OF NOTATIONS

ANN: Artificial Neural Network
BBN: Bayesian Belief Network
CDCI: Crime Detection and Criminal Identification
CRISP-DM: Cross-Industry Standard Process for Data Mining
CSR: Crime Situation Recognition
EDA: Exploratory Data Analysis
GIS: Geographic Information System
HOT: Hotspot Optimization Tool
HSA: Hot Spot Analysis
IACA: International Association of Crime Analysts
PREDPOL: Predictive Policing
SCDA: Spatial Crime Data Analysis
SEMMA: Sample, Explore, Modify, Model, Assess
STCA: Spatio-Temporal Crime Analysis
SVM: Support Vector Machine
TCDA: Temporal Crime Data Analysis
TDB: Transaction Database

Chapter 2
A Classification Framework for Data Mining Applications in Criminal Science and Investigations

Mahima Goyal
Ambedkar Institute of Advanced Communication Technologies and Research, India

Vishal Bhatnagar
Ambedkar Institute of Advanced Communication Technologies and Research, India

Arushi Jain
Ambedkar Institute of Advanced Communication Technologies and Research, India

DOI: 10.4018/978-1-5225-0463-4.ch002

ABSTRACT

The importance of data analysis across different domains is growing day by day. This is evident in the fact that crucial information is retrieved through data analysis, using different available tools. The usage of data mining as a tool to uncover the nuggets of critical and crucial information is evident in modern day scenarios. This chapter presents a discussion on the usage of data mining tools and techniques in the area of criminal science and investigations. The application of data mining techniques in criminal science help in understanding the criminal psychology and consequently provides insight into effective measures to curb crime. This chapter provides a state-of-the-art report on the research conducted in this domain of interest by using a classification scheme and providing a road map on the usage of various data mining tools and techniques. Furthermore, the challenges and opportunities in the application of data mining techniques in criminal investigation is explored and detailed in this chapter.

INTRODUCTION

In recent years, there has been an alarming increase in the volume of crimes in different applications like finance, credit card fraud, theft, violent crime, cybercrime, intrusion detection, and online fraud. It is a challenge for researchers to develop a crime analysis tool that can identify crime patterns accurately and efficiently. Thus crime science and investigation plays an important role in accounting such challenges of crime control and maintenance of public order.

Data mining is a field of extracting knowledge from huge amounts of data stored in Data warehouse and repositories. It is often used to uncover the latent truths behind huge volumes of data. It extracts interesting patterns which helps in detecting crimes and decision making. Thus, various advancements in crime data applications adopt data mining techniques to follow the task of crime investigation.

This chapter has three targets to achieve. The first target presents a framework which classifies the applications of data mining to Criminal Science and Investigations (CSI). The second is to provide a rigorous and extensive review of existing work on the applications of data mining to CSI. The third is to develop a road map for the researchers in this field. The major applications of CSI include financial frauds like credit card and money laundering, violent crime like sex and drug offense, theft and intrusion detection. Crime detection uses data mining techniques like classification, clustering, prediction, association, neural networks and genetic algorithms. The literature review shows that data mining techniques have been applied in detecting different types of crime, although, financial fraud and cyber crime are favored among the researchers.

The three subtasks of CSI involves extracting named entities from narrative reports, detecting deceptive criminal identities and identifying criminal group and key members of the group (Kevyanpour et al., 2011). The important algorithms used in 'Clustering' are k-means and AK-mode algorithm, in' Association', Apriori and Frequent Pattern (FP) growth algorithm, in 'Classification', Naïve Bayes Algorithm and Support Vector Machines (SVM). Other data mining techniques like neural networks and genetic algorithm have also made their way in appealing to the criminal investigators in the recent times.

The chapter is divided into various subtopics. The sections include an introduction, framework for data mining applications in CSI, data mining based layered framework, opportunities of data mining techniques associated with the criminal science and investigation and challenges of data mining associated with the criminal science and investigation. The framework for research includes the research methodologies used in writing the review. The framework for data mining applications includes classification of data mining techniques and classification of CSI. The analysis for CSI includes the steps performed while analyzing the classification.

RESEARCH DESIGN

Data mining techniques in Criminal Science Investigations is the field of study which has enormously gained huge popularity in a few years. It is a diverse discipline on which extensive research has been done. This field attracts a lot of researchers because of its wide applications in different domains. This chapter is dispersed across diverse journals and conferences. This diverse search comprises 16 research journals, 25 conference proceedings, two book chapters and lecture notes. The articles were reviewed with publication limit starting from 2008 to 2015. The various journal sites, which were chosen for the catalogue of the literature in this area are:

- IEEE Electronic Library,
- Science Direct,
- Springer Link Libraries,
- ACM Digital Library,
- IGI Global.

The articles were searched on the keywords 'data mining techniques' and 'criminal science investigation'. Every article was classified according to these two combined topics. Each article was reviewed extensively before including it in the chapter. It was then reviewed further for its inclusion in the final selection if any ambiguity arrived.

CLASSIFICATION FRAMEWORK FOR DATA MINING TECHNIQUES IN CRIME PATTERN DETECTION

The framework used for this review is classified into different levels of crime patterns and the data mining techniques associated with them. The framework extensively reviews past literature review and aims at providing impressive implication of the research. The authors have tried to unveil the potential of data mining techniques in crime data (Chen, 2004).

The classification of different levels of crime data is explained in Table 1. Different types of crime data are enlisted as sexual crime, financial fraud, traffic violations, theft, violent crimes and cybercrime. The classification framework is adopted from the article (Ngai et al., 2010) for Financial Fraud. A brief explanation of the framework along with the types of crimes and different data mining techniques

Figure 1. Classification framework based on criminal science applications in data mining
Adopted from Ngai, 2010.

Table 1. Classification of different types of crimes

Name of the Crimes	Types of the Crimes
1. Financial Fraud	Bank fraud, money laundering, insurance fraud, corporate fraud, security and commodities
2. Violent crime	Murder, honor-killing
3. Cyber crime	Online credit card fraud, suspicious emails, phishing, spam, DDOS, identity threat
4. Theft	Robbery, burglary, snatching
5. Traffic violations	Breaking of traffic rules
6. Sexual crimes	Rape, harassment

used, is described below. The major data mining classes are Classification, Clustering, Neural Network (NN), Genetic Algorithm (GA), Pattern and Prediction, Visualization, Regression and Fuzzy Logic.

Classification of Crime Data

1. **Financial Fraud:** This includes crime related to extortion of money by different illegitimate ways. It includes bank fraud, money laundering and insurance fraud.
    a. Bank fraud is the way of extorting money from a genuine user by the criminals posing as a bank.
    b. The three basic steps to money laundering are 'placement', 'layering' and 'integration' . In placement step, cash is introduced to a banking system or legitimate account. In the second step, layering is done by passing the money through several financial transactions to separate it from the criminal origins. In the third step, funds will be aggregated with legitimately obtained money(Gray & Debreceny, 2014)
    c. Insurance fraud means experiencing unauthorized benefits and insurance by introducing false claims and misconceptions. The most common ways of performing insurance crimes are:
        i. False claims,
        ii. Illegal Billing,
        iii. Inappropriate Testing,
        iv. Personal Injury Mills,
        v. Miscoding.

2. **Cyber Crime:** cybercrime involves criminal activities which are being performed by the means of computer or internet. This type of crime is increasing at an alarming rate due to the rapid increase of internet during the day to day lives. The major type of cyber crimes are credit card fraud, suspicious emails, phishing and Distributed Denial of Service Attacks (DDOS) and Identity Crimes. Identity crime is a way of deception in which criminals gain unauthorized access to the user's information through social networking and e-commerce sites, etc. It also includes forgery of identity documents motivated by the economic gain. The main application of identity crime is a credit card and Transaction Application. Phishing is the type of fraud in which perpetrators send e-mails to the legitimate users posing as trusted users in order to gain access to the users' credentials and financial profit. DDOS is the type of Denial of Service attack in which multiple sources attack an online service in order to make the services unavailable to the legitimate users by jamming the service.
3. **Violent Crime:** Violent crimes are those crimes in which some force is acted upon by the criminals. The extreme scenario of it would be the murder of a person. This type of crime is very dangerous.
4. **Traffic Violations:** It means breaking of the rules of the traffic by not adhering to them. This includes drink and drive, jumping red lights, road rage and damage of the property. Data mining techniques like Pattern and Prediction can be applied to detect such violations of traffic.
5. **Sexual Crime:** This covers heinous crimes against women. It includes rape, molestation, sexual assault and domestic violence.
6. **Theft:** It includes the crimes like chain snatching, robbery, burglary which involves illegal gain of the possessions of the legitimate people by physical means.

Classification of Data Mining Classes

1. **Classification:** It is a supervised learning based technique in which different items are classified into target classes. This technique is used in the cases where the exact prediction is required. In this, a training set is prepared which finds the association between the values of predictors and target. The target is the value assigned to the class and the predictor is the value associated with the domain whose target class needs to be found. The major classification techniques employed are Naïve Bayes Algorithm, Decision Tree and Support Vector Machines (SVM). This technique finds the significant applications in detection of Credit card fraud, suspicious emails, Theft and Sexual Crime
2. **Clustering:** It is used to group the objects in the meaningful clusters in order to maximize the intra class similarity and minimize the interclass similarity. It

means that the objects within the same cluster are highly similar to each other and the objects of the different clusters are dissimilar to each other according to some parameter. It is a type of unsupervised learning technique as the target variable cannot be identified. The main algorithm for this is K-means algorithm where K is the number of clusters. The main applications of this technique are in the detection of Robbery, Crime Profiling, Money Laundering

3. **Neural Network (NN):** A Neural Network is used to recognize patterns in data. The data can be specified according to the different domains like Financial Fraud including Credit Card Fraud detection and Phishing etc. NN are used for those problems where exact solution is not required as this technique is not sensitive to errors. Some common types of NN are Artificial Neural Network (ANN) and Multilayer Artificial Neural Network (MNN). An another type of NN is Granular Neural Network (GNN) which is used for fuzzy sets. NN solve problems in the similar way a human brain performs it. The increase computation leads to increase in complexity and hidden layers of the NN. It is designed by the interconnection of different nodes where each node has some weight and the output is calculated by multiplying the weight of different nodes with each other until we get the final output. It can be used for both supervised and unsupervised techniques.
4. **Genetic Algorithm:** It is used for the purpose of prediction to generate logic rules and fitness function in order to detect financial fraud and suspicious e-mails. The major steps which are used iteratively are Mutation, Inheritance, Selection and Crossover. GA and NN can be used in combination to solve a complex problem. Every model inherits traits from previous models and compares it with the other models. It is based on the theory of the fittest of the survival which means that the model which is fit will survive to the next generation and the others will not be applied to the next level.
5. **Visualization:** It is a way to present the complex data in an easy and understandable manner. The purpose is to understand the relationships between different patterns uncovered in data mining techniques. It can be visualized using tools and applications that use different graphs, color, size, positions and other visual techniques.
6. **Regression:** It is known to be used for estimating the relationships among variables. It is mainly used to predict some value based on different variables. It works by measuring the difference between the expected and predicted values of the dependent variables. This value is termed as 'regression coefficient'. The independent variables are the predictors and the dependent variables are the targets. It is mainly used for the detection of financial fraud, particularly credit card fraudulent detection. It consists of two sampling approaches-oversampling of minority and under sampling of majority class.

7. **Prediction:** This is also called Association Rule Mining. It involves finding relationships and frequent patterns among different entities. A frequent pattern means a sequence that appears frequently within the data. There are three types of association rule mining-Positive, Negative, Constraint Based. The main algorithm applied in this is Apriori and FP growth Algorithm. The major applications that fall in this data mining method is Cyber Crime, Violent Crime and Crime against women etc.
8. **Fuzzy Logic:** The word fuzzy means 'not crisp'. It gives the understanding that the solution is not definite but approximate and this fuzziness is removed using fuzzy logic in data mining. Fuzzy methods can be applied in clustering, Neural Network, Genetic Algorithm to make the solution crisper. It is a technique that assigns a data to a particular category based on some parameter. The performance of fuzzy logic can be extended by the numerical representation of unclear terms and by decreasing sensitivity to outliers. It can also be used to identify frauds in insurance and banking etc. The applications of data mining techniques in criminal fraud have been discussed in Table 2.

DATA MINING BASED LAYERED FRAMEWORK FOR CRIME INVESTIGATION

The data mining based layered framework is shown in Figure 2. The data mining techniques to be implemented in a criminal data follows the same procedure as followed by the generic data mining framework. The authors have tried to extend it to different criminal fraud. It includes special features of different data mining techniques in criminal fraud. It can be implemented by using all the four layers as described below:

Figure 2. Data mining based layered framework
Adopted from Sharma & Panigrahi, 2012.

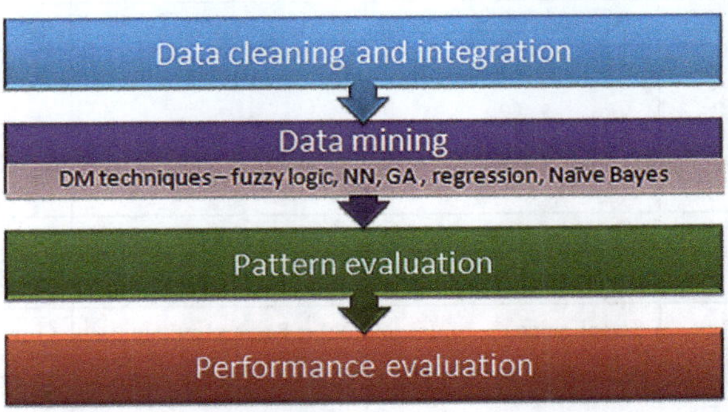

Table 2. A review of application of data mining techniques in criminal sciences

Reference	Year	Data Mining Technique	Algorithm Applied	Applications in Criminal Science
Isafiade et al	2015	Pattern and Prediction	FP growth algorithm	Crime datasets
Iqbal et al	2014	Classification	ID3 algorithm for decision tree	Suspicious e-mails
Sharma. M	2014	Fuzzy logic	Evolving Fuzzy grammar	Violent crime
Sharef and Martin	2013	Classification, Neural Network	Decision tree	Financial fraud
Ku and Leroy	2013	classification	Naïve Bayes	Crime reporting
Bogahawatte et al.	2013	Classification, clustering	Naïve Bayes	Theft
Gonzalez et al	2013	Pattern and Prediction	FP growth algorithm	Theft
Isafiade and Bagula	2012	Pattern and prediction	Apriori algorithm	Violent crimes
Iqbal et al.	2010	Clustering, pattern	K-means, FP growth	Cyber crime
Hussain et al	2013	Fuzzy logic	Fuzzy logic	Terrorist activities
Vishwakarma et al	2011	Fuzzy logic	Graph mining method	Money laundering
Michalak et al	2013	Pattern and prediction	Apriori and Predictive Apriori	Crime against women
Bansal et al	2013	Pattern, clustering	Apriori algorithm	Robbery, homicide
Sandig et al	2014	Classification, prediction	Naïve Bayes, Apriori algorithm	Theft, sexual crime
Sathyadevan et al	2010	Classification, Regression, GA	SVM, Probabilistic NN	Financial fraud
Ravisankar et al	2010	Clustering, neural network	Back Propogation method	Money laundering
Le et al	2013	Pattern and prediction	Apriori algorithm	Crime against women
Bansal et al	2013	Association rule mining	Apriori algorithm	Network Forensics
Zhong et al	2013	classification	J48 algorithm	Sexual crime
Sindhu et al	2012	Pattern and prediction	Apriori algorithm	Cyber crime
Sujatha et al	2014	Clustering	k-means algorithm	Crime profiling
Gera et al	2013	Clustering	k-means algorithm	robbery
Khan et al	2011	NN, classification	SVM	financial fraud
Ravisankar et al	2011	NN, classification	Bayesian network	financial fraud
Perols et al	2011	NN, classification	SVM	financial fraud
Zhou et al	2015	Clustering	K-means algorithm	Cyber crime
Patange	2015	Classification, clustering	KNN,K-means	Theft, Violent crime
Tayal	2013	Association Rule mining	Apriori algorithm	Cyber crime(Phishing)
Kadam	2014	Classification	Naïve Bayes Algorithm	Criminal Profiling
Sathyevedan Ranjan	2014	Association Rule Mining	Apriori algorithm	Cyber Attacks

Layer 1: It is the data cleaning and integration layer. In this, first data integration is performed in which the data is collected from different sources. Different sources from where data can be extracted are financial statements, audit reports, crime reports, arrest reports, police calls etc. Next is 'data selection'. In this we select the data on which data mining is performed. After that cleaning is performed by removing inconsistencies and missing values.

Layer 2: It is the data mining layer in which a technique is chosen for data mining from the different techniques available. The next step is to choose the algorithm for that chosen technique. The different data mining techniques available are NN, GA, Classification, clustering, etc. Different algorithms can be applied to different cases of crime data as shown in the Table 2. These algorithms are then applied to gain useful information so that different types of crimes can be detected.

Layer 3: It is the pattern evaluation layer. It includes transformation, visualization and removing inconsistent and redundant patterns. In this layer, useful patterns representing knowledge are extracted. E.g.: The clustering technique enables the extraction of useful information about the group of persons involved in credit card fraud. This layer extracts these patterns after the data mining techniques are applied.

Layer 4: It is the performance evaluation layer. It includes reviews of the patterns so that a better decision can be taken. This chooses different measures like Precision, Recall and F-measure to evaluate the performance of the extracted pattern.

OPPORTUNITIES OF DATA MINING TECHNIQUES ASSOCIATED WITH THE CRIMINAL SCIENCE AND INVESTIGATION.

Table 3 shows the various opportunities of data mining techniques associated with the criminal science and technology.

Criminology is the most suitable field for applying data analysis because of voluminous data and complex relationship among different parts of data. Data mining is the analytical process for analyzing and exploring large data sets to find hidden rules, associations and patterns among the parts of data. It helps to formalize and plan the future decision making process which is enabled by the knowledge feature. In this section, we discussed about the various opportunities and challenges of data mining in CSI, which focuses on extraction of named entities from reports, detecting criminal identities from existing crime datasets and identifying criminal groups. To safeguard against fraud, anti crime organizations are liable to select the best methods to cater their needs.

Table 3. Data mining techniques

Data Mining Technique	Underlying Structure	Basic Process	Validation Method	Example
Cluster Detection	In n-vector space distance is calculated	Similar objects are grouped together.	To verify accuracy cross validation method is used	Market analysis for example market basket analysis
Decision Trees	Binary Tree	At decision points data sets are branched based on their entropy.	Cross validation	Risk Assessment: Credit card upgrades
Memory-based Reasoning	On the basis of distance and combination functions predictive structure is formulated.	In this technique unknown occurrence is associated with known occurrence.	Cross validation	Mortgage Loans, Customer Retention
Link Analysis	Different nodes are linked together.	Relationship among various nodes are identified.	Not applicable	Customers likely to churn.
Neural Networks	Large processing elements are working in parallel to solve a specific problem.	Weights are assigned at each input node.	Not applicable	Trend analysis.
Genetic Algorithms	Not applicable	Based on survival of the fittest.	Mostly cross validation	Customer Relationship Marketing.

Paulraj, 2011; Palshikar, 2002.

CHALLENGES OF DATA MINING ASSOCIATED WITH THE CRIMINAL SCIENCE AND INVESTIGATION

Key challenges of data mining associated with the criminal science and investigation that needs to be addressed are listed below:

1. **Mounting Data Mining Algorithm:** New algorithms are required to deal with distributed, parallel, and out-of-memory versions of mining algorithms. As a technology, data mining is too "ad-hoc" and is designed for discrete problems. The question rises whether to build a relational database or multidimensional database structure. In relational database data is stored in column wise fashion while in multidimensional structure data is stored in the set of cubes. The more powerful, the data mining query is, larger the data is being collected and maintained. This enhances the need for speedy system, which are too costly.

2. **Expanding Data Mining Algorithms to New Data Types:** In data mining, data is obtained from different sources possessing different data formats. Due to the varying data formats, no single data mining algorithm can be applied to all the application (Jiang et al.,1999). The most suitable algorithm is selected on the basis of goal of the application and data fittability. It is important to transform the various data formats into the target which is a complex task in the real world. It is a challenge to enlarge data mining algorithms to work with variant data types. Generalized data types will reduce the transformation complexity and user could able to select the suitable mining algorithm to successfully achieve the goal (Jiang, Tseng, & Liao, 1999).
3. **Evolving Distributed Data Mining Algorithms:** The rapid growth of communication networks results into the generation of voluminous datasets from various sources such as supermarket, banking, stock market and mobile service. Distributed Data Mining (DDM) can be implemented using any one of the four approaches,(Hammouda & Kamel, 2009). The first approach is to carry data together, to mine in a single and centralized data warehouse, but this is highly costly and is a possible violation of privacy. The second approach is to perform mining locally at each site to build a local model. The local models built are then combined into a global model. (Samatova, Ostrouchov, Geist, & Melechko, 2002) . This approach deals with the scalability problem with the increase in the number of sites. The third approach is using samples where a small set of illustrative data is carefully sampled at each site to form one global illustrative dataset. The data mining can then be performed on the global representative data set (Nair, Judith, & Jayakumari, 2011). The fourth approach is to perform data mining on peer to peer(P2P) networks, where sites communicate directly with each other without involving a central server (Datta et al., 2005)
4. **Ease of Use:** The data mining tools are far from the understanding of the average analyst as the tool was generally designed for expert statisticians. A root challenge is to refine data mining systems which is easier to use.
5. **Data Must Be Available, Adequate, Clean and Relevant to be Used:** The data should be accessible, sufficient and crisp. When we select data from the data warehouse, it is assumed that all the errors have been removed and the varying data format is transformed into the target one (Pooniah Paulraj, 2011). Data mining techniques produce good results when voluminous data is available at the lowest grain. Data mining is the analytical process of discovering and extracting unseen patterns and relationship among parts of data, allowing making productive and useful decision. Mining erroneous data leads to the discovery of wrong patterns and relationship (Paulraj, 2011).

6. **Data Mining Problem Must Be Well Defined:** The problem domain must be clearly defined to accurately and efficiently analyze the growing data volume but organizing proper questions and condition attributes is not an easy task. The data mining tool must be able to access data sources and should quickly bring the required datasets to the environment. The objective of data mining is to analyze and explore large data sets to find hidden rules, associations and patterns among the parts of data, which helps to formalize and plan the future decision making process which is enabled by knowledge feature(Paulraj, 2011).
7. **High Degree of Missing Data Limits Prediction Accuracy:** Data mining means discovering, exploring and extracting unseen patterns and relationship between large data sets. Mining erroneous data leads to the discovery of wrong patterns and relationship. Thus, false information will be gained resulting into the production of imprecise results. The actions taken based on the uncertain discoveries will produce significant imprecise results so the data warehouse quality of the data must be maintained (Paulraj, 2011).
8. **Are Data Mining Tools Are Sufficient for Detecting and Preventing Crime?:** The tool must be compatible with the overall framework of metadata. The tool must be able to explain the rules and the discovery of patterns. (Paulraj, 2011).

CLASSIFICATION OF PAPERS

Distribution of Papers According to the Crime Type

The Figure 3 shows the distribution of the articles discussed in the chapter according to the different types of crime. It is clearly evident that the number of crimes in the financial fraud and cybercrime is increasing at a rampant rate. Both of these are followed by Sexual crime and Theft. The least number of papers was found in violent crime.

Distribution of Papers Asccording to the Data Mining Techniques

The Figure 4 shows the distribution of papers according to the different data mining techniques like Classification, Clustering, Pattern and Prediction, NN, GA, Fuzzy Logic, Regression, Visualization. The chart shows that the numbers of papers found in Pattern and Prediction are maximum followed by Classification, Clustering, NN and Fuzzy Logic. The least number of papers is in GA, Regression and Visualization.

Figure 3. Frequency of papers according to crime type

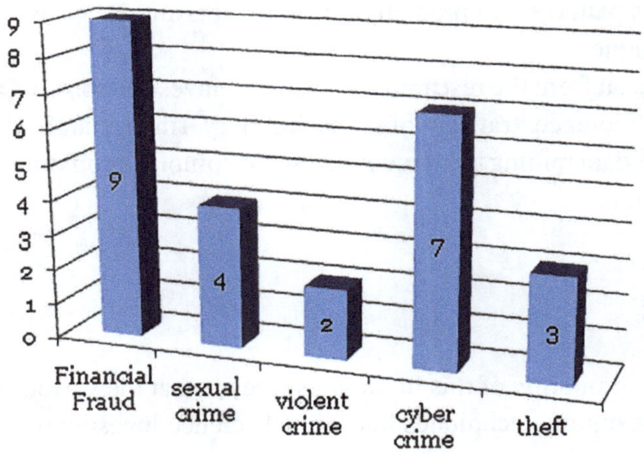

Figure 4. Frequency of papers according to data mining techniques

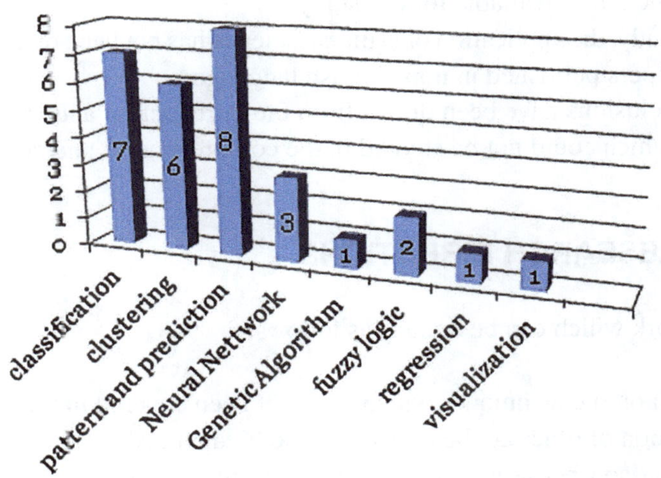

IMPLICATION OF RESEARCH AND IMPLEMENTATION

1. The rampant research going on in the field of CSI covers different application areas like cyber crime and financial fraud.
2. It is quite clear from our study that the type of crime which attracts the most researchers is financial fraud and cyber crime.
3. It can be understood that the two data mining techniques can be combined to perform detection and prevention of criminal data.

4. The hottest data mining technique which is quite evident from the above research is patterns and prediction with Apriori and FP growth Algorithm of this technique.
5. It can be seen from the research that criminal investigation covers all the areas including violence, traffic violations, burglary, finance and cyber.
6. The use of data mining techniques can solve complex problems in the criminal investigation.

LIMITATION

1. The major limitation of this literature survey is that the various papers related to the data mining techniques in criminal science investigation are limited to a few authors.
2. It was tried to cover all the available papers of the mentioned authors, but we cannot claim encompassing research as there may be some other techniques and applications available for our study.
3. In this study, the application of criminal science has not been discussed related to the papers published in non-English languages.
4. The conclusions have been drawn from the introduction and abstract of such papers which could not be studied in the comprehensive and complete way.

FUTURE RESEARCH DIRECTIONS

The future work which can be done is as follows:

- Research on the techniques which have not been covered in the research.
- Exploration of other applications can also be included.
- A comparison between new and improved methodology can be done with existing work of proving the said work.

CONCLUSION

It is quite clear from this research that criminal investigation is an ongoing field that has attracted a lot of researchers and academicians in the recent times. The classification by the author will make new avenues for the researchers to gain in-sight knowledge about the subject. The existing research will be beneficial for the other authors to implement their requirements in an easy manner. The literature was extensively reviewed across different articles to construct a good classification framework. It is evident from the graph in Figure 4 that very few articles have been discussed on the techniques 'Visualization' and 'Regression'. It is due to the fact that less work has been done on these techniques. On the other hand, 'clustering' and 'classification' are a favorite among the different authors as much work has been done on it. The authors have not only identified different techniques of data mining but also provided a systematic review of their applications in different types of frauds. Although an exhaustive review for this chapter cannot be asserted, the chapter will be useful to anyone who is interested in this study.

REFERENCES

Bansal, D., & Bhambhu, L. (2013a). Usage of Apriori Algorithm of Data Mining as an Application to Grievous Crimes against Women. *International Journal of Computer Trends and Technology*, *4*(9), 3194–3199.

Bansal, D., & Bhambhu, L. (2013b). Execution of APRIORI Algorithm of Data Mining Directed Towards Tumultuous Crimes Concerning Women. *International Journal of Advanced Research in Computer Science and Software Engineering*, *3*(9), 54–62.

Bogahawatte, K., & Adikari, S. (2013). Intelligent criminal identification system. In *Computer Science & Education (ICCSE), 8th International Conference on* (pp. 633-638). doi:doi:10.1109/ICCSE.2013.6553986doi:10.1109/ICCSE.2013.6553986

Chen, H., Chung, W., Xu, J. J., Wang, G., Qin, Y., & Chau, M. (2004). Crime data mining: A general framework and some examples. *Computer*, *37*(4), 50–56. doi:10.1109/MC.2004.1297301

Datta, S., Bhaduri, K., Giannella, C., Wolff, R., & Kargupta, H. (2006). Distributed data mining in peer-to-peer networks. *IEEE Internet Computing*, *10*(4), 18–26. doi:10.1109/MIC.2006.74

Gera, P., & Vohra, R. (2014). City Crime Profiling Using Cluster Analysis. *International Journal of Computer Science & Information Technologies*, *5*(4), 5145–5148.

González, P. C., & Velásquez, J. D. (2013). Characterization and detection of taxpayers with false invoices using data mining techniques. *Expert Systems with Applications*, *40*(5), 1427–1436. doi:10.1016/j.eswa.2012.08.051

Gray, G. L., & Debreceny, R. S. (2014). A taxonomy to guide research on the application of data mining to fraud detection in financial statement audits. *International Journal of Accounting Information Systems*, *15*(4), 357–380. doi:10.1016/j.accinf.2014.05.006

Hammouda, K. M., & Kamel, M. S. (2009). Hierarchically distributed peer-to-peer document clustering and cluster summarization. *Knowledge and Data Engineering. IEEE Transactions on*, *21*(5), 681–698.

Hussain, K. Z., Durairaj, M., & Farzana, G. (2012). Criminal behavior analysis by using data mining techniques. In *Advances in Engineering, Science and Management (ICAESM), International Conference on,* (pp. 656-658).

Iqbal, F., Binsalleeh, H., Fung, B. C., & Debbabi, M. (2010). Mining writeprints from anonymous e-mails for forensic investigation. *Digital Investigation*, *7*(1), 56–64. doi:10.1016/j.diin.2010.03.003

Isafiade, O., Bagula, A., & Berman, S. (2015). A Revised Frequent Pattern Model for Crime Situation Recognition Based on Floor-Ceil Quartile Function. *Procedia Computer Science*, *55*, 251–260. doi:10.1016/j.procs.2015.07.042

Isafiade, O. E., & Bagula, A. B. (2013). Citisafe: Adaptive spatial pattern knowledge using fp-growth algorithm for crime situation recognition. In *Ubiquitous Intelligence and Computing, IEEE 10th International Conference on and 10th International Conference on Autonomic and Trusted Computing (UIC/ATC)* (pp. 551-556).

Jiang, M. F., Tseng, S. S., & Liao, S. Y. (1999). Data types generalization for data mining algorithms. In *Systems, Man, and Cybernetics, 1999. IEEE SMC'99 Conference Proceedings. IEEE International Conference on,* (pp. 928-933).

Kadam, A. S., & Pawar, S. S. (2013). Comparison of association rule mining with pruning and adaptive technique for classification of phishing dataset. In *Computational Intelligence and Information Technology, CIIT Third International Conference on,* (pp. 61-67). doi:doi:10.1049/cp.2013.2573 doi:10.1049/cp.2013.2573

Keyvanpour, M. R., Javideh, M., & Ebrahimi, M. R. (2011). Detecting and investigating crime by means of data mining: A general crime matching framework. *Procedia Computer Science*, *3*, 872–880. doi:10.1016/j.procs.2010.12.143

Le Khac, N. A., Markos, S., & Kechadi, M. (2010). A data mining-based solution for detecting suspicious money laundering cases in an investment bank. In *Advances in Databases Knowledge and Data Applications (DBKDA), Second International Conference on,* (pp. 235-240).

Michalak, K., & Korczak, J. (2011). Graph mining approach to suspicious transaction detection. In *Computer Science and Information Systems (FedCSIS), 2011 Federated Conference on,* (pp. 69-75).

Nair, V. V., Judith, J. E., & Jayakumari, J. (2011). Secured distributed document clustering & keyphrase extraction algorithm in structured Peer to Peer networks. In *Signal Processing, Communication, Computing and Networking Technologies (ICSCCN), International Conference on,* (pp. 151-156). doi:doi:10.1109/ICSCCN.2011.6024533 doi:10.1109/ICSCCN.2011.6024533

Ngai, E. W. T., Hu, Y., Wong, Y. H., Chen, Y., & Sun, X. (2011). The application of data mining techniques in financial fraud detection: A classification framework and an academic review of literature. *Decision Support Systems*, *50*(3), 559–569. doi:10.1016/j.dss.2010.08.006

Palshikar, G. K. (2002). The Hidden Truth -Frauds and Their Control: A Critical Application for Business Intelligence. *Intelligent Enterprise*, *5*(9), 46–51.

Patange, D. V., & Butey, P. K. (2015). Analyze Cluster Techniques for Web Crime Patterns of Web Users. *International Journal of Advanced Research in Computer Science and Software Engineering*, *5*(4), 128–131.

Perols, J. (2011). Financial statement fraud detection: An analysis of statistical and machine learning algorithms. *Auditing: A Journal of Practice & Theory, 30*(2), 19-50.

Ponniah, P. (2004). *Data warehousing fundamentals: a comprehensive guide for IT professionals*. John Wiley & Sons.

Ranjan, P., & Vaish, A. (2014). Apriori Viterbi Model for Prior Detection of Socio-Technical Attacks in a Social Network. *In Engineering and Telecommunication (EnT), International Conference on.*

Ravisankar, P., Ravi, V., Rao, G. R., & Bose, I. (2011). Detection of financial statement fraud and feature selection using data mining techniques. *Decision Support Systems*, *50*(2), 491–500. doi:10.1016/j.dss.2010.11.006

Samatova, N. F., Ostrouchov, G., Geist, A., & Melechko, A. V. (2002). RACHET: An Efficient CoverBased Merging of Clustering Hierarchies from Distributed Datasets. *Distributed and Parallel Databases*, *11*(2), 157–180.

Sandig, J. D. E., Somoba, R. M., Concepcion, M. B., & Gerardo, B. D. (2013). Mining Online GIS for Crime Rate and Models based on Frequent Pattern Analysis. In *Proceedings of the World Congress on Engineering and Computer Science*.

Sathyadevan, S., Devan, M. S., & Surya Gangadharan, S. (2014). Crime analysis and prediction using data mining. *In Networks & Soft Computing (ICNSC), First International Conference on.*

Sharef, N. M., & Martin, T. (2015). Evolving fuzzy grammar for crime texts categorization. *Applied Soft Computing*, *28*, 175–187. doi:10.1016/j.asoc.2014.11.038

Sharma, A., & Panigrahi, P. K. (2013). *A review of financial accounting fraud detection based on data mining techniques.* arXiv preprint arXiv:1309.3944

Sharma, M. (2014). Z-CRIME: A data mining tool for the detection of suspicious criminal activities based on decision tree. In *Data Mining and Intelligent Computing (ICDMIC), International Conference on* (pp. 1-6). doi:doi:10.1109/ICDMIC.2014.6954268 doi:10.1109/ICDMIC.2014.6954268

Sindhu, K. K., & Meshram, B. B. (2013). Digital Forensics and Cyber Crime Data mining. *Journal of Information Security*, *3*(3), 196–201. doi:10.4236/jis.2012.33024

Sujatha, R., & Ezhilmaran, D. (2013). A Proposal for Analysis of Crime Based on Socio–Economic Impact using Data Mining Techniques. *International Journal of Societal Applications of Computer Science*, *2*(2), 229–231.

Tayal, D. K., Jain, A., Arora, S., Agarwal, S., Gupta, T., & Tyagi, N. (2015). Crime detection and criminal identification in India using data mining techniques. *AI & Society*, *30*(1), 117–127. doi:10.1007/s00146-014-0539-6

Vishwakarma, R. K., & Shankar, R. (2013). Modeling brain and behavior of a terrorist through fuzzy logic and ontology. In *Industrial Engineering and Engineering Management (IEEM), IEEE International Conference on* (pp. 857-861). doi:doi:10.1109/IEEM.2013.6962533 doi:10.1109/IEEM.2013.6962533

Zhong, X. (2013). The Application Of Apriori Algorithm For Network Forensics Analysis. *Journal of Theoretical and Applied Information Technology*, *50*(2), 430–434.

Zhou, W., & Kapoor, G. (2011). Detecting evolutionary financial statement fraud. *Decision Support Systems*, *50*(3), 570–575. doi:10.1016/j.dss.2010.08.007

ADDITIONAL READING

Bharathi, A. S., & Shilpa, R. (2014). A Survey on Crime Data Analysis of Data Mining Using Clustering Techniques. *International Journal of Advance Research in Computer Science and Management Studies*, *2*(8), 9–13.

Chen, H., Chung, W., Xu, J. J., Wang, G., Qin, Y., & Chau, M. (2004). Crime data mining: A general framework and some examples. *Computer*, *37*(4), 50–56. doi:10.1109/MC.2004.1297301

Devesh, B. (2012). Emerging Trends in Utilization of Data Mining in Criminal Investigation: An Overview. *Journal of Environmental Science. Computer Science and Engineering & Technology*, *2*, 124–131.

Dutta, S., Gianella, C., & Kargupta, H. (2005). K-means clustering over peer-to-peer networks. In 8th international workshop on high performance and distributed mining, SIAM international conference on data mining.

Eck, J., Chainey, S., Cameron, J., & Wilson, R. (2005). Mapping crime: Understanding hotspots.*1-71*.

Oatley, G., Ewart, B., & Zeleznikow, J. (2006). Decision support systems for police: Lessons from the application of data mining techniques to "soft" forensic evidence. *Artificial Intelligence and Law*, *14*(1-2), 35–100. doi:10.1007/s10506-006-9023-z

Wang, T., Rudin, C., Wagner, D., & Sevieri, R. (2015). Finding Patterns with a Rotten Core: Data Mining for Crime Series with Cores. *Big Data*, *3*(1), 3–21. doi:10.1089/big.2014.0021

KEY TERMS AND DEFINITIONS

Classification: A supervised learning based technique in which different items are classified into target classes.

Clustering: Used to group the objects in the meaningful clusters in order to maximize the intra class similarity and minimize the interclass similarity.

Cyber Crime: Cyber crime involves criminal activities which are being performed by the means of computer or internet.

Financial Fraud: This includes crime related to extortion of money by different illegitimate ways. It includes Bank Fraud, Money Laundering and Insurance Fraud.

Neural Network: NN are used for those problems where exact solution is not required, such that this technique is not sensitive to errors.

Pattern and Prediction: Involves finding relationships and frequent patterns among different entities.

Violent Crime: Violent crimes are those crimes in which some force is acted upon by the criminals

Section 2
HotSpot, Spatial, and Visual Analytics

Chapter 3
Visual Analytics for Crime Analysis and Decision Support

Chih-Hao Ku
Lawrence Technological University, USA

Alicia Iriberri
California State University, Fresno, USA

Goutam Jena
Lawrence Technological University, USA

ABSTRACT

Today, the amount of digital data increases exponentially due to the rapid growth of the Internet, mobile, and sensory data. Crime data are arriving from multiple sources and formats. The major challenge for crime analysis is to store, manipulate, manage, and analyze data efficiently. To gain useful insight from a great amount of raw data, visual analytics techniques have been drawn attention to law enforcement agencies and researchers. The visual analytics applications do not erase the need for crime analysts' insight. To make better predictions and smarter decisions, data mining, text mining, information visualization, human-computer interaction, and analytics techniques are important to explore. This book chapter provides an overview of different types of crime data, discusses how to analyze and visualize different types of data, and explores popular visualization toolkits that have been used for crime analysis.

DOI: 10.4018/978-1-5225-0463-4.ch003

INTRODUCTION

Motivation

A massive volume of structured and unstructured data posts great challenges on data processing, search, analysis, and visualization. Crime data such as crime reports and criminal information are digitized and stored for later use. However, raw crime data have limited value in itself. Data mining and information visualization techniques enable users to explore data and hidden patterns and relationships, and use interactive graphical tools to gain an understanding of data by highlighting, comparing information and even revealing patterns, trends, and outliers (Heer, Bostock, & Ogievetsky, 2010; Purchase, Andrienko, Jankun-Kelly, & Ward, 2008). More recently, the term visual analytics (Stone, 2009) has been emphasized to analyze extremely large volumes of data to gain insight and facilitate decision making. Graphical presentation requires careful selection of colors, sizes, positions, and typography to avoid graphical distortion and inadequate presentation (Stone, 2009). Today, human-computer interaction (HCI) attracts considerable attention to better understand human's requirements and perceptions and to enhance design of visual interfaces. Basic design techniques such as zoom, filter, and details-on-demand are prevalent approaches for effective visual displays.

Objective

This chapter explores visual analytics for crime analysis; in particular, how information visualization can be used to display different types of crime data and support decision making. The sections present various visual representations that have been used to reveal the meaning of crime data.

The emphasis is on reviewing data analysis techniques and toolkits for visualization that can be used for crime analysis and on introducing a variety of graphical representations such as force-directed layout, histogram, arc diagram (Heer et al., 2010), network visualization (Didimo, Liotta, & Montecchiani, 2014), heatmap visualization, tag clouds (Wang et al., 2012), and GIS-based solutions that can be used to create effective crime data visualizations.

The review of visual analytics for crime analysis follows the framework shown in Figure 1. Visualization tools that have been used in the analysis of crime data allows four types of data analysis: statistical, textual, multimedia, and spatio-temporal. The four types of data analysis are discussed in this chapter along with example cases where these have been used and the toolkits that support these analyses.

Figure 1. A framework of visual analytics for crime analysis

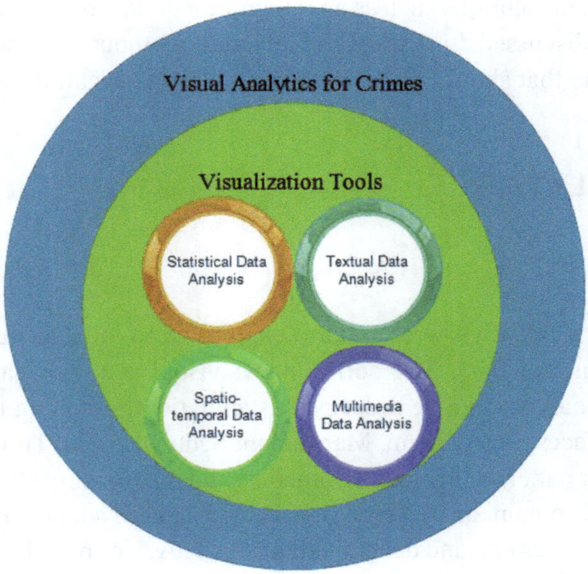

The toolkits that can be used for crime analysis include for example the toolkits D3 (M. Bostock, Ogievetsky, & Heer, 2011) and Visualization Toolkit (Heer et al., 2010). These toolkits have been studied and used frequently to visualize datasets. The review of current research studies shows that tools have been used in combination to further extend the analysis of datasets. However, these combination requires extra effort and time to import and export data from one tool to another. A more desirable solution is to use platforms that offer added capabilities – the one that combines data mining algorithms with visualizations techniques.

In this chapter, the authors explore the following questions:

- How visual analytics can be used to facilitate crime analysis and gain insights of crime data?
- What types of visual graphics have been used to visualize the various types of crime data?
- What open-source and proprietary tools and toolkits have been used for crime analysis and information visualization?

The outline of this chapter is the following. Visual analytics and information visualization is first introduced. A classification of crime data analysis is then provided: statistical data analysis, textual data analysis, multimedia data analysis, and spatio-temporal data analysis. After discussing four types of data analysis, visualization tools including popular open-source and proprietary toolkits are examined. Next, the combined solutions such as an integration of data mining and information visualization are discussed. Last, principles of human computer interaction (HCI) and human perception that should guide the creation of visualizations are emphasized.

VISUAL ANALYTICS

Principle

Visual analytics is a fast-growing field to explore and synthesize information and gain understanding of data. The definition of visual analytics can be varied. In general, visual analytics can be described as analytical reasoning techniques with interactive interfaces (D. A. Keim, Mansmann, Schneidewind, Thomas, & Ziegler, 2008) to discover patterns, changes, anomalies, and relationships (Cook, Earnshaw, & Stasko, 2007), to gain and develop new insight, and to support data processing, knowledge representation, and decision making (D. A. Keim et al., 2008). The goal of visual analytics research for crime analysis is thus to turn a large volume of data into useful and actionable knowledge for prevention, forecasting, management, and eventually solution of crime.

Visual analytics is a multi-disciplinary field. Keim, Kohlhammer, and Ellis (2010) illustrated the general scope and disciplines that contribute to visual analytics. The building block includes data management, data mining, human perception and cognition, visualization, and spatial-temporal data analysis. The main focus of this chapter is on information visualization and data analysis, including spatial-temporal data analysis and visual representations, in the crime domain.

For financial crime detection, Didimo, Liotta, & Montecchiani (2014) used network diagrams combined with ad-hoc clustering techniques to discover criminal patterns such as money laundering and frauds. The system has been used for two years and a survey study was conducted with four users and received positive feedback from the users.

Luo and MacEachren (2014) contend that space and social networks should be studied simultaneously when trying to explain human activities and added that visual analytics provides the methods to understanding the interaction of these two fields of study. The value of the combination of space, social network, and visual analytics is exemplified by research on crime analysis. White and Roth (2010) designed TwitterHitter.com, a prototype that generates map-timeline views of recent activities of suspects on Twitter and generates network graphs of suspect's known associates. White and Roth (2010) contend that this prototype could be used to support crime analysis, and decision making on information gathering and personnel deployment.

Information Visualization and Data Analysis

Information visualization is a discipline that exploits interactive graphics to help people comprehend data and facilitate communications or decision making (Louis Engelbrecht, 2014). Visual analysis enables users to develop insights through an interactive process of viewing, exploring, and refining visual graphs. Visual properties such as size, color contrast, shape, and position are frequently used to help users discover patterns and relationship and make sense of data. Heer & Shneiderman (2012) provide a taxonomy of tools that support interactive, visual analysis. For example, the data & view specification includes visualizing data by selecting visual encodings, filtering out data, sorting items, and deriving values.

In the crime domain, a great variety of visual representations and tools have been used to analyze the equally varied types of data that may be available. Crime data may include spatial and temporal descriptors, personal characteristics of suspects, characteristics of property or vehicles involved, and even actions and circumstances that were present when incidents occurred. Therefore, it is generally difficult to use one graph to represent the diversity of crime data. In this section, the authors provide an overview of the different data, graphs and tools used in crime analysis and classify visual analysis for crime into four major categories: statistical or numeric, textual, multimedia, and spatial-temporal data analysis as shown in Table 1.

The outline of this section is the following, statistical and data analysis including data from the National Incident-Based Reporting System (NIBRS), Uniform Crime Reports (UCR), National Crime Victimization Survey (NCVS) is first introduced. Textual and multimedia data Analysis is then discussed. Finally, spatio-temporal Data Analysis including hot spot, graduate, pin, chart, and buffer maps is presented.

Table 1. A classification of crime data analysis for visual analytics

Type of Crime Data	Description
Statistical/numeric data	Population, crime rate, values (e.g., similarity scores), frequency, number of occurrences.
Textual data	Text reports, notes, crime tips, extracted crime entities such as vehicle, gun, clothing, crime reports, type of crimes, names, locations (e.g., hospital, school, etc.), phone numbers, address (e.g., city, zip code, and state).
Multimedia	Audio, video, image, 3D
Spatio-temporal data	Latitude, longitude, and time.

Statistical or Numeric Data Analysis

Statistical or numeric data for crime incidents is available from government institutions, law enforcement agencies, cities, and schools. The granularity of these data varies from very detailed to very general including aggregated, summarized, and calculated data. In the United States, two major sources of data are the NIBRS and UCR published by the Federal Bureau of Investigation (FBI). An additional source is the NCVS that represents a firsthand source of information of crimes that may not have been reported or detected.

- **NIBRS:** NIBRS is an incident-based reporting system for crimes and known to law enforcement agencies. Data include demographic characteristics of the offender(s) and victim(s), specific incident offenses, and value of stolen properties. The NIBRS data include detailed information on each single crime occurrence. These data are collected by law enforcement agencies and include more than 200 variables such as type of incident date/year/month/day of occurrence, location type, city submission, criminal activity, type of weapon / forced involved, automatic firearm, among others. Under the type of weapon/ force, the weapons are classified into a firearm, handgun, rifle, shotgun, other firearm, knife, blunt object, personal weapons, poison, and explosive.
- **UCR:** The FBI UCR program provides national crime report data obtained by law enforcement agencies. The participating agencies submit a crime index including different types of crimes such as violent and property crimes, assault, and fraud. The FBI collects crime statistics from law enforcement agencies and publishes the results yearly. The statistics include violent crime (e.g., aggravated assault, murder, and robbery) and property crime (e.g., arson, burglary, and motor vehicle theft).
- **NCVS:** The NCVS survey enables the Bureau of Justice Statistics (BJS) to estimate the number of unreported crimes. The NCVS is the primary source of criminal victimization. The data has been collected from 1973 to 2013 from a nationally representative sample of appropriately 90,000 households. The NCVS has a large number of variables. Variables include weapons such as a handgun (e.g., pistol, revolver, etc.) or other guns (e.g., rifle, shotgun, etc.), types of injuries suffered (e.g., rape, knife, stab wounds, etc.), property description (e.g., something taken, attempt theft, etc.), and location information (e.g., city, county, etc.). The reliability of the NCVS data is limited since they depend on victims' ability or willingness to accurately recall the crime incident in which they were involved. Data are from individuals who are at least 12 years old and does not include homicides or crimes committed against children.

The analysis of existing data from the National Archive of Criminal Justice Data (NACJD) is a priority of BJS. The NACJD, administered by the Data Resource Program (DRP), makes data available for researchers to conduct new research, reproduce original findings, replicate results, and test new hypotheses. In recent search, the authors found that visual analytics techniques have not been used extensively to analyze the available data resources.

Statistical analysis packages are often used to represent trends and patterns found in large datasets. Statwing developers demonstrate the capabilities of this statistical analysis tool using crime data from 2001 to 2013 in Chicago (Laughlin, 2014). The demonstration shows visualizations including time of day and month of the year and various types of crime occurred. The visualization includes bar charts and heatmaps. Examples of their findings include criminal sexual assault in Chicago that are strongly associated with New Year's Day and homicides and gambling arrests that are most common in the warmer months.

LaValle, Haas, Turley, and Nolan (2013) used graphical analysis to supplement the automated outlier detection methods to evaluate data quality. These analyses included standard deviation and box plot thresholds to identify outliers in the data from the Huntington Police Department (PD), obtained from West Virginia (WV)'s Incident-based Reporting data. Three different plots were used for data visualizations, a histogram, dot plot, and line chart (see Figure 2 right). In their results, La Valle et al. used histograms (see Figure 2 left) to display the data distribution, with the left-skewed distribution suspected to have anomalies. They used a dot plot (see Figure 2 middle) to show the spread and clustering pattern of data with isolated points or small clusters separated from the main cluster representing outliers. The line chart illustrated the agency's data trend over time, with a peak or valley point indicating higher or lower crime counts for seasonal data visualization.

Wheeler (2015) used crime statistics published by the New York City Police Department (NYPD) and provided an overview on how to construct tables with different color schemes (see Table 2) and graphs. Five colors were used for table

Figure 2. Outlier plots for Huntington PD property crime counts
LaValle et al., 2013.

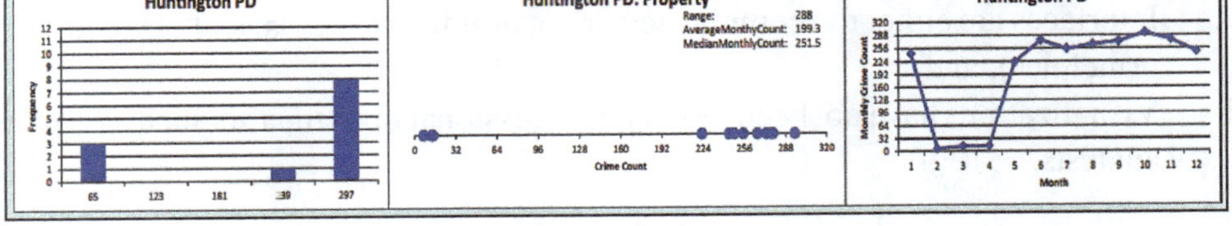

Table 2. Table visualization of NYPD's crime statistics

Ward	Month to Date			Year to Date		
	2012	2013	% Chg	2012	2013	% Chg
Ass-Agg	12	14	16.7%	93	94	1.1%
Auto Thft	4	1	-75.0%	26	25	-3.8%
Burg-Non	3	1	-66.7%	11	9	-18.2%
Burg-Res	36	30	-16.7%	191	189	-1.0%
Burg-Bus	7	2	-71.4%	23	16	-30.4%
Hom	0	0	0.0%	0	2	200.0%
Larceny	42	36	-14.3%	262	262	0.0%
Rape	1	0	-100.0%	5	4	-20.0%
Rob-Bus	0	1	100.0%	1	4	300.0%
Rob-In	3	3	0.0%	31	46	48.4%
Totall	108	88	-18.5%	643	651	1.2%

Wheeler, 2015.

visualization: blue for row and column headers, green for a sharp decline, yellow for a lesser decline, orange for a small increase, and red for a sharp increase in the number of crimes and the percentage change from 2012 to 2013.

Textual Data Analysis and Text Mining

Text mining or text data mining is a process of extracting textual data from textual documents or pages. The amount of textual data has exponentially increased during recent decades and unstructured data might make up more than 80% of all organizations' data. To extract information from unstructured documents and to conduct textual analysis, natural language processing (NLP) and data mining techniques are frequently used. Text mining techniques involve multi-disciplinary approaches such as information extraction, information retrieval, clustering, classification, data mining, and information visualization.

Digitized crime reports can be derived from online crime tip submission, transcriptions from recordings such as phone calls, and patrol officers' notes and incident reports. Three factors that complicate text visualization for investigative analysis are:

1. Text is nominal data and is more difficult to display visually than ordinal and quantitative data (Hearst, 2009),
2. Interfaces are either too complicated or not user friendly (a lack of clear design principles), and
3. Visualizations have not been tested by professional investigators such as crime analysts.

For crime report visualization, Ku, Nguyen, & Leroy (2012) developed an online, decision support system, which includes information extraction, natural language processing, visualization techniques, and similarity algorithms to classify same and different crimes and thus enhance decision support for crime analysts. The system offers different views of data. The visualization view includes an interactive, circular graph or sunburst graph (see Figure 3a) to display similarity among documents with different colors and sizes of lines connected. The document view (see Figure 3b) enables crime analysts to compare and contrast selected crime reports with a highlighting function. Ku et al. (2012) conducted a case study with a crime analyst to compare a paper-based approach to a system-based approach. The overall results demonstrate how the proposed system can significantly shorten the time for crime analysis and maintain the same quality compared to the traditional paper-based approach.

For textual relationships in forensic evidence, Holzinger et al. (2013) present a visual analytic framework to explore the relationship of textual evidence for computer forensics. The visualization system includes three major panes

1. A hierarchy view (see Figure 4a),
2. Tag-cloud terms in the selected files (see Figure 4b), and
3. A search interface (see Figure 4c).

Figure 3. (a) Crime report visualization of similar crimes; (b) a document view with text highlight
Ku et al., 2012.

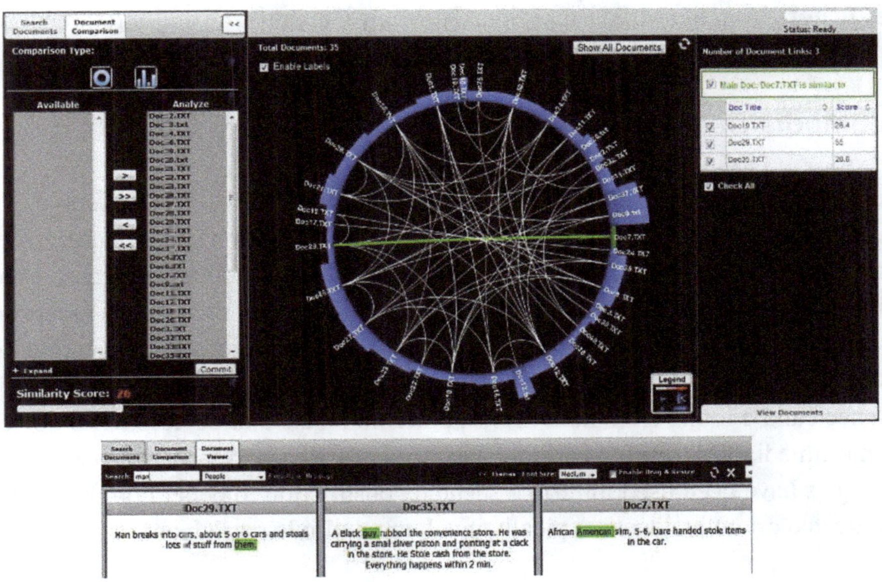

Figure 4. Text forensics visualization: (a) tag-cloud terms in selected files; (b) direct search interface; (c) file metadata with search functions and cluster visualization
Holzinger et al., 2013.

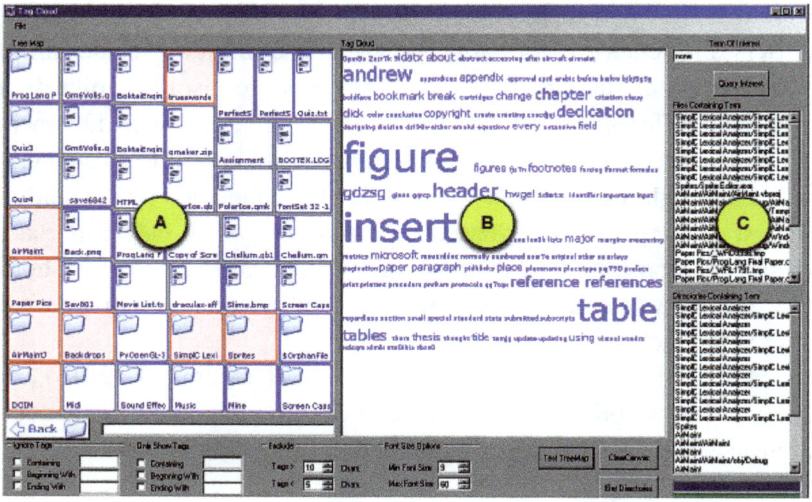

The hierarchical view is a treemap-like depiction and enables forensics officers to explore files dynamically (search sensitive). Tag-cloud terms are then displayed in conjunction with selected files. The word size depends upon the frequency of words. The search interface is an alternative starting point to explore files and offers a cluster view to display information located on the physical disk. Holzinger et al. conducted a case study of fraud cases and received positive feedback from two investigators from the Mississippi State Attorney General's Office and three forensics instructors at the National Forensics Training Center.

Multimedia Data Analysis

To solve crimes, audio-visual evidence can be useful and found in diverse sources such as restaurants, banks, shopping malls, and any location with a surveillance camera. Many law enforcement agencies such as New York State Police's Forensic Video/Multimedia Service Unit have been establishing a digital and multimedia unit or section. The primary goal of such unit is to perform computer forensic examinations and provide supporting information to Federal, State, and local law enforcement. Digital evidence can be found from hard drives, portable media and devices, GPS devices, and multimedia files from web sites and cameras. Recent years, 3D visualization techniques have been used for crime scene reconstruction to better comprehend the complicated crime incidents, typically involving multiple participants.

Figure 5. Three-dimensional model of the crime scene from different views simulated from potential witnesses' observation points
Maksymowicz et al., 2014.

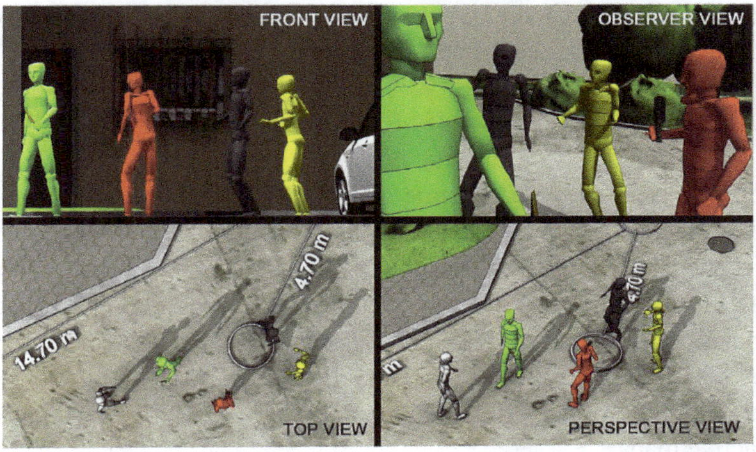

Maksymowicz, Tunikowski, and Kościuk (2014) demonstrate the use of 3D crime scene and event reconstruction based on incomplete or fragmentary evidence being collected. The collected evidence materials include witnesses' testimonies, a recording video from the crime scene, photographic documentation, Google Maps and Street View, and construction archive documentation. To provide an animated version of evidence, the authors used the applications - Autodesk Image, Modeler, 3D modeling, and animation software including Autodesk 3D Studio Max and Bentley MicroStation to reconstruct the crime scene from different views (see Figure 5). Five participants, including their testimonies have been collected. From the given case, the 3D reconstruction helped the court access the likelihood of opposite testimonies. The authors believe the animations can be used for evidence investigation and provide a holistic view of the event.

Spatio-Temporal Data Analysis

Spatio-temporal data represent crime incidents that happen at locations and occur at some point in time. Hot spot analysis, cluster and outlier analysis, and grouping analysis are frequently used techniques to exploit spatio-temporal data. Spatial data is the data or information of a physical object that can be represented by numerical values in a geographic coordinate system and usually stored as coordinates and can be mapped. Spatial data can be accessed, visualized and analyzed through Geographic

Information Systems (GIS), while temporal data are the data that vary with time. It denotes the evolution of an object's characteristics over a period of time and time is an integral dimension in most GIS applications.

In this section, five different types of maps will be introduced: hot spot maps, graduate maps, pin maps, chart maps, and finally buffer maps.

Types of Spatio-Temporal Maps for Crime Analysis

Crime mapping techniques enable crime analysts and researchers to better understand crime patterns and victimization. Researchers from Purdue University developed VALET, a visual analytic tool to allow visualization of spatio-temporal crime data. They further developed this tool to allow local law enforcement agencies to identify potential crime hotspots (Malik, Maciejewski, Collins, and Ebert, 2011). Santos (2012) classified crime maps into six categories: density (hot spot) maps, graduated (choropleth) maps, single-symbol (pin) maps, chart maps, buffer maps, and interactive maps.

- **Hot Spot Maps:** Crime hot spots refer to areas of high crime intensity on a map. For crime mapping, John, Spencer, James, Michael, & Ronald (2009) from the National Institute of Justice provide a report discussing how to use crime mapping to detect high-crime-density areas, also called hot spots. A comprehensive overview of hot spot analysis techniques and software such as CrimeStat and GeoDa has been discussed in this report. In addition, Google Maps API has been used to visualize crime concentrations in the Chicago area (Giaccardi & Fogli, 2008).
- **Graduate Maps:** The basic form of hot spots indicates that the number of crimes happened in a place. To identify high-crime locations, graduated dots with different colors or sizes can be used. For example, a color gradient (see Figure 6) – white (no crimes) through red (greater than 15 crimes) can be used to illustrate the density of crimes in each location.
- **Pin Maps:** Pin maps or single-symbol maps use point symbols to represent crime-related information. Lodha and Verma (1999) used the Virtual Reality Modeling Language (VRML) to create an animated pin map (see Figure *7*), which gives an observer a great picture of the density and distribution of crimes. Pin maps can be rotated, tilted and zoomed in to be viewed from any angle. Spheres of different diameter can be used to aggregate the crimes at the same location to highlight the hotspots. In addition, SpotCrime (see Figure 8) provides national crime information and uses different symbols to represent arrests, arsons, assaults, burglaries, robberies, shootings, thefts, and vandalisms on a Google Map.

- **Chart Maps:** Chart maps display values in a selected variable such as robbery. Pie charts, stacked histograms, and bar charts are regularly used together with crime maps. Multi-view displays enable crime analysts to view data from different perspectives. Brushing and linking techniques can be used to process selected data in a view and highlight corresponding data in the other views (Michael Bostock & Heer, 2009). The city of Overland Park in Kansas provides an interactive map (see Figure 9) with a pie chart and bar chart to display major crimes such as kidnapping, murder, rape, and robbery in the city. The pie chart shows the distribution of different types of crimes, while the bar chart shows the crime trend over time. For example, with kidnapping being selected in the pie chart, the corresponding information with yellow, overlapping circles is displayed in the map. However, there is no suspect information and crime descriptions available.
- **Buffer Maps and Interactive Maps:** A buffer map allows users to create a buffer layer and set a perimeter around a given address or city to see the number of crimes committed within the buffer, while an interactive map enables users to manipulate the view being displayed based on personal needs. Popular interactive techniques include focusing/filtering (increasing or decreasing the details over the map), viewpoint manipulation (panning, zooming, view changing), brushing and linking, and color-map manipulation (adjusting symbols, colors and sizes on the map items (Roth, Ross, Finch, Luo, & MacEachren, 2013). Figure 10a shows an interactive map from RAIDSONLINE.com with a buffer set on one-mile perimeter (a black circle). RAIDSONLINE.com, a commercial crime visualization software, leads the way in demonstrating the usefulness of visualizing crime data in combination with spatial data. Figure 11a renders point data and heatmaps of crime data provided by law enforcement agencies. These visualizations are available to the public who can filter crime data by locations. When an incident is selected, a pop-up message shows information including type of crime, location, date, time, public address and law enforcement agency. The analytics tab (see Figure 10b) displays types of crimes in a pie chart, the crime frequency, timeline and in a bar chart, and a heatmap of crimes in a week by hours.

VISUALIZATION TOOLS

An increasing number of open-source and proprietary visualization tools are available in the market. However, most of them are ad hoc solutions for specific domains. Harger and Crossno (2012) conducted a comprehensive evaluation of open-source visual analytics tools. They evaluated visualization functions, analysis capabilities,

Figure 6. Vehicle crimes mapped by census tract
John et al., 2009.

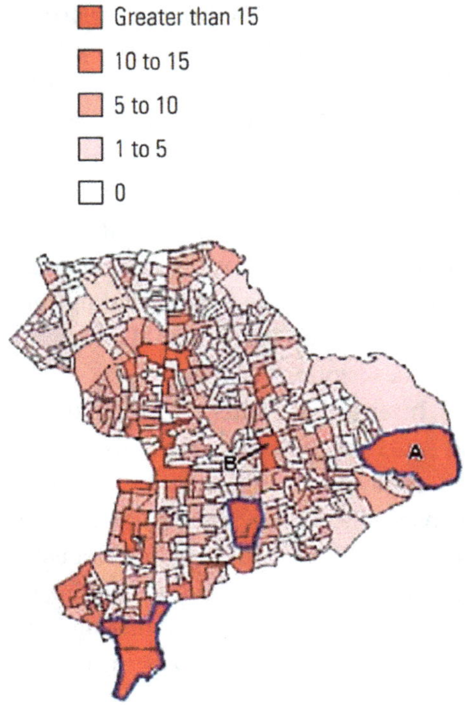

Figure 7. A pin map showing urban crime distribution patterns
Lodha & Verma, 1999.

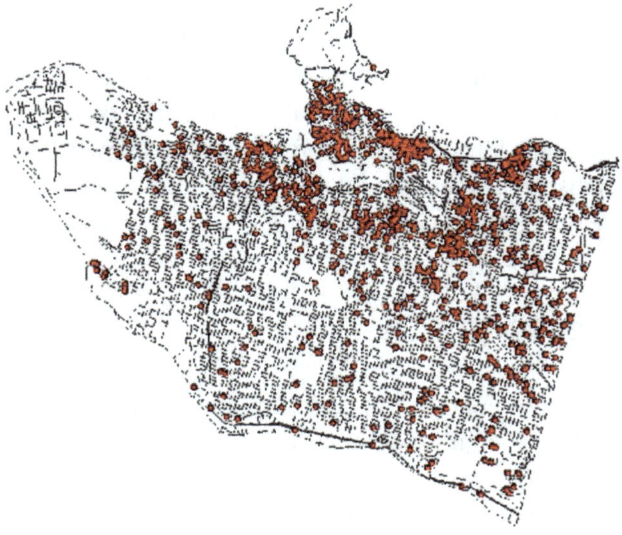

Figure 8. Crime incidents in the Detroit area
"SpotCrime," n d.

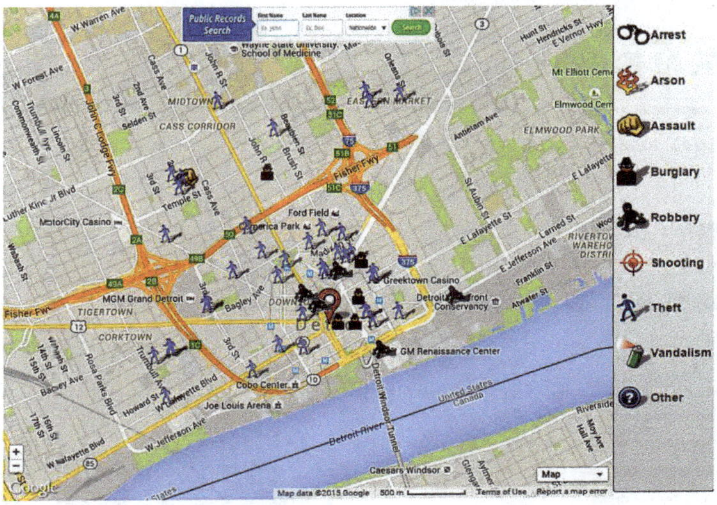

and development environment for more than twenty toolkits including Axiis, birdeye, Flare, Gephi, Google Visualization API, GraphViz, Improvise, Infovis Toolkits (IVTK), JavaScript Infovis Toolkit (JIT), JFreeChart, JUNG, Prefuse, Protovis, and R. Twenty-five different types of basic graphs were identified among the toolkits. They found that the toolkits Protovis and birdeye offer powerful features, while other toolkits JGraph and JUNG offer strong analysis functionality. This section highlights popular toolkits that have been applied or have potential to be used in crime analysis. In this section, both open-source and proprietary toolkits are explored and combined solutions are provided.

More than 300 different types of graphics are available from open-source tools ("D3 gallery", n.d.; Harger & Crossno, 2012). In this chapter, the authors classify those graphs into 7 different groups (see Table 3) based on the features and shapes of graphics. Each type of graph corresponds to four data types. The plot, chart, bar, and scatterplot are basic charts and frequently used to present statistical data. However, they also can be applied to the other three data types, which depends upon the purpose of research study. The circle, chord, and sunburst graphics with different thickness of links, colors, and sizes can be used to present relationships between given entities. Such relations also can be presented in force-directed and network graphs that may pay more attention to distance and grouping. To classify information, tree, clustering, and treemap are popular approaches. To show pairwise data, table and matrix graphs are commonly used. Map-related graphics can be combined with basic charts such as pie charts to display statistical data. Other

Figure 9. City of Overland Park uses the map and charts to display major crimes and crime patterns from 06/03/2015 to o7/03/2015
"Major Crimes from Overland Park," n.d.

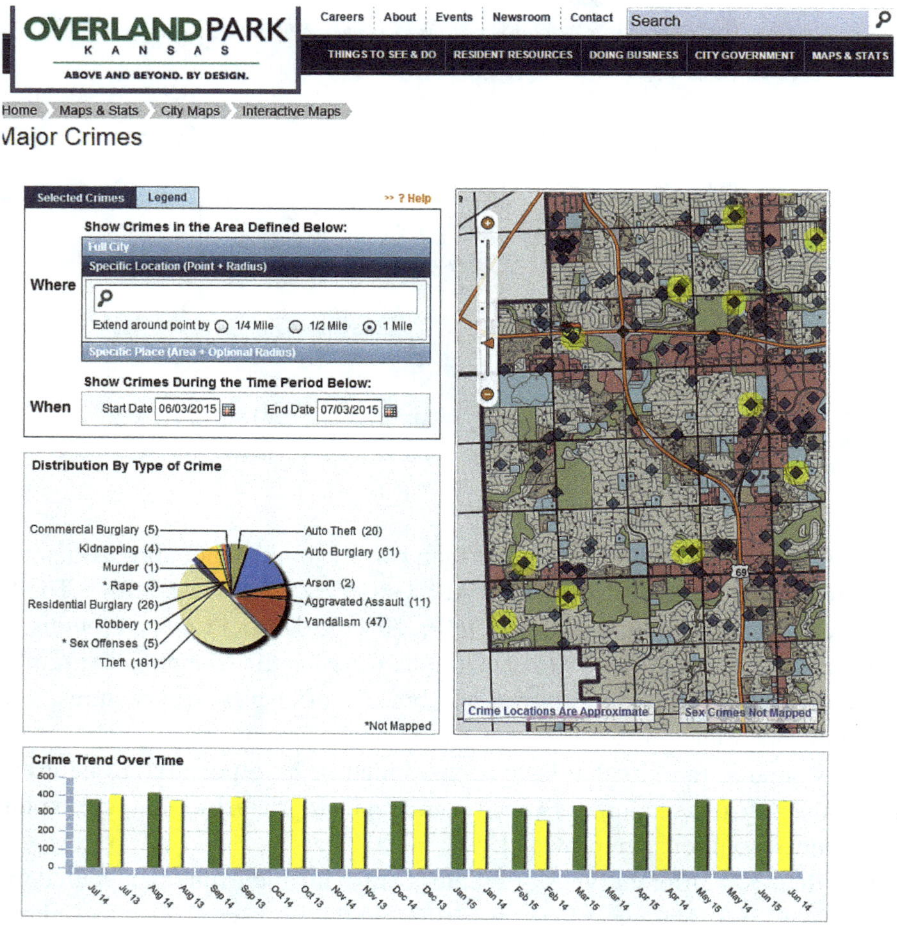

visual presentations such as word/tag cloud can be used to display the frequency or importance of words, while 3D, animations, and self-developed graphs can be applied to all four data types.

JavaScript(JS)-Based Toolkits

- **D3:** ("D3," n.d.) stands for Data-Driven Document. D3.js is a JS library/ framework, which can be used in HyperText Markup Language (HTML), Scalable Vector Graphics (SVG), and Cascading Style Sheets (CSS), for data

Figure 10. (a) RAIDSONLINE for crime mapping with buffer on 1 mile, in Industry, California; (b) crime analytics for the city being searched
"RAIDSONLINE," n.d.

visualization. Protovis is a JS tool used to display data in bars and dots; however, it is no longer updated and the same team develops D3 based on the concepts in Protovis. Even though D3.js has not been widely used for crime information visualization in research projects, the D3 gallery (see Figure 11) provides rich examples including a variety of animated and interactive graphs, which will be valuable for crime information visualization.

- **JavaScript InfoVis Toolkit:** provides tools for developers to create interactive data visualization. The toolkit includes area, bar, and pie charts, sunburst, icicle, force directed, treemap, space tree, RGraph, and Hyper tree, etc. Ku et

Figure 11. D3 gallery
"D3 gallery ", n.d.

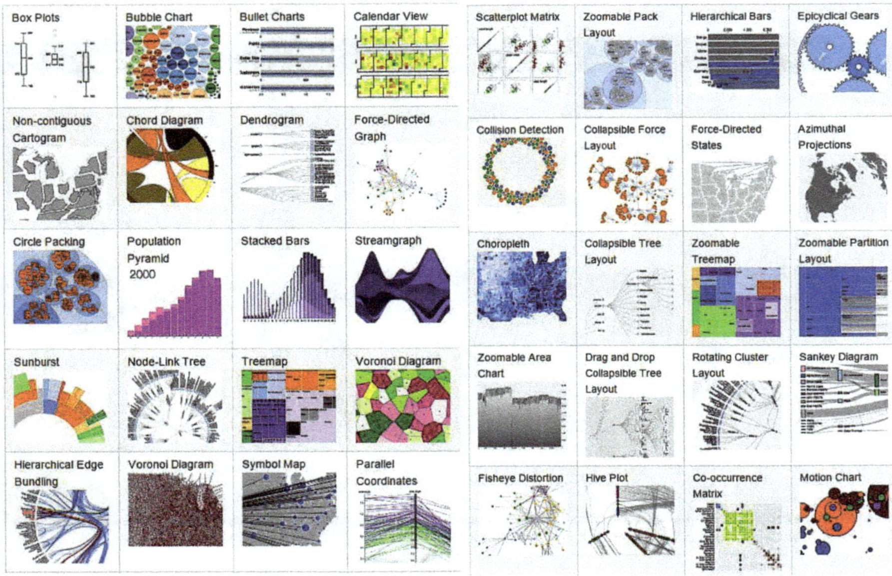

Table 3. Types of visual presentations

Chart Type		Statistical	Textual	Multimedia	Spatio-Temporal
Plot, Chart, Bar, Scatterplot	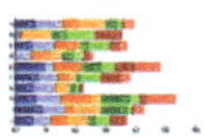	X	X	X	X
Circle, Chord, Sunburst	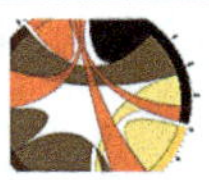	X	X	X	
Force-Directed, Network	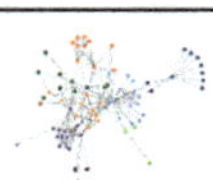		X		X
Tree, Clustering, Treemap	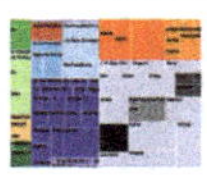	X	X	X	
Table, matrix, calendar	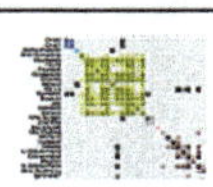	X			
Map-related		X			X
Others		X	X	X	X

"D3 gallery", n.d.; Harger & Crossno, 2012.

al. (2012) used its sunburst graph together with jQuery ("jQuery," n.d.) techniques to visualize crime reports and their relationship indicated by similarity scores.

- **Gephi:** ("Gephi," n.d.) is an interactive visualization toolkits and provides a platform for exploratory data analysis, link analysis, social network analysis, and biological network analysis. It is available for most operating systems such as Windows, Linux, and Mac OS X. Rasheed and Wiil (2014) used the Gephi toolkit to develop a framework called PREVNT for visualization of criminal networks. The framework was used to observe the crime activity during the first quarter of 2011 in a Chicago Narcotics data set.

Proprietary Toolkits

Tableau is business analytics software used to visualize data, which provides interactions with data, and support decision making. It allows users to combine databases and computer graphs to visualize information without programming skills. The

Figure 12. District of Columbia crimespotting
"District of Columbia Crimespotting by Tableau," n.d.

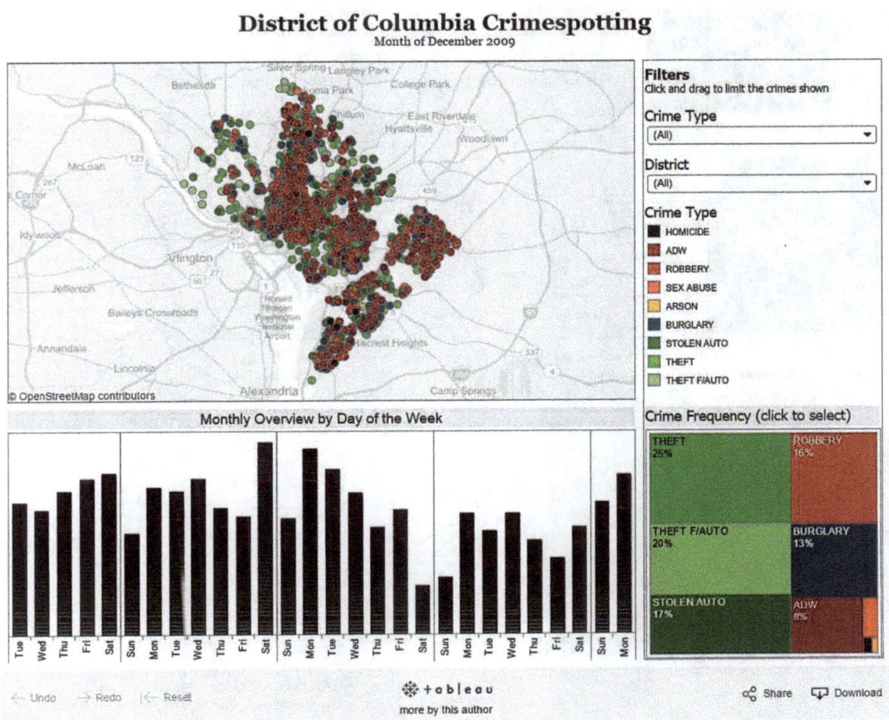

software has been widely used in business- and research-related purposes. For crime analysis, it has been used to display crime spots in the District of Columbia (Figure 12), including filter functions, crime frequency, and weekly overview of crimes. In addition, it provides dashboard including crosstab headings, bar and line charts, state map, and interactive functions. Figure 13 shows 2012 U.S. crime in a dashboard and indicates that the crime rates have steadily declined over last twenty years. It offers the ability to filter crimes rates and numbers by state, region, type of crime, and date and offers comparisons by year and by state. These platforms are not specifically designed to generate visualizations of crime data, but are available for use with any large data set that requires analysis.

ArcGIS is geographic information system (GIS) software, provided by ESRI, for developing and using maps, analyzing mapped information, and visualizing data on the map. It provides Web APIs such as JavaScript and runtime software development kits (SDKs) - iOS and Android for developers. Developers can create thematic interactive maps that allow users to explore and better understand the data.

Figure 13. 2012 U.S. crime dashboard
"2012 U.S. Crime Dashboard by Tableau," n.d.

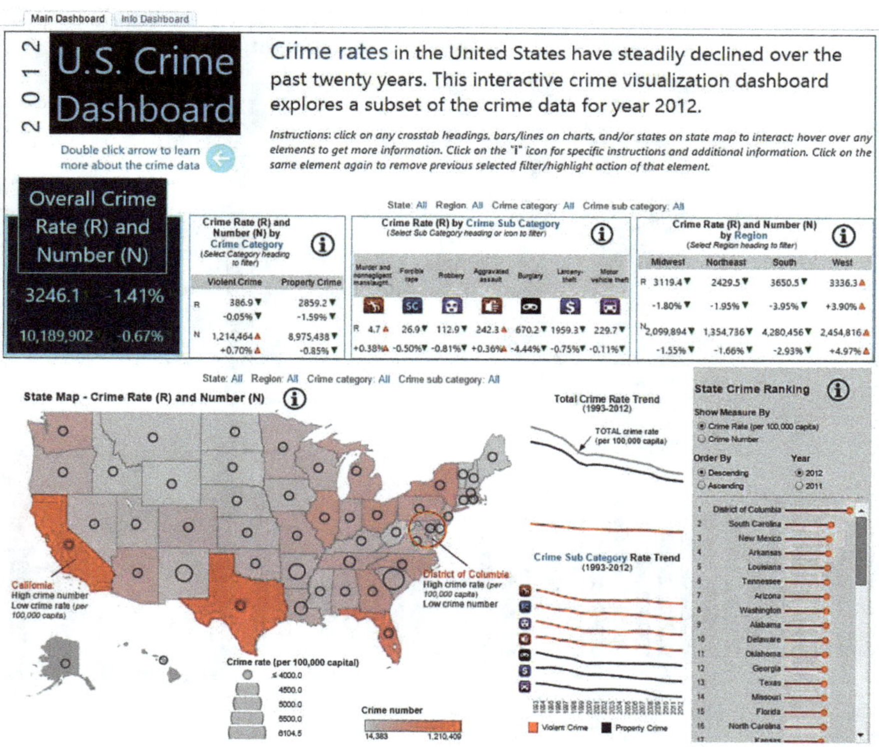

Figure 14. Crime hot spots generated from vandalism data for Lincoln, Nebraska
Scott & Warmerdam, 2005.

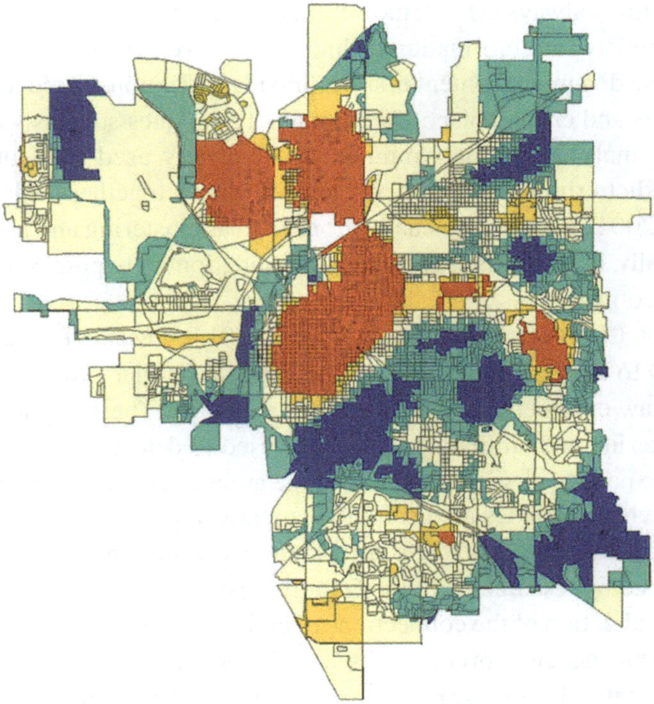

In addition, it supports spatial analysis to detect patterns and outliers, explore trends, and even make decisions. ArcGIS has been frequently used for crime analysis (Scott & Warmerdam, 2005). Figure 14 shows crime hot spots for Lincoln, Nebraska. The crime hot spots were generated from vandalism data without normalization. The bright-red spots indicate high incidence of vandalism, e.g., downtown Lincoln, while the dark-blue spots indicate low vandalism areas.

Combined Solutions

Data mining is the computational process of exploring and analyzing *structured data* to identify patterns and relationships between given variables. Common data mining techniques include outlier detection, clustering, classification, association rule, and regression. Text Mining, described in the section of textual data analysis, is a process of extracting information from *unstructured data*. Text mining generally involves techniques such as NLP, information extraction, and computational algorithms to discover previously unknown information. The authors are typically interested in combined solutions and tools supporting crime analysis.

Crime data are a fertile field for data visualizations and data mining. Many examples of frameworks, tools, and products have made their way to the public eye. Visualization tools always offer demos of their capabilities using crime data, while computer scientists and information technologists have advanced crime data visualization, crime document content relationship identification, crime data triangulation techniques and crime hotspot forecasting. Techniques such as social network analysis, link analysis, and data mining are frequently used to identify criminal networks, predict criminal activity, and cluster crimes together (Giles, Bollacker, & Lawrence, 2004). Scientific visualizations such as clustering and network graphics are generally used for data exploration, validation of hypotheses, and system performance comparison.

Borg, Boldt, Lavesson, Melander, and Boeva (2014) presented a decision support system (DSS) to analyze gathered 2,416 residential burglary reports, which were collected by law enforcement officers over six months. The analytical framework contains clustering and similarity algorithms used to detect serial residential burglaries. Two experiments were conducted. The authors found that spatial proximity or residential characteristics are useful to compare and detect crimes.

Another application of interactive visualization for crime analysis includes Jigsaw, a tool developed by researchers of the Georgia Institute of Technology. Jigsaw has presented visualization of the connections of entities across documents, which help law enforcement agencies sort out and search for documents that relate to common entities. Using natural language processing techniques, Jigzaw interprets the content of the various textual documents written in common English, like news reports and crime reports, and is able to identify common information. Jigzaw then presents the connections using various views like list, graphs, and scatter plots (Stasko, Görg, & Liu, 2008). Adding to the scope of connecting documents, researchers from the Claremont Graduate University, developed TASC (Ku et al., 2012). TASC goes beyond the abilities of Jigzaw in terms of being able to identify crime reports that refer to the same crimes and presents these connections using an interactive circle graph where documents that relate to the same crimes are linked.

Lastly, several frameworks and platforms to visualize crime data are available. Many of these platforms are available commercially and most offer a demonstration of interactive crime data visualizations. Examples of these platforms include Tableau, QlikView, and SAS. These platforms offer graphing and visualization capabilities that can be used for any type and size of the data source. Crime data can be analyzed based on various dimensions and using various display formats.

Similarly, the world of open-source software offers frameworks for the analysis of datasets. Weka and OpenedEyes are two prominent open-source platforms. Weka offers several data mining algorithms with scientific visualization capabilities, while OpenedEyes offers bar and bubble charts, choropleth and circle maps. OpenenEyes is JavaScript based and is available for use on the Web (Almeida & Júnior, 2012).

VISUALIZATIONS AND HUMAN PERCEPTION

The major challenge of visual analytics for crimes is how to analyze the high volume and complexity of crime data efficiently under time pressure, uncertainty, and the requirement of intensive coordination. In law enforcement, rather than documents visual presentations are frequently used for decision making (Martin & Roland Andreas, 2014). However, a common problem of information visualization is information overload, too much information in a diagram. The implications from the aforementioned situations highlight the need to consider a variety of design principles, human factors such as cognition and perception, and visualization techniques. A good graphical representation enables users to reduce the cognitive effort and provides practical and actionable insights. For example, brushing and linking, selecting and marking (Andrews, Endert, Yost, & North, 2011), aggregation, elimination, virtual navigation technique such as zooming (Andrews et al., 2011), focus+context, and details-on-demand techniques have been studied and used (Andrews et al., 2011) to overcome an over cluttered screen.

Human-Computer Interaction (HCI) is a study of designing a user interface to facilitate interaction between users and computers. Both human cognition principles and design principles are equally important for visual analytics. For example, field studies are frequently conducted on domain experts' working and cognitive activities (Zhao et al., 2006). The well-known general design principles have been identified and explained in Johnson (Johnson, 2010), Shneiderman and Plaisant (Shneiderman & Plaisant, 2009), and Krug's (Krug, 2005) books. Frequently used principles include 'don't make me think', 'proximity', 'consistency and repetition', 'contrast', 'avoid complex reading', and 'users' feedback'.

- **Don't Make Me Think:** Things that make people think include bad names, unfamiliar technical names, and cute or clever names. This principle is to get rid of users' "question marks."
- **Proximity:** The relative distance between elements affects people's perception. Thus, similar elements should be grouped in the same place to avoid confusion.

- **Consistency and Repetition:** This is to repeat certain elements such as a logo, color scheme, basic layout, and navigation to avoid confusion. Graphs and elements should be placed consistently in the same locations.
- **Contrast:** The contrast is different from the brightness. Distinctive colors include black, white, red, green, yellow, and blue. People's visual system can distinguish those six colors easily and quickly.
- **Avoid Complex Reading:** Most users do not have the patience and time to read long text. Removing needless words also reduces the noise level of the interface and saves the screen space.
- **Users' Feedback:** Watch how people use the interface and obtain feedback from users. A small focus group (3-5 people) discusses the prototype design and determines what potential users want. Usability test can be completed by showing the visual graph to one user each time and ask users' opinions.

CONCLUSION

Data mining and visualization techniques enable law enforcement agencies to process and analyze crime data efficiently. This chapter provides a comprehensive overview of visual analytics for different types of crime data, which can be used for crime pattern discovery and decision making. The chapter includes an exploration of design principles and human factors, such as cognition and perception, and visualization techniques for information visualization.

In the review of existing studies and practices, the authors found that combining various techniques and tools provides a more exhaustive analysis of the various types of crime data. Specifically, the combination of visualization techniques with text and data mining seems to offer added benefits in crime data analysis. Further study of crime data analysis should focus on exploring and comparing existing integrated solutions and identifying the best combination of tools for specific analysis requirements. These explorations should include comparisons of such solutions and toolkits such as KNIME, RapidMinder, Japster, Weka, R, OpenNLP, and General Architecture for Text Mining (GATE). These tools may offer integrated solutions to combine data mining, natural language processing, or statistical functions together with visual representations.

REFERENCES

D3. (n.d.). Retrieved from http://d3js.org/

D3 Gallery. (n.d.). Retrieved from https://github.com/mbostock/d3/wiki/Gallery

Almeida, C. S. d. B., & Júnior, A. L. A. (2012). *OpenedEyes: Developing an Information Visualization Framework Using Web Standards and Open Web Technologies*. Academic Press.

Andrews, C., Endert, A., Yost, B., & North, C. (2011). Information Visualization on Large, High-Resolution Displays: Issues, Challenges, and Opportunities. *Information Visualization, 10*(4), 341-355. Retrieved from http://ivi.sagepub.com/content/10/4/341.abstract

Borg, A., Boldt, M., Lavesson, N., Melander, U., & Boeva, V. (2014). Detecting Serial Residential Burglaries Using Clustering. *Expert Systems with Applications, 41*(11), 5252–5266. doi:10.1016/j.eswa.2014.02.035

Bostock, M., & Heer, J. (2009). Protovis: A Graphical Toolkit for Visualization. *IEEE Transactions on Visualization and Computer Graphics, 15*(6), 1121–1128. doi:10.1109/TVCG.2009.174 PMID:19834180

Bostock, M., Ogievetsky, V., & Heer, J. (2011). D[3] Data-Driven Documents. *IEEE Transactions on Visualization and Computer Graphics, 17*(12), 2301–2309. doi:10.1109/TVCG.2011.185 PMID:22034350

Bureau of Justice Statistics (BJS). (n.d.). Retrieved from http://www.bjs.gov/

Cook, K., Earnshaw, R., & Stasko, J. (2007). Guest Editors' Introduction: Discovering the Unexpected. *IEEE Computer Graphics and Applications, 27*(5), 15–19. doi:10.1109/MCG.2007.126 PMID:17913020

Didimo, W., Liotta, G., & Montecchiani, F. (2014). Network Visualization for Financial Crime Detection. *Journal of Visual Languages and Computing, 25*(4), 433–451. doi:10.1016/j.jvlc.2014.01.002

District of Columbia Crimespotting by Tableau. (n.d.). Retrieved from http://www.tableau.com/learn/gallery/crime-spotting

Gephi. (n.d.). Retrieved from http://gephi.github.io/

Giaccardi, E., & Fogli, D. (2008). *Affective Geographies: Toward a Richer Cartographic Semantics for the Geospatial Web*. Academic Press.

Giles, C. L., Bollacker, K. D., & Lawrence, S. (2004). *CiteSeer: An Automatic Citation Indexing System.* Paper presented at the third ACM conference on Digital libraries, Pittsburgh, PA.

Harger, J. R., & Crossno, P. J. (2012). *Comparison of Open-Source Visual Analytics Toolkits*. Academic Press.

Hearst, M. A. (2009). *Information Visualization for Search Interfaces Search User Interfaces*. Cambridge University Press. doi:10.1017/CBO9781139644082

Heer, J., Bostock, M., & Ogievetsky, V. (2010). A Tour Through the Visualization Zoo. *Communications of the ACM*, *53*(6), 59–67. doi:10.1145/1743546.1743567

Heer, J., & Shneiderman, B. (2012). Interactive Dynamics for Visual Analysis. *Communications of the ACM*, *55*(4), 45–54. doi:10.1145/2133806.2133821

Holzinger, A., Stocker, C., Ofner, B., Prohaska, G., Brabenetz, A., & Hofmann-Wellenhof, R. (2013). Combining HCI, Natural Language Processing, and Knowledge Discovery - Potential of IBM Content Analytics as an Assistive Technology in the Biomedical Field. In A. Holzinger & G. Pasi (Eds.), *Human-Computer Interaction and Knowledge Discovery in Complex, Unstructured, Big Data* (pp. 13–24). Springer Berlin Heidelberg.

JavaScript InfoVis Toolkit. (n.d.). Retrieved from http://philogb.github.io/jit/

John, E., Spencer, C., James, C., Michael, L., & Ronald, E. W. (2009). *Mapping Crime: Understanding Hot Spots*. Retrieved from https://www.ncjrs.gov/pdffiles1/nij/209393.pdf

Johnson, J. (2010). *Designing with the Mind in Mind: Simple Guide to Understanding User Interface Design Rules*. Morgan Kaufmann.

jQuery. (n.d.). Retrieved from https://jquery.com/

Keim, D. A., Mansmann, F., Schneidewind, J., Thomas, J., & Ziegler, H. (2008). Visual Analytics: Scope and Challenges. In S. J. Simoff, M. H. Böhlen, & A. Mazeika (Eds.), *Visual Data Mining* (pp. 76–90). Springer Berlin Heidelberg. doi:10.1007/978-3-540-71080-6_6

Keim, E. D., Kohlhammer, J., & Ellis, G. (2010). *Mastering the Information Age: Solving Problems with Visual Analytics*. Eurographics Association.

Krug, S. (2005). *Don't Make Me Think: A Common Sense Approach to Web Usability* (2nd ed.). New Riders Press.

Ku, C. H., Nguyen, J. H., & Leroy, G. (2012). *TASC - Crime Report Visualization for Investigative Analysis: A Case Study*. Paper presented at the Information Reuse and Integration (IRI), 2012 IEEE 13th International Conference on. Retrieved from http://ieeexplore.ieee.org/ielx5/6294629/6302564/06303045.pdf?tp=&arnumber=6303045&isnumber=6302564

Laughlin, G. (2014). *Crime Over Time: Visualizing Crime Data in Chicago*. Retrieved from http://www.socrata.com/blog/crime-time-visualizing-crime-data-chicago/

LaValle, C. R., Haas, S. M., Turley, E., & Nolan, J. J. (2013). *Improving State Capacity for Crime Reporting: An Exploratory Analysis of Data Quality and Imputation Methods Using NIBRS Data*. Academic Press.

Lodha, S. K., & Verma, A. (1999). Animations of Crime Maps Using Virtual Reality Modeling Language. *Western Criminology Review (now Criminology, Criminal Justice, Law & Society), 1*(2), 1-19.

Louis Engelbrecht, A. B. (2014). *Information Visualisation View Design: Principles and Guidelines*. doi:10.13140/2.1.1822.8808

Luo, W., & MacEachren, A. M. (2014). Geo-social visual analytics. *Journal of Spatial Information Science, 8*, 27–66.

Major Crimes from Overland Park. (n.d.). Retrieved from http://map.opkansas.org/crime-map/#

Maksymowicz, K., Tunikowski, W., & Kościuk, J. (2014). Crime Event 3D Reconstruction Based on Incomplete or Fragmentary Evidence Material – Case Report. *Forensic Science International, 242*, e6–e11. doi:10.1016/j.forsciint.2014.07.004 PMID:25132528

Martin, J. E., & Roland Andreas, P. (2014). Best of Both Worlds: Hybrid Knowledge Visualization in Police Crime Fighting and Military Operations. *Journal of Knowledge Management, 18*(4), 824–840. doi:10.1108/JKM-11-2013-0462

National Crime Victimization Survey (NCVS). (n.d.). Retrieved from http://www.bjs.gov/index.cfm?ty=dcdetail&iid=245

New York State Police. (n.d.). *Forensic Video/Multimedia Services Unit*. Retrieved from https://troopers.ny.gov/Academy/Multimedia_Services_Unit/

Protovis. (n.d.). Retrieved from http://mbostock.github.io/protovis/

Purchase, H. C., Andrienko, N., Jankun-Kelly, T. J., & Ward, M. (2008). Information Visualization. In A. Kerren, J. T. Stasko, J.-D. Fekete, & C. North (Eds.), *Theoretical Foundations of Information Visualization* (Vol. 1, pp. 46–64). Berlin, Heidelberg: Springer-Verlag. doi:10.1007/978-3-540-70956-5_3

RAIDSONLINE. (n.d.). Retrieved from https://www.raidsonline.com

Rasheed, A., & Wiil, U. K. (2014). *PEVNET: A Framework for Visualization of Criminal Networks*. Paper presented at the 2014 IEEE/ACM International Conference on Advances in Social Networks Analysis and Mining (ASONAM). doi:10.1109/ASONAM.2014.6921689

Roth, R. E., Ross, K. S., Finch, B. G., Luo, W., & MacEachren, A. M. (2013). Spatio-temporal Crime Analysis in U.S. Law Enforcement Agencies: Current Practices and Unmet Needs. *Government Information Quarterly*, *30*(3), 226–240. doi:10.1016/j.giq.2013.02.001

Santos, R. B. (2012). Crime Analysis With Crime Mapping (3rd ed.). Thousand Oaks, CA: SAGE Publications, Inc.

Scott, L., & Warmerdam, N. (2005). Extend Crime Analysis with ArcGIS Spatial Statistics Tools. *ArcUser, 8*.

Shneiderman, B., & Plaisant, C. (2009). *Designing the User Interface: Strategies for Effective Human-Computer Interaction* (5th ed.). Addison Wesley.

SpotCrime. (n.d.). Retrieved from http://www.spotcrime.com/

Stasko, J., Görg, C., & Liu, Z. (2008). Jigsaw: Supporting Investigative Analysis Through Interactive Visualization. *Information Visualization*, *7*(2), 118–132. doi:10.1057/palgrave.ivs.9500180

Stone, M. (2009). *Information Visualization: Challenge for the Humanities*. Paper presented at the Promoting Digital Scholarship: Formulating Research Challenges in the Humanities, Social Sciences and Computation, Washington, DC.

2012 . U.S. Crime Dashboard by Tableau. (n.d.). Retrieved from http://public.tableau.com/profile/wee3190#!/vizhome/USCrimeAnalysisDashboard120814-1/MainDashboard

Wang, B., Dong, H., Boedihardjo, A. P., Lu, C.-T., Yu, H., Chen, I.-R., & Dai, J. (2012). *An Integrated Framework for Spatio-Temporal-Textual Search and Mining*. Academic Press.

Wheeler, A. P. (2015). *Tables and Graphs for Monitoring Temporal Crime Patterns (ID 2551472)*. Retrieved from Rochester; http://papers.ssrn.com/abstract=2551472

White, J., & Roth, R. (2010). *TwitterHitter: Geovisual Analytics for Harvesting Insight from Volunteered Geographic Information*. Paper presented at the GIScience 2010, Zurich, Switzerland.

Zhao, J. L., Bi, H. H., Chen, H., Zeng, D. D., Lin, C., & Chau, M. (2006). Process-Driven Collaboration Support for Intra-Agency Crime Analysis. *Decision Support Systems*, *41*(3), 616–633. doi:10.1016/j.dss.2004.06.014

KEY TERMS AND DEFINITIONS

Crime Analysis: Crime analysts systematically analyze crime-associated reports and police phone calls to identify crime patterns and trends, predict future occurrences, and devise solution to crime problems.

Data Mining: Data mining is the process of exploring data to find patterns or relationships and gain new insight from datasets. Common tasks include anomaly detection, association rule learning, clustering, classification, regression, and summarization.

Decision Support System (DSS): A DSS is a computerized system that support decision making through an interactive information system.

Human Computer Interaction (HCI): HCI is a study of designing usable interfaces and enhances the interaction between users and computers.

Information Visualization: Information visualization involves a set of techniques to create visual representations for users to explore and understand a massive amount information.

Natural Language Processing (NLP): NLP uses a set of algorithms to process, analyze, and understand human's natural language.

Visual Analytics: Visual analytics is the process to explore and synthesize information and gain understanding of data through visual analytics tools.

Chapter 4
Crime Hotspot Detection: A Computational Perspective

Emre Eftelioglu
University of Minnesota, USA

Shashi Shekhar
University of Minnesota, USA

Xun Tang
University of Minnesota, USA

ABSTRACT

Given a set of crime locations, a statistically significant crime hotspot is an area where the concentration of crimes inside is significantly higher than outside. The motivation of crime hotspot detection is twofold: detecting crime hotspots to focus the deployment of police enforcement and predicting the potential residence of a serial criminal. Crime hotspot detection is computationally challenging due to the difficulty of enumerating all potential hotspot areas, selecting an interest measure to compare these with the overall crime intensity, and testing for statistical significance to reduce chance patterns. This chapter focuses on statistical significant crime hotspots. First, the foundations of spatial scan statistics and its applications (i.e. SaTScan) to circular hotspot detection are reviewed. Next, ring-shaped hotspot detection is introduced. Third, linear hotspot detection is described since most crimes occur along a road network. The chapter concludes with future research directions in crime hotspot detection.

DOI: 10.4018/978-1-5225-0463-4.ch004

INTRODUCTION

Analyzing crime locations and using the spatial information associated with them is a fundamental task of environmental criminology since the main goal of a crime investigation is to locate the criminal and/or prevent more crimes from occurring. Two important spatial theories in environmental criminology are routine activity theory and crime pattern theory. *Routine activity theory* states that a crime location is related to a serial criminal's frequently visited areas (Burn, 1982). *Crime pattern theory* extends routine activity theory on a spatial model (Brantingham & Brantingham, 1993). When crime analysts study the locations of crime sites and make inferences that help track down a serial criminal or that identify areas where extra police presence is needed, they are using these theories. Thus, the motivation of crime hotspot detection can be summarized as:

1. To detect current/emerging crime hotspots to focus the deployment of police forces, and
2. To predict the location of a serial criminal's residence.

Previously, most analysis of crime locations was done manually. However, the task of enumerating potential hotspots by hand and detecting meaningful patterns in the data is arduous, even for experienced analysts. Rising crime numbers in larger cities increase analysts' workload and compound their stress. For example, a typical crime dataset of the continental United States includes around 10^7 crimes annually (FBI, 2015). Therefore, law enforcement agencies need computational tools that can automate hotspot detection. Moreover, these tools should eliminate the chance patterns (false positives). Most police departments and similar entities have limited resources for crime mitigation and prevention. Therefore, false positive results, that is, hotspots that occur only by chance, risk causing real harm. If a police department diverts money and manpower to a chance hotspot location that don't need it, may leave other areas less protected. *Chance hotspots* can have other harmful consequences as well. When police increase their presence in a location identified as a crime hotspot, people naturally begin to avoid the area out of fear for their safety, and the neighborhood may become stigmatized.

Hence there is a growing need for crime hotspot analysis tools which can handle large crime datasets as well as eliminate chance patterns. Such tools may help crime analysts accomplish their law enforcement goals with optimal resource allocation (Eck & others, 2005).

Many computational techniques (Spencer Chainey & Ratcliffe, 2013; Eck & others, 2005; Levine, 2006) are used for hotspot detection. One of the most common methods is to enumerate hotspots with clustering techniques. These techniques are highly scalable and widely used in many societal applications (Ester & others, 1996; Ilango & Mohan, 2010; Liao, Liu, & Choudhary, 2004; Sarmah, Das, & Bhattacharyya, 2007; Wu et al., 2008). Nevertheless, clustering has two important limitations for hotspot detection. First, these techniques require the user to input the number of clusters beforehand. This does not conform well to hotspot detection, whose aim is to search for an abnormality that may or may not exist in the data. In other words, the user does not know beforehand whether a hotspot exists, or if so, how many. A second limitation is that most clustering techniques lack a statistical significance test to eliminate chance occurrences of hotspots.

This chapter focuses on statistically significant hotspot detection techniques that aim to remove chance patterns. The shape of the desired hotspot, determines the enumeration technique used to generate candidate hotspots and spatial scan statistics is used to assess the statistical significance of each candidate.

Three representative techniques for discovering significant crime hotspots are presented and each technique is illustrated using sample case studies on real crime datasets collected from different states in the U.S. However, it is important to note that there are many statistically significant hotspot detection techniques with different outputs that are designed to be used in different application domains, such as epidemiology, animal foraging, medical imaging etc. (Agarwal, McGregor, Phillips, Venkatasubramanian, & Zhu, 2006; Coleman et al., 2009; Janeja & Atluri, 2005a; Kulldorff, Huang, Pickle, & Duczmal, 2006; McCullagh, 2006; Neill & Moore, 2004; Neill, 2009; Patil & Taillie, 2004; Prates, Assunção, & Costa, 2012; Shi & Janeja, 2011; Walther, 2010; Zhang, 2010).

Formally, a crime hotspot can be defined as an area where the concentration of crimes inside is significantly higher than the number of activities in any other place in the study area. The hotspot can be circular (partial/full), rectangular, ring-shaped or linear depending on the goal of the hotspot analysis, the geographic features associated with the study area and the crime type. Circular hotspots occur when the crimes are spread around an anchor point of a criminal. For example, narcotics crimes tend to occur in a circular pattern causing a circular hotspot around the criminal narcotics manufacturer (Belenko & Spohn, 2015). Similarly, linear hotspots can be seen for some crimes that are committed along a road network. For example, street robbery cases can be seen on the road network and crime activities tend to be on specific road segments where a criminal selects as his base crime location. Finally, ring-shaped hotspots can be seen for serial criminals, who try not to commit crimes too close to home and try to spend least effort to travel causing a ring-shaped crime pattern around their residence.

SCOPE

This chapter provides and overview of statistically significant crime hotspot detection and outlines its capabilities for aiding in law enforcement with the primary intent of reducing chance patterns in crime hotspot detection. Hence this chapter does not focus on presenting computational performance evaluation. Also there are a number of clustering techniques that are used for crime hotspot detection, but this chapter just focuses on statistically significant crime hotspot detection using spatial scan statistics.

BACKGROUND

This section reviews basic concepts related to statistically significant hotspot detection and formally define the crime hotspot detection problem.

Basic Concepts

- **Activity Set:** An activity set *A* is a collection of geo-located points (i.e. crime locations). Each activity $a \in A$ is associated with a pair of coordinates (*Lat, Lon*) representing its location in two-dimensional Euclidean space.
- **Study Area:** Study area *S*is territorial area of responsibility of a public safety agency. *S* is assumed to be the minimum orthogonal bounding rectangle of the activity set *A*in this chapter.
- **Spatial Bi-Partitioning:** Spatial bi-partitioning is the division of an area into two non-overlapping subsets. The key point of spatial bi-partitioning is the notion of "inside" and "outside". Any activity point $a \in A$ is either inside or outside but not both.
- **Spatial Comparison:** Spatial comparison is the comparing of two populations after spatial bi-partitioning, i.e., the population "inside" and the population "outside" which have been partitioned in the spatial bi-partitioning phase. This comparison can be done by different metrics such as difference or ratio; by different interest metrics such as disease rate, areal density or linear density; or by different significance tests such as parametric (Poisson) test or non-parametric test.

Spatial Scan Statistics

Spatial scan statistics is a widely used tool to detect hotspots in a point process and it's widely used in epidemiology to determine disease outbreaks (Neill & Moore,

Figure 1. A circular window enumerating zones in a study area

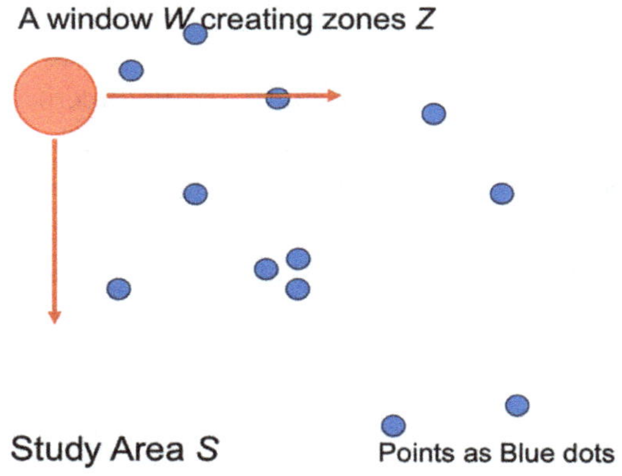

2004). It was first studied for one-dimensional data and then extended to multi-dimensional data (M. Kulldorff, 1999; Kulldorff, 1997). Spatial scan statistics has proved to be the most powerful statistical test to detect hotspots in an activity set (M. Kulldorff, 1999).

Suppose there is a point process N in a study area S. The aim is to find a hotspot in this point process. First, candidate hotspot regions are enumerated using a window W, which moves around the study area and creates candidate hotspot regions referred to as zones Z. For each of these zones, the number of observed and expected observations is noted. For example, Figure 1 shows a circular window moving in the study area S and creating zones. Note that each created zone will be a candidate hotspot to be evaluated for being an actual hotspot.

The fundamental question asked for each of the zone Z is "Is there any difference between inside the zone and outside?" In order to answer this question, a Hypothesis Test is constructed with two outcomes. The null hypothesis (H_0) states that the activity points are distributed randomly according to a homogeneous Poisson process over the study area S. The alternative hypothesis (H_1) states that the inside of a zone Z has higher activities than outside (Martin Kulldorff, 2014).

The hypothesis test has two important requirements. The first is a metric to give a score for each zone Z. If the window had a fixed size and thus all zones Z had the same size, then the test statistic would be the count of the points inside the zone. Since the actual size of the hotspot in a crime scenario is not known beforehand, the window should have a variable size and thus created zones Z will not have the same size. Therefore, a *log likelihood ratio test* is the metric used to determine the test statistic. The second requirement of hypothesis testing is a distribution of the test statistic under the null hypothesis of no clusters. This distribution will show what one should expect when there is no hotspot in the dataset. This distribution is acquired using a *randomization test*. Finally, the test statistic score of each zone is compared with the distribution of the test statistic to determine the statistical significance (*p-value*). Given a required significance level (α_p), if a zone Z has a *p-value* lower than α_p, it can be concluded that the zone Z is a significant hotspot (Kulldorff, 1997b). These concepts are described in more detail next.

Likelihood Ratio Test

The likelihood ratio test determines the test statistic of a candidate zone Z. It is computed by dividing the likelihood of the activities in zone Z under the alternative hypothesis (H_1) by the likelihood of the zone Z under the null hypothesis (H_0). This comparison gives the following equation:

$$LR_Z = \frac{L(Z)_{H_1}}{L(Z)_{H_0}}$$

In order to find the maximum likelihood of a zone Z, the parameters in $LR(Z)$ are selected to maximize the likelihood ratio. These terms are used as the supremum (least upper bound) when likelihood ratios are computed. Thus, the Likelihood Ratio is derived as follow. Note that *Log* values are used to make the interpretation easier.

$$Log\ LR_Z = Log\left(\left(\frac{c}{B}\right)^c \left(\frac{|A|-c}{|A|-B}\right)^{|A|-c} I()\right),$$

where $B = \dfrac{|A|\, area(Z)}{area(S)}$ and $I() = \begin{cases} 1, & if\ c > B \\ 0, & otherwise \end{cases}$.

Here, B is the expression of the expectation of number of activities in a particular zone Z. The observed number of activities is denoted as c. Total number of activities is the cardinality $|A|$ of set A. The final term $I()$ denotes the indicator function. $I()=1$ when a zone Z has more activity points than expected ($c > B$) and otherwise it is set to 0 to prevent the detection of low activity areas (Martin Kulldorff, 2014).

Randomization Test

Once the enumeration of the candidate hotspots (zone *Z*) is done and the test statistic of each candidate is computed, a randomization test is done to determine the distribution of the test statistic under the null hypothesis (H_0). This distribution later helps to determine the statistical significance of a candidate hotspot and will help determine whether the candidate hotspot occurred by chance or is truly anomalous. Although other methods exist, in this chapter the randomization test with Monte Carlo simulations will be explained.

For Monte Carlo simulation, *m* random activity sets $A_{1...m}^{random}$ are created in the same study area *S*. The locations of the activities are determined using complete spatial randomness (CSR). In other words, points inside each activity set are randomly thrown into the study area. For each of these random activity sets $A_{1...m}^{random}$, new zones *Z*are generated and their test statistics (log likelihood ratio) are computed using almost the same method as for the original activity set *A*.The only difference is that only the maximum log likelihood ratio is stored. Thus, at the end of this process a list of *m* test statistic values are obtained from *m* random activity sets $\left(A_{1...m}^{random}\right)$. These values are used to determine the statistical distribution of the log likelihood ratios.

Hypothesis Test

The null hypothesis states that activity points are distributed randomly according to a homogeneous Poisson process over the study area *S*(Kulldorff, 1997a). In order to accept or reject the null hypothesis (accept H_1), we need to determine the significance level (*p-value*) of the candidate hotspots. We do this by comparing a candidate's test statistic with the distribution of test statistics obtained from the randomization test, and then dividing its position by the number of Monte Carlo simulation trials *m*. If the computed p-value is higher than the desired significance level (α_p), the H_1 hypothesis is rejected; otherwise, it is said that H_1 can't be rejected, indicating the detected hotspot is significant.

With this background, we are ready to consider three representative approaches to statistically significant hotspot detection. Case studies on real crime data are included to illustrate each approach. We also briefly explain each method's limitations.

CIRCULAR HOTSPOT DETECTION

Criminal activity in an area tends to spread in a circular process similar to that described by the diffusion model in physics and chemistry. Diffusion means that molecules or heat will move away from their sources once they are discharged. The diffusion model provides a natural way to describe the circular spreading of cases (i.e. crimes). This gives rise to the notion of circular footprints of hotspots in isotropic geographies. Therefore, the ability to detect a circular hotspot is an important task in environmental criminology.

In formal terms, circular hotspot detection can be defined as follows: Given a set of geo-located points (e.g. crime reports) and a significance threshold, circular hotspot detection finds circular shaped areas where the concentration of points inside a circle is significantly higher than the number of points outside. Circular hotspot detection requires the following inputs specified by an analyst:

1. A spatial crime dataset with a collection of crimes, each associated with geo-location information (i.e., latitude, longitude),
2. A statistical significance threshold (α_p).

Based on the above inputs, the goal of circular hotspot detection is to report a collection of circular hotspot areas with p-values lower than the specified statistical significance threshold (α_p).

Case Study on a Real Crime Data

A typical input to circular hotspot detection is a spatial crime dataset that contains crime reports each associated with geo-location. For example, Figure 2 shows a crime dataset from Chicago, Illinois (City of Chicago, 2013). The dataset includes 384 homicides (by first degree murder) crimes committed in Chicago, Illinois between March 2013-March 2014. Each crime location is shown as blue dots and the map is created using QGIS Software (Quantum GIS Development Team, 2012), and the Open Street Plugin (Haklay & Weber, 2008). Study area is selected as the minimum orthogonal bounding rectangle of the crime dataset. Note that the study area could be the territorial area of responsibility for a public safety agency. The aim is to find circular hotspots with a statistical significance level of $\alpha_p = 0.001$. Figure 3 shows the output of SaTScan with two hotspot areas having log likelihood ratio of 107.10 and 48.26 respectively. These hotspots have p-value = 0.001 which indicates statistical significance at the 99.9% confidence level.

Figure 2. First degree murder cases in Chicago between March 2013 and March 2014; dataset includes 384 Homicide cases shown in blue dots

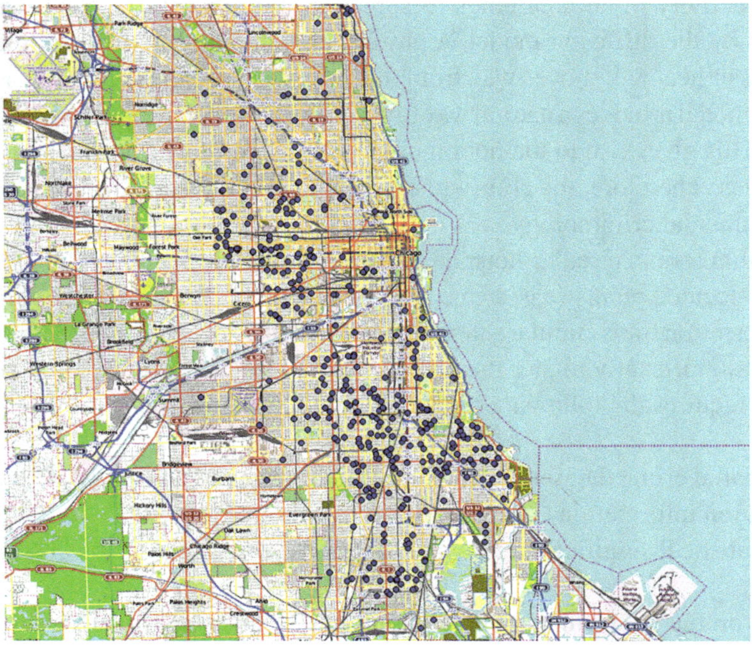

Figure 3. Output of SaTScan with two circular hotspots shown in blue

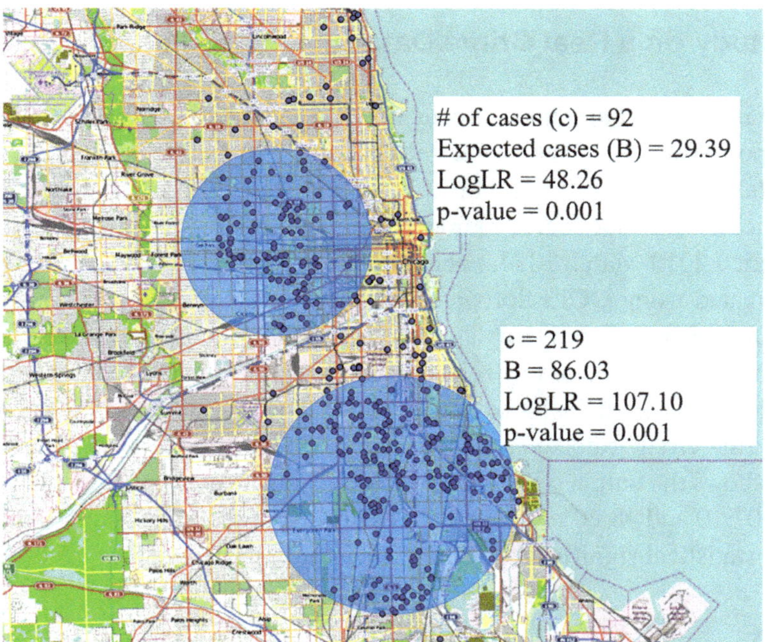

SaTScan Circular Hotspot Detection Algorithm

SaTScan is a state-of-the-art software package that uses spatial scan statistics to detect circular hotspots. It is used extensively in epidemiology to detect circular disease hotspots.

In its simplest form SaTScan uses a three-step approach to detect statistically significant circular hotspots:

1. Enumeration of Circles,
2. Log likelihood ratio test, and
3. Monte Carlo simulation and Hypothesis test.

Although indexing and optimization techniques exist for the circle enumeration and Gumbel Approximation (Martin Kulldorff, 2014) and Early Monte Carlo termination for the Monte Carlo simulation step can be used to improve the scalability of the SaTScan algorithm, this chapter describes these three steps without any algorithmic refinements.

Step 1: Enumeration of circles.

When enumerating candidate circular hotspots, SaTScan uses activity points in the activity set ($a \in A$) as the centers. In other words, SaTScan searches only the circles centered on each of the activity points in the dataset. Whenever a point is selected as a circle center, distances from the rest of the points to this center are used as radii to enumerate the circles. For example, given an activity set with $|A|$ = 100 activity points, $|A|(|A|-1) = 10099 = 9900$ circles are enumerated.

Step 2: Log likelihood ratio test.

The computation of $Log\ LR_Z$ requires the area and the number of points inside a zone *Z*. Suppose the zones are enumerated as circles in Step 1. Using the area of each circle and number of activity points inside, Log Likelihood Ratio of circles are computed. Note that among the overlapping circles, SaTScan returns only the circle with the highest Log Likelihood Ratio since most clusters of this type provide little additional information, but their existence means that while it is possible to pinpoint the general location of a cluster, its exact boundaries must remain uncertain (Kulldorff, 2010).

For example, the crime dataset set in Figure 2 includes 384 crime locations and the study area S is a 0.09 square degrees. The area of the circular hotspot in the north is $\pi r^2 = 3.140.047^2 = 0.0069$ and thus B = 29.39 and likelihood ratio is 48.268

Step 3: Monte Carlo Simulation and Hypothesis Test.

For the circles created in Step 1, a p-value is computed by doing a Monte Carlo simulation. First, m random datasets with Poisson distribution are generated. For each random dataset, new circles are enumerated and the maximum log likelihood ratio of each random dataset is stored in decreasing order. Then, log likelihood ratio of each circle enumerated in Step is compared with this list and its corresponding position is determined. This position is divided into the number of Monte Carlo simulations m to determine the p-value of a circle. Finally, all non-overlapping circles with p-value lower than the specified significance threshold α_p, are returned by the algorithm.

Limitations

As demonstrated, SaTScan relies on points as the centers. However, in cases where the center is sparse, SaTScan may not recognize a hotspot. Therefore, in cases when the contiguities of circular hotspots are disturbed by geographic features (i.e. rivers, roads, jurisdiction boundaries), these hotspots may not be detected by SaTScan. In addition, elliptical or imperfect circular (i.e. quarter/half circle) hotspots caused by geographic features may also be missed by this approach.

Another issue arises when two points occur too close to each other. SaTScan may detect them as significant hotspots since the log likelihood ratio function depends on the number of activity points and the area of the hotspot.

Finally, a hotspot detected by SaTScan has strict boundaries. However, most crimes tend to show a diffusion process where moving further from the center results in fewer observations of activities. Therefore, strict boundaries may not fully represent a crime hotspot. For these reasons, SaTScan should not be thought of as the sole tool to determine crime hotspots.

RING-SHAPED HOTSPOT DETECTION

In this section, ring shaped hotspot detection with a statistical significance will be defined and it will be illustrated with an example based on a crime dataset from San Diego, California. Formally, given a set of geo-located points (e.g. crime reports) and a significance threshold, ring-shaped hotspot detection aims to find ring-shaped hotspot areas where the concentration of points inside is significantly higher than the number of points outside. Ring-shaped hotspot detection requires the following inputs specified by an analyst:

1. A spatial crime dataset with a collection of crimes each associated with geo-location information (i.e. Latitude, Longitude).
2. A statistical significance threshold (α_p).

Based on the above inputs, the goal of ring-shaped hotspot detection is to report a collection of ring shaped hotspot areas with p-value lower than the specified statistical significance threshold (α_p).

In geographic profiling, two concepts are widely used to predict a potential location for a criminal. These concepts are distance decay and buffer zone as shown in the Figure 4. Distance decay is the result of a basic behavior caused by the requirements of time, effort and money to travel. Distance decay explains why most crimes occur relatively close to the offender's home (Brantingham & Brantingham, 1993). For example, 70% of arson crimes occur within two miles of a serial arsonist's home (Estepp, 1987). Second concept is the buffer zone, which is the basic result of the anonymity principle. In other words, buffer zone is an area where crimes are less likely, because of the increased risk of recognition by the neighbors. Geographic profiling uses the opposing effects of distance decay and buffer zone to predict the potential residence (location) of a criminal. Ring-shaped hotspots are also known as doughnut hole patterns or distance-decay zones.

Previous work on doughnut hole patterns focused on serial crime and used a formulation known as Rossmo's formula (Rossmo, 1995). Although it is a widely accepted method to determine the search area for a serial criminal's residence, Rossmo's formula has some limitations. It assumes a single crime source (e.g. serial criminal) and it lacks a statistical significance test.

Figure 4. Distance decay and buffer zone as described in environmental criminology
Burn, 1982.

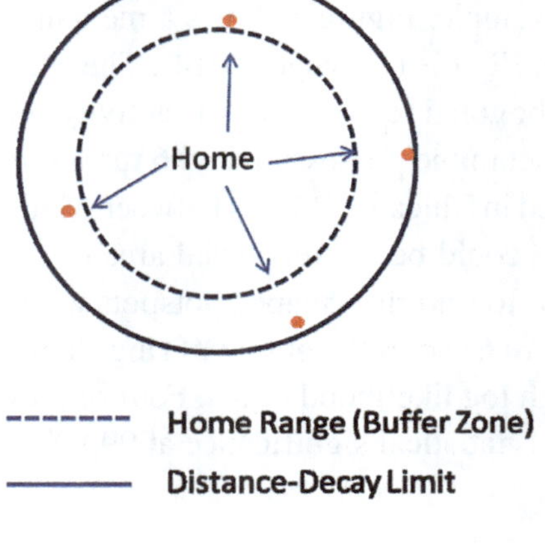

Figure 5. Methamphetamine possession (48 cases shown in red dots) and methamphetamine manufacture/deliver crimes (6 cases shown in yellow stars) committed in Chicago between March 2013 between March 2014

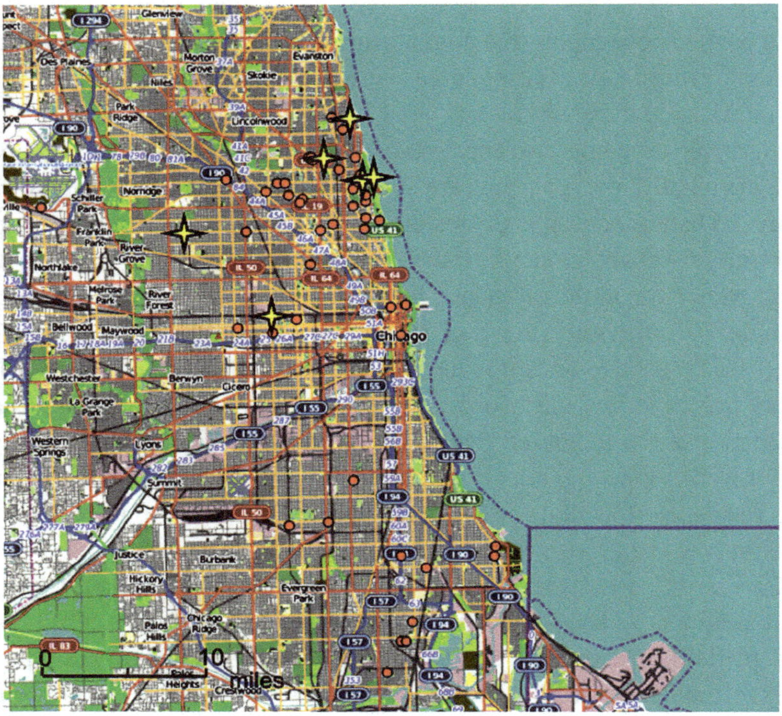

Case Study on a Real Crime Data

Similar to the Circular Hotspot Detection, Ring-shaped hotspot detection (RHD) uses an activity set (i.e. crime locations) as input to detect ring-shaped hotspots in the study area. For example, Figure 5 shows a methamphetamine crime dataset collected from Chicago, Illinois (Chicago, 2014). The study area is selected as the minimum bounding orthogonal rectangle of the activity set. Activity set includes a sample of 48 methamphetamine possession and 6 methamphetamine manufacture/deliver crimes committed in Chicago, Illinois between March 2013 and March 2014. Note that the study area could be the territorial area of responsibility for a public safety agency. The aim is to find ring-shaped hotspots with a statistical significance level of $\alpha_p = 0.001$. Figure 6 shows the output of ring shaped hotspot detection with 5 hotspot areas with high log likelihood ratios. Four of these hotspots have p-value = 0.001 which indicates statistical significance at 99.9% confidence level.

Figure 6. Output of ring shaped hotspot detection with 5 ring-shaped hotspots enumerated from the methamphetamine crime dataset in Figure 5

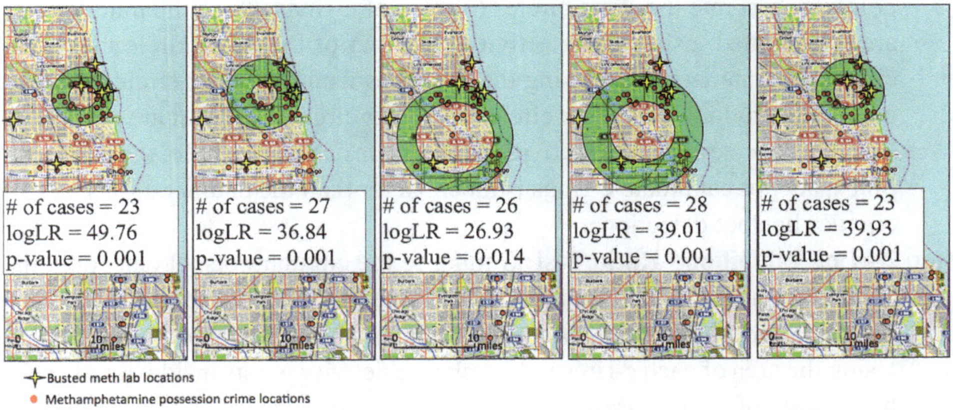

Ring-Shaped Hotspot Detection Algorithm

A ring shaped hotspot can be defined by a variety of techniques; here a ring is defined as a concentric ring (c-ring) (Eftelioglu et al., 2014) in this section.

Basic Concepts

- **C-Ring:** Any three non-collinear activities a_1, a_2, $a_3 \in A$ can uniquely identify a circle $circle_i$. For any activity point $a \in A$ outside $circle_i$, we can identify another circle $circle_o$ where a is on the circle and $circle_o$ is concentric with $circle_i$. The shape between any pair of such concentric circles $circle_i$ and $circle_o$ is defined as a C-Ring, denoted as R. Each C-Ring R has four parameters: the x and y coordinate of the center, the outer circle radius r_o, and the inner circle radius r_i. The area of the shape R is *area (R)*. Note that, for a given inner circle $circle_i$ with (x, y, r_i), there are many outer circles $circle_o$ (each defined by a distinct activity point a outside inner circle) and many c-rings R. (Eftelioglu et al., 2014)

Naïve Ring Shaped Hotspot Detection Algorithm

A naïve approach to ring shaped hotspot detection uses a three-step algorithm to detect statistically significant hotspots: (1) Enumeration of C-Rings, (2) Log likelihood ratio test and (3) Monte Carlo simulation and Hypothesis test. This chapter describes these three steps without any algorithmic refinements. In addition to the naïve algorithm, a faster approach with prune and refine steps will be shown.

Step 1 - Enumeration of Rings: Every three non-collinear points can define a unique circle. Using this notion, RHD enumerates every three non-linear points to generate the inner circles ($circle_i$) of c-rings. Once the inner circles are enumerated, using every activity point out of the inner circle, the outer circles are enumerated by using the distances from the inner circle center as outer circle radii. Using inner circles and outer circles c-rings R are generated. In RHD, since every three activity point creates an inner circle, the enumeration space for candidate c-rings is much larger than the enumeration space of circular hotspot detection.

Step 2 - Log Likelihood Ratio Test: Similar to the circular hotspot detection, the computation of $Log\ LR_Z$ requires the area and the number of points inside a zone Z. Suppose the zones are enumerated as ring-shaped hotspots in Step 1. Using the area of each c-ring and number of activity points inside, Log Likelihood Ratio of c-rings are computed.

Step 3 - Monte Carlo Simulation and Hypothesis Test: Monte Carlo simulation uses as similar algorithm to get the distribution of the log likelihood ratios under the null hypothesis. However, in Monte Carlo simulation, instead of the original input activity set A, random activity sets are generated under the null hypothesis and then Step 1 and Step 2 of the algorithm are run on these datasets. Among all c-rings enumerated using the random activity sets, only the c-ring with the highest likelihood ratio is stored for each random activity set. Then, the log likelihood ratio of each c-ring enumerated from the original activity set A is compared with this list and its corresponding position is determined. This position is divided into the number of Monte Carlo simulations m to determine the p-value of a c-ring. Finally, all non-overlapping c-rings with a p-value lower than the specified significance threshold α_p, are returned by the algorithm.

In a naïve approach to RHD problem, c-rings are enumerated by using circumcircle of all possible triplets of activities. Since each inner circle is created by three activities, outer circles are enumerated starting from the fourth activity. Thus the total number of inner circles is $\binom{|A|}{3}$ where |A| is the cardinality of the activity set A. For example, given an activity set with $|A| = 100$ activity points, $\binom{100}{3} = 161700$ inner circles are enumerated. Additionally, outer circles are enumerated using every point outside every inner circle. Therefore, the total number of candidate c-rings is high. For example, using an activity set of 1000 crime incidents, this number increases to approximately 10^{12} c-rings and computation time becomes exorbitant.

Dual Grid Based Pruning Algorithm

In order to address scalability limitation caused by the high number of c-rings generated by a naïve approach, Dual Grid based Pruning (DGP) algorithm namely DGP is proposed (Eftelioglu et al., 2014).

Simply, DGP algorithm defines an upper bound on the likelihood ratio of the c-rings. *The pruning phase* uses a dual grid approach, which keeps the number of activities in a geometric grid and enumerates c-rings in a parametric grid. For each ring enumerated in the parametric grid space an upper bound likelihood ratio is computed. Note that a c-ring in the parametric space represents a collection of actual c-rings in Euclidean space. Once the upper bound likelihood ratios are computed, the parametric grid cells which survive a given log likelihood ratio threshold are saved and the associated activity points are sent to the refine phase. *Refine phase* enumerates the actual c-rings and computes their likelihood ratios using the same enumeration technique described in the naïve approach. Finally, the candidate c-rings are tested for statistical significance using *Monte Carlo simulation phase.*

Limitations

The enumeration technique used in ring-shaped hotspot detection is costly. Although the DGP algorithm reduces the cost significantly, its refine phase still uses the same enumeration technique whereby triplets of points are used to enumerate inner circles and a fourth point to enumerate outer circles. An algorithm, which does not do extensive enumeration of rings, would be beneficial for efficient detection of c-rings.

A second limitation of RHD is that rings are assumed to be concentric. This is a very restrictive assumption. Imperfect rings and non-concentric rings which have occurred due to geographic features should be taken into account.

Finally, a ring shaped hotspot detected by Ring Shaped Hotspot Detection has strict boundaries. However, the diffusion of crimes described in circular hotspot detection holds in ring-shaped hotspots as well. Therefore, most crimes tend to show a diffusion process where moving further from the inner circle will cause less observation of activities.

Finally, a hotspot detected by Ring Shaped Hotspot Detection has strict boundaries. However, the diffusion of crime activity described in circular hotspot detection holds for ring-shaped hotspots as well. Since most crimes tend to show a diffusion process, moving further from the inner circle will cause less observation of activities. However, ring shaped hotspot detection does not take this into account.

LINEAR HOTSPOT DETECTION

The problem of linear hotspot detection (LHD) focuses on hotspots on network space. This problem is motivated by the fact that many types of crime only happen on road networks (e.g., street robbery). This section is organized as follows: First, a formal definition to the linear hotspot detection is introduced. Second, a motivating example for Linear Hotspot Detection is shown by a Case study on real data. Next, algorithms to solve the linear hotspot detection problem are introduced. Finally, the limitations of the proposed approaches are discussed.

Formally, given a spatial network (i.e. road network), a set of geo-located activities (i.e. crime reports), and a significance threshold, linear hotspot detection aims to find linear hotspots where the concentration of activities is significantly higher than other road segments. Detection of linear hotspots requires the following inputs specified by an analyst:

1. A spatial network (i.e. road network)
2. A spatial crime dataset with a collection of crimes each associated with a road segment,
3. A statistical significance threshold (α_p).

Based on the above inputs, the goal of linear hotspot detection is to report a collection of linear hotspot areas with p-value lower than the specified statistical significance threshold (α_p).

Case Study on a Real Crime Data

Linear hotspot detection will be illustrated with an example based on a crime dataset collected from Orlando, Florida in May 2015. Linear hotspot detection (LHD) uses activity locations and road network as input to detect the paths (road segments) where the number of activities is significantly higher than other road segments. For example, Figure 7 shows 44 street robbery crimes occurred in Orlando, Florida in May 2015. In this example, crime activities are shown by red dots (Orlando & FL, 2014). The input spatial network is the road network of the Orlando area. The aim is to find the linear hotspot areas with a statistical significance level of $\alpha_p = 0.03$. Figure 8 shows the output of Linear Hotspot detection with two significant paths. These paths are shown in blue and green and p-value is 0.02 and 0.01 respectively, which indicates statistical significance at 97% confidence level.

Figure 7. Street robbery cases in Orlando, Florida in May 2015. Crime dataset includes 44 reported theft cases as shown in red

Figure 8. Output of linear hotspot detection

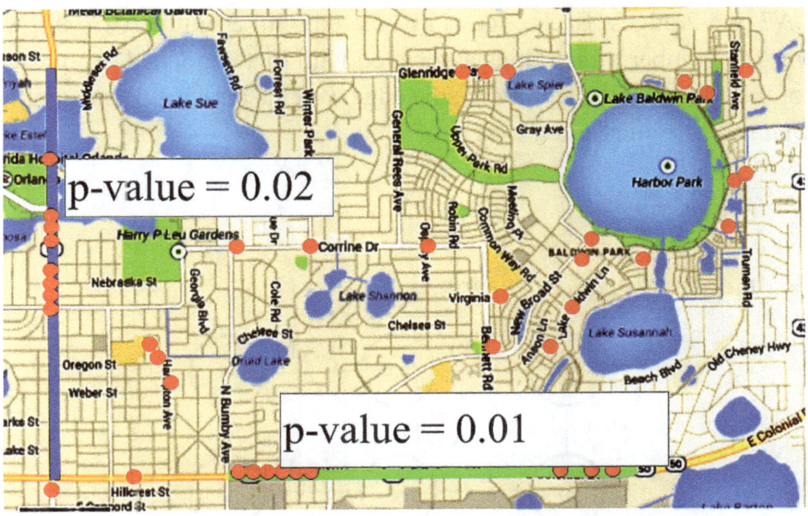

Linear Hotspot Detection Algorithm

Since linear hotspot detection is slightly different from hotspot detection in Euclidean space, related basic concepts will be introduced first, then a naïve and enhanced algorithm will be presented.

Basic Concepts

- **Spatial Network:** $G = (N, E)$ consists of a node set N and an edge set E, where each element u in N is associated with a pair of real numbers (x, y) representing the spatial location of the node in a Euclidean plane. Edge set E is a subset of the cross product N x N. Each element $e = (u, v)$ in E is an edge that joins node u to node v. Each edge has a weight w, which may represent its length or traffic density, etc. Note that each activity in the activity set A is associated with a specific edge in the spatial network $G = (N, E)$.
- **Distance:** Distance between any nodes in the spatial network is defined by the shortest path between the nodes. The triangle inequality of distance metric holds for this definition. Note that, the shortest path between two nodes could be not unique because there may be several paths with the same weight. However, the distance between two nodes is unique.

Figure 9 shows an example of spatial network, which contains 7 nodes denoted by 1, *N*2…*N*7 and 7 edges. Each edge is associated with 2 numbers (a, w), where a represents the number of activities associated with that edge, and w represents the weight of the edge. For the simplicity, the edge weights are set 1. For example, edge (*N*1, *N*2) has 6 activities and a weight of 1.

Figure 9. An example spatial network

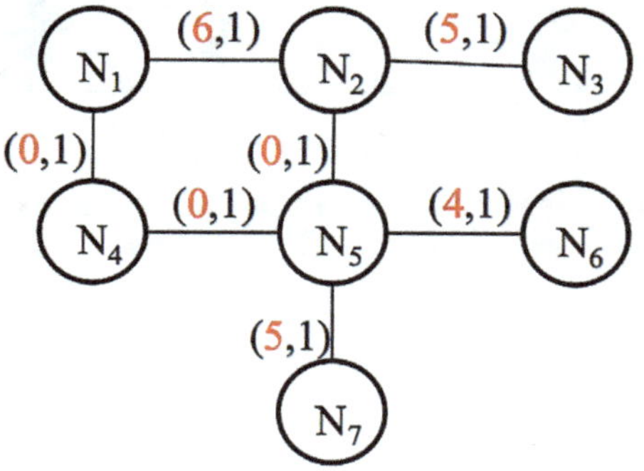

- **Likelihood Ratio of a Path:** In the linear hotspot detection, the likelihood ratio function is used as described in Linear Semantic Likelihood Ratio computation (Janeja & Atluri, 2005b). The linear semantic likelihood ratio (LR_p) function is described as following:

$$LR_p = \frac{\frac{a_p}{w_p}}{\frac{|A| - a_p}{|W| - w_p}}$$

As can be seen from the equation, the likelihood ratio of a path *p*, is the ratio of the activity density inside path *p* to the activity density outside *p*. In Figure 9, likelihood ratio of the path N_1, N_2, N_3, can be computed as

$$LR_p = \frac{\frac{11}{2}}{\frac{9}{5}} = 3.05$$

Note that although likelihood ratio of a path described in this section is different that the log likelihood ratio function described in Circular and Ring-Shaped Hotspot Detection, both functions can be used to assess the test statistic of an enumerated path.

Naïve Linear Hotspot Detection Algorithm (Oliver et al., 2014)

The basic idea behind linear hotspot detection algorithm is to find all statistically significant shortest paths in the spatial network whose likelihood exceeds θ. Note that the shortest paths returned are constrained so that they are not sub-paths of any other path in the output. This constraint aims to improve solution quality by reducing redundancy in the paths returned. The output is also constrained such that the shortest paths returned start and end with active nodes. This constraint also aims to improve solution quality by ignoring edges at the start and/or end of a path that do not have any activities.

Similar to the previous algorithms Naïve Linear Hotspot Detection algorithm (Oliver et al., 2014) consists of three steps.

Step 1 - Enumeration of Road Segments: In its first step naïve linear hotspot detection algorithm gets the spatial network as input and calculates the all pair shortest path for this spatial network.

Step 2 - Log Likelihood Ratio Test: For each enumerated road segment, this step computes the likelihood ratio if the starting and ending nodes are active nodes, meaning that the road segments should have activities associated with them. If any of the road segments has likelihood ratio higher than the specified threshold, they are saved into a candidate list for hypothesis test.

Step 3 - Monte Carlo Simulation and Hypothesis Test: In the Monte Carlo simulations, each activity in the original spatial network graph G is randomly associated with an edge so that the number of activities on each edge is shuffled, forming a new graph G_s. Note that all the activities in G are present in G_s, with no activities added or removed; the original activities in G are now shuffled so they may be on different edges in G_s. Then the highest likelihood of randomized G_s is compared with the highest likelihood ratio of original G. If the original one is smaller, then $p = p + 1$. The above process repeats m times and after it terminates, the p-value is subsequently p/m. Paths whose p-values are less than or equal to the given p-value threshold are deemed statistically significant and the null hypothesis is rejected.

LHD problem is challenging from computational perspective for several reasons. First, given a spatial network, the computation of all pair shortest paths is a costly operation. Moreover, the randomization test with Monte Carlo simulations (typically with 1000 trials) multiplies this cost. Second, log likelihood ratio function does not have monotonicity, which means given a path, its log likelihood ratio depends on both the number of activities and the weight of the path. Thus, monotonicity based pruning algorithms do not apply in LHD problem.

Smart Significant Route Miner Algorithm (Oliver et al., 2014)

A likelihood ratio pruning based algorithm is proposed to overcome the challenges of LHD problem. SmartSRM proposes an upper bound pruning approach to avoid computing all shortest paths of a graph. The framework of SmartSRM is similar to Dijkstra's algorithm, which uses a shortest path tree to represent the shortest paths from a source node (root of the tree) to all the other nodes. It stops growing a branch in the tree if the likelihood ratios of any shortest path on that branch must smaller than a specified likelihood ratio threshold $\alpha 1$. SmartSRM proposes a novel linear likelihood ratio upper bound to determine such branches. In addition, a Monte

Carlo Simulation (MCS) early stop algorithm is used in SmartSRM. The key idea is stopping a MCS trial once a linear likelihood ratio is found higher than the highest one in the candidate paths.

Limitations

Linear hotspot detection (LHD) has a high computational cost due to the extensive all pair shortest path enumeration. Moreover, Monte Carlo simulation multiplies this cost. Another problem with LHD arises from the definition of a Linear Hotspot. LHD defines linear hotspots as starting and ending with Nodes. However, long paths between two nodes may cause missing a dense linear hotspot if the activities are in a specific part of a path. For instance, in Figure 9, although activities are dense in a part of the returned path LHD returned a longer path which starts and ends with Nodes in the Spatial Network. Finally, some road crimes occur when a criminal travels from one location to another, causing a linear hotspot, which moves in the network over time. However, LHD described in this section cannot evaluate linear hotspots that take the temporal dimension into account.

CURRENT HOTSPOT DETECTION TOOLS

This chapter focused on three representative techniques that use spatial scan statistics for crime hotspot detection. However, these are just the tip of the iceberg and there are many tools that modern police enforcement uses for crime mitigation as well as research on hotspot detection that are going on. In the following paragraphs, those tools will be presented. More detailed information on spatial aspect of crime can be found in (Brimicombe, 2005; Cohen & Felson, 1979; Gonzales, Schofield, & Hart, 2005; Levine, 2006; Ratcliffe & McCullagh, 1999; Wang et al., 2013; Yu, Ward, Morabito, & Ding, 2011).

Today, public security officials use crime analysis software for to improve their efficiency and reaction time (Spencer Chainey & Ratcliffe, 2013; Gonzales et al., 2005). Software, which are used by public security officials, depends on the crime type (i.e., fraud, cyber crime, gun related crime). For example, a fraud detection software may audit the stock exchange movements and determine fraudulent activity on stock market whereas a cyber crime software may focus on the detection of cyber crimes. Since this chapter is focused on crime hotspot detection, the following examples will focus on the "spatial" aspect of crime.

GIS tools (ESRI ArcGIS, QGIS, Python GDAL/OGR, etc.) can be used to determine locations for new police deployment, detect suspicious activities, integrate 911 emergency call locations, perform resource (i.e. patrol) allocation to incidents, and analyze the crime locations (Mitchell, 1999). Modern GIS software integrates the statistical analysis tools in order to determine hotspots of crime as well as the days and times of high crime activities. Although some crime specific features may be added to those GIS software (Goetz, n.d.), they are not specialized in crime activities. Therefore, several softwares (i.e. CrimeStat) were developed to analyze the spatial aspect of crime. CrimeStat (Lavine, 2013), a software package for spatial analysis of crime locations, incorporates several methods to determine the crime hotspots in a study area. CrimeStat package has k-means tool, nearest neighbor hierarchical (NNH) clustering, Risk Adjusted NNH (RANNH) tool, STAC Hot Spot Area tool, and a Local Indicator of Spatial Association (LISA) tool that are used to evaluate potential hotspot areas (Leong K, 2015). Urban Growth Simulator (UGS), which is developed at Kent State University, aims to estimate changes in crime rates as induced by urban growth (Lee, Brody, Zhang, Kim, & Bradac, 2002). Rigel software, which depends on Rossmo's Formula, uses crime locations, suspect information, case details and investigator details to analyze a series of linked crimes and determine the most probable locations of the offender's residence (Beauregard, Proulx, & Rossmo, 2005; Devlin & Lorden, 2007). Hotspot Detective, which is (was) an add-on for MapInfo Software, uses a grid based approach together with kernel density estimation to determine hotspot locations (S Chainey, Tompson, & Uhlig, 2008).

Apart from the software above, several spatial statistical analysis tools are also used for the analysis of the spatial aspect of crime. For example, GeoDa, a spatial data analysis software, can be used to do multivariate exploratory data analysis, global and local spatial autocorrelation analysis, and basic linear regression with crime data (Anselin, Syabri, & Kho, 2006). In addition, several R software packages (spatstat, geoR, spdep, etc.) are widely used for spatial analysis of point referenced data (e.g. crime locations) (R Development Core Team, 2011). Finally, it is worth noting that there are many web-based crime analysis and visualization tools thanks to the spatial abilities of HTML5 (Holdener, 2011).

FUTURE RESEARCH DIRECTIONS

Although there are a variety of techniques (Ester & others, 1996; Ilango & Mohan, 2010; Karypis, Han, & Kumar, 1999; Levine, 2006; Wu et al., 2008) which are developed to be used in different domains, the techniques described in this chapter are representative approaches to detect circular, ring-shaped and linear hotspots given an activity set. In this section, some important research topics that include methodological advancements that may be needed to analyze crime hotspots are reviewed.

Crime occurrences are always associated with a population. However, the techniques described here do not take the population into account. For example, in most of the crime datasets used in this chapter, crime activities are dense near downtowns since these locations are dense in population. When detecting crime hotspots, the underlying population should be taken into account to reflect this.

In addition, the circular and ring-shaped hotspot detection techniques described here are based on the Euclidean space. However, people tend to use road networks to travel. Similarly, criminals tend to use the road network to travel to the crime sites. Thus, even a hotspot detection technique which focuses on circular hotspots should take road network distances into account. Detecting hotspots on a road network may provide additional insights that crime analysts can use to identify patrolling districts after taking a variety of other factors into consideration. Linear hotspot detection technique described in this section considers spatial network nodes as the starting and ending nodes of a significant road path. In order to detect partial road segments with high number of activities, activities on a spatial network can be considered as dynamic nodes, and the edges can be segmented accordingly. Linear hotspot detection on this new "dynamic segmented" spatial network may be able to give more precise location of hotspots. Techniques described in this chapter focus on the spatial dimensions of crime hotspots in either in Euclidean Space or Spatial Networks. However, new hotspot detection techniques are required which can evaluate the temporal space and detect hotspots using a constant flow of new crime activities.

Furthermore, fuzzy statistically significant hotspot detection techniques are needed to better represent the diffusion of crimes. Techniques described in this chapter detect crime hotspot areas with strict boundaries. Since the crime activities are similar to the diffusion processes in Physics and Chemistry, the crime activities become sparser when moving further from the center. Therefore, new fuzzy hotspot detection techniques are needed.

Given the current rate of crimes each year (e.g. annual 10^7 crimes U.S.), any crime hotspot detection technique should also consider the scalability of the designed algorithms. For example, the circular hotspot detection technique (i.e. SaTScan) described in this chapter is limited to a couple of thousands of activity points (i.e. crimes) due to the extensive circle enumeration using points as centers. Therefore, there is a need for new scalable algorithms to handle the high number of crime activities.

In this chapter, hotspot detection using the locations of crime incidents (geo-located crimes) is discussed. However, in the light of the technological advances, digital crimes (i.e. cyber crimes) are starting to get prevalent among crimes (Fei, Eloff, Olivier, & Venter, 2006). Such crimes include child abuse, hacking, financial theft, stealing private and/or confidential data etc. (Robert W. Taylor, Tory J. Caeti, D. Kall Loper, Eric J. Fritsch, 2006). Although these crimes do not have a specific location information (i.e., longitude, latitude), an approximate location can be captured from suspects' internet address (i.e. IP address) (Kao & Wang, 2009). However, since the locations of these crimes will be approximate (unlike a crime location in geographic space), new hotspot detection techniques are required to capture these events. Moreover, social media posts (Twitter, Facebook etc.) and geo-tags can be leveraged as well as the social network connections (i.e. friends, buddies) to have a sense of a criminal's location (Surette, 2010). Such opportunities can be new frontiers for hotspot detection.

CONCLUSION

This chapter explored crime hotspot detection methods, which is an important task in environmental criminology. When evaluating hotspot detection techniques, this chapter focused on the statistically significant hotspot detection techniques, to reduce false positive rates (i.e. hotspot areas which are occurred by chance). The chapter started with the foundations of Spatial Scan Statistics and the applications using Spatial Scan Statistics to find statistically significant circular hotspots. Next, ring-shaped hotspot detection is described. Finally, since most crimes occur and diffuse along a road network, linear hotspots are illustrated. Finally, chapter is concluded with future directions and opportunities for the crime hotspot detection task.

ACKNOWLEDGMENT

This material is based upon work supported by the National Science Foundation under Grant Number 1029711, IIS- 1320580, 0940818 and IIS-1218168, USDOD under Grant Number HM1582-08-1-0017, HM0210-13-1-0005, and University of Minnesota via U-Spatial. We would like to thank Kim Koffolt and the members of the University of Minnesota Spatial Computing Research Group for their comments.

REFERENCES

Agarwal, D., McGregor, A., Phillips, J. M., Venkatasubramanian, S., & Zhu, Z. (2006). Spatial scan statistics. In *Proceedings of the 12th ACM SIGKDD international conference on Knowledge discovery and data mining - KDD '06* (p. 24). http://doi.org/ doi:10.1145/1150402.1150410

Anselin, L., Syabri, I., & Kho, Y. (2006). GeoDa: An introduction to spatial data analysis. *Geographical Analysis*, *38*(1), 5–22. doi:10.1111/j.0016-7363.2005.00671.x

Beauregard, E., Proulx, J., & Rossmo, D. K. (2005). Spatial patterns of sex offenders: Theoretical, empirical, and practical issues. *Aggression and Violent Behavior*, *10*(5), 579–603. doi:10.1016/j.avb.2004.12.003

Belenko, S. R., & Spohn, C. (2015). *Drugs, crime, and justice*. Academic Press.

Brantingham, P. L., & Brantingham, P. J. (1993). Environment, Routine, and Situation: Toward a Pattern Theory of Crime. *Routine Activity and Rational Choice: Advances in Criminological Theoy*, *5*, 259–294.

Brimicombe, A. J. (2005). *Cluster Detection in Point Event Data having Tendency Towards Spatially Repetitive Events*. Intl. Conf. on GeoComputation.

Burn, O. (1982). *Environmental criminology. Journal of Criminal Justice* (Vol. 10). Sage Publications. http://doi.org/<ALIGNMENT.qj></ALIGNMENT>10.1016/0047-2352(82)90028-9

Chainey, S., & Ratcliffe, J. (2013). *GIS and Crime Mapping*. GIS and Crime Mapping; doi:10.1002/9781118685181

Chainey, S., Tompson, L., & Uhlig, S. (2008). *The Utility of Hotspot Mapping for Predicting Spatial Patterns of Crime*. http://doi.org/<ALIGNMENT.qj></ALIGNMENT>10.1057/sj.2008.6

City of Chicago. (2013). *City of Chicago Data Portal*. Retrieved from https://data.cityofchicago.org/

City of Chicago. (2014). Methamphetamine Possession Cases Chicago 2013. Chicago.

City of Orlando, FL. (2014). *Orlando Crime Dataset*. Author.

Cohen, L. E., & Felson, M. (1979). Social Change and Crime Rate Trends: A Routine Activity Approach. *American Sociological Review*, *44*(4), 588. doi:10.2307/2094589

Coleman, M., Coleman, M., Mabuza, A. M., Kok, G., Coetzee, M., & Durrheim, D. N. (2009). Using the SaTScan method to detect local malaria clusters for guiding malaria control programmes. *Malaria Journal*, *8*(1), 68. doi:10.1186/1475-2875-8-68 PMID:19374738

Devlin, K., & Lorden, G. (2007). *The Numbers Behind NUMB3RS: Solving Crime with Mathematics*. Academic Press.

Eck, J., & others. (2005). *Mapping crime: Understanding hotspots*. Academic Press.

Eftelioglu, E., Shekhar, S., Oliver, D., Zhou, X., Evans, M. R., & Xie, Y., ... Farah, C. (2014). Ring-Shaped Hotspot Detection: A Summary of Results. In *2014 IEEE International Conference on Data Mining* (pp. 815–820). doi:10.1109/ICDM.2014.13

Estepp, I. (1987). Motived-based Offender profiles of arson and fire-related crimes. *FBI Law Enforcement Bulletin, 56*(4), 17–23.

Ester, M. et al. (1996). *A density-based algorithm for discovering clusters in large spatial databases with noise* (pp. 226–231). AAAI Press.

Fei, B. K. L., Eloff, J. H. P., Olivier, M. S., & Venter, H. S. (2006). The use of self-organising maps for anomalous behaviour detection in a digital investigation. *Forensic Science International, 162*(1-3), 33–37. doi:10.1016/j.forsciint.2006.06.046 PMID:16876359

Goetz, S. L. (n.d.). *ArcGIS Tool Implementation of Risk Terrain Modeling.*

Gonzales, A. R., Schofield, R. B., & Hart, S. V. (2005). Mapping Crime: Understanding Hot Spots. National Institute of Justice, 79.

Haklay, M., & Weber, P. (2008). OpenStreetMap – User Generated Street Map. *IEEE Pervasive Computing / IEEE Computer Society [and] IEEE Communications Society, 7*(4), 12–18. doi:10.1109/MPRV.2008.80

Holdener, A. T. (2011). HTML5 Geolocation. *Online*, 114. Retrieved from http://books.google.com/books?id=9aIA5P6dp2cC&pgis=1

Ilango, M., & Mohan, V. (2010). A survey of grid based clustering algorithms. *International Journal of Engineering Science, 2*(8), 3441–3446. Retrieved from http://www.ijest.info/docs/IJEST10-02-08-17.pdf

Janeja, V. P., & Atluri, V. (2005a). LS3: a Linear Semantic Scan Statistic technique for detecting anomalous windows. *Proceedings of the 2005 ACM Symposium on Applied Computing*, (pp. 493–497). http://doi.org/http://doi.acm.org/10.1145/1066677.1066790

Janeja, V. P., & Atluri, V. (2005b). LS3: a Linear Semantic Scan Statistic technique for detecting anomalous windows. In *Proceedings of the 2005 ACM symposium on Applied computing* (pp. 493–497). http://doi.org/http://doi.acm.org/10.1145/1066677.1066790

Kao, D.-Y., & Wang, S.-J. (2009). The IP address and time in cyber-crime investigation. *Policing: An International Journal of Police Strategies & Management, 32*(2), 194–208. doi:10.1108/13639510910958136

Karypis, G., Han, E.-H. H. E.-H., & Kumar, V. (1999). Chameleon: Hierarchical clustering using dynamic modeling. *Computer*, *32*(8), 68–75. doi:10.1109/2.781637

Kulldorf, M. (1999). *Spatial Scan Statistics: Models, Calculations and Applications. Scan Statistics and Applications*. Springer; doi:10.1007/978-1-4612-1578-3_14

Kulldorff, M. (1997). A spatial scan statistic. *Communications in Statistics. Theory and Methods*, *26*(6), 1481–1496. doi:10.1080/03610929708831995

Kulldorff, M. (2010). *SaTScan User Guide v. 9.0*. Academic Press.

Kulldorff, M., Huang, L., Pickle, L., & Duczmal, L. (2006). An elliptic spatial scan statistic. *Statistics in Medicine*, *25*(22), 3929–3943. doi:10.1002/sim.2490 PMID:16435334

Lavine, N. (2013). *Introduction to CrimeStat IV (CrimeStat IV: A Spatial Statistics Program for the Analysis of Crime Incident Locations, Version 4.0)*. Academic Press.

Lee, J., Brody, T. M., Zhang, R., Kim, H., & Bradac, M. (2002). *Simulating Urban Growth on the Web*. Academic Press.

Leong K, S. A. (2015). A review of spatio-temporal pattern analysis approaches on crime analysis. *International E-Journal of Criminal Sciences, 9*.

Levine, N. (2006). Crime mapping and the crimestat program. *Geographical Analysis*, *38*(1), 41–56. doi:10.1111/j.0016-7363.2005.00673.x

Liao, W., Liu, Y., & Choudhary, A. (2004). A grid-based clustering algorithm using adaptive mesh refinement. *Proc. of the 7th Workshop on Mining Scientific and Engineering Datasets*.

Maguire, M. (2008). *Crime statistics*. Retrieved January 1, 2015, from https://www.fbi.gov/stats-services/crimestats/

Martin Kulldorff. (2014). *SaTScan User Guide for Version 9.3*. StatScan. Retrieved from http://www.satscan.org/

McCullagh, M. (2006). Detecting hotspots in time and space. *Isg06*, 1–18. Retrieved from http://citeseerx.ist.psu.edu/viewdoc/download?doi=10.1.1.158.2442&rep=rep1&type=pdf

Mitchell, A. (1999). The ESRI guide to GIS analysis. Volume 1: Geographic patterns & relationships. *Annals of Physics*, *54*, 87–88. Retrieved from http://books.google.com/books?id=FOj8L-iDMq0C&pgis=1

Neill, D. B. (2009). An empirical comparison of spatial scan statistics for outbreak detection. *International Journal of Health Geographics*, *8*(1), 20. doi:10.1186/1476-072X-8-20 PMID:19371431

Neill, D. B., & Moore, A. W. (2004). Rapid detection of significant spatial clusters. In *Proceedings of the 2004 ACM SIGKDD international conference on Knowledge discovery and data mining - KDD '04* (p. 256). http://doi.org/ doi:10.1145/1014052.1014082

Oliver, D., Shekhar, S., Zhou, X., Eftelioglu, E., Evans, M. R., & Zhuang, Q. … Farah, C. (2014). Significant Route Discovery: A Summary of Results. In Proc. of GIScicence (pp. 284–300). Springer.

Patil, G. P., & Taillie, C. (2004). Upper level set scan statistic for detecting arbitrarily shaped hotspots. *Environmental and Ecological Statistics*, *11*(2), 183–197. doi:10.1023/B:EEST.0000027208.48919.7e

Prates, M. O., Assunção, R. M., & Costa, M. (2012). Flexible scan statistic test to detect disease clusters in hierarchical trees. *Computational Statistics*, *27*(4), 715–737. doi:10.1007/s00180-011-0286-9

Quantum GIS Development Team. (2012). Quantum GIS Geographic Information System. *Open Source Geospatial Foundation Project*. Retrieved from http://qgis.osgeo.org

R Development Core Team. (2011). R Language Definition. *Web*, *0*, 62. doi:10.1016/0164-1212(87)90019-7

Ratcliffe, J. H., & McCullagh, M. J. (1999). Hotbeds of crime and the search for spatial accuracy. *Journal of Geographical Systems*, *1*(4), 385–398. doi:10.1007/s101090050020

Rossmo, D. K. (1995). *Geographic profiling: Target patterns of serial murderers. ProQuest Dissertations and Theses. Theses (School of Criminology)*. Simon Fraser University.

Sarmah, S., Das, R., & Bhattacharyya, D. K. (2007). Intrinsic Cluster Detection Using Adaptive Grids. *15th International Conference on Advanced Computing and Communications (ADCOM 2007)*. http://doi.org/ doi:10.1109/ADCOM.2007.18

Shi, L., & Janeja, V. P. (2011). Anomalous window discovery for linear intersecting paths. *IEEE Transactions on Knowledge and Data Engineering*, *23*(12), 1857–1871. doi:10.1109/TKDE.2010.212

Surette, R. (2010). *Media, Crime, and Criminal Justice*. Retrieved from http://books.google.com/books?id=geK4L1Q7fqAC&pgis=1

Walther, G. (2010). Optimal and fast detection of spatial clusters with scan statistics. *Annals of Statistics*, *38*(2), 1010–1033. doi:10.1214/09-AOS732

Wang, D., Ding, W., Lo, H., Stepinski, T., Salazar, J., & Morabito, M. (2013). Crime hotspot mapping using the crime related factors - A spatial data mining approach. *Applied Intelligence*, *39*(4), 772–781. doi:10.1007/s10489-012-0400-x

Wu, X., Kumar, V., Ross Quinlan, J., Ghosh, J., Yang, Q., Motoda, H., … Steinberg, D. (2008). Top 10 algorithms in data mining. *Knowledge and Information Systems* (Vol. 14). http://doi.org/<ALIGNMENT.qj></ALIGNMENT>10.1007/s10115-007-0114-2

Yu, C.-H., Ward, M. W., Morabito, M., & Ding, W. (2011). Crime Forecasting Using Data Mining Techniques. *2011 IEEE 11th International Conference on Data Mining Workshops*, (pp. 779–786). http://doi.org/ doi:<ALIGNMENT.qj></ALIGNMENT>10.1109/ICDMW.2011.56

Zhang, Y. (2010). *Hotspot Analysis of Highway Accident Spatial Pattern Based on Network Spatial Weights*. Academic Press.

Chapter 5
Visual Data Mining:
A Great Opportunity for Criminal Investigation

Mehrdad Ghaziasgar
University of the Western Cape, South Africa

Antoine Bagula
University of the Western Cape, South Africa

Nathan De La Cruz
University of the Western Cape, South Africa

James Connan
Rhodes University, South Africa

ABSTRACT

Current generation criminal justice relies mostly on manual procedures and processes which are time-consuming and error-prone. A polygraph test consists of only "yes" or "no" questions and depends several physiological responses in subjects. It's effectiveness and accuracy have been questioned due to the possibility of swaying the examiner by individuals that are capable of controlling their physical reactions in order to defeat the lie detection exercise. The criminal justice of the future is expected to be empowered by the most modern information and communication technologies to provide various participants in the justice system with a rich set of services such as virtual court presence and hearing participation through visual sensor networks. This chapter revisits the issue of deception detection by proposing visual data mining as a non-invasive alternative to deception detection in next generation criminal justice. Image processing and machine learning techniques are used to accurately detect facial micro-expressions which have been shown to be strong indicators of deception.

DOI: 10.4018/978-1-5225-0463-4.ch005

INTRODUCTION

Current generation criminal justice relies mostly on manual procedures and processes which are time-consuming, hard to scale, error-prone and sometimes invasive. For example, the polygraph commonly referred to as the "lie detector test" is based on a process that measures and records several physiological indices such as blood pressure, pulse, respiration, and skin conductivity while the subject is asked and answers a series of questions. The expectation is that deceptive answers will produce physiological responses that can be differentiated from those associated with non-deceptive answers. A polygraph test consists of only "yes" or "no" questions which are dependent on the ways in which several physiological activities are simultaneously recorded during a test and aims to monitor at least three bodily reactions to determine whether a person is truthfully answering questions. These reactions include the respiratory rate, sweat gland activity, and cardiovascular activity. The polygraph test has been at the heart of debates between proponents and opponents of the system, some claiming a 90% success rate while others questioning its accuracy due to many factors, including 1) not being reliable and unable to tell the examiner whether the subject is telling the truth or lying as they depend on the physiological reactions to the questions asked and 2) possibly swaying the examiner as they rely on the physiology of individuals who may be very nervous, unshakable or capable of controlling their physical reactions in order to defeat the lie detection exercise.

The criminal justice of the future is expected to be empowered by the most modern information and communication technologies (ICTs) to provide magistrates, advocates, judges, members of the jury and the police force a rich set of services such as virtual court presence and hearing participation through visual sensor networks (VSNs). These networks will be equipped with camera sensors and communication capabilities to enable recording and streaming to places where virtual participation is required. In addition, machine learning techniques and statistical methods can be leveraged in order to detect and provide a rich set of indicators to these participants, including lip-shape and facial micro-expressions, among others. In this regard, facial micro-expressions have been shown to be strong indicators of deception, giving rise to the possibility of detecting deception automatically. This chapter revisits the issue of deception detection by proposing visual data mining (VDM) as a non-invasive alternative to deception detection in next generation criminal justice.

Micro-Expressions and Deception Detection

Facial expressions contain non-verbal cues and help in conveying tone in conversation. Micro-expressions are facial expressions that have two characteristics: they appear over a very short duration and have a much lower intensity than normal facial expressions i.e. they are subtle. While there is no consensus on the correct duration of micro-expressions, it is generally believed that they span, on average, between $^1/_5$th and $^1/_{25}$th of a second (Shreve, Godavarthy, Goldgof, & Sarkar, 2011), with the longest generally accepted duration considered to be half a second (Wang, Yan, Li, Zhao, & Fu, 2014).

Micro-expressions have been researched extensively in the field of Psychology (Haggard & Isaacs, 1966; Endres & Laidlaw, 2009; Ekman, 2009; Russell, Chu, & Phillips, 2006) and to a limited extent in Computer Science (Wang, Yan, Li, Zhao, & Fu, 2014; Shreve, Godavarthy, Goldgof, & Sarkar, 2011; Wu, Shen, & Fu, 2011; Pfister, Li, Zhao, & Pietikainen, 2011). Ekman was one of the pioneers of facial micro-expression research and has played a major role in identifying and characterizing various micro-expressions (Ekman & Friesen, Nonverbal leakage and clues to deception, 1969; Ekman, 2009). The micro-expressions that have been characterized are: sadness, anger, contempt, disgust, fear, happiness and surprise. However, contempt and happiness may appear similar in many cases, both expressed with a smiling face, and the micro-expressions may be thought of as totaling to six categories (Wu, Shen, & Fu, 2011).

All of these categories of micro-expressions have macro counter-parts, from which they are distinguished in terms of the much shorter period of time over which they are expressed and the reduced intensity of the expression.

Research has shown that micro-expressions are strong indicators of deception. Subjects have been shown to express one or more micro-expressions after a deceptive statement is made, and these micro-expressions are more likely to occur in high stake scenarios in which there may be grave consequences if the deception is discovered (Li, Pfister, Huang, Zhao, & Pietikainen, 2013).

The pioneers of this idea were Haggard and Isaacs (1966) who were the first to report the observation of micro-expressions as linked to deception. Shortly after, Ekman and Friesen (1969) also reported observing micro-expressions independently. The study by Ekman and Friesen involved a video of a psychiatric patient who deceived her psychiatrist about, and concealed, her intentions to commit suicide. While the patient appeared to be normal and perhaps even cheerful throughout the interview, a careful frame-by-frame examination of the video revealed two frames in which the subject expressed sadness, lasting a total of $^1/_{12}$th of a second. This was one of the pioneering studies of the idea that the presence of micro-expressions can be used as a strong indicator of deception in a conversation or interrogation, an idea that was developed in subsequent studies (Ekman, 2009). The type of micro-expression is irrelevant in this regard. It is sufficient to detect the presence of any one of the types of micro-expressions to this end. Therefore, the ability to detect micro-expressions implies the ability to detect deception.

Ekman's research has been used to inform and train expert human micro-expression detectors, with applications to criminal and clinical investigations and interrogations (Russell, Chu, & Phillips, 2006; Endres & Laidlaw, 2009; Warren, Schertler, & Bull, 2009; Frank, Herbasz, Sinuk, Keller, & Nolan, 2009). Human detectors have been shown to achieve relatively low accuracy detection of no higher than 40%(Frank, Herbasz, Sinuk, Keller, & Nolan, 2009). The speed at which some micro-expressions occur, typically 20 to 25 frames per second, may exceed the speed at which the human eye is capable of capturing information, typically 10 to 12 frames per second (Read & Meyer, 2000). In many cases, the remedy employed is to freeze-frame prerecorded video feeds and analyze them on a frame-by-frame basis. A typical video with a duration of 1 minute has 1500 frames. Considering that an interrogation or interview may last between 10 minutes and an hour, it is clear that freeze-framing is exceptionally slow, inefficient and tiresome (Wu, Shen, & Fu, 2011).

Typical web cameras do not have this limitation, and are capable of capturing 20 frames per second and above. Specialized cameras may achieve between 60 and 300 frames per second. Coupling this with computer vision and machine learning techniques provides the prospect of automatically detecting deception in a fast, scalable, accurate and efficient manner.

Contribution and Outline

Research studies that have focused on using computer vision to automatically recognize micro-expressions in video feeds are very limited (Li, Pfister, Huang, Zhao, & Pietikainen, 2013), especially as compared to systems that recognize facial macro-expressions. This is attributed mainly to the difficulty of the detection problem and the lack of readily available and open labelled micro-expression data sets. Of those studies that exist, varied feature extraction techniques have been proposed and investigated to achieve varied levels of detection success (Wang, Yan, Li, Zhao, & Fu, 2014; Wu, Shen, & Fu, 2011; Shreve, Godavarthy, Goldgof, & Sarkar, 2011; Pfister, Li, Zhao, & Pietikainen, 2011).

The Local Binary Pattern (LBP) operator is a computationally efficient texture descriptor that has shown significant promise in facial macro-expression detection and recognition (Mushfieldt, Ghaziasgar, & Connan, 2013; Moore & Bowden, 2011). It is expected that the operator can achieve similarly promising results in the detection of micro-expressions.

This chapter investigates the automatic detection of micro-expressions from a video feed using LBPs as a facial feature descriptor and Support Vector Machines (SVMs) as a classifier into one of two categories, namely: "micro-expression" and "neutral expression". The "micro-expression" category here is a combination of all seven facial expression types that have been described by Ekman and others. This has important applications in the criminal justice system of the future.

This chapter is structured as follows: The "Related Work" section describes select related work in the field of automatic micro-expression detection and the use of the LBP operator in facial macro-expression recognition; The "Visual Data Mining Framework" section describes the proposed micro-expression recognition implementation and its context within a VDM framework; the experimentation and subsequent results are provided and discussed in the "Experimental Setup and Results" section; the discussion on automatic micro-expression recognition is concluded in the section that follows.

RELATED WORK

In this section, related studies are discussed. The first subsection describes select related work in the field of micro-expression detection. The second subsection discusses select studies that used LBPs to achieve accurate macro-expression recognition.

Automatic Micro-Expression Detection

Micro-expression detection systems generally employ a three-step processing procedure: determining the location of and segmenting the face; feature extraction from the face; and classification of the extracted features into one of two classes: "micro-expression" and "neutral expression". Once micro-expression detection has been carried out, micro-expression recognition can be carried out, that is, determining which specific class of micro-expressions the detected expression belongs to. Concretely, detection involves a binary decision as to whether or not a micro-expression of any type exists in the frame under examination, while recognition involves determining the type of the micro-expression present.

As mentioned previously, the type of micro-expression is relevant to the task of deception detection only as a Boolean indicator of the presence or absence of a specific micro-expression. While the type of micro-expression provides the ability to carry out a deeper analysis of the nature and intent of deception taking place, the mere presence of any type of micro-expression is sufficient to provide a strong indication of deception in and of itself. As such, this discussion limits itself to micro-expression detection only and discussions of micro-expression recognition strategies are omitted. Where relevant, however, whether or not a recognition strategy was proposed is mentioned to allow the interested reader to refer to the literature for an extended reading.

Wu et al. (2011) developed a fully automatic micro-expression detection and recognition system. The system processes every frame of a video sequence to detect micro-expressions. Once micro-expressions have been detected, micro-expression recognition is carried out.

The face segmentation method proposed by Kienzle et al. (2004) is used to locate and segment the face in each frame. Gabor filters are used as a facial feature descriptor. SVMs are used to classify expressions as either micro-expressions or the neutral expression. In training and testing the system, images from various macro-expression databases were compiled. Training and testing sequences were manually generated by inserting a small number of macro-expression frames in between a number of neutral frames. This was aimed at mimicking the short duration of micro-expressions. However, the low intensity of micro-expressions was not represented as the frames inserted contained macro-expressions which are of much higher intensity than micro-expressions. The system achieved a very high accuracy of 95.83%. This is a very impressive and commendable result but it should be noted that the use of true micro-expressions complicates the task of detection and will very likely reduce the accuracy.

Gabor filters and the LBP operator have been co-characterized as appearance-based or texture-based feature descriptors, since both highlight texture features (Mushfieldt, Ghaziasgar, & Connan, 2013). Gabor filters have been shown to achieve a somewhat higher accuracy than LBPs in some facial macro-expression detection and recognition tasks. However, Gabor filters are a significantly more complex and computationally expensive technique, especially as the number of kernels used increases. A large number of kernels are typically required to achieve a high accuracy (Mushfieldt, Ghaziasgar, & Connan, 2013).

Shreve et al. (2011) used a combination of skin motion tracking and skin strain computation to detect micro-expressions. Manually constrained facial images are used such that it is unnecessary to locate or segment the face in the images. This simplifies the detection process but introduces the need for manual intervention on every frame of a sequence in any application of the system. Skin motion tracking is achieved by means of dense optical flow tracking. The strain on the facial skin is determined by means of an approximation of the finite difference in skin motion. Finally, a dynamic threshold on the skin strain is applied to portions of the video containing significant skin motion to determine whether or not a micro-expression occurred.

The system successfully detected all micro-expression frames, seven to be exact, contained in a test video, with 1 false positive also reported. Although the result is promising, it is evident that the experimentation carried out was limited and further testing is required. The researchers conclude by noting that a major challenge in this area of research is a lack of micro-expression data sets for training and testing (Shreve, Godavarthy, Goldgof, & Sarkar, 2011; Wu, Shen, & Fu, 2011).

Polikovsky et al. (2009) used micro-muscle movements in the face to detect micro-expressions. The system detects micro Action Units (AUs), as defined by the Facial Action Coding System (FACS), originally proposed by Hjortsjö (1969), and later modified by Ekman (1977). The FACS defines key muscles in the face—referred to as AUs—that are the constituent units of, and are combined to form, all facial expressions.

A static mask is used to filter out all non-facial pixels in every frame of a video sequence and achieve face segmentation. The assumption made is that the video sequence contains a face that is located in the centre of every frame and remains static across the frames of the video sequence. The face is divided into 12 regions. Histograms of the spatial and temporal gradient vectors are used to represent the facial features of each region in each frame. Finally, a combination of a k-means classifier and an AU voting procedure is used to determine whether a micro-AU is contained in each region of each frame, which in turn determines if a micro-expression has occurred.

It should be noted that only specific AUs can be present or absent in each region. For example, the region around the eyes (and only this region) can contain AUs 4, 7 and 43. This localizes the voting procedure to limit classifier confusion and achieve a high accuracy. The system was tested on a manually collected data set. The system obtained an impressive average accuracy of 86% for 11 AUs over 15000 frames of video. However, it should be noted that the data set used consists of subjects rapidly performing micro-expressions and returning to the neutral facial expression, i.e. the micro-expressions are posed and intense, whereas micro-expressions are spontaneous and subtle. Therefore, the data set used is similar in nature to that used by Wu et al. Working with true micro-expressions that are far less intense complicates the task of detection and is expected to result in a much reduced accuracy.

Automatic Macro-Expression Recognition Using Local Binary Patterns

Mushfieldt et al. (2013) investigated the use of LBPs in the context of automatic facial macro-expression recognition. The system is fully automatic and applies macro-expression recognition on every frame in a video sequence.

A novel dynamic face segmentation procedure was proposed which results in an image of only the facial region for both frontal and profile facial images. The segmented face is scaled to a resolution of 40×60 pixels. The LBP operator is applied to the resulting image to highlight texture features of the facial image.

The LBP image is divided into 8×5-pixel regions and a histogram of each region is computed. The histograms of all the regions are concatenated into a single histogram set. Dividing the image into regions ensures that both local- and global-feature information is preserved and represented in the final histogram set. SVMs are used to classify the facial features into six prototypic macro-expression categories, namely: neutral, anger, disgust, fear, happiness, sadness and surprise.

The system was trained on a manually collected data set of videos of 10 subjects of mixed gender and varied skin tone performing each of the macro-expressions twice. For testing, videos of ten different subjects of mixed gender and varied skin tone performing each of the six expressions once were collected. For each video, the system response was recorded. On average, the system achieved an impressive facial macro-expression accuracy of 85%.

Moore and Bowden (2011) also used LBPs and SVMs in facial macro-expression recognition. The face segmentation strategy used is unclear from the literature. Several variants of the LBP operator were used and compared to determine the most efficient variant for facial macro-expression recognition. The following LBP variants were considered: uniform rotation invariant LBPs (LBPriu2); rotation invariant LBPs (LB-Pri); uniform LBPs obtained from the gradient magnitude image (LBPgm); standard local uniform LBPs (LBPu2); multi-scale LBPs (LBPms) and LBPs extracted from Gabor images (LGBP). In each case, the relevant LBP operator was applied to the facial image. Similar to the previous study, the resulting LBP image in each case was divided into regions and a histogram set for each image was computed by computing and concatenating histograms of each region of the LBP image.

Classification was carried out by means of an SVM. A number of different region sizes and LBP image resolutions were investigated. It was found that different LBP operator-variants may require different region sizes and LBP resolutions to achieve optimum accuracy.

Two databases were used to test the system: The Binghamton University 3D facial expression (BU3DFE) database and the Multi-pie database. The training set consisted of 90 subjects and the test set consisted of 10 subjects doing the six prototypic expressions at different angles. The two operator-variants that achieved the highest accuracy were the LGBP and the LBPms with average accuracies of 67.96% and 65.02% respectively.

It can be concluded from these studies that the LBP descriptor is a potentially powerful feature representation technique in the context of facial expression recognition.

THE VISUAL DATA MINING FRAMEWORK

Visual sensor networks (Soro and Heinzelman (2009), Tavli et al (2011)) have been extensively researched during the last decades. However, to the best of our knowledge, their combined use with machine learning techniques to achieve situation recognition in criminal investigation is still in its infancy. This section presents a framework for VDM and describes the procedure used to segment the face, extract and represent facial features and classify expressions as either "neutral expression" or "micro-expression". The proposed VDM framework can be seen as an application visual sensor networks' concepts and principles to improve criminal investigation by taking advantage of camera sensors and machine learning techniques. Figure 1 depicts the framework. It has been designed around four layers:

Figure 1. Proposed multi-layer framework for VDM

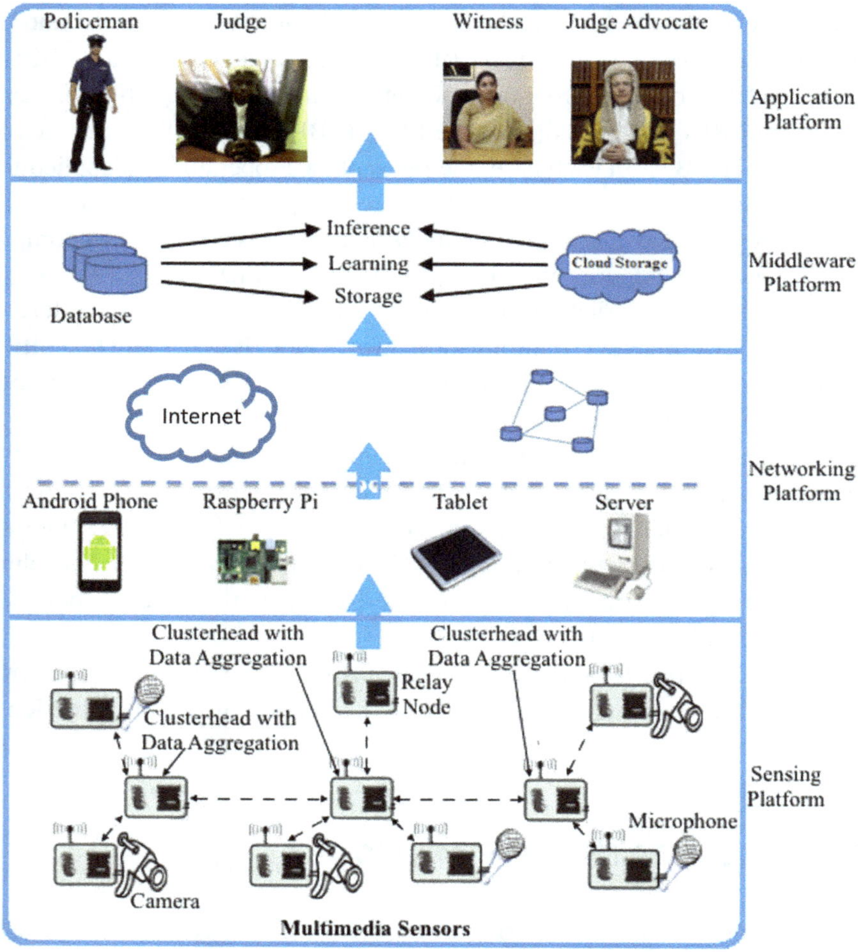

- **Sensor Layer:** Defines the interaction with the physical by embedding multimedia devices including cameras into the environment being studied (magistrate court, police interrogation rooms, *etc*.) to record images that will be analyzed using micro-expression detection.
- **Communication Layer:** Defines the communication model and protocols used to disseminate the images to places where virtual presence is required. Note that in contrast to traditional sensor networks, the VSN communication system underlying such image dissemination process may be a power hungry system that requires higher bandwidth capabilities in case the images are collected at the source and transmitted to the destination where VDM is performed. Note also that as implemented, our system makes opportunistic networking a viable option as data don't need to be communicated in real-time.
- **Middleware Layer:** Where the micro-expression detection process is performed. It is the layer that is closest to the service/application layer and includes storage, data mining and adaptation processes which are translated into services to the users. Note also that this layer serves to hide the complexity of the lower layers to the end users through user-friendly interfaces and translation mechanisms such as text-to-speech recognition for illiterate users.
- **Application Layer:** The layer where different services are provided to different users through different applications. In our case, they include virtual presence/participation services provided to different crime prevention bodies including the police, witnesses, judges and other lawyers who are involved in a court case but are unable to physically participate in the hearings.

While all the four layers of the VDM framework are equally important, the focus of this chapter lies in the middleware layer where micro-expression detection is performed according to the procedure in Figure 2.

Figure 2 depicts the proposed processing work flow that is carried out on every frame. The novel work flow results in very effective segmentation of the facial region and elimination of unrequired regions of the face such as the ears, hair and neck. The work flow can be divided into four procedures: face segmentation; normalization; feature extraction; and classification. The following subsections describe each of these procedures in greater detail.

A brief overview of the proposed workflow is provided. Referring to the box labelled "Frame" in the top-left of Figure 2. Proposed processing work flow and working down through the work-flow, the system continuously reads in frames from the camera. Face detection is carried out to find the face which is the region of interest. If a face is not found, processing moves on to read in the next available frame, that is, the frame is skipped. If the face is found, eye-pair detection is carried out on the facial region. Once again, if the eye-pair is not found, processing moves

Figure 2. Proposed processing work flow

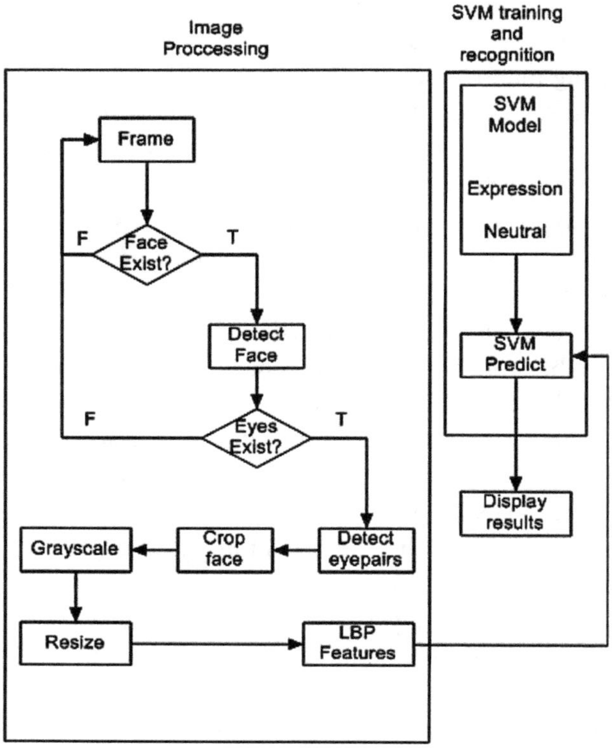

on to the next available frame. Once the eyes are located, the face is cropped using the width of the eye-pair, grayscaled and resized to achieve a normalized image. LBPs are computed on the resulting image to generate a feature vector which is then used as input to SVMs for classification into one of the two categories "micro-expression" or neutral expression". The subsections below describe each of the steps in greater detail.

Face Segmentation

The Viola-Jones face detection classifier (Jones & Viola, 2003) is applied to the frame to detect and locate the face, as illustrated in Figure 3. If the face cannot be found, such as in cases where the face is partially or completely occluded or facing completely away from the camera, all subsequent steps are skipped and processing moves on to the next frame in the sequence.

Figure 3. Face detection (left) and eye-pair detection (right)

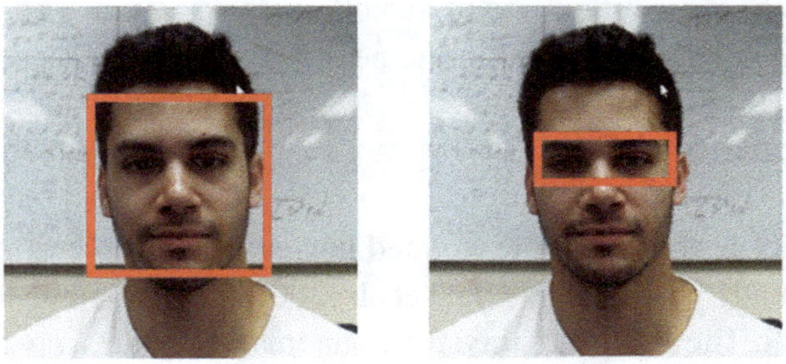

An eye-detection Haar Classifier is simultaneously applied to the frame to detect the eye pair, as illustrated in Figure 3. Similar to the face detection component, if the eyes cannot be detected, all subsequent steps are skipped and processing moves on to the next frame in the sequence.

Once the face and eye pair are located, the height of the facial frame and the width of the approximate eye region are taken as the height and width, respectively, of the region of interest and the frame is cropped using these dimensions. This significantly reduces sources of noise in the original facial frame detected by the face detector. Unnecessary regions of the head, hair and ears are removed. The resulting isolated face can be seen in Figure 4.

Normalization

Normalization involves scaling the isolated face to a pre-determined size. This ensures that the feature vector used in classification is dimensionally consistent.

The normalization procedure used involves converting the isolated face to grayscale, and scaling it to a pre-determined optimum size. Mushfieldt et al. (2013) showed that using a resolution size of 40×60 pixels and subsequently optimizing

Figure 4. Isolated face (left), normalized face (centre) and resulting LBP image (right)

the number of regions into which the LBP image must be divided, yielded a high accuracy. As such, a resolution size of 40×60pixels was used. The optimization of the number of regions is explained in the next subsection.

Feature Extraction

The LBP operator is applied to the isolated normalized facial frame. The LBP operator was originally proposed by Ojala et al. (2000). It was shown to be a powerful texture descriptor. The algorithm transforms an image into an array of integer labels describing small-scale appearance features of the image. Figure 4demonstrates the result of applying the LBP operator to an isolated and normalized facial image. The operation of the algorithm is now clarified.

The operator is applied to every pixel in the isolated facial image. For each pixel I_c, the eight pixels I_p in the 3×3 neighbourhood around the pixel I_c are each thresholded with the value of I_c using a thresholding function *f*, provided in the equation below:

$$f\left(I_p, I_c\right) = \begin{cases} 1 \ if \ I_p \geq I_c \\ 0 \ if \ I_p < I_c \end{cases}$$

where $p = \{0,\ldots 7\}$ are the indices of the neighbouring pixels.

The LBP value LBP (I_c) for pixel I_c is then computed by concatenating the threshold values of the neighbouring pixels. By convention, the concatenation procedure starts at the pixel in the top-left corner of the 3×3 neighbourhood and proceeds in a clock-wise order, but the start position and ordering are irrelevant so long as it is carried out consistently. The resulting number is taken to be a binary number—a LBP for pixel I_c. This procedure is illustrated graphically in Figure 5.

Figure 5. Graphical illustration of the LBP operator

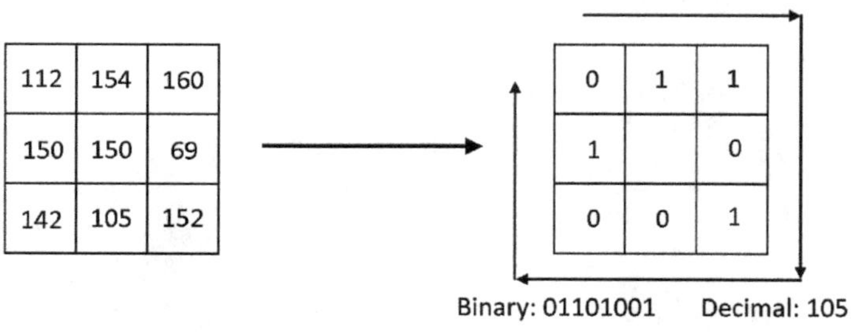

It is expressed mathematically as in the equation below:

$$LBP\left(I_c\right) = \sum_{p=0}^{7} f\left(I_p, I_c\right) 2^p$$

This procedure is repeated for every pixel with a 3×3 neighbourhood in the facial image. A histogram set is used to represent local and global LBP texture features. The LBP image is divided into regions of a pre-determined size. The size of these regions is henceforth referred to as the "region size". As mentioned in a previous section, determining an optimum region size is a process of trial-and-error.

The optimization of the region size went hand-in-hand with the optimization of the SVM. The Grid Search function in Lib SVM (Chang & Lin, 2011) was used to determine the values of the $\gamma$and C parameters of the Radial-Basis Function (RBF) kernel used with the SVM that yield the highest leave-one-out cross validation accuracy for several region size combinations.

The r-fold cross-validation procedure divides the training set into r sets, in which (r–1) images of each set are used to train the SVM and the remaining image in the set is used to test the accuracy of the resulting model. This procedure is repeated for all r set combinations and the cross-validation accuracy is computed as the average accuracy achieved across all r sets. This provides an accurate measure of the accuracy of the system. Table 1 summarizes the results of this optimization procedure for a number of different region size combinations (w×h).

The results indicate that the resolution size used is appropriate since it provides very high cross-validation accuracies for all the region sizes used. The highest accuracy obtained is 98.81%, which is obtained for a number of different region sizes. All factors equal, a region size of 10×20was used since this is the most proportional to the resolution size of 40×60 pixels used. The optimum value of the (C, γ) pair at this region size was determined to be (8.0, 0.0001221). These values are used to train the SVM in the subsequent classification step.

Table 1. Cross-validation accuracy (%) for region size (w×h)

		h		
		5	**10**	**20**
w	**5**	98.81	98.81	98.52
	10	98.81	98.81	98.81
	20	98.81	98.81	97.33

The LBP image is divided into regions of the size mentioned. A histogram of each region is computed. The histograms of all the regions are concatenated into a histogram set. This is used as the final feature vector for the subsequent classification step.

Classification

A SVM is used to classify the frame into one of two categories, better known as 'classes': "micro-expression" and "neutral expression".

Given a set of training examples, each marked as belonging to one of the two classes, an SVM training algorithm builds a model that assigns new examples into one of the categories. The model is a representation of the examples as points in space, mapped such that the examples of the classes are divided by a margin that achieves maximum separation between the two classes. New examples are then mapped into the same space and predicted as belonging to one of the two classes.

A manually collected data set was used to train the SVM. Videos of ten subjects were recorded. Each subject was asked to perform each of the six types of micro-expressions—sadness, anger, contempt/happiness, disgust, fear and surprise—once. For each expression, a single video was recorded. In each case, the subject started from a neutral facial expression, performed the facial expression and moved back to the neutral expression. This resulted in six videos per subject, and a total of 60 videos across all ten subjects. Five frames of each video were selected for use in training the system. The five frames were chosen from the peak of the expression in each video. This formed an initial training set of 50frames per expression—a total of 300 frames.

In order to ensure that the data was of a high quality, three independent assessors were asked to evaluate each of the training images, having first seen a benchmark of the expression in the image. Images of four of the subjects were marked as incorrectly performed. As such, all of the images of these subjects—120images— were removed from the data set. The final prototypical expression training data consisted of 30 frames per expression, and a total of 180 frames.

A number of neutral frames were inserted into the training data to represent the neutral expression class. It was decided to ensure that the ratio of neutral frames to frames representing micro-expressions in the data set was1:1. This prevents a bias towards either class in the eventual data model. As such, 30 frames of the neutral expression for each subject—a total of180 frames—were used in the data set.

In summary, the final training data set consisted of 30 frames of each prototypical micro-expression—a total of 180 frames—and 180 frames of the neutral expression.

EXPERIMENTAL SETUP AND RESULTS

This section describes the experiment that was carried out to collect testing data and assess the micro-expression detection accuracy of the proposed system. The section is divided into two subsections: experimental setup; and results and analysis.

Experimental Setup

It was mentioned in a previous section that a major challenge to automatic micro-expression detection is the lack of data sets to train, but more importantly, test on. Many systems (Shreve, Godavarthy, Goldgof, & Sarkar, 2011; Wu, Shen, & Fu, 2011; Polikovsky & Kameda, 2013) that attempt to automatically recognize micro-expressions have been criticized on the nature of the testing data used i.e. such data contains micro-expressions that are posed and significantly more intense than real micro-expressions. This is attributed to the unfortunate lack of micro-expression data sets produced in truly high-stake scenarios such as criminal investigations.

Recently, a data set of spontaneous micro-expressions has been made available, but was published subsequent to the conclusion of this research and the micro-expressions in the data set are performed while watching various emotionally-enticing videos, not in the context of deception in a high-stake scenario (Li, Pfister, Huang, Zhao, & Pietikainen, 2013).

A novel experiment involving a guessing game was used in this study to collect realistic spontaneous micro-expression data in the context of deception in this research as a next-best alternative. Attempts were also made to raise the stakes in the experiment as far as possible as will be explained. This is the first data set of its kind to our knowledge.

Eight subjects, not used in the training set, were used in this experiment. Figure 6 depicts the eight subjects used. Table 2 provides additional information about the subjects. It is important to note that the subjects represented a wide variety of skin colours, from very light-skinned to very dark-skinned. Each subject was asked to sit at a desk, facing and keeping eye contact with a camera. Each subject was given six cards. The subject was instructed to lift the cards one-by-one, acknowledge the card, and then decide whether to lie or tell the truth about the identity of the card to the investigator. They were informed that their main objective was to "try and fool the interrogator".

At this point, it is important to make a distinction between a lying and deception in the context of this experiment, keeping in mind that subjects were instructed to try to deceive the interrogator about the identity of all six cards.

Figure 6. Images of the eight test subjects

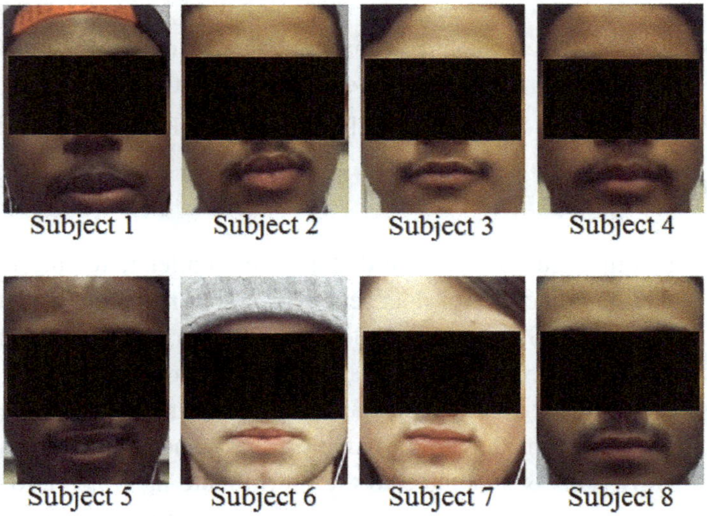

For each card, the subject was given the option to tell the truth about the identity of the card or lie about it. Regardless, the internal intent of the subject was to deceive the interrogator. For example, the card may have been a Jack of diamonds and the subject may have stated this, but with the intent of giving the interrogator the impression that he/she is lying. Although the statement was true, the intent was deceptive. Conversely, the card may have been a Jack of diamonds and the subject may have stated that it is an Ace of spades, with the intent of giving the interrogator the impression that he/she is telling the truth. Therefore, regardless of whether

Table 2. Test subjects used in the experimentation

Subject	Gender	Age
1	M	21
2	M	23
3	M	27
4	M	18
5	M	25
6	M	24
7	M	24
8	M	29

or not a lie was told about the identity of each card, deception was taking place. Based on the discussion in the Introduction section, this setup aimed to produce micro-expressions for every card.

In each case, the subject made a statement as to the identity of the card and the subject was given the impression that the interrogator would then try to determine if the subject had lied or told the truth. For each time that the interrogator was deceived, the subject was rewarded with a sum of money. The subject was also informed that if their deception was caught out at any time by the interrogator i.e. their deception failed, all their winnings would be forfeit and the game would be over. In reality, the interrogator had prior knowledge of all of the cards and appeared to be deceived in all cases in order to keep the experiment running, and none of the winnings were forfeit.

This polarised reward-punishment structure was put in place to attempt to raise the stake of the scenario as far as possible outside an actual disciplinary or criminal interrogation setting. As previously mentioned, deception in a high-stake situation increases the probability of performing micro-expressions.

A total of 8 videos were recorded, 1 video for each subject. Each video contained the interrogation across all six cards for a specific subject. For each video, the 30 frames that immediately followed the completion of a statement about the identity of each of the six cards were extracted. This is the time period in which it is most likely that one or more micro-expressions may be performed (Haggard &Isaacs, 1966; Li, Pfister, Huang, Zhao, & Pietikainen, 2013). This initially resulted in a total of 1440 frames—30 frames for each of the 6 cards by each of the 8 subjects.

Each of these frames were then used as input into the system, and the detection procedure described in the previous section was applied to these frames. This resulted in a system prediction of either "Micro-expression" or "Neutral" for each frame. A total of 68 frames were ignored by the system due to an inability of the face detection or eye-pair detection procedures to successfully locate the face or eyes. Therefore, results for a total of 1372 frames were obtained. Each of these frames was then manually inspected to determine whether or not the system response was correct.

RESULTS AND ANALYSIS

The following subsections provide a detailed analysis of the results.

Overall Accuracy and Comparison

Table 3 summarizes the number of correctly recognized frames for both expression classes. For ease of reference, the neutral facial expression and micro-expression classes are henceforth referred to as 'Neutral' and 'Mic. Exp.' respectively. Further-

Table 3. Overall recognition results: total number of frames in the data set for each class (Total Frames), number of correctly classified frames (Correct) and number of correctly classified frames as a percentage of the total (Correct %)

	Total Frames	Correct	Correct (%)
Mic. Exp.	365	326	89.3
Neutral	1007	832	82.6
Total	1372	1158	84.4

more, frames containing the neutral facial expression are henceforth referred to as 'neutral frames' and those containing micro-expressions, 'micro-expression frames'.

Referring to the table, the majority of the frames—1007 of the 1372 frames—were neutral frames. Nevertheless, a large number of micro-expression frames—365 frames—were obtained from the data. The results clearly demonstrate that the system correctly classifies micro-expression frames at a very high accuracy of 89.3%. Furthermore, it is also very important to note that the system classifies neutral frames with a similarly high accuracy of 82.6%. Overall, the system achieves a high accuracy of 84.4%.

This result was compared to the results obtained by relevant studies in the literature, namely Wu et al. (2011) and Polikovsky et al. (2013) discussed in a previous section. Shreve et al.'s (2011) experimentation and results were very limited and a comparison with their results is omitted. A summary of our results and their results is provided in Table 4.

Wu et al. obtained a very high and commendable accuracy of 95.83%. Polikovsky et al.'s accuracy of 86% was similarly very high and comparable to the accuracy of the proposed approach. However, it should be noted that both of these approaches were tested on data containing posed micro-expressions of much higher intensity than actual micro-expressions. A higher intensity greatly reduces the similarity of such expressions to the neutral expression and simplifies the detection task. It is

Table 4. Comparison of results of the proposed system with results obtained by Wu et al. (2011) and Polikovsky et al. (2013)

System	Correct	Correct (%)
Proposed	84.4	Spontaneous
Wu *et al.*	95.83	Posed
Polikovsky *et al.*	86	Posed
Human Expert	40	Spontaneous

expected that the use of true micro-expression data would result in accuracies that are reduced. In such a case, the proposed approach would most likely out-perform Polikovsky et al.'s system, and perform at a similar or better accuracy to Wu et al.'s system.

Currently, in spite of using data containing micro-expressions of very low intensity, the proposed system achieves an accuracy that is quite comparable to both related systems. Finally, the accuracy of the proposed system is at least twice that of human experts (Frank, Herbasz, Sinuk, Keller, & Nolan, 2009). This is a very encouraging result.

Precision and Recall

In order to analyse the precision and recall of the Mic. Exp. class, a confusion matrix of the two classes for predicted system response against the actual observation is provided in Table 5. Referring to the table, only 39 of the 365 micro-expression frames and 175 of the 1007 neutral frames were incorrectly classified.

Using the information in the confusion matrix, the precision and recall of the Mic. Exp. class were determined to be 0.65 and 0.89 respectively. This precision value implies that the false-alarm rate i.e. the number of cases that the system predicts as being micro-expression frames that are actually neutral frames, is relatively, but not very, low. This is attributed to the low intensity of micro-expressions and the difficulty in discerning them from the neutral expression. This causes some neutral frames to be incorrectly confused with micro-expression frames. The recall rate is very high and implies that the system is very comprehensive and correctly identifies almost all of the micro-expressions in the test data.

In practice, additional information would be required in order to trade off the precision and recall towards a specific target application. A higher recall ensures that very few deceitful cases go unnoticed, at the expense of marking a number of truthful cases as deceitful. A higher precision ensures that the system avoids marking cases as deceitful if they are not, at the expense of overlooking a number of actual deceitful cases.

Table 5. Confusion matrix of system response ('Predicted') against the actual observation ('Actual')

		Actual	
		Mic. Exp.	**Neutral**
Predicted	**Mic. Exp.**	326	175
	Neutral	39	832
Total		365	1007

In a high-stake criminal interrogation context, a higher recall may be more desirable. The slightest micro-expression can prove to be of great help to the interrogator and a higher recall ensures that very few are missed, at the expense of having to verify cases incorrectly marked as neutral. On the other hand, in a context in which the stakes are not high such as in a primary school disciplinary interrogation in which it may be beneficial and desirable to give children the benefit of the doubt, a higher precision may be more appropriate.

As it currently stands, the proposed system allows very few actual deceptive cases to go unnoticed, at the expense of marking a number of non-deceptive cases, albeit not very large, as being deceptive. It is configured to limit false negatives.

A more detailed analysis of the results is carried out to provide answers to three key questions involving the robustness of the proposed approach to variations in test subjects, which will guide the remainder of the discussion. It is undoubtedly better for the proposed approach to be robust to such variations. These are:

1. How is the number of ignored frames related to and distributed across test subjects?
2. How is the micro-expression and neutral recognition accuracy of the system related to and distributed across test subjects?
3. How is the number of actual micro-expressions related to and distributed across test subjects?

Relationship between Ignored Frames and Test Subjects

The first question that arises is: how is the number of ignored frames, henceforth referred to as "dropped frames", distributed across test subjects? This can reveal whether the dropping of frames is related to test subjects, or is a random occurrence.

Table 6 summarizes the number of frames dropped per subject across all cards and the percentage of dropped frames to the total number of frames per subject—180 frames to be exact. The largest number of dropped frames (24) is registered for Subject 2. It is important to observe that this is only 13% of the frames for this subject. More importantly, it should be noted that Subjects 2, 3 and 4 are of similar skin colour and relatively similar facial structure, but only 5 dropped frames are registered for Subject 3, and no dropped frames are registered for Subject 4. Therefore, the number of dropped frames cannot be attributed to skin colour or facial structure.

For the scope of this experiment, it can be said that the number of dropped frames is very small and approximately randomly distributed across the subjects, averaging at a mere 4%. As such, it can be said that the proposed system is robust to variations in skin colour and facial structure in terms of the number of frames dropped. A larger number of subjects and frames in a future experiment may shed more light on the issue.

Table 6. Number of dropped frames per test subject

Subject	Dropped Frames	Percentage Dropped (%)
1	8	4
2	24	13
3	5	2
4	0	0
5	12	6
6	11	6
7	8	4
8	0	0
Total	68	4

The dropping of frames can be attributed to two factors: slight random tilting of the head by test subjects in some instances, or sudden changes in lighting from the nearby window. The Viola-Jones frontal face detector and eye-pair detector are incapable of detection in faces that are rotated or tilted past a specific angle. The algorithm is known to be intolerant and highly sensitive to rotations or tilting of the head (Mushfieldt, Ghaziasgar, & Connan, 2013). Also, changes in lighting cause the camera to re-adjust and refocus, momentarily distorting the input image and preventing the face detector from locating the required features. Given the number of dropped frames is very small, these occurrences do not significantly affect the system performance.

Relationship between Detection Accuracy and Test Subjects

The second question that requires analysis is: how is the micro-expression and neutral recognition accuracy of the system distributed across test subjects? An investigation of the recognition accuracy distribution across test subjects provides an indication as to whether or not the system generalizes well to a variety of skin colours, facial structures *etc.*

In order to analyse the recognition accuracy, it should first be noted that a simple computation of the percentage recognition accuracy per test subject and comparison thereof is inappropriate with this data. The number of neutral and micro-expression frames varies sharply across test subjects. As an example, Subject 5 performed 105 micro-expressions, 97 of which were correctly recognized—a 92% accuracy—whereas Subject 6 only performed a total of 2 micro-expressions, 1 of which was correctly recognized—50% accuracy. It is observed that subjects with fewer micro-expression totals incorrectly appear to perform poorly.

Figure 7. The number of correctly and incorrectly recognized micro-expression frames per test subject

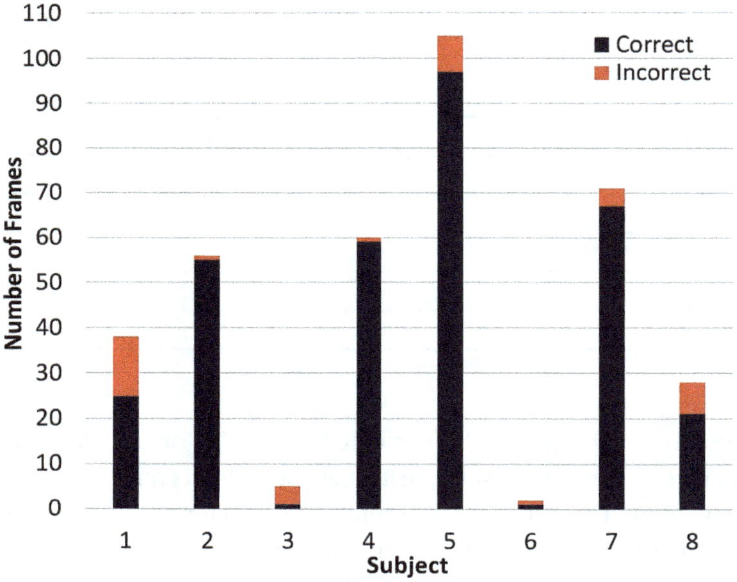

An unbiased discussion requires that the number of frames in each case be taken into account. As such, the discussion adheres to the quantity of frames, as opposed to the percentage of the total, in each case, as a true reflection of the results. Figure 7 depicts a stacked bar graph that summarizes the number of correctly and incorrectly recognized micro-expression frames for each subject, both as portions of the total number of micro-expression frames for that subject.

The graph clearly demonstrates that the number of correctly classified micro-expression frames is generally very high across all test subjects. Subjects 2 and 4 clearly perform better than all other Subjects, with 55 out of 56 and 59 out of 60 micro-expression frames correctly recognized, respectively. Subjects 1 and 5 perform at a lower accuracy than other subjects. However, it should be observed that only 13 and 8 frames, respectively, are misclassified for these subjects. This is a relatively small number of frames. The majority of micro-expression frames are correctly classified for both of these subjects.

Figure 8 is similar to Figure 7 The number of correctly and incorrectly recognized micro-expression frames per test subject for neutral frames per subject. It can be seen from the graph that the system correctly recognizes all of the neutral frames for three of the eight test subjects. The system recognizes the majority of the frames correctly for three additional subjects—2, 7 and 8. The system appears to struggle

Figure 8. Number of correctly and incorrectly recognized neutral frames per test subject

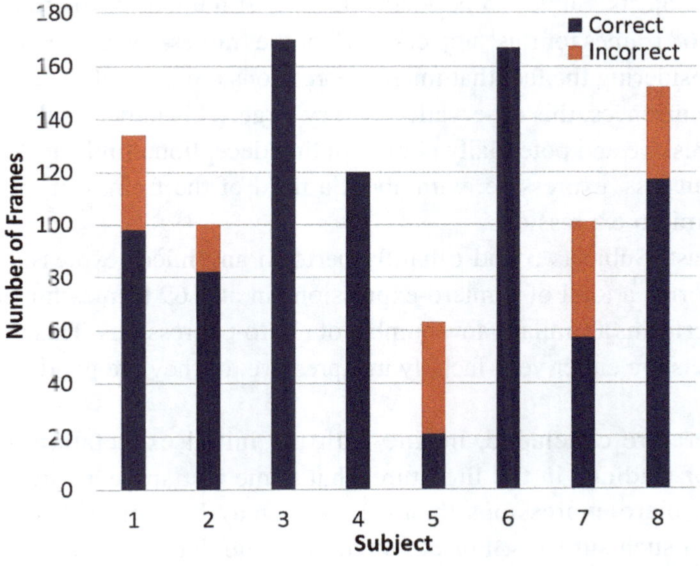

to recognize neutral frames for Subject 5, but is still able to correctly recognize 21 of the 63 neutral frames. Given this is not observed for any of the other subjects, it cannot be attributed to subject-dependence. It should further be noted that this subject achieves a very high micro-expression recognition accuracy. As such, it is concluded that the system is highly robust to variations in test subjects in terms of detection accuracy.

Relationship between Occurrence of Micro-Expressions and Test Subjects

The final question that is analysed in this discussion is: how is the number of actual micro-expressions observed distributed across test subjects. This investigation alludes to whether or not some test subjects are more likely to perform micro-expressions than others. This may well be the case since it is known that about half of all people do not perform micro-expressions in any situation (and the cause of this is unknown) (Ekman, 2009) and of those that do perform micro-expressions, some are better at concealing their deception than others, meaning that they are able to conceal their micro-expressions if they actively try to keep a straight face.

Analysing the number of micro-expressions observed per test subject, Figure 7 clearly demonstrates that there are sharp variations in the number of micro-expressions across test subjects. Subject 5 performs the largest number of micro-expressions. 105 of the 168 frames for this subject—62% of the frames—were micro-expression frames. Considering the fact that micro-expressions are generally regarded as momentary occurrences, this observation is very large. This indicates that the subject is very expressive and potentially poor at hiding deception. Subjects 2, 4 and 7 are similarly, but less, expressive, with about a third of the frames of these subjects containing micro-expressions.

In contrast, Subjects 3 and 6 hardly perform any micro-expressions. Subject 6 only performs a total of 2 micro-expressions in all 169 frames for that subject. Subject 3 performs a similarly low number of micro-expressions. This indicates that these subjects are either very facially inexpressive, or they are good at concealing deception.

It is therefore concluded, in line with the initial expectation and in confirmation of findings in the literature, that some test subjects are more likely to perform micro-expressions than others. It may be more difficult to detect deception in such subjects. For completeness, the data of Figure 7 and Figure 8 is provided in Table 7.

Table 7. Summary of recognition results: total number of frames in the data set (Total) and number of correctly classified frames (Correct) per subject for each class (Mic. Exp. and Neutral)

Subject	Mic. Exp.		Neutral	
	Total	Correct	Total	Correct
1	38	25	134	98
2	56	55	100	82
3	5	1	170	170
4	60	59	120	120
5	105	97	63	21
6	2	1	167	167
7	71	67	101	57
8	28	21	152	117
Total	365	326	1007	832

CONCLUSION

This research aimed to investigate the use of LBPs as an effective feature extraction technique in the context of micro-expression recognition. A novel experiment was used to obtain natural and spontaneous facial micro-expression data. The data was used to evaluate the recognition accuracy of the system.

It was demonstrated that the proposed strategy yields highly accurate results, with the ability to detect true micro-expressions which are of very low intensity and short duration. It performs comparable to or better than currently existing related systems which carry out a simpler detection task using posed micro-expressions of much higher intensity than true micro-expressions. It was further demonstrated that the system is highly robust to variations in skin colour and facial dimensions among test subjects. It was also shown, in confirmation of findings in the literature and expectation, that certain test subjects are more prone to performing micro-expressions than others.

Overall, the results presented in this chapter reveal the relevance of using LBPs for micro-expression recognition in VDM for criminal investigation. The work presented in this paper complements the work done by Isafiade and Bagula (2013) which similarly relies on machine learning techniques but relies on data for crime investigation. As part of a full criminal investigation tool to be developed by the authors in the context of an innovation project, the integration of QoS-aware routing models defined by Bagula (2006, 2007, 2010) and Bagula and Krzesinski (2001) in the communication layer of the VDM framework proposed in this paper is an avenue for future work.

ACKNOWLEDGMENT

The authors would like to thank Telkom SA Ltd., Cisco, THRIP and Aria Technologies for generous funding towards the Centre of Excellence at the Department of Computer Science at the University of the Western Cape and making this research possible.

REFERENCES

Bagula, A. (2006). Hybrid routing in next generation IP networks. *Elsevier Computer Communicationsg*, *29*(7), 879–892. doi:10.1016/j.comcom.2005.08.009

Bagula, A. (2007). On achieveing bandwidth-aware LSP/lambdaSP multiplexing/separation in multi-layer networks. *IEEE Selected Areas in Communications*, *25*(5), 987–1000. doi:10.1109/JSAC.2007.070611

Bagula, A. (2010). Modelling and implementation of QoS in wireless sensor networks: A multiconstrained traffic engineering model. *EURASIP Journal on Wireless Communications and Networking*, *2010*(1), 468737. doi:10.1155/2010/468737

Bagula, A., & Krzesinski, A. E. (2001). Traffic engineering label switched paths in IP networks using a pre-planned flow optimization model.*Proceedings of the IEEE Ninth International Symposium on Modeling, Analysis and Simulation of Computer and Telecommunication Systems*, (pp. 70-77). doi:10.1109/MASCOT.2001.948855

Chang, C.-C., & Lin, C.-J. (2011). LIBSVM: A library for support vector machines. *ACM Transactions on Intelligent Systems and Technology*, *2*(3), 27. doi:10.1145/1961189.1961199

Ekman, P. (2009). Lie catching and microexpressions. *The philosophy of deception*, 118-133.

Ekman, P., & Friesen, W. V. (1969). Nonverbal leakage and clues to deception. *Psychiatry*, *32*(1), 88–106. PMID:5779090

Ekman, P., & Friesen, W. V. (1977). *Facial action coding system*. Academic Press.

Endres, J., & Laidlaw, A. (2009). Micro-expression recognition training in medical students: A pilot study. *BMC Medical Education*, *9*(1), 47. doi:10.1186/1472-6920-9-47 PMID:19619307

Frank, M., Herbasz, M., Sinuk, K., Keller, A., & Nolan, C. (2009*). I see how you feel: Training laypeople and professionals to recognize fleeting emotions.* The Annual Meeting of the International Communication Association, New York, NY.

Haggard, E. A., & Isaacs, K. S. (1966). Micromomentary facial expressions as indicators of ego mechanisms in psychotherapy. In *Methods of research in psychotherapy* (pp. 154–165). Springer. doi:10.1007/978-1-4684-6045-2_14

Hjortsjö, C.-H. (1969). *Man's face and mimic language*. Studentlitteratur.

Isafiade, O., & Bagula, A. (2013). CitiSafe: Adaptive Spatial Pattern Knowledge Using Fp-Growth Algorithm for Crime Situation Recognition.*Proceedings of the IEEE International Conference on Ubiquitous Intelligence and Computing*, (pp. 551-556). doi:10.1109/UIC-ATC.2013.72

Jones, M., & Viola, P. (2003). Fast multi-view face detection. *Mitsubishi Electric Research Lab TR-20003-96, 3*, 14.

Kienzle, W., Bakir, G. H., Franz, M. O., & Schölkopf, B. (2004). Face Detection-Efficient and Rank Deficient. *NIPS, 17*, 673–680.

Li, X., Pfister, T., Huang, X., Zhao, G., & Pietikainen, M. (2013). A spontaneous micro-expression database: Inducement, collection and baseline. *Automatic Face and Gesture Recognition (FG), 2013 10th IEEE International Conference and Workshops on*, (pp. 1-6).

Moore, S., & Bowden, R. (2011). Local binary patterns for multi-view facial expression recognition. *Computer Vision and Image Understanding, 115*(4), 541–558. doi:10.1016/j.cviu.2010.12.001

Mushfieldt, D., Ghaziasgar, M., & Connan, J. (2013). Robust facial expression recognition in the presence of rotation and partial occlusion.*Proceedings of the South African Institute for Computer Scientists and Information Technologists Conference*, (pp. 186-193). doi:10.1145/2513456.2513493

Ojala, T., Pietikäinen, M., & Mäenpää, T. (2000). Gray scale and rotation invariant texture classification with local binary patterns. In *Computer Vision-ECCV 2000* (pp. 404–420). Springer. doi:10.1007/3-540-45054-8_27

Pfister, T., Li, X., Zhao, G., & Pietikainen, M. (2011). Recognising spontaneous facial micro-expressions. *Computer Vision (ICCV), 2011 IEEE International Conference on*, (pp. 1449-1456).

Polikovsky, S., Kameda, Y., & Ohta, Y. (2009, Dec). Facial micro-expressions recognition using high speed camera and 3D-gradient descriptor. *Crime Detection and Prevention (ICDP 2009), 3rd International Conference on*, (pp. 1-6).

Polikovsky, S., Kameda, Y., & Ohta, Y. (2013). Facial Micro-Expression Detection in Hi-Speed Video Based on Facial Action Coding System (FACS). *IEICE Transactions on Information and Systems, 96*(1), 81–92. doi:10.1587/transinf.E96.D.81

Read, P., & Meyer, M.-P. (2000). *Restoration of motion picture film*. Butterworth-Heinemann.

Russell, T. A., Chu, E., & Phillips, M. L. (2006). A pilot study to investigate the effectiveness of emotion recognition remediation in schizophrenia using the micro-expression training tool. *The British Journal of Clinical Psychology, 45*(4), 579–583. doi:10.1348/014466505X90866 PMID:17076965

Shreve, M., Godavarthy, S., Goldgof, D., & Sarkar, S. (2011). Macro-and micro-expression spotting in long videos using spatio-temporal strain. *Automatic Face & Gesture Recognition and Workshops (FG 2011), 2011 IEEE International Conference on*, (pp. 51-56).

Soro, S., & Heinzelman, W. (2009). A survey of visual sensor networks. *Advances in Multimedia*, *2009*, 640386. doi:10.1155/2009/640386

Tavli, B., Bicakci, K., Zilan, R., & Barcelo-Ordinas, J. M. (2011). A survey of visual sensor network platforms. *Springer Multimedia Tools and Applications*, *60*(3), 689–726. doi:10.1007/s11042-011-0840-z

Wang, S.-J., Yan, W.-J., Li, X., Zhao, G., & Fu, X. (2014). Micro-expression Recognition Using Dynamic Textures on Tensor Independent Color Space. *Pattern Recognition (ICPR), 2014 22nd International Conference on*, (pp. 4678-4683).

Warren, G., Schertler, E., & Bull, P. (2009). Detecting deception from emotional and unemotional cues. *Journal of Nonverbal Behavior*, *33*(1), 59–69. doi:10.1007/s10919-008-0057-7

Wu, Q., Shen, X., & Fu, X. (2011). The machine knows what you are hiding: an automatic micro-expression recognition system. In *Affective Computing and Intelligent Interaction* (pp. 152–162). Springer. doi:10.1007/978-3-642-24571-8_16

KEY TERMS AND DEFINITIONS

Automatic Lie Detection: The use of data mining techniques to determine if a subject is telling the truth.

Facial Action Coding System: A system that defines key muscles in the face that are the constituent units of, and are combined to form, all facial expressions.

Local Binary Pattern Operator: An algorithm to convert an image into an alternate representation of that image in which texture features are significantly more pronounced. The Local Binary Pattern representation can be used in a variety of visual recognition problems and has been shown to be effective due to its robustness to lighting and chrominance variations.

Macro-Expression: A clearly visible facial expression, generally categorized as being one of the facial expression types: "Anger", "Contempt", "Disgust", "Fear", "Happiness", "Sadness" or "Surprise".

Micro-Expression: An involuntary facial expression of very low intensity and lasting only a fraction of a second performed by a person when he/she attempts to conceal his/her deception. Micro-expressions are also categorized as being one of the seven facial expression types mentioned under the definition of "Macro-expression". Micro-expressions are more likely to occur in high-stake scenarios in which there may be grave consequences for the person if his/her deception is discovered.

Precision: The ratio of correctly identified frames to the sum of the total number of frames predicted to be positively identified. The precision provides an indication of how accurate the positive predictions of the system are.

Recall: The ratio of correctly identified frames to the sum of the frames correctly predicted to be positively identified and the frames incorrectly predicted to be negatively identified. The re provides an indication of how accurate the positive predictions of the system are.

Visual Data Mining: The combination of traditional mining methods and image processing and machine learning techniques towards extracting useful information from images or video streams.

Section 3
Forensics, Suspect Modeling, and Intelligence Gathering

Chapter 6
On the Use of Bayesian Network in Crime Suspect Modelling and Legal Decision Support

O. E. Isafiade
University of Cape Town, South Africa

A. B. Bagula
University of the Western Cape, South Africa

S. Berman
University of Cape Town, South Africa

DOI: 10.4018/978-1-5225-0463-4.ch006

ABSTRACT

Predictive policing (Pp) relates to identifying potentially related offences, similar criminal attributes and potential criminal activity, in order to take actionable measures in deterring crime. Similarly, Legal Decision Making Process (LDMP) considers some level of probabilistic reasoning in deriving logical evidence from crime incidents. Bayesian Networks (BN) have great potential in contributing to the area of Pp and LDMP. Being based on probabilistic reasoning, they can assess uncertainty in crime related attributes and derive useful evidence based on crime incident observations or evidential data. For example, in a particular context of crime investigation, BN based inference could help collect useful evidence about a crime scenario or incident. Such evidence promotes effective legal decision making process and can assist public safety and security agencies in allocating resources in an optimal fashion. This chapter reports on various application areas of BN in the crime domain, highlights the potential of BN and presents "thought experiments" on how offender characteristics could be modelled for decision support in legal matters. The chapter further reports on the performance of empirical analysis in the legal decision support process, in order to elucidate the practical relevance and challenges of using BN in the crime domain.

1. INTRODUCTION

The foundation and motivation for repeat victimisation study (RVS) relates to the fact that repeat crime is much more likely to happen in a short interval of time after the first incident, and often within a close proximity (Evett et al., 2006 & Riesen et al., 2009). RVS is also associated with the notion that crime is mostly initiated and perpetuated "where and when" there is a "conducive" environment for a potential offender and the presence of a suitable (vulnerable) target victim. This notion is corroborated by the long-established routine activity theory (RAT) in criminology depicted in Figure 1 (Clarke et al, 1993), which stipulates that a crime can only be committed when three specific criteria are involved. These criteria are that there must be a motivated offender, a suitable target or vulnerable victim (available at an appropriate location and time), as well as the absence of a capable guardian. RAT is a sub-field of crime opportunity theory that focuses on situations or circumstances of crimes. Jury members also consider such circumstances when probing crime scenarios, in order to justify the legal decision process.

Furthermore, judges or jury members often make legal decisions based on their instinct and/or experience (Milgram A., 2013). Such legal decision making process considers some level of probabilistic reasoning in deriving logical evidence, although

Figure 1. A model of routine activity theory

the mathematical rigour for such probabilistic evidence is sometimes ignored or ill-defined.

One aspect that stimulates interest is whether a crime *X* that previously occurred or repeatedly happens in location *K* is committed by the same individual suspect in that location, another location of close proximity or geographically close domestic dwellings, given observations of certain exculpatory or incriminating evidence or findings. For example, exculpatory or incriminating evidence could be footwear or footprint marks found at both points of entry of the crime scenes, particular items recovered from the points of entry at both crime scenes, type of victim information repeatedly reported and Modus Operandi (MO) involved. The degree of similarity between the evidence in two crimes can further motivate a number of research questions:

1. How does the evidence transfer between previous and current crimes?
2. To what extent can we attribute the crime observations or offender characteristics in the current crime to the previous one, for example in terms of MO reported?

Such probing or investigative research questions are also at the intersection of efforts in predictive policing.

Predictive policing deals with the usage of analytical and predictive techniques in law enforcement to identify and curb potential criminal activity. Existing software technology called PredPol is a good sample application in the area of predictive policing (Predpol, 2013). However, PredPol does not predict a potential offender, but helps in identifying and preventing potential crime incidents by predicting the next probable crime location. Predictive policing approaches are categorised into four distinct methods, these are:

- Methods for predicting perpetrators' identities,
- Methods for predicting offenders' characteristics,
- Methods for predicting crimes,
- Methods for predicting victims of crime.

It is widely recognised that Bayesian Networks (BNs), also known as Bayesian belief networks (BBNs), or Probabilistic Directed Acyclic Graphical Model (PDAGM), have great capacity for contributing to the area of predictive policing and crime suspect modelling (Zoete et al, 2014). Being based on probabilistic reasoning, they can derive useful probabilistic dependencies and inferences about the crime subject. Such probabilistic inference can ultimately assist public safety agencies in identifying mitigation priorities and allocating security resources in an optimal fashion, during investigative crime procedures. The terms Bayesian network (BN) and Bayesian belief network (BBN) shall be used interchangeably throughout the chapter.

A BN is a graphical mathematical model that encodes probabilistic relationships and conditional independence relationships between crime variables in the graph structures. A BN can be used to model suspect/offender behaviour as presented in Figure 2, a simple (4-nodal) BN, where a crime "suspect" variable encodes information about who the "offender" would most likely be, and the offender has a direct influence on both crime type and victim(s) involved. The offender encodes information about the crime committed and has a direct impact on the victim.

A Bayesian network is potentially useful in the following ways:

- Acquiring useful knowledge (probabilistic dependencies) from crime data.
- Assessing uncertainty in crime related attributes or characteristic features.
- Combining crime knowledge sources or observations.
- Deriving actionable crime evidence and mitigation priorities.

Figure 2. A simple (4-nodal) Bayesian network

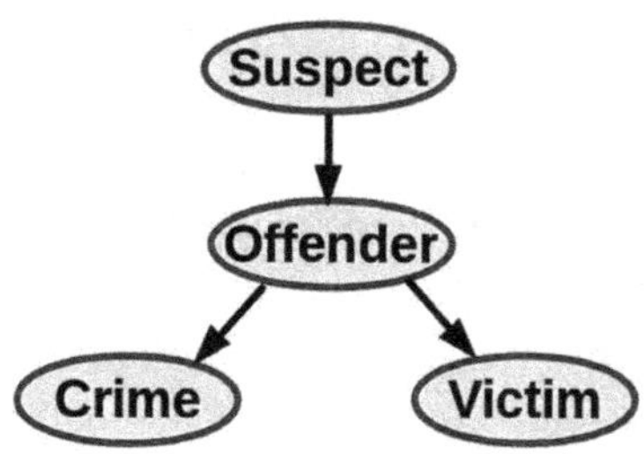

BNs are of practical significance in real life scenarios, especially where domain experts are not available or in limited supply for knowledge acquisition. Its usefulness is further evident in the fact that it is a compact representation of the joint probability distribution over the crime variables and encodes the conditional independence relationships between the variables in the graph structure (BN).

Current criminal justice systems and legal decision making processes are mostly dependent on a jury's intuition and experience. Judges have the best interest of the community at heart when they make legal decisions, but decisions made with instincts and/or experience have not significantly helped to promote the public safety of many nations (Milgram, 2013). However, a BN can assist a jury with reasoning under uncertainty (Sjoerd et al, 2014), in order to make a decision that makes the community and nation at large safer.

BNs have received widespread acceptance in academia and industry and proven useful as practical applications of artificial intelligence in solving real-life problems. For example, BNs have practically and successfully been adopted in speech recognition (Nefian et al., 2002), spam filtering/text mining (Raghuram et al., 2009), image classification systems (Jayech et al, 2010) and smart home activity prediction (Nazerfard, 2013), to mention a few.

Furthermore, BNs have over the years received much attention in the public safety and crime domain, and successfully been applied in the areas of offender behavioral modeling (Baumgartner et al., 2008), predicting victimisation (Riesen et al, 2009), crime linkage analysis (Zoete et al, 2014) and Forensic science (Sjoerd et al, 2014), among others. The BN approach to crime profiling typically draws on the fields of criminology, offender modeling and knowledge-based systems. The adoption of probabilistic networks make it practical to represent multidimensional relationships between all relevant crime or offender variables that may be identified at a crime scene. Hence, a valid BN model is a probabilistic directed acyclic graphical model (PDAGM) and can be used to predict unknown crime variables composing an offender profile based on observational variables from a crime scene.

1.2 Contributions and Outline

BNs have been employed for deriving crime knowledge from information in various capacities. This chapter explores various implementation of BN for crime knowledge discovery and delivery, and presents "thought" experiments that focus on understanding the underlying arguments regarding crime or offender modeling using BNs, as well as support in legal decision making process.

The organization of the chapter is as follows: Section 2 presents a brief review of background concepts on BN and further reports on current implementation or adoption of BN in the public safety and crime domain. Section 3 describes methods of exploring the application of BNs in modeling a simple offender scenario. In section 4, a more complex scenario is presented alongside the types of knowledge that can be derived from the BN. The performance of the empirical analysis in legal decision support is also reported. Section 5 summarizes and concludes the chapter.

2. BACKGROUND CONCEPTS AND RELATED STUDY

2.1 Theory and Notation of Bayesian Network Models

A Bayesian belief network (BBN) is a directed acyclic graph (DAG), that encodes probabilistic quantities to derive statistical inference based on probabilities (Jensen, 1996). Essentially, a BBN combines graph theory and probability theory to map variable interdependences in a stochastic system. Nodes in the network (graph) depict variables, while edges represent conditional dependencies between those variables (Vlek et al., 2013a). The DAG $\nabla=\{\chi,\gamma\}$ comprises a set of directed arcs γ that denote the dependencies among a set of nodes (variables) $\chi = \{X_{1,} \ldots, X_n\}$ such that:

$$\gamma = \{(X_i, X_j); X_j \in \chi \wedge X_i \neq X_j, j > i\}.$$

Given a set of discrete random variables $X_1 \ldots X_n$ in the Bayesian network, their joint probability density distribution is mathematically defined as follows, in Equation 1:

$$P(\chi) = p(X_1, \ldots, X_n) = \Pi P(X_i = x_i \,/\, Parents(X_i)) \tag{1}$$

where $Parents(X_i)$ represent the values of the parents of the node X_i with respect to the graph. Bayesian probability, from Bayesian statistics, is the underlying concept in Bayesian networks. Bayesian probability is based on the assumption that probabilities are dependent on prior events or incidents. It then follows that in a Bayesian crime network, the strengths of the conditional crime dependencies would be calculated with the help of the Bayes' Rule equation. The probabilities $P(X_i)$ are derived from Bayes' theorem (Equation 2) and correspond to degrees of belief of a crime observation. Bayes' rule allows the computation of the probability of a crime event, given prior knowledge of a variable that the event is conditionally dependent on. As new information regarding a crime is obtained, the probabilities of certain characteristics of the unidentified subject are updated with Bayes' Rule.

Bayes' theorem is mathematically stated in Equation 2 as follows:

$$P(X/Y) = \frac{P(Y/X)P(X)}{P(Y)} \tag{2}$$

where *X* and *Y* are "effect" and "cause" events respectively.

- $P(X)$ and $P(Y)$ are independent probabilities of *X* and *Y*.
- $P(X/Y)$ is the conditional probability of *X* given that *Y* is true.
- $P(Y/X)$ is the conditional probability of *Y* given that *X* is true.

BN application in a crime domain typically relies on four major steps, which are

1. Identify crime variables of interest, which become nodes in the network.
2. Specify prior probabilities over observable crime scenarios or incidents.
3. Compute posterior probabilities based on prior specifications, using Bayes' rule and all observed crime information.
4. Make predictions or inference according to the posterior quantities.

Figure 3 is a depiction of how crime evidence is influenced by hypothesis (i.e. extracting inference from crime observations or scenarios).

Given the following:

- Evidence/manifestations of crime: $E_1 \ldots E_p$,
- Hypotheses/observed crime features: $H_1 \ldots H_n$

Suppose we know the prior probability of the hypothesis $P(H_i)$ and the conditional probability $P(E_j/H_i)$ and want to compute the posterior probability $P(H_i/E_j)$, applying Bayes' theorem from Equation 2 results in Equation 3

Figure 3. Model setting of investigative Bayesian inference

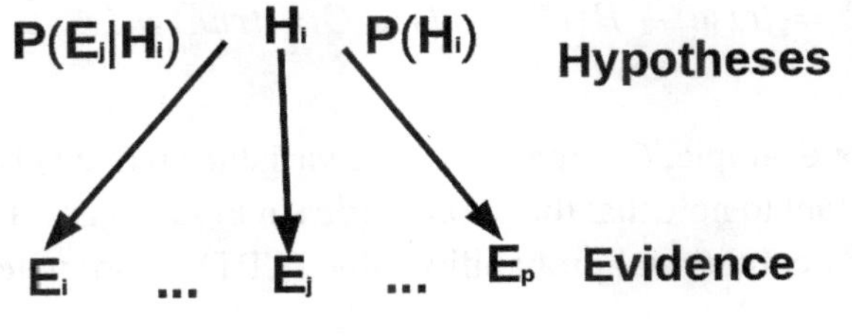

$$P\left(H_i / E_j\right) = \frac{P\left(E_j / H_i\right) P\left(H_i\right)}{P\left(E_j\right)} \tag{3}$$

For a simple Bayesian investigative reasoning, the goal is to determine the hypothesis H_i with the highest posterior, i.e. $\mathrm{Max}_i P(H_i/E_1 \ldots E_p)$. However, the simple Bayesian inference is limited in handling very large sets of crime information or data. In spite of their significant power and potential to address inferential procedures, there are some inherent limitations and liabilities to Bayesian networks (Fenton et al, 2014). It is computationally expensive, and sometimes specifying an appropriate or actual prior is not straightforward. Some researchers often just specify a convenient prior for computational purposes, not the actual prior. Further problem centers on the quality and extent of the prior beliefs used in Bayesian inference processing. A BBN is only as useful as the strength or reliability of such prior knowledge or belief. Either a pessimistic or an excessively optimistic expectation of the quality of these prior beliefs could distort the entire network and invalidate the results. Vlek et al. (Vlek et al, 2013c) noted that constructing a BN for complex scenarios is sometimes cumbersome and proposed a tool for exploring crime scenarios in a step-wise manner by building a BN in a step-by-step fashion. This notion exploits unfolding crime scenarios with variations. The idea only focuses on crime scenarios of interest at any given time of the investigative procedure and expands each scenario as crime event or evidence unfolds. Such an approach therefore results in a relatively more rigorous network of crime incident observations.

Using a Bayesian network to compute probabilities is called inference. Figure 4 presents a representation of Figure 2 with the conditional probability distribution for each variable of interest, where the names of the variables have been abbreviated to S = Suspect, Offender (O), Crime (C) and Victim (V). Each node X_i (in Figure 4) has a conditional probability table (CPT) representing its probability distribution $P(X_i/Parents(X_i))$, which quantifies the effect of the parents on the node or relationship between variables. The parameters are the probabilities in the CPTs. Therefore, for a given combination of values of the parents *O* in the analogy, the entries for $P(C{=}true/O)$ and $P(C{=}false/O)$ must add up to 1, satisfying one of the axioms of probability as shown in Equation 4 below (Vlek et al., 2013a).

$$P\left(C = true \,/\, O = false\right) + P\left(C = false \,/\, O = true\right) = 1 \tag{4}$$

In this case for example, *C* is the "evidence variable" while *O* is the query "variable". It is important to note that the probabilities in Figure 4 are chosen for illustrative purposes of a conditional probability table (CPT). Also, note that suspect in-

Figure 4. A Bayesian network with CPTS for Figure 2

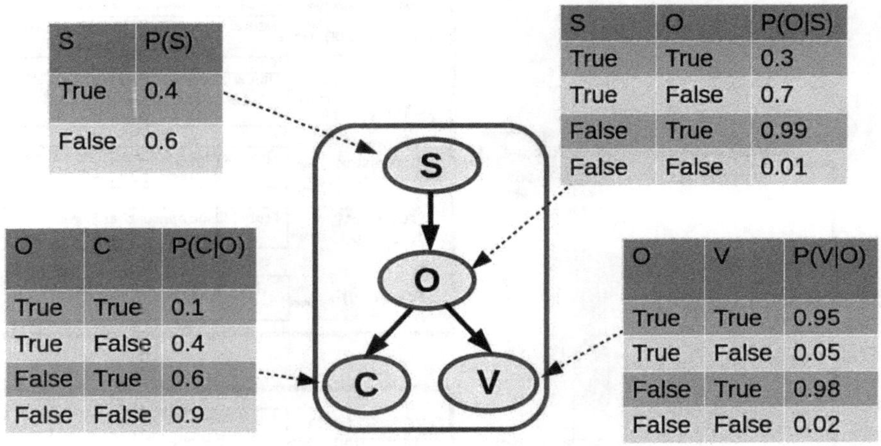

formation (depicted as "*S*" in the table) is the so-called "root node" with no parent(s), so there is only a single probability distribution for the node, *S*, while for nodes with parents there is a conditional distribution for each possible instantiation of its parents. Hence the varying CPTs in Figure 4.

2.2 Practical Applications of BN Model in Crime Domain

There is a wealth of research in the field of crime data mining and with a number of different techniques and approaches for achieving different tasks in this field. Figure 5 presents different techniques or approaches of data mining available for exploration.

The strength of Bayesian Belief Networks (BBNs) as a powerful predictive probabilistic model (PPM) in the crime domain is evident in its different areas of real world application (Vlek et al, 2013b), which includes criminal profiling, forensic science, prediction of victimization characteristics, crime linkage and crime series detection, to mention a few. Furthermore, there exists a number of software technologies available for building and/or modeling BN (Korb et al, 2011). These include Netica, software used to program BNs in Java (Woodberry et al, 2015), CaMML (Causal discovery via Minimum Message Length), a machine learning program used for learning causal BNs from data (Chris et al, 1999), HUGIN model-based decision support software, and BayesiaLab software, to mention a few. It is important to note that most of these are however commercial (not free) software. There are a few open source BN tools available, such as the BN implementation in

Figure 5. A taxonomy of crime data mining techniques

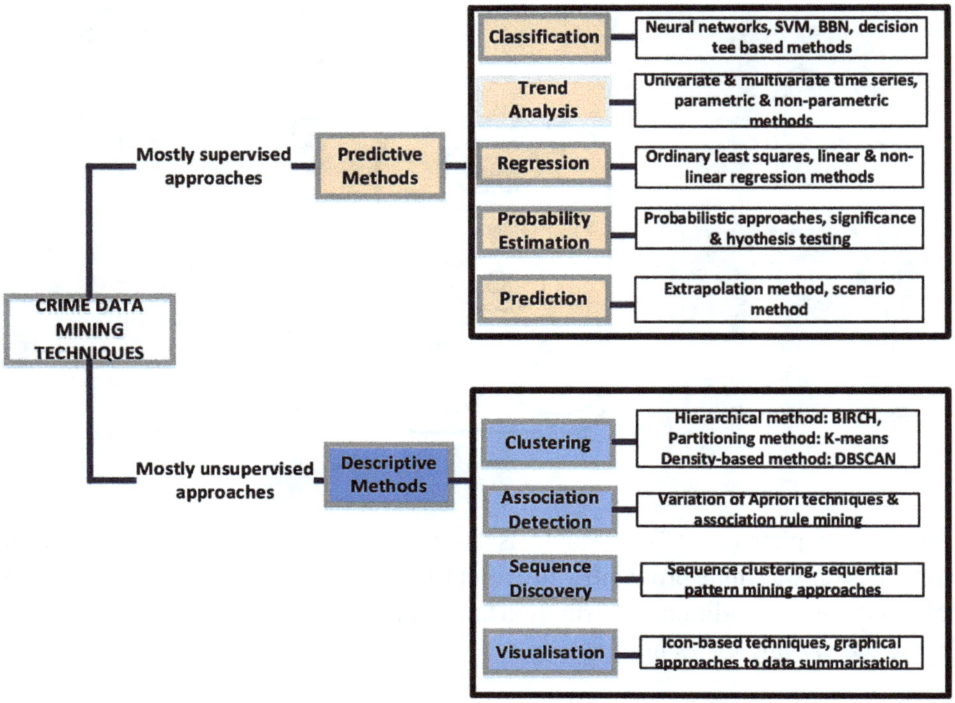

the Weka Machine Learning Workbench for data mining (Hall et al, 2009). We hereafter present a non-exhaustive summary of existing application areas of BN in the crime domain.

2.2.1 Criminal Profiling

BNs offer several advantages in criminal profiling and received significant attention in this area (Stahlschmidt et al, 2013). Criminal profiling deals with identifying the attributes or behavioural characteristics of an unknown offender, what motivates the crime committed and principal personality from a crime scene (Baumgartner et al, 2008). As such it is an important consideration in crime investigation since it provides useful gain in psychological and social profiling of the suspect. This generally promotes crime detection and criminal identification (CDCI), since identified characteristics of the offender can narrow the number of potential suspects and reduce investigative efforts by excluding those not showing the specific traits inferred. For example, if a crime investigator initially has three suspects on his list to investigate, and thereafter realises that only two of the suspects match all the crime observations he has gathered to date, he can easily focus more of his attention on those two whose characteristics correlate with his current observations.

Security agencies do background work by filtering or sniffing through a crime scene for observational evidence, because they have some degree of belief that careful observation and analysis of the crime scene can produce useful information that could help apprehend an unknown offender or understand "why" such crime occurred. Essentially, the three major approaches to modeling reasoning with evidence are argumentative, narrative and probabilistic approaches. The work of Vlek et al. (Vlek et al, 2014) reports that integrating these three approaches could arguably enhance the communication between an expert and a judge or jury. Their approach combined the three techniques (argumentative, narrative and probabilistic) in order to form a design method for constructing a Bayesian network based on narratives. Related research has however proposed techniques to represent narratives in a Bayesian network and to use narratives as a basis for systematizing the construction of a Bayesian network for a legal case (Sjoerd et al, 2015).

While Stahlschmidt et al (Stahlschmidt et al, 2013) report on using BN for criminal profiling and prediction in sex-related homicides, the work of Baumgartner et al. present a novel Bayesian network approach to criminal profiling (Baumgartner et al, 2008). Their approach learns a BN model from crime data, which is one of the options for constructing a BN, and then implements the model for profiling means. The variables used as nodes include "offender" and "evidence" variables. The offender variables are characteristics of the offender, which includes attributes such as military history and sex crime history. Evidence variables are characteristics of the crime scene, such as possibility of committing arson, stabbing the victim, and so on. The strengths of edges between nodes are calculated using a combination of a database of offender and crime data and expert knowledge from actual criminal profilers. The more data, the more iterations of Bayes' rule can be applied, and the more accurate the interdependences between offender variables and evidence variables. Once the preliminary conditional probabilities have been calculated, the network can be instantly used to narrow down criminal profiles in unsolved cases in an automated structure. Once evidence/crime scene data are supplied as input, characteristics/attributes that are closely correlated to the variables of interest are observed. Conditional probabilities are re-computed based on new crime data. Their research presents a significant use of BN and Bayes' rule in real world scenarios.

2.2.2 Prediction of Victimisation Characteristics

Riesen et al. (Riesen et al, 2009) developed a Bayesian network classifier for predicting a victimisation attribute value from a crime data set. They identified that a scoring function, suitable structure-learning algorithm and parameter learning algorithm are necessary in order to induce a Bayesian network from a dataset. The dataset they considered was the National Crime Victimisation Survey dataset with 216,000 and 250 data points and attributes respectively. Their model implemented the local hill-climbing and k2 algorithms in the parameter and structural learning phase using the Weka machine learning software workbench, while ensuring reasonable bounds for time-space complexity (Hall et al, 2009).

Related work of Axelrad et al (Axelrad et al, 2013) focuses on predicting insider threat using a BN model. Their paper which consists of five different phases reports on a Bayesian network model for the prediction of level of interest in a malicious insider. Authors investigate the motivation and psychology of the malicious insider by first developing an initial model based on results in the research literature, thereby highlighting essential variables for the prediction of level of interest in a potentially malicious insider. Second, a survey was conducted to measure these predictive variables in a regular sample of normal participants. Third, the original model was used to construct a structural equation model. The model was updated based on a split-half sample of the empirical survey data and validated against the remaining half of the dataset. Fourth, the Bayesian network was updated in view of the results of the empirical analysis. Lastly, the updated model was used to develop an upper limit on the quality of model predictions of its own simulated data. When empirical data regarding psychological predictors were input to the model, predictions of counterproductive behavior approached the upper bound of model predictiveness.

To validate the BN constructed, a hypothesized structural equation model (SEM) was developed, which incorporated as many of the variables from the Bayesian network as it was feasible to measure. Then the data was split in half, randomly assigning cases to a development sample and a holdout sample. SEM was then fit to the first data sample and model adjusted in light of the results so as to test it on the holdout sample. Data was then aggregated to fit a final structural model.

2.2.3 Crime Linkage

Crime linkage focuses on identifying possibly related crime incidents in relation to perpetrator attribute characteristics, different (incriminating) crime scene observations such as Modus Operandi, and victim information. When two distinct similarities are identified in two or more different crimes, it becomes of interest to know whether the crimes were committed by the same culprit or group of culprits. Bayesian networks can be used to model varying evidential structures in linking two or more crimes using different crime attributes as metrics.

Space and time metrics have been considered as parameters for estimating crime linkage. Tonkin et al (Tonkin et al., 2012) used crime location and time between two crime events as yardsticks for identifying linked and unlinked crime cases. They focused on how far apart (in time) were two crimes committed or length of space between two related crimes. They resolved that temporal and/or spatial proximity and/or crime incident locations can achieve statistically significant levels of discrimination between crimes that are linked and unlinked. A related attempt by Zoete et al (Zoete et al, 2014) also reports on modeling crime linkage using Bayesian networks. Their work is motivated by the lack of adequate mathematical treatment in defining the degree of crime similarity in practical casework. They investigated how evidential information derived in one case can influence the probability of hypotheses about who the offender is in another case. It was reported that the usual procedure in law enforcement where only cases with evidence pointing to a suspect are considered and other cases discarded, could be misleading because those discarded cases can generate evidence with important practical consequences if considered.

2.3 Limitations and Challenges of Bayesian Network

A BN has a significant computational cost (an NP hard task) because one needs to explore all parent crime nodes or variables, in order to explore an unknown crime network. Missing dependencies could affect crime results or evidence provided. It potentially requires initial knowledge or prior probabilities of certain crime variables, which may be extremely difficult to obtain and is sometimes falsified. Furthermore, it is sometimes insufficient to derive conclusions for a specific case from an initially developed network (Vlek et al, 2013c). Often there is a need to further explore sub-scenarios of crime in order to update the developed model or network and uncover new crime evidence, especially in a very complex BN model. Furthermore, since each crime is unique, there is a need to investigate how useful a scheme for a general situation is, when dealing with a peculiar crime situation.

3.0 BAYESIAN NETWORKS ADOPTION IN OFFENDER MODELLING

In this section we present a "thought experiment" on how a BN can be used to model a simple offender's behaviour and present a scenario of offender modelling in the subsequent section. We focus more on the logic of the argumentation which presents the essence of the problem and application of BN in reality. There exist various methods of obtaining Bayesian Network (e.g have an expert design it or learn it from data), but that is not the focus of this chapter. We refer the reader to comprehensive textbooks on Bayesian networks for more theoretical arguments or information on BN (Korb et al, 2011 & Woodberry et al, 2015).

3.1 A Simple Case of Offender Modelling

One of the major goals of offender modeling is to identify mitigation priorities in the crime investigation procedure. When related characteristics of an offender are identified it helps to narrow down an investigative procedure by eliminating suspects with characteristics unrelated to those in the identified profile list. Suppose two separate crimes have been committed, not necessarily by the same offender, and you are trying to determine whether an individual is a serial criminal who committed both (Evett at al, 2006 & Zoete, et al, 2013). You observe the following (how likely a suspect is a serial offender given certain conditions, for example prior offences, prior arrests):

- The suspect appears to have previously committed "crime "A".
- The suspect appears to have previously committed "crime "B".
- The suspect appears to have previously committed "crime "C".

Note that we are not 100% certain that the person is a serial offender because of these "observations". Thus, we are dealing with uncertainty at this stage. While there is no similarity evidence at this point of observation, one would assume that knowledge of the culprit or offender in case A would not necessarily affect the uncertainty related to case B or C.

Consider the simple Bayesian offender modeling (from Figure 2). Given a set of observations (evidence (E)), we have the following hypothesis for a single crime scenario:

H1: The suspect (S) is the offender (O).
H2: The suspect (S) is not the offender (O).

3.1.1 Properties of a Hypothesis

1. Must be mutually exclusive (non-overlapping).
2. Must consider all possible scenarios (i.e. exhaustive).

In a "two-crime scenario" (crime A and crime B), however, the following hypothesis is considered (Zoete et al, 2014).

H1: The suspect (S) is the offender (O) in both crime cases.
H2: An unknown person (U) is the offender (O) in both cases.
H3: An unknown person (U) is the offender in the first case and the suspect is the offender in the second case.

H4: The suspect is the offender in the first case and an unknown person (U) is the offender in the second case.

H5: An unknown person (U) is the offender (O) in the first case and another unknown person (U') is the offender (O) in the second case.

In any case, the goal is to find the hypothesis (H_i) with the highest posterior probability. The resulting output further strengthens, weakens or nullifies the *a priori* belief regarding the initial hypothesis considered. In light of the fact that BN is a PPM, it has the capability of approximating the posterior probability distribution of any attribute of interest in a crime domain (Riesen et al, 2009).

In general, each of the five hypotheses (crime propositions) has a unique probability. In theory the probabilities must sum up to one. However, one is much more interested in how the probabilities would change as they are updated with corresponding evidence. The question that follows then is "how does the *posterior* probability $P\left(H_1 / E, A\right) = k'$ change or evolve as it is updated with the computation from the prior probability $P(H_1/A)=k$, where H_1 is the hypothesis, A is the crime scenario considered and E is the evidence.

Going by Bayes' rule, we obtain the following equation:

$$P\left(H_1 / E, A\right) \propto p\left(E / H_{1,}A\right) P\left(H_1 / A\right).$$

The same expression could be derived for the remaining joint propositions or hypotheses. For example, if the *posterior* value $k' > k$, then it becomes clear that there is a higher chance that hypothesis H_1 is true, i.e. the suspect is most likely to be the offender in both cases. The *posterior* probability is being updated as new evidence is derived, computed and updated; eventually an effective decision would result.

It is important to note that more work needs to be done in terms of modeling complex scenarios of crime using BN. Such effort has been demonstrated in the work of Vlek et al (Vlek et al, 2013c), which deals with unfolding (sub) crime scenarios in an attempt to make a scenario more precise. This precision is achieved by modeling several connected sub-scenarios to enhance the network and derive more inclusive evidence. They implemented a three-stage approach idiom which exploits "scenario", "sub-scenario" and "merged-scenario" idioms, in order to further complement and strengthen the derived evidence. This is one of the ways by which inference could be extracted from observations in a BN, which greatly relies on prior belief and observations from a crime scene or about a specific crime. Depending on the level or strength of the incriminating evidence, the jury may then be able to reach one of the following decisions:

1. Charge the suspect with case 1; drop case 2.
2. Charge the suspect with case 2; drop case 1.
3. Charge the suspect with both cases.
4. Drop both cases.

3.2 Complexity of Inference in Bayesian Belief Networks

Inference in a BBN corresponds to calculating the conditional probability, $P[A/B=b]$, where $A, B \subset \left\{X_{1,} \ldots, X_{n}\right\}$ are sets of latent and observed crime variables, respectively. Cooper (Cooper, G. F., 1990) proved that exact inference in BBNs is NP-hard. In general, the size of the problem is given by the total size of the probability tables needed to represent the BN. Dagum and Luby (Dagum, P., Luby, M.,1993) further showed that even approximate inference is NP-hard (note: the mathematical detail of the proof is not explicitly highlighted in this chapter).

There exist three main inference tasks for BBNs. These include:

1. **Inferring Unobserved Variables:** Since BN is a PDAGM, it can be used to answer probabilistic queries about variables and their relationships. It therefore helps in deriving probabilistic inference, which is a process that derives updated knowledge of the state of a subset of crime variables when other variables (the *evidence* variables) are observed.
2. **Parameter Learning:** It is necessary to specify for each node *X* the probability distribution (CPT) for *X* conditional upon *X*'s parent, in order to fully specify the BBN and therefore completely represent the joint probability distribution of the random variable. The conditional distributions sometimes include unknown crime parameters which must be estimated from the available crime data, sometimes using the maximum likelihood approach.
3. **Structure Learning:** The structures of BBNs are either learned from data or specified by an expert in the corresponding domain and afterwards used to perform inference. In applications where the task of defining the network is too complex for humans, the network structure and the parameters of the local distributions are usually learned from data. An alternative method of structural learning uses optimization based search, which requires a scoring function and a search strategy. A typical scoring function is *a posterior* probability of the structure given the training crime data.

4.0 COMPLEX SCENARIOS OF BAYESIAN LEARNING AND OFFENDER MODELLING

In this section, we present relatively more complex scenarios of offender modeling using Bayesian networks and corresponding implications for deriving valid results.

More generally, BN probabilistic reasoning can result in a powerful combination of predictive, diagnostic and explanatory reasoning. Considering the fact that several levels of scenarios could be explored in the figurative explanation of a relatively complex BN (Figure 6), which may also have different levels of precision, it is worth noting that the validity of evidence that can be derived would to a large extent depend on the level of this exploration.

The general approach to a complex crime scenario or offender information, such as in Figure 6 usually considers evaluating different kinds of evidence. Such evidence includes information from crime attractors (e.g. vulnerable victims), eye witnesses, scientific processes and results and alibis, to mention a few. Most of the evidence is usually not quantified but could be used by the jury to follow a quantitative means of reaching a fair and effective decision, among several.

The BN in Figure 6 can be used to derive useful inference such as the following:

1. Can combine evidence from various crime attributes.
2. Can predict a crime suspect from the observational crime features.
3. Can explain the model's belief in a crime investigation scenario.
4. Can identify specific characteristics of suspects based on the nature of their crimes.
5. Can model information such as the crime spatial dispersion pattern and suspect apprehension.

Figure 6. A more complex Bayesian network of suspect modelling

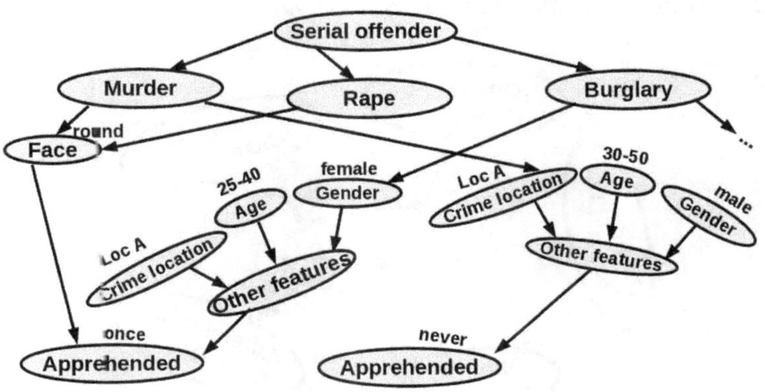

4.1 Generating Candidate and Extraction Rules

Candidate items in our "thought experiment" refer to attributes of crime incidents of interest, which a jury or crime analyst is very much interested in investigating or probing further. Consider five different crime scenarios or types as follows: Crime A, Crime B, Crime C, Crime D, Crime E, with Figure 7 depicting how each crime might be linked to a suspect.

Now, for each scenario, suppose we are interested in how many crimes relate to a particular suspect (e.g identifying a serial offender), assuming we already have prior knowledge of certain incriminating evidence or observations from each crime scene. In real life scenarios, one may observe that residential burglars tend to return to previously victimized locations, or to their close vicinities, after having acquired information on the schedules of inhabitants, the properties, and possible surveillance systems. For example, in Figure 6, a once apprehended offender may be suspected of another related crime in a location of close proximity to the previous crime.

However, depending on how much incriminating evidence is attributed to a suspect, the jury may then be able to make one or more of the following decisions:

- The suspect is not guilty of any of the crimes.
- The suspect is guilty of only one crime, say crime k, $k \in \{A, B, C, D, E\}$.
- The suspect is guilty of only two of the crimes, say crimes *A* and *B*, etc.

We could model possible scenarios of allegations that can be made to a suspect in a 5-crime scenario as presented in Table 1. Since there are five crimes, then there are $S=2^5$ possible states related to the suspect in question. Variables A, B, C, D, E depict the five different crime types thought to have been committed by the suspect, S_i, $i \in \{1,2,\ldots,32\}$.

Figure 7. BN model for crime suspect decision support in real life scenarios

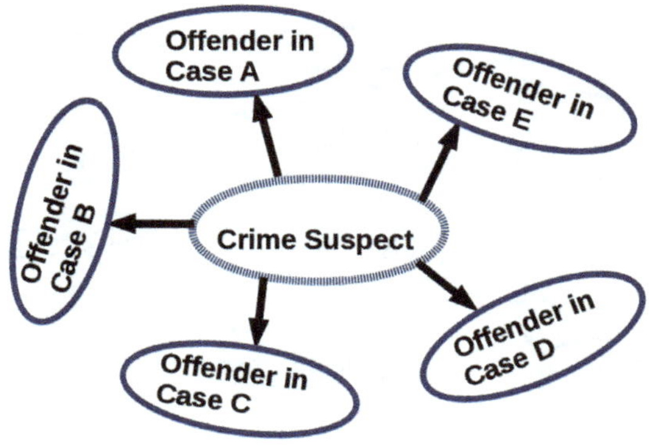

Table 1. Possible scenarios of suspect allegations in legal decision making

	A	B	C	D	E	GWM
S1	N	N	N	N	N	N/A
S2	N	N	N	N	G	1/5
S3	N	N	N	G	N	1/5
S4	N	N	N	G	G	2/5
S5	N	N	G	N	N	1/5
S6	N	N	G	N	G	2/5
S7	N	N	G	G	N	2/5
S8	N	N	G	G	G	3/5
S9	N	G	N	N	N	1/5
S10	N	G	N	N	G	2/5
S11	N	G	N	G	N	2/5
S12	N	G	N	G	G	3/5
S13	N	G	G	N	N	2/5
S14	N	G	G	N	G	3/5
S15	N	G	G	G	N	3/5
S16	N	G	G	G	G	4/5
S17	G	N	N	N	N	1/5
S18	G	N	N	N	G	2/5
S19	G	N	N	G	N	2/5
S20	G	N	N	G	G	3/5
S21	G	N	G	N	N	2/5
S22	G	N	G	N	G	3/5
S23	G	N	G	G	N	3/5
S24	G	N	G	G	G	4/5
S25	G	G	N	N	N	2/5
S26	G	G	N	N	G	3/5
S27	G	G	N	G	N	3/5
S28	G	G	N	G	G	4/5
S29	G	G	G	N	N	3/5
S30	G	G	G	N	G	4/5
S31	G	G	G	G	N	4/5
S32	G	G	G	G	G	5/5 = 1

Variables G and N in Table 1 represent *guilty:G* and *not guilty:N* respectively. Note that certain allegation scenarios states S_i, $i \in \{1,2,\ldots,32\}$ appear to share the same value in terms of general weight measure (GWM), where $0 < GWM \leq 1$. They may however not necessarily share the same aggregate weight measure (AWM). There are two "exceptional" cases S_1 having no weight since the suspect is not guilty of any of the (five) crimes and S_{32} where the suspect is guilty of all allegations. For example scenarios $S_2, S_3, S_5, S_9, S_{17}$ have a general weight measure (GWM) of 1 in 5 crimes. However, suppose the unique weight (w) for each crime is depicted as W_A, W_B, W_C, W_D, W_E respectively. Then each scenario S_i would have different weight values. A special case would then be if all the crimes have the same weight measure, in which there is a high probability that a suspect has committed a crime repeatedly five times. In summary, we have the following states or scenarios sharing the same GWM as presented in Figure 8 and Equations 5, 6, 7, and 8. However, note that every scenario has only one GWM.

$$1/5 = \{S_2, S_3, S_5, S_9, S_{17}\} \tag{5}$$

$$2/5 = \{S_4, S_6, S_7, S_{10}, S_{11}, S_{13}, S_{18}, S_{19}, S_{21}, S_{25}\} \tag{6}$$

$$3/5 = \{S_8, S_{12}, S_{14}, S_{15}, S_{20}, S_{22}, S_{26}, S_{27}, S_{29}\} \tag{7}$$

$$4/5 = \{S_{16}, S_{24}, S_{28}, S_{30}, S_{31}\} \tag{8}$$

Thus the Aggregate Weight Measure (AWM) for each state S_i is computed as the sum of the corresponding weights $c_W \in \{W_A, W_B, W_C, W_D, W_E\}$ for which the suspect is guilty (G), as depicted in Equation (9)

$$AWM_{\{S_i\}} = \sum_{G_i} \{C_W\} \tag{9}$$

The weight information could be regarded as indicating the gravity of the crime committed, which is further defined by the AWM for every suspect scenario S_i, especially for a serial offender. The suspect could then be charged for correspond-

Figure 8. Correlated GWM of possible scenarios of suspect allegation

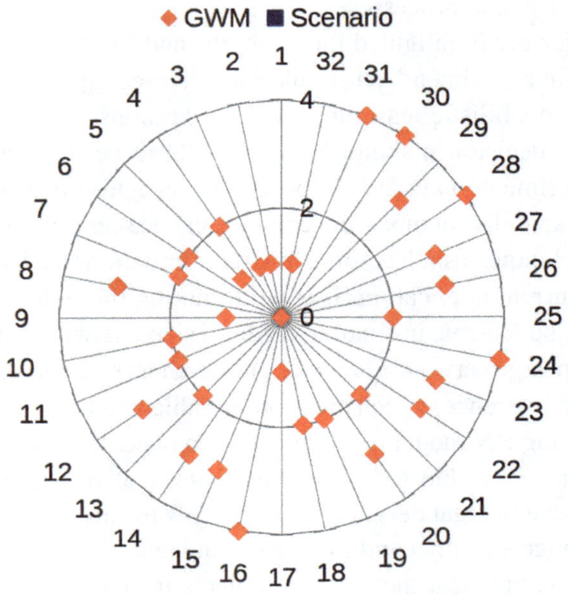

ingly identified scenario(s) accordingly. It is important to recognise that the reported idea does not eliminate or exclude the jury's intuition but serves to complement their overall decision.

5. SUMMARY AND CONCLUDING REMARKS

The public safety agencies collect a great deal of crime information which can be explored for evidence-based solutions in deterring crime. Also legal cases involve, to a great extent, reasoning with evidence. Thus, employing Bayesian networks (BNs) in the crime domain is a recognised application that can model different crime scenarios and assist in mitigation priorities or investigative procedures for solving crime, since it is based on probabilistic reasoning.

The strength of BNs as a Predictive Probabilistic Model (PPM) is evident in its wide acceptance and application in solving real world problems, both in academia and industry. A BN is particularly useful for classification and prediction tasks and has thus received significant attention in several domains, including the crime domain. This chapter has described various means by which BNs have been employed in the crime mining domain. The various applications areas discussed include crime suspect modeling, crime linkage, criminal profiling and repeat victimisation studies, which can assist in understanding criminal identification or apprehension, crime control and legal decision processes.

This chapter further highlighted the strengths and limitations of BNs and also reported a "thought experiment" on simple and "near-complex" offender modeling cases using BN probabilistic reasoning, with discussions of the logic of evidence interpretation and decision making. While BNs have been explored in different capacities in the crime domain, it is important to recognise that there is still room for exploring its capability in modeling complex crime scenarios and advancing the strength of the technique, as it has some inherent limitations such as computational difficulty in its current application. It is worth noting that inference from BNs is quite convenient and feasible in small to medium sized networks and could be very time consuming in large networks. However, researchers resort to various techniques for approximating inference, which are more reliable and faster.

Also the resulting BN model is not intended to make final decisions or conclusions about a crime case, but to assist in the investigative process and advise or assist a jury or judge in legal decision making. This means that we do not propose eliminating the judge's instinct and experience in legal decision making and crime control. We however present the fact that judge's instinct and experience can be complemented and strengthened using BN, as presented in current applications of BN in the crime domain. There is a great deal more to BNs when building an actual network of any complexity, which can be studied in depth in Bayesian Network focused textbooks. This work illustrates the future potential and opportunities of applying Bayesian Networks in this field and can be explored further in different forms in future practical research. This chapter however could further serve as a reference guide to understanding key issues and underlying framework of BN application in Crime Detection and Criminal Identification (CDCI) or crime mining field in general.

LIST OF NOTATIONS

BBN: Bayesian Belief Network
BN: Bayesian Network
CaMML: Causal discovery via MML
CPT: Conditional Probability Tables
CDCI: Crime Detection and Criminal Identification
DAG: Directed Acyclic Graph
DBN: Dynamic Bayesian Network
EDA: Exploratory Data Analysis
LDMP: Legal Decision Making Process

MO: Modus Operandi
PDAGM: Probabilistic Directed Acyclic Graphical Model
PPM: Predictive Probabilistic Model
RVS: Repeat Victimisation Study
SCDA: Spatial Crime Data Analysis

ACKNOWLEDGMENT

The authors gratefully appreciate the financial support from an AIMS-DAAD Fellowship, L'oréal-UNESCO Women in Science Fellowship and resources made available by the University of Cape Town and the University of the Western Cape.

REFERENCES

Axelrad, E. T., Sticha, P. J., Brdiczka, O., & Shen, J. (2013). A Bayesian Network Model for Predicting Insider Threats. In *Proceedings of Security and Privacy Workshops* (pp. 82–89). IEEE. doi:10.1109/SPW.2013.35

Baumgartner, K., Ferrari, S., & Palermo, G. (2008). Constructing Bayesian Networks for Criminal Profiling from Limited Data. Journal of Knowledge-Based Systems. doi:10.1016/j.knosys.2008.03.019

Baumgartner, K., Ferrari, S., & Salfati, C. (2005). Bayesian Network Modeling of Offender Behavior for Criminal Profiling. In *Proceedings of the 44th IEEE Conference on Decision and Control*. doi:10.1109/CDC.2005.1582571

Chris, S. W., & Kevin, B. K. (1999). Learning Linear Causal Models by MML Sampling. In *Causal Models and Intelligent Data Management* (pp. 81–11). Springer-Verlag.

Clarke, V. R., & Felson, M. M. (1993). Introduction: Criminology, Routine Activity, and Rational Choice. *Advances in Criminological Theory Routine Activity and Rational Choice*, *5*, 1–14.

Cooper, G. F. (1990). The computational complexity of probabilistic inference using Bayesian belief networks. *Artificial Intelligence*, *42*(2-3), 393–405. doi:10.1016/0004-3702(90)90060-D

Dagum, P., & Luby, M. (1993). Approximating probabilistic inference in Bayesian belief networks is NP-hard. *Artificial Intelligence*, *60*(1), 141–153. doi:10.1016/0004-3702(93)90036-B

Evett, L. W., Jackson, G., Lindley, D. V., & Meuwly, D. (2006). Logical Evaluation of Evidence When a Person is Suspected of Committing two Separate Offences. *Science & Justice*, *46*(1), 25–31. doi:10.1016/S1355-0306(06)71564-7 PMID:16878782

Fenton, N. E., Neil, M., & Hsu, A. (2014). Calculating and understanding the value of any type of match evidence when there are potential testing errors. *Artificial Intelligence and Law*, *22*(1), 1–28. doi:10.1007/s10506-013-9147-x

Hall, M., Frank, E., Holmes, G., Pfahringer, B., Reutemann, P., & Witten, I. H. (2009). "The WEKA data mining software: An update". In ACM Digital Library. *SIGKDD Explorations*, *11*(1), 10–18. doi:10.1145/1656274.1656278

Jayech, K., & Mahjoub, M. A. (2010). New approach using Bayesian Network to improve content based image classification systems. *International Journal of Computer Science Issues.*, *7*(6), 53–62.

Jensen, F. V. (1996). *Introduction to Bayesian Networks*. New York: Springer.

Korb, K. B., & Nicholson, A. E. (2011). Bayesian Artificial Intelligence. Chapman & Hall/CRC.

Milgram, A. (2013). Why smart statistics are the key to fighting crime. *TED Video*. Retrieved from https://www.ted.com/talks/anne_milgram_why_smart_statistics_are_the_key_to_fighting_crime

Nazerfard, E., & Cook, D. J. (2013). Using Bayesian Networks for Daily Activity Prediction. Association for the Advancement of Artificial Intelligence. Retrieved from www.aaai.org

Nefian, A. V., Liang, L., Pi, X., Liu, X., & Murphy, K. (2002). Dynamic Bayesian Networks for Audio-Visual Speech Recognition. *EURASIP Journal on Applied Signal Processing*, *11*, 1–15.

Papoulis, A. (1984). Bayes' Theorem in Statistics and "Bayes' Theorem in Statistics (Reexamined). In Probability, Random Variables, and Stochastic Processes (2nd ed.). New York: McGraw-Hill.

Predpol. (2013). *PredPol Predicts Gun Violence*. Retrieved from http://cortecs.org/wp-content/uploads/2014/10/predpol_gun-violence.pdf

Raghuram, S., Xia, Y., Palakal, M., Jones, J., Pecenka, D., Tinsley, E., & Geesaman, J. et al. (2009). Bridging Text Mining and Bayesian Networks. In *Proceedings of the IEEE International Conference on Network-Based Information Systems*.

Riesen, M., & Serpen, G. (2009). A Bayesian Belief Network Classifier for Predicting Victimization in National Crime Victimization Survey. In *Proceedings of the IEEE International Conference on Artificial Intelligence*.

Sjoerd, T., Charles, M., Hendrik, P., Silja, R., & Bart, V. (2015) A Structure-guided Approach to Capturing Bayesian Reasoning about Legal Evidence in Argumentation. In *Proceedings of the ICAIL international conference.*ACM.

Sjoerd, T., Hendrik, P., Charles, M., Silja, R., & Bart, V. (2014) Extracting Legal Arguments from Forensic Bayesian Networks. In *Legal Knowledge and Information Systems.JURIX 2014: The Twenty-seventh Annual Conference.*

Stahlschmidt, S., Tausendteufel, H., & Härdle, W. K. (2013). Bayesian Networks for Sex-related homicides: Structure Learning and Prediction. *Journal of Applied Statistics*, *40*(6), 1155–1171. doi:10.1080/02664763.2013.780235

Tonkin, M., Woodhams, J., Bull, R., & Bond, J. W. (2012). Behavioural Case Linkage with Solved and Unsolved Crime Crimes. *Forensic Science International*, *222*(1-3), 146–153. doi:10.1016/j.forsciint.2012.05.017 PMID:22704669

Vlek, C., Prakken, H., Renooij, S., & Verheij, B. (2013a). Modeling Crime Scenarios in a Bayesian Network. *The 14th International Conference on Artificial Intelligence and Law (ICAIL 2013).Proceedings of the Conference*, (pp. 150-159). New York: ACM.

Vlek, C., Prakken, H., Renooij, S., & Verheij, B. (2013b). Representing and Evaluating Legal Narratives with Sub-scenarios in a Bayesian Network.*Workshop on Computational Models of Narrative*. OASICS Schloss Dagstuhl Publishing.

Vlek, C., Prakken, H., Renooij, S., & Verheij, B. (2014). Building Bayesian networks for legal evidence with narratives: a case study evaluation. Journal of Artificial Intelligence and Law, 22(4), 375-421. doi:10.1007/s10506-014-9161-7

Vlek, C. S., Prakken, H., Renooij, S., & Verheij, B. (2013c). Unfolding Crime Scenarios with Variations: A method for building a Bayesian network for legal narratives. In Legal Knowledge and Information Systems - JURIX.

Woodberry, O., & Mascaro, S. (2015). Programming Bayesian Network Solutions with Netica. Bayesian Intelligence. Retrieved from http://bayesian-intelligence.com/programming-bns/

Zoete, J. D., Sjerps, M., Lagnado, D., & Fenton, N. (2014). Modelling Crime Linkage with Bayesian networks. *Journal of Science and Justice, Elsevier, Ireland*, *7*(5), 1–9. PMID:25934374

KEY TERMS AND DEFINITIONS

Bayesian Network: A directed acyclic graph that encodes probabilistic reasoning of an event or a compact representation of probability distribution over a set of propositional random variables.

Crime Linkage: The process of verifying whether two or more crimes, say A and B, committed at possibly separate times and/or locations are linked by some related features.

Criminal Profiling: The process of identifying behavioural characteristics of a crime offender and motivations for committing the crime.

Crime Pattern: An observable recurring trend of crime attributes or characteristics.

Crime Tactical Analysis: A crime analysis that is carefully planned in order to combat a specific crime.

Dynamic Bayesian Networks (DBNs): These are Bayesian networks that include directed edges pointing in the direction of time.

Modus Operandi: This characterises the process or mode of operation of an offender or group of offenders.

Probabilistic Reasoning: The process of summarising uncertainty from various sources or using probability theory and information about interdependencies to derive statistical inference.

Serial Crime: A set of two or more related crimes identified to have been committed in a successive time interval and mostly within close proximity.

Serial Offender: An offender that has been identified to commit related crime offences in a successive time interval, mostly with the same Modus Operandi.

Victimization Prediction: The process of identifying principal attributes, characteristics or features that surrounds a crime victim and using such observation to identify potential victims.

Chapter 7
Forensic Investigation of Digital Crimes in Healthcare Applications

Nourhene Ellouze
University of Carthage, Tunisia

Slim Rekhis
University of Carthage, Tunisia

Noureddine Boudriga
University of Carthage, Tunisia

ABSTRACT

Healthcare applications are increasingly being used due to the safety and convenience brought to patients' life and healthcare professionals, respectively. Nevertheless, the use of weak authentication techniques and vulnerable communication protocols makes these applications threatened by specific classes of security attacks and e-crimes. The latter threaten the privacy, the safety and even the life of the persons using these applications, due to the fact that they handle sensitive information and implement complex and critical features. This chapter focuses on postmortem investigation of crimes on healthcare applications. After classifying crimes targeting healthcare applications, the requirements for the design of appropriate postmortem investigation system, are discussed. A literature review of proposals related to the investigation of crimes in healthcare applications together with a discussion of the advanced issues are also provided in this chapter.

DOI: 10.4018/978-1-5225-0463-4.ch007

INTRODUCTION

The advances in Information and Communications Technologies have led to the release of a wide set of healthcare applications, including, but are not limited to, remote monitoring of patients in hospitals, real time detection of emergency situations threatening chronically ill patients, and continuous monitoring of elderly people. Healthcare applications are increasingly being used owing to the great efficiency and quality of service they offer to elderly persons, patients, and healthcare professionals. They have contributed to the enhancement of patients' autonomy, and the improvement of clinical treatment and remote health surveillance through the development and implementation of several technologies and equipment like, Wireless Sensor Networks (WSN), Implantable Medical Devices (IMDs), and cloud services.

Healthcare applications exhibit significant security weaknesses including the use of weak authentication techniques and the lack of appropriate security mechanisms. These weaknesses make them unprotected and subject to several criminal attacks threatening the safety and the privacy of patients, especially as these applications handle sensitive medical data and provide life-sustaining functions. Among the most common crimes targeting healthcare applications, we cite the unauthorized access to the medical records. Such type of attacks may induce serious threats on the privacy of the victims through the disclosure of their medical records, or even may threaten their life through the malicious modification of their medical records to make further medical prescription by physicians erroneous. In this context, the design of a system for postmortem investigation of criminal incidents threatening healthcare systems is becoming a key requirement.

A set of challenging issues should be addressed during the design of a postmortem investigation system tailored to healthcare applications. The first challenge is related to the storage of the huge amount of evidential traces that can be provided by healthcare systems, as these traces require an unlimited storage space when collected over a long period of time. The second challenge is related to the integrity and the trustworthiness of the provided evidence, especially as healthcare systems are connected to open environments (e.g., internet) through vulnerable communications protocols. The third is related to the complexity of medical evidence collection and processing, especially as healthcare systems implement different technologies and equipment that may provide heterogeneous evidence. The fourth challenge is related to the need that an investigation on healthcare digital crimes collects and analyzes two types evidence collected from the IT system under investigation. The first type contains information related to authentication, access, sensitive events execution, while the second type contains the medical information related to the victim health status.

Several research works have focused on the identification of criminal attacks targeting healthcare applications, and the development of security techniques protecting them from security attacks. Other research works focused on the development of secure audit and accounting tailored to healthcare applications to prepare for a postmortem investigation. A set of postmortem investigation techniques were also proposed in the literature to address medical and physical crimes. An overview of these research works will be provided in this chapter.

The remaining part of this chapter is organized as follows. The next section provides an overview of e-health systems. In Section 2, we identify and classify crimes targeting healthcare systems. Section 3 discusses the main requirements for the design of postmortem investigation of e-crimes on healthcare applications. In Section 4, we review the literature related to the design of techniques and methodologies for the checking of audit logs and the analysis of incidents on Wireless Body Area networks. We also discuss in this section digital investigation scope and techniques considering attacks on Implantable Medical Devices. Section 5 reviews investigation techniques tailored to physical crimes. In Section 6, we discuss advanced issued related to the investigation of criminal attacks on healthcare applications.

SECTION 1: OVERVIEW OF E-HEALTH SYSTEMS

E-health systems refer to the systems providing healthcare services (e.g., diagnosis, treatment, monitoring) using Information and Communication Technologies (ICTs). These systems can largely serve patients safety by making healthcare services more efficient and improving the work of healthcare professionals (e.g., physicians and caregivers). There are several types of healthcare applications such as remote monitoring of patients, and real time detection of emergency situations which can improve the quality of life of elderly and chronically ill persons, as they reduce the amount of travelling (e.g., to book diagnosis appointments) and avoid hospitalization. In the remaining part of this section, an overview of healthcare applications will be provided.

Generic Architecture of E-Health Systems

Typically, e-health systems involve three principal stakeholders: a) the healthcare service providers, which are responsible of managing and providing healthcare services; b) the patient, who represents the person eligible for the provided healthcare services; and c) the healthcare professionals (e.g., physicians and caregivers) which use e-health systems to perform their healthcare functions, such as the remote diagnosis of patients.

Figure 1. Generic architecture of e-health systems

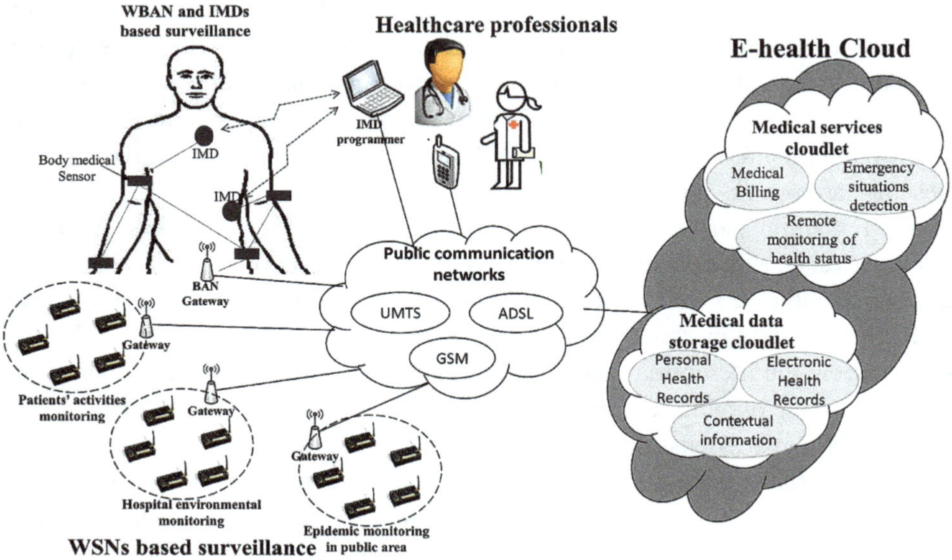

Several architectures of e-health systems were proposed in the literature. They vary according to the type of the designed healthcare applications, the provided services, and the implemented technologies. In the sequel, we provide a generic architecture of e-health systems that is able to implement the majority of applications and technologies. Figure 1 illustrates the generic architecture of an e-health system which mainly integrates the following described components.

- **Wireless Sensor Network (WSN):** Consists of a set of environmental sensor nodes including, but are not limited to video cameras, gas, pressure, temperature, humidity, and locations sensors. These nodes are typically deployed around the monitored person (e.g., home, hospital) to provide rich contextual information about him and identify the environmental conditions where he is located. Nodes of the same network communicate through a multi-hop wireless technology (e.g., ZigBee) to forward the sensed data to the sink node or the gateway.
- **Wireless Body Area Network (WBAN):** Represents a specific type of Wireless Sensor Network, which consists of a set of medical sensor nodes (e.g., physiological, cardiac, and glucose sensors) that are deployed on the body of a person to monitor its vital signs. These nodes can be interconnected through a wireless network by means of different technologies, such as IEEE 802.15.4. Body medical nodes belonging to the same WBAN cooperate to-

gether to forward the performed measurements to the BAN gateway, which will be in charge of transmitting these data through a public communication network to be stored in the corresponding medical data storage cloud/cloudlet.

- **Implantable Medical Device (IMD):** Is a medical device that is surgically implanted inside the body of a patient who suffers from chronic ailments, such as cardiac arrhythmia, diabetes, and Parkinson's disease. Such a device is in charge of measuring the vital signs of the patient (e.g., heart rate, glucose level, or blood pressure) and applying specific medical therapeutic functions when abnormal physiological conditions appear. Because they are surgically implanted, IMDs require a wireless connection to allow healthcare professionals to collect of data stored in them (e.g., the history of the patient's vital signs and the history of responses undertaken by the IMD), monitor in real time the patient's vital signs, adjust the therapy configuration, and update the device firmware. To this end, IMDs can be wirelessly configured using an external programmer through the 402-405 MHz Medical Implant Communication Service (Savci et al., 2005) band. Thanks to the integration of IEEE 802.15.4 and 6LoWPAN (Hui & Culler, 2008) technologies, future IMDs would also be wirelessly connected to the public communication network (Astorga et al., 2014) through a BAN gateway.
- **Gateway:** Ensures the adaptation layer between the Internet Protocol (IP) stack's link and Wireless Body Area and Sensor networks, so that IP packets could be sent and received over these networks. A gateway is in charge of forwarding the data received from WBANs or WSNs through the public communication network to the medical data storage cloudlet to be stored. It is also responsible of transmitting the data requests received from healthcare professionals to the corresponding entity (i.e., WSNs or WBAN).
- **Public Communication Networks:** They ensure the interconnection between the WSNs (as well as the WBAN) part of the e-health system, the healthcare professionals, and different used cloudlets. Several IP and packet switched and cellular networks can be used to offer a fixed or mobile broadband access. The selection of the communication technologies to be used depends on the specific requirements regarding the quality of service and security to be provided. In healthcare applications, where medical equipment need to transfer patients' medical using wireless communication, while reducing communication interference, prioritizing access to the wireless channel by remote medical equipment, protect medical services from unavailability and harmful interferences, cognitive radio networks can be provided as a solution for e-health applications in hospitals.

- **E-Health Cloud:** There are several types of clouds which are designed to provide a large scale of services and applications. Among the most common types of cloud services, we cite: Cloud Storage as a Service (StaaS) and Cloud Software as a Service (SaaS). StaaS ensures an infinite remote storage of data and allows users to access them any time from any place. It also allows cloud applications to share data between them and scale beyond their limited servers. SaaS makes available a set of applications running on a cloud infrastructure and accessible to the user through a thin client interface without requiring to manage or control the underlying cloud infrastructure (e.g., network, storage, and operating systems).

As depicted in Figure 1, two main types of interaction scenarios may be distinguished: regular and emergency. While communication in the first scenario is periodically performed by the e-health system, the second scenario is only used in emergency situations (when the healthcare professionals notice a deterioration of the health status of the patient, and need to get a real-time data information to identify the actual health status of the patient).

In the regular scenario, the WBAN and the deployed WSNs collect periodically a set of medical and contextual information. After that, the collected information is forwarded by the gateways of these networks to the medical data storage cloud/cloudlets through public communication networks. After being stored in the medical data storage cloud/cloudlet, these data will be accessible to the healthcare professionals. Generally, healthcare professionals use third-party applications to get access to/analyze the data related to the supervised patients.

In the emergency scenario, which is triggered by the detection of bad health parameters, the healthcare professionals need to collect instantaneous information about the patients' health status, and be able to remotely order immediate medication, intervention, or emergency ambulance transportation. All the emergency requests exchanged with the different healthcare professionals and the WSNs/WBANs should be timely transmitted via the communication system, while ensuring a high level of quality of service to control the end-to-end delay and network throughput. Therefore, at least two levels of quality need to be provisioned by the network depending in the interaction scenario: regular, or emergency.

Wireless Sensor Networks for Healthcare

Thanks to the continuous monitoring of the vital functions that can be offered by sensor nodes, WSNs for healthcare applications have the potential to offer a set of benefits to patients, healthcare professionals, and the society. First, they provide a continuous long-term monitoring of chronically ill patients, confirm the adherence of these patients to treatment guidelines, and monitor the effects of drug therapy. Second, they provide a real time feedback of the health status of patients. Third, they allow the early detection of life-threatening and emergency situations, so that a proactive reaction could be undertaken by the medical staff. Fourth, WSNs for healthcare applications allow the collection of context aware information (e.g., location, motions, and activities) which are useful to identify unusual patterns of the monitored persons. Fifth, they provide the early detection of serious external threats on patients' safety such as air pollution and presence of virus, as they are able to perform a continuous monitoring of a wide set of environmental and physiological parameters. Because of the benefits offered by WSNs for healthcare, a set of WSN based healthcare applications was proposed in the literature. Among these applications, we cite:

1. Tracking and monitoring of patients inside hospitals;
2. Monitoring the physiological parameters of chronically ill persons; and
3. Surveillance of the behavior and activities of children and elderly peoples.

A set of prototypes of WSN based healthcare systems was also designed to monitor the health status of patients and transmit his/her physiological data. Among them, we cite:

1. Medical Emergency Detection in Sensor Network (Ko et al., 2010) system. Such a system ensures the monitoring of the physiological parameters of patients inside hospitals;
2. Medical Ad hoc Sensor Network (Hu et al., 2008) system which is in charge of ensuring the real-time surveillance of patients who suffer from heart diseases; and
3. A body area network based system (Felisberto et al., 2015) for the recognition of human activities and the detection of harmful events.

Several issues should be addressed during the design of WSNs for healthcare applications. One of the principal issues is the preservation of power consumption, since sensor nodes use a battery with limited lifetime whose replacement is a burdensome task. To this end, it is required to extend the availability of sensor nodes by minimizing to the maximum possible the energy overhead induced by the implemented algorithms. Privacy and security are also among the critical issues that should be addressed. In fact, the unauthorized collection and use of the sensitive data collected by sensor nodes can cause life threatening risks to the proprietary patient.

Implantable Medical Devices for Healthcare

Implantable Medical Devices (IMDs) are increasingly being used by chronically ill patients, due to the benefits, the life-sustaining, and the therapeutic functions they offered. In fact, they have improved the quality of life of patients by making it possible the continuous control of their health status and the automatic delivery of therapy when abnormal physiological conditions appear. Pacemakers, for example, are implanted in the heart tissue of a patient to regulate its heart rhythm through the delivery of electric shocks.

A generic architecture of an IMD mainly integrates:

1. A set of sensing devices to measure the physiological parameters useful to identify the health status of the patient;
2. A processing unit to manage the functionalities of the device;
3. A stimulator to deliver the required therapy;
4. A memory to store the collected measurements and therapy settings;
5. A transceiver to enable the wireless communication with the programmer used by physicians; and
6. A battery which is in charge of powering the device components.

The principal issues of IMDs are the preservation of energy consumption and the guarantee of the privacy and the security of the patients carrying them. In fact, an IMD should remain operational as long as possible, despite the fact that it uses a limited battery whose replacement requires a surgical intervention. In addition, due to the use of wireless communication, IMDs are threatened by a set of security attacks, where most of them could be a serious source of death of patients carrying these devices. For instance, since an IMD automatically reacts to treat the detected cardiac anomalies, with respect to therapy settings which is generally adjusted by authorized physicians, a malicious modification of these settings may lead to a future inappropriate reaction, and thus harming the health status of the patient.

Cloud Based Services for Healthcare

Cloud computing can be considered as a promising paradigm for the enhancement of healthcare services. First, it allows coping with the limited storage of the traditional local healthcare servers, as it provides an infinite storage of medical data. Second, it ensures a continuous availability and sharing of e-health data that are managed by different healthcare providers. Third, it allows providing virtualized healthcare services (generally using a third-party application) independently of the geographic locations of the involved healthcare professionals. In fact, when medical data are stored in cloud, there is no need to perform clinical tasks in the same hospital where these data are generated. Fourth, it offers a set of benefits regarding data management like scalability, Quality of Service (QoS), cost effectiveness, and ease of access.

Cloud Storage as a Service (StaaS) is among the existing cloud computing types. It provides several services, including the storage of Electronic Health Records (EHRs) and Personal Health Records (PHRs) which represent the digital version of the health information of a patient, such as medical history, medication and allergies, and vital signs. The migration of the EHRs and PHRs to the cloud offers several advantages. First, it is possible to ensure an infinite storage of data. Second, thanks to the use of cloud storage, healthcare services will be able to interoperate between them to improve the quality of healthcare services through sharing information across healthcare organizations. In fact, the patients' EHR can be distributed at various locations due to the fact that a patient may be examined by many healthcare professionals of different specialties (e.g., primary care physicians, specialists, and therapists) and register with a set of different health insurance companies according to the insurances types. Third, the use of cloud storage relieves healthcare professionals and organizations from the infrastructure management tasks.

Typically, healthcare services generate and manage sensitive personal data (e.g., medical records) that have strict confidential, privacy and security concerns. In this context, the security of cloud based services for healthcare is a challenging issue that should be addressed during their development. For instance, a long term storage of healthcare data in a cloudlet belonging to a third party organization requires robust security solutions that ensure secure access controls, audit controls, authentication, and storage privacy, in order to avoid exposing theses data to unauthorized entities and security threats (e.g., disclosure, theft). Trustworthiness of cloud environment is another security issue which depends on the cloud deployment model (e.g., private, public). Private clouds seem to be trusted and more secure than public clouds, due to the fact that the security control of the physical infrastructure and the access to data is mitigated to the owner of the private cloud. Nevertheless, the owner of the private cloud needs to call for security expertise to handle the security of the cloud infrastructure, which is a heavy and expensive task. In the other side, the organization owning the public cloud infrastructure is responsible of enforcing a sufficient security policy that guarantees the protection of data in public clouds. The use of public cloud by a healthcare provider may therefore introduce additional security risks and threats, especially as security depends on the degree of trustworthiness to the provided security mechanisms in the public cloud.

Table 1. Classification of healthcare applications

Application Classes	References	Monitored Parameters	The Area of Surveillance	Quality of Service
Emergency detection and response	(Ko et al., 2010)	Physiological parameters	Hospital	Optimized rate control protocols
	(Felisberto et al., 2015)	Movement Parameters	Home	-
	(Almadani et al., 2015)	Health status parameters	Ambulance	Real time transmission
Disease and safety surveillance	(Chen et al., 2014)	ECG	Home	-
	(Al-Qurishi et al., 2015).	Multimedia and medical Information	Home	-
	(Aquino-Santos et al., 2013)	ECG	-	-
Medication and assistance in prescription solution	(Kaur & Chana, 2014)	Health data	Home	Resource elasticity mechanisms
	(Maia et al., 2014)	Vital signs of patients	Home	-

A wide set of healthcare applications was proposed in the literature. These applications can be classified with respect to the services they offer to the patients. In this context, we distinguish three classes. The first, denoted by "emergency detection and response", groups the healthcare applications that are in charge ensuring a real time surveillance of specific types of parameters (e.g., physiological, movement) allowing to proactively detect emergency situations, locate patients, and provide them with the necessary health support (e.g., alert generation toward doctors which can issue remote prescriptions, or order sending ambulance to the patient's location). The second class, "disease and safety surveillance", includes healthcare applications that are designed for the surveillance of patients and elderly persons who suffer from chronic illness and need a continuous monitoring of their health status, or need to be monitored during a recovery period after a surgery or an acute event. The third class, "medication and assistance in prescription solution", groups healthcare applications, which are in charge of managing and processing the stored electronic medical records to identify the patient's disease and assist physicians in remotely delivering the appropriate healthcare prescription.

Table 1 classifies a set of references related to healthcare applications, with respect to five criteria, namely the monitored parameters, the area of surveillance, and the provided quality of service.

SECTION 2: DIGITAL CRIMES TARGETING HEALTHCARE SYSTEMS

As emerging healthcare systems rely on mobile networks and internet to provide and improve healthcare services (e.g., remote monitoring of patients, storage and sharing of medical records), they become unprotected and vulnerable to a set of security threats due to the lack of appropriate security mechanisms. A Compromised security of such type of systems could disrupt the critical functions they perform and expose the patients to privacy and life threats. Recent research works have demonstrated that healthcare systems are targeted by several types of digital crimes that can be classified according to their goals and their impact on the patients. Four classes of crimes are described hereinafter.

Crimes Threatening the Privacy of Patients

As healthcare applications have significant security weaknesses, several attacks ranging from eavesdropping to location tracking could be executed to discover and disclose the personal information of the victim patient. Using the discovered information, a set of crimes targeting the patients' privacy may be performed. Below, we present some examples.

Eavesdropping attack can be performed by simply snooping on the radio communication and analyzing the intercepted traffic. If the latter contains sensitive information about persons, such an attack may threaten their privacy. For instance, we consider the case of WBAN based health monitoring application. When executing an eavesdropping attack on the traffic exchanged between wearable sensor nodes and the BAN gateway, an adversary would be able to discover a set of health information (in the form of values of some physiological parameters). This can be achieved through the analysis of the intercepted traffic, if the latter contain clear text data. However, when the exchanged traffic is secured using the same cryptographic keys for a long period of time, the adversary can execute some attacks in persistent mode (e.g., brute-force attacks) to discover the used encryption keys, and therefore he will be able to decrypt the intercepted traffic. One of the criminal consequences of eavesdropping attack is the disclosure of the discovered health information which may cause significant harms to the victim, especially if these data information show the presence of chronic illnesses or other types of serious diseases. For example, a person may fail physical exams for employment (e.g., a footballer) due to the diffusion of its health information showing the presence of chronic diseases. The disclosure of health information can also cause financial harms to the victim, if for instance, his/her personal health information, which exhibits a chronic illness (e.g., cardiac arrhythmia), is disclosed and forwarded to the insurance organization which provides to him the healthcare coverage. If such a situation happens, the health insurance premium cost will be increased.

Fingerprint and Timing-based Snooping attack (Srinivasan et al., 2008) is one of the side channel attacks that can also threaten the privacy of persons who use WSN based e-health system. Such an attack can be performed by simply eavesdropping and analyzing the wireless transmission of the traffic of the sensor nodes which are deployed in home to collect contextual information. Even if all wireless communication between sensor nodes and the gateway are fully encrypted, the execution of this attack remains possible. In fact, its execution requires only the identification of timestamp and the fingerprint (in the form of a set of features of a Radio Frequency waveform that are particular to unique transmitter) of each radio message. An adversary, who performs fingerprint and timing-based snooping attack, would be able to infer the private activities of a person (e.g., cooking, showering, or sleeping). Nevertheless, the tracking of the persons' private activities in his/her home constitutes a significant invasion of privacy, which can reveal many things about his/her life, and thus can prepare for several serious harms. For instance, an adversary can post the daily activities of the victim on a social site. This would make the victim in embarrassing position, especially if he is a famous person (e.g., actor or politician).

Crimes Targeting the System Availability

Crimes targeting the availability of healthcare systems are those that are intended to eliminate the system capacity of performing the expected functions, so that the threatened medical systems would not be able to react properly during emergency situations. These crimes can be typically achieved by disrupting the performance of the deployed network or by altering the functionality of the system components. Below, we detail some examples of crimes targeting the availability of e-health systems.

Jamming is defined as the continuous emission of high power interference to disrupt the wireless communication between two communicating entities. When executed, this attack may disrupt the availability of the system, affecting the instantaneous response of the system, which is needed to ensure the patients safety. Typically, when executed on e-health monitoring applications, jamming attack can target the traffic exchanged between sensor nodes belonging to the same network or between the wireless network (e.g., WSN or WBAN) and the gateway to prevent the collected data from being transmitted to the gateway, and thus from being forwarded to the analysis center. Nevertheless, if the jammed traffic contains information showing the detection of an emergency situation, the system could not trigger the appropriate reaction to such situation. By the way of example, we consider a Home Care Monitoring System (Magaña-Espinoza et al., 2014) which allows monitoring the heart rate of patients in their home and triggering alerts to physicians or family members when detecting emergency situations (i.e., rapid physiological changes due to falls or occurrence of some types of fatal arrhythmias like tachycardia). By executing jamming attack on the messages exchanged between the nodes monitoring the patient and the gateway, the sensed data could not be delivered to the gateway, so that it may become impossible to detect the occurrence of emergency situations, and thus it will be impossible to generate instantaneous alerts towards the involved physicians.

Sensor worm attack (Tan et al., 2011) can also be classified among the security attacks threatening the availability of WSNs for healthcare applications. Such an attack consists in discovering and exploiting software vulnerabilities of sensor nodes. It can be executed as follows. The adversary discovers exploitable software vulnerabilities (this may be achieved through the analysis of the libraries of the popular operating systems running on sensor nodes). Then, he exploits the vulnerabilities of the implemented software update mechanisms to inject a malicious program into the firmware of the sensor node. For example, when sensor nodes implement an over-the air-programming mechanism to update the healthcare applications, the adversary can exploit the self-programming routines in the bootloader to inject a malicious program into these sensor nodes. Typically, the injected malicious codes allow tampering the logic of sensor nodes and altering the expected sensing and processing functions they implement. For instance, when performing counterfeit software updates of medical sensors belonging to healthcare WBANs, these nodes would not able to accurately measure and collect physiological parameters.

Crimes Targeting the Life of Patients

As discussed in the previous section, Implantable medical devices are autonomous medical devices. They are wirelessly accessible through an external programmer. Nevertheless, because of the use of insecure and vulnerable communication protocols, IMDs are threatened by a set of security attacks, where most of them could be a serious source of crimes targeting the life of patients carrying them. In the sequel, we detail some of these security attacks.

Battery depletion attack can exhaust the battery of IMDs by flooding these devices with a large amount of bogus encrypted traffic. In fact, for security purposes, an IMD is required to verify the authenticity of every received message using cryptographic computations before proceeding with acceptance or rejection. By receiving a huge amount of encrypted messages, the IMD consumes a lot of energy, due to the intensive execution of the implemented cryptographic algorithms. Consequently, its battery may be depleted, as it has a limited lifespan. When the battery depletion attack targets some types of IMDs, such as defibrillators, the consequences of the battery depletion attack may be fatal. In fact, the defibrillators could not perform the implemented life-sustaining functions including the detection of arrhythmias and the delivery of therapies. In (Hei et al., 2010), it was shown that a depletion attack on an Implantable Cardiac Defibrillator (ICD) can be easily launched by an adversary who uses a radio software platform to conduct a reverse-engineering of the communication protocol used by the ICD and execute the attack.

Exposing some types of IMDs, such as pacemakers, to electromagnetic interference (EMI) can be also classified among fatal attacks threatening patients carrying these devices. The use of EMI within a frequency spectrum being detected by the sensing circuitry of the pacemaker, can affect the pacemaker functioning in different ways. When exposing the pacemaker to a magnetic field that is within the heart rate range, the pacemaker will stop the delivery of the stimulating pulses that regulate the heart's rhythm. Consequently, patients will be susceptible to lightheadedness, syncope, or even death according to the duration of the EMI and the cardiac rhythms. Otherwise, when the pacemaker is exposed to a strong magnetic field, it contiguously delivers stimulating pulses at a fixed rate (which can be rapid or low rate pacing) regardless the real heart's rhythm. This can threaten the safety of the patient, since a very rapid pacing can induce the occurrence of ventricular fibrillation, which is one of the fatal arrhythmia.

Another fatal security attack consists in using a relay node to repetitively replay old messages which are typically exchanged between an implanted device or sensor node, and a remote controller. The reception of old messages that contains old values of the sensed physiological parameters leads the remote controller to order the delivery of erroneous treatment (e.g., mistreatment or overtreatment) which can endanger the health status or even the life of the patient. For instance, insulin delivery systems are vulnerable to replay attack (Li et al., 2011), due to the weakness of protection against replay attack (every packet showing a counter different to the one received in the last packet is accepted). In fact, by replaying in an altering fashion two intercepted packets, an outdated glucose level can be reported to the insulin pump. Moreover, the replay of an old message to the insulin pump showing high blood glucose level will cause the delivery of an overdose of insulin.

Crimes Targeting Medical Records

Medical records of a patient may refer to Personal Health Information (PHI), Electronic Medical Record (EMR), or Electronic Health Record (EHR). Typically, these records include very sensitive data that should be properly protected against security and privacy threats, since their unauthorized alteration or disclosure can induce serious consequences to the victim ranging from financial to life threatening harms. Nevertheless, due to the complexity of the architecture of e-health systems managing these records and the lack of security solutions that ensure end to end protection of medical records (during transmission, storage, and access), medical records are threatened by a set of security attacks.

The use of unsecure end-user systems to access to medical records makes them vulnerable. End-user systems (e.g., personal computers or Smartphone) are generally used by an authorized patient or physician to retrieve or update medical records. However, access to medical records using end-user systems is sometimes performed using weakly protected operating systems, or even weak authentication techniques that are implemented by third party applications for securing access to medical records. As discussed in the work of Dmitrienko et al. (2013), an adversary may exploit the vulnerabilities of the software running on the end-user system to get unauthorized access to medical records, by inducing this victim user to install malicious software (e.g., malware) or faked third party applications. When the victim user uses a fake third party application to log, the credential he enters will be sent to the adversary.

Medical identity theft is one of the serious consequences of unauthorized access to medical records. It presents one of the vicious new kinds of crimes threatening medical records. Medical identity theft is defined as the fraudulent use of personal health information to obtain medical services or goods such as prescription drugs, medical treatment, or Medicare reimbursement. It often aims to alter or inject false medical records (e.g., false diagnosis, falsified medical history) to make healthcare professionals unable to provide the appropriate treatments. Medical identity theft can also lead to a fraudulent acquisition of medical services, inducing an important financial loss to the victim.

SECTION 3: REQUIREMENTS AND CHALLENGING ISSUES FOR A POSTMORTEM INVESTIGATION OF HEALTHCARE CRIMES

A postmortem digital investigation system of healthcare crimes should at least fulfill the following requirements.

Ubiquity and Diversity of Collected Evidence

To be investigable, a healthcare system should provide a variety of accurate ubiquitous evidence. In fact, due to the diversity of the implemented technologies and services in healthcare systems, a postmortem investigation of these systems should address the investigation of the entire system components including networks, databases, embedded sensor nodes, and medical devices. To this end, the following types of evidence should be at least available:

1. Evidential traces collected from sensor nodes. These traces could help identifying the source of the malicious nodes, and the malicious forged/exchanged information, which are used to prepare for the crime execution;
2. Evidence data provided by wireless access devices (e.g., gateways or access points). Typically, these data contain traces related to the sensitive activities (e.g., authentication, database update) performed by remote users. They can help identifying potential crimes on networked healthcare systems;
3. Digital traces collected from autonomous medical devices, capable of automatically ordering/delivering therapy (e.g., Implantable Medical Devices). This type of evidence would allow identifying inappropriate functionalities performed by these devices and representing the root of the incident damages;
4. Database evidence traces (e.g., EHR, contextual information, physiological parameters) which include the data collected by healthcare devices. They could allow identifying potential crimes targeting the life of patients, since they would be useful to determine how and when the health of the victim was deteriorated;
5. Digital evidential traces related to the third-party applications. The latter traces may be useful in some circumstances (e.g., when the involved third-party application is malicious or indirectly used to facilitate the execution of the crime), since they would allow identifying the potential attacks exploiting these applications and determining their objectives;
6. Evidential traces provided by physical authentications devices (e.g., smart cards). In fact, since these devices are used to authenticate users, they store various information including authentication keys, and some user-generated sensitive activities. Such type of information would be useful to determine the behavior of the user carrying the physical authentication device; and
7. Evidential traces provided by virtual infrastructures. Since in some cases, a virtual infrastructure (e.g., virtual cloud instance) can be the place where the incident happened or originated, it can provide useful information for forensic investigation.

Hypothetical Investigation Tolerant to Data Incompleteness

Typically, an investigated system cannot totally detect and record all executed events. To this end, evidential data provided to the investigator may be incomplete. In some circumstances, investigators may also be faced to new types of security attacks targeting the system under investigation. Moreover, the implemented library of attacks can also exhibit the absence of some security attacks targeting the investigated system. Nevertheless, to enable the reconstruction of potential crime scenarios, the postmortem investigation system should be tolerant to the incompleteness of the provided information related to evidential traces, investigator knowledge, and the library of attacks. To do this, such a system should allow hypothesizing missing events and generating hypothetical actions when needed.

Accuracy and Correctness of the Postmortem Investigation System

Because of the diversity of the collected evidence and the complexity of crime scenarios, the results of postmortem investigation may become prone to errors. To cope with this, postmortem investigation should be based on formal techniques and methodologies. The latter are time-saving and able to automatically infer provable potential crime scenarios starting from the collected evidence, and provide accurate and relevant results, even with a huge amount of evidential data.

Trustworthy and Evidentiary Aspect of Evidence

In order to enable an efficient postmortem investigation, the trustworthy and integrity of the provided evidential traces are stringent requirements. Moreover, once gathered, digital evidence should fulfill the same legal requirements. They should be:

1. **Complete:** Contain enough information allowing proving or disproving the occurrence of the crime;
2. **Reliable:** Have not been changed after their creation and they are collected using reliable techniques from a physically protected device that ensures at least tamper proof evidence;
3. **Believable:** Convincing to juries; and
4. **Admissible:** Collected using procedures that are conform to the common law and legislative rules.

To this end, it becomes crucial to protect the evidential traces against security attacks, especially from anti-forensic attacks which are intended to alter the generated evidence to hide information related to the executed attack, and mislead the investigator. The use of tamper-evident mechanisms in e-health system could be a promising solution. In fact, such a mechanism could allow tracking and recording all actions (e.g., removal, modification) that may be performed on the digital traces, so that the integrity of these traces can be checked before postmortem analysis. Moreover, it is also required to implement a security solution, which allows the protection of e-health systems against security attacks and the provision of a secure environment for the measurement, the collection, and the storage of the evidential traces.

Aggregation of the Pathologists and Healthcare Providers' Efforts, and Digital Forensic Investigators Efforts

As digital crimes on healthcare applications may affect the life of patients, a postmortem investigation of crimes on healthcare systems requires fitting together the efforts and the decisions of healthcare experts (e.g., physicians, pathologists) and digital forensic investigators. In fact, when a digital crime was conducted on a healthcare system and led to the deterioration of the health status of the victim, digital investigators can only demonstrate its occurrence and reconstruct plausible crime scenarios starting from the collected digital evidence. On the other side, healthcare experts can only prove that the inappropriate functioning of the healthcare system induced the deterioration of the patient health status. Nevertheless, none of them (i.e., healthcare experts and investigators) could prove or disprove whether the death is a consequence of a digital crime, unless the causality between them is identified. This can only be achieved by conducting a collaborative postmortem analysis between forensic investigators and healthcare experts. Nevertheless, to provide accurate results, forensic investigators and healthcare experts need to make accessible and share between them the collected evidential data and the obtained results. The development of forensic as a service cloud-based solution can be a promising for the collaborative postmortem investigation. In fact, such a service would allow benefiting from the expertise of investigators, as it makes collaborative investigation available anytime at any place. In addition, it can also help constructing a large library of investigated crimes scenarios, which can be useful to improve the efficiency and the productivity of the forensic experts. A postmortem investigation can also benefit from the storage as a service, as it allows coping with the storage limitation of the provided evidential data. In fact, such a service can provide an infinite storage space of evidential data. Moreover, it could also allow sharing evidential data across the involved investigators.

SECTION 4: AUDITING AND INVESTIGATING CRIMES ON E-HEALTH SYSTEMS

E-health systems provide convenience and efficiency to elderly and chronically ill persons through the healthcare services they implement. Nevertheless, as discussed in Section 2, healthcare systems are vulnerable to a set of digital crimes, which can threaten the privacy, the safety, and even the life of persons using these systems. To cope with this, it becomes crucial to develop forensic readiness e-health systems that enable the secure auditing and the postmortem investigation of crimes on these systems. In the context of digital crimes targeting healthcare systems, a pre-mortem investigation could not be applied because of the need of the presence of forensic pathologists to collect the medical evidence. The latter are essential for the reconstruction of medical scenarios.

The existing postmortem investigation approaches (Carrier & Spafford, 2006) tailored to general types of digital systems cannot be applied directly to investigate digital crimes on e-health systems, for the following reasons. First, contrary to the general types of digital systems, where a crime affects only the hardware of software assets, crimes on e-health systems affect these types of assets as well as the patient. The consequences of these crimes are more serious, as they affect the health status of the patient and may even cause its death. Second, when reconstructing the potential executed scenarios, the classical digital investigation techniques assume that the consequence of an action (malicious or legitimate) part of the scenario is deterministic. This is not the case for the investigation of several types of healthcare crimes. In fact, the consequences of an action may vary (i.e., is probabilistic) depending on the behavior, the health status, and the physiological state of the patient. Third, conducting an investigation of digital crimes on e-health systems requires the collaboration of forensic pathologists and digital investigation experts. The forensic pathologists will be in charge of examining the status of the victims and determining the cause of death and/or injuries, while the forensic digital investigation experts will be in charge of examining digital evidence and reconstructing the scenarios of attacks (e.g., illegal modification of sensors configuration), determining the source of the attack, and identifying the types of exploited vulnerabilities. Proving that an illegal modification of the e-health system is the root cause of an unsuitable medication that leads to the death cannot be done unless the conclusions derived by the two types of experts are correlated together. Fourth, a healthcare attack could take a long time to impact the patient. For example, an illegal modification of the electronic healthcare records a patient may lead to an unsuitable medical several months or years after. Reconstructing the whole scenarios and finding the traces related to the illegal modification, requires storing the evidential data for a very long time. Such a feature, introduces additional challenges related to the long-term secure storage of evidence.

Several research works were proposed in the literature to address the secure auditing and the postmortem investigation of digital crimes on e-health systems. In the sequel, we provide an overview the most important ones of these research works.

Auditing the Health Information Exchange

Health Information Exchanges (HIEs) systems refer to distributed systems ensuring the sharing of medical records between healthcare institutions. As discussed in Section 2, the inappropriate sharing of medical records, which are highly sensitive data, could threaten the privacy and the safety of patients. It is therefore essential to implement techniques and mechanisms, which allow providing secure accountability and auditing of the exchanges of these sensitive data, especially as evidential traces (i.e., audit data) could be useful to conduct postmortem investigation of crimes on e-health systems. These techniques will be in charge of monitoring the exchanges and the sharing of health information, and logging sensitive action executed on e-healthcare systems, including access, share, and transfer of healthcare records. To allow tracing the entire sharing path of a patient's health records, the logged data should contain a wide set of information, including, but are not limited to, the identities of the entities (e.g., the physician, the hospital) involved in the creation of the health record, the timestamp of these records, and the identities of the entities updating them.

To improve the accountability of actions executed in e-health systems and enable the identification of data breach, Mashima and Ahamad (2012) developed a patient-centric scheme allowing the establishment of robust information accountability in electronic health record (EHR) sharing systems. The proposed system introduces the use of a secure metadata, namely "accountability tag", which is attached to each copy of EHR record. An accountability tag implements a cryptographically-verifiable evidence of the involved entities (e.g., the repository that creates the copy of the healthcare record, the sharing source, and the sharing destination). Thanks to the use of accountability tags, the proposed scheme offers the benefit of patients' awareness to the access and the sharing of EHR in the e-healthcare system, so that a patient can determine whether sharing is appropriate and even identifies the involved entities when detecting a suspicious disclosure or sharing of its healthcare data. Accountability tags are managed by a trusted agent, namely "patient-centric monitoring agent". They are verified and logged each time the "Accountable Update" or the "Accountable Usage" protocol is executed, so that the monitoring agent will be able to reconstruct the sharing path and identify the involved entities. Accountable Update protocol is initiated when a health record is created or updated. In fact, when the record issuer creates or updates a health record, he attaches his digital signature, which is encrypted using the public key of the monitoring agent, to the created record. After that, he sends them to the repository which will be in charge of obtaining the proof of patient's authorization through the monitoring agent. After accepting the creation or the update of the record, the repository generates and sends verifiable receipts to the monitoring agent and the record issuer. The Accountable

Usage protocol is executed when the consumer receives the healthcare record. Since the consumer needs to decrypt the received signature, he sends a verification request to the monitoring agent. The latter logs this action, decrypts the signature, and creates a non transitive signature using Universal Designated Verifier Signature scheme (Steinfeld et al., 2003). Such a signature can be only verified by the specific consumer. After that, the monitoring agent sends back the generated signature along with a transaction proof to the consumer which verifies this signature using the issuer's public key.

For the sake of privacy preservation, Oh et al. (2014) proposed a Health Information Exchange (HIE) audit system which allows limiting the amount of accessible logs' information to only those that are required to provide evidence for audits process. This system implements together the use of Hierarchical Identity Based Encryption (HIBE) algorithm, which is an encryption algorithm ensuring the encryption of the data stored on audit logs, and a logic-based audit algorithm, which is able to handle the incompleteness of the available logs and generate formal explanations using only the available decrypted information. The proposed audit system uses two types of logs: internal Audit Trail and Node Authentication (ATNA) logs, which represent standard audit logs providing infrastructure for HIE audits, and external audit logs which include supplementary information (e.g., patient registration, medical billing) retrieved from healthcare organizations to enhance the results of HIE audits. The audit system mainly integrates four components: the audit data processor (ADP), the audit agent, the audit algorithm, and the auditor viewer. The ADP is in charge of encrypting external audit logs using HIBE algorithms, aggregating ATNA logs and external logs together, and making them available to the audit agent. When receiving a set of accesses of audit interest from the auditor through the auditor viewer, the audit agent transmits audit logs together with the policy and the requested access of interest to the audit algorithm, which will be in charge of verifying whether the requested access of interest complies with the policy. Since audit logs are encrypted, the audit algorithm may not be able to decide about compliance or violation. To this end, starting from the residual policy, the audit agent identifies the minimum data information required for audits, requests the corresponding decryption keys from the ADP, decrypts these data information, and then makes them available to the audit algorithm. Based on the available decrypted data, the audit algorithm generates the formal explanations for accesses and then sends them to the auditor viewer, which will be in charge of translating these explanations in human readable information. After that, it returns them to the viewer. When detecting incompliance, the auditor sends a notification to the involved healthcare organizations.

Forensics in Wireless Medical Body Area Networks

As detailed in Section 2, wireless medical Body Area Networks (BANs) are vulnerable to specific classes of security attacks that can be exploited to perform crimes threatening the privacy and the safety of patients who use them. In this context, it becomes crucial to address forensic investigation of security attacks on wireless medical BANs. Several research works investigated the possibility of using wireless medical BANs for healthcare applications. Nevertheless, to the best of our knowledge, there is no postmortem investigation system proposed in the literature, which is tailored to wireless Medical BANs. The work of Cusack and Kyaw (2012) discussed only the need of developing a forensically ready and secure wireless Medical BANs based systems, which allows investigating events after their occurrence. However, it is possible to customize the forensic systems, proposed in the literature to investigate security attacks on Mobile Ad hoc and Sensor Networks (MASNets), to the investigation of healthcare security attacks and crimes in wireless medical BANs, especially as wireless medical BANs are specific classes of MASNets.

Since Mobile Ad hoc Sensor Networks (MASNets) are typically characterized by the absence of infrastructures and the mobility of nodes, techniques and mechanisms developed for the investigation of attacks on wired networks cannot be efficient to investigate attacks on MANets. In fact, as attacks targeting such type of networks are generally mobile, traditional evidence collection techniques for wired networks could not allow tracing and tracking mobile attacks. To cope with this, a digital investigation in MASNets needs to implement new techniques allowing a distributed supervision of the network, so that it becomes possible to collect digital evidence from different locations in the network and the victim system. In this context, Rekhis and Boudriga (2011) developed a new architecture and evidence collection technique in MANets which ensures an efficient collection of mobility-based information. In addition to the user nodes (i.e., mobile devices of patients) which are randomly distributed over the network, the proposed technique integrates the use of a set of mobile trusted nodes, namely observers, which are responsible of supervising the mobile networks. As depicted in Figure 2, observer nodes, denoted by $\left\{O_i, i \in [1, n]\right\}$ where is the number of observers, are distributed over the network in a way that they form an observation network allowing the supervision of every pair of communicating user nodes, denoted by u_i. Each deployed observer is responsible of monitoring the traffic exchanged within its transmission range, storing the observable parts of the detected datagrams and actions as network evidential traces, and forwarding them to the node in charge of investigation (selected among the observer nodes).

Figure 2. Variation of the network topology during an attack scenario

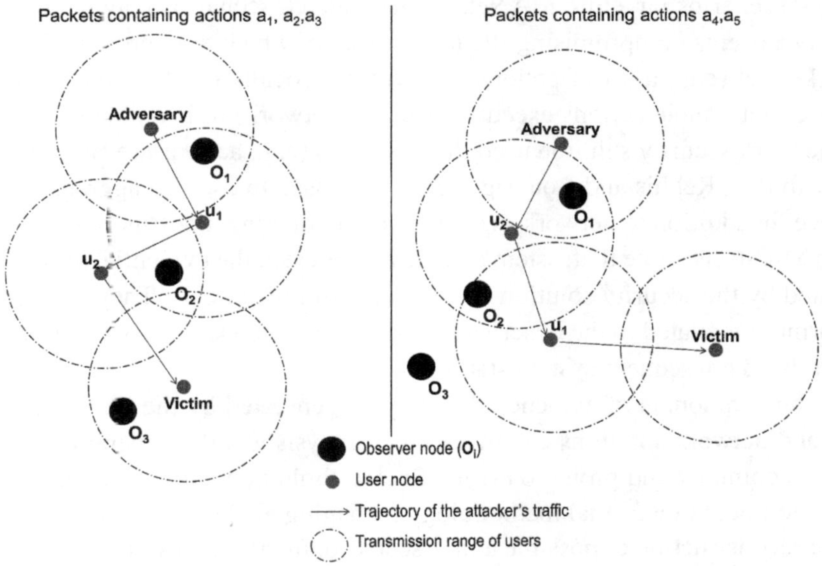

Because of the mobility of observer nodes and the scheduling algorithm they implement to minimize energy consumption, an observer node will not be able to detect all the datagrams sent by the attacker. In fact, the observer node may go out of the attacker transmission range or change its state to inactive, so that some of the attacker datagrams will be invisible. Nevertheless, datagrams, which are invisible to a given observer, can be visible to another, and thus observer nodes can generate redundant or/and complementary evidential traces which need to be merged and aggregated by the node in charge of investigation before reconstructing the occurred scenario. An example of nodes mobility and topology variation during an attack scenario is depicted in Figure 2. During the occurrence of the attack scenario, user nodes as well as observer nodes change their positions, where two paths are used to forward the datagrams sent by the adversary to the victim node. While the first path (Adversary _ $u_{1\rightarrow}$ $u_{2\rightarrow}$ victim) is used to forward packets containing actions a_1, a_2, and a_3, the second path (Adversary $_{\rightarrow}$ $u_{2\rightarrow}$ $u_{1\rightarrow}$ victim) is used to forward packets containing actions a_4, and a_5. Observer nodes take two different positions during the execution of the attack scenario. In the first position, O_1 is under the coverage of adversary and u_1 nodes, O_2 is under the coverage of u_1 and u_2 nodes, and O_3 is under the coverage of the victim node. In this position, all observers O_1, O_2, and O_3 detect the datagrams containing the actions a_1, a_2, and a_3. In the second positions, while O_1 and O_2 detect the datagrams containing the actions a_4, and a_5, since they are under the transmission coverage of adversary and u_2, and u_2 and u_1, respectively, O_3 cannot detect any packet.

Network evidence could not provide sufficient information related to some type of attack scenarios targeting MANets. In fact, attack scenarios may include some suspicious events compromising the target system, which are unobservable at the network level (e.g., a set of actions are executed locally on the target system, in response to a remote actions executed over the network) or invisible to the developed network security solution used the observers (e.g., actions are encrypted). To cope with this, Rekhis and Boudriga (2011 proposed to use and aggregate system evidence, in addition to network evidence, for conducting a postmortem investigation on MASNets. Note that, sstem evidences represent the evidential digital traces generated by the security solution that the system implements. They provide a set of information related to the observable parts of executed actions and a description of the related consequent system states.

The huge amounts of evidence that may be generated by the implemented security and network solutions can make their analysis and the generation of attack scenarios complex and prone to errors. Such a limitation can be handled through the development of a formal methodology managing evidence and ensuring an automatic reconstruction of possible attack scenario. In this context, the methodology for investigation of security attacks proposed in the work of Rekhis and Boudriga (2011) implements an inference system that integrates network and system evidence and copes with the incompleteness and duplication of the information to generate the possible and provable attack scenarios. The proposed methodology is organized into four principal steps described as follows. During the first step, the node in charge of investigation will be in charge of collecting the available evidence from the victim system and the observer nodes deployed in the network under investigation. The network evidence should be also filtered to include only the digital traces related to the attack under investigation. In the second step, an aggregation of the collected network evidence is performed. This can be achieved through the execution of a set of inference rules allowing the generation of merged and optimal network evidence. Heuristics, which are based on information appended by nodes during the generation of their observations, are also implemented to retain plausible sequences. The third step consists in the generation of the set of possible attack scenarios based on the provided network and system evidence. The fourth step consists in determining the provable actions and scenarios among the generated possible attack scenarios. All of the previous detailed steps are automatically performed through the execution of a specific set of inference rules, which allows aggregating the generated network evidence, inferring possible attack scenarios, and generating provable actions and scenarios.

In the case when the fourth step fails to determine a provable attack scenario, investigators are expected to select from the potential evidence a plausible attack scenario. Three techniques can be used. In the first technique, the set of information, which profiles the attacker, is extracted from every possible attack scenario. Based on the collected information, the scenario showing the most malicious profile will be selected as the plausible attack scenario. In the second technique, the set of information, which indicates the estimated degree of damage of every attacked system resource, is extracted from every generated possible attack scenario. The scenario showing the highest degree of system damage will be considered as the most plausible attack scenario. In the third technique, every action in a possible attack scenario is labeled by the probability value of its occurrence from the state in which it is enabled. According to the probability values, the plausible attack scenario will be selected.

The inference conducted in this research is a sort of data mining by which the investigator can access to a knowledge base describing known attacks on systems, and the description of the investigated system, detect interesting dependencies in a very noisy data, and infer more elaborated scenarios involving the execution of several actions that argument the content of the collected evidence. The use of data mining for the purpose of investigation is developed in other chapters of the same book.

Digital Investigation of Criminal Attacks on Implantable Medical Devices

As discussed in Section 2, IMDs are vulnerable to a set of attacks threatening the life of patients carrying them. Some of these attack scenarios are illustrated in the graph depicted in Figure 3. Every node in the graph specifies the state of the IMD, which can be secure (safe configuration) or unsecure (safe configuration). Every arrow in this graph represents an elementary attack action (e.g., eavesdropping, modify therapy, data analysis). An example of a lethal attack scenario depicted in this figure is described as follows. An attacker intercepts the traffic exchanged between the IMD and an authorized programmer (A_1: eavesdropping), and analyzes the intercepted data to disclose the credentials used for authentication (A_2: data analysis). Having identified the credentials, the attacker authenticates himself to the IMD and gets a privileged access to the IMD (A_3: authentication). After that, he modifies the therapy settings (A_4: modify therapy), so that the IMD configuration becomes unsafe. A further reaction of the IMD in the case of heart arrhythmia, would be inappropriate, and could harm the health of the patient.

In this context, the design of a postmortem investigation system of lethal attacks on cardiac IMDs becomes crucial. This system would enable the identification and the reconstruction of potential attack scenarios source of death of the victim. Such a system should combine together medical and technical notices. While the techni-

Figure 3. Examples of lethal attack scenarios targeting IMDs

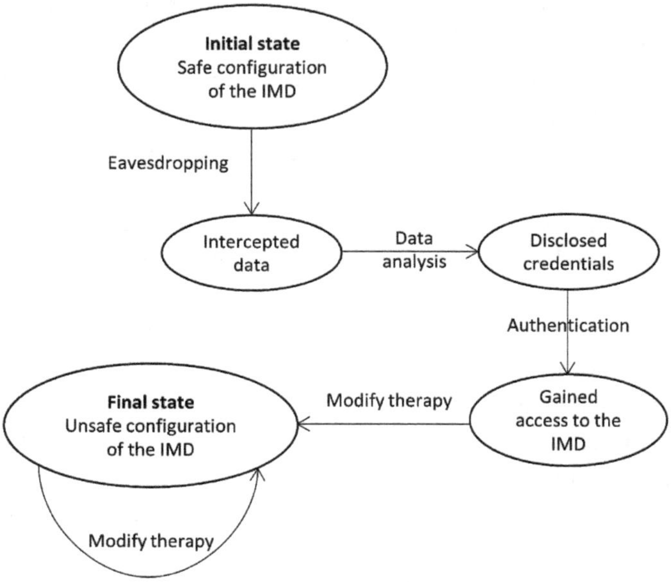

cal investigator conducts forensic analysis to prove or disprove the occurrence of malicious attacks, the medical expert performs forensic analysis to prove that the IMD malfunction is the source of death of the victim.

Typically, cardiac IMDs (e.g., pacemakers and cardiac defibrillators) provide a set of digital traces such as, the history of electromyogram and the history of the delivered therapy. These traces could be useful to conduct a forensic investigation. In fact, starting from these traces, pathologists can derive some conclusions about the primary cause of death. Nevertheless, these traces are insufficient to provide accurate investigation results. They need to be extended to include the sensitive events that may be executed on the IMD. Moreover, they should be authenticated and secured against tampering and forging. In addition, since a cardiac IMD may provide a huge amount of evidential traces, it becomes necessary to develop appropriate mathematical and formal analysis techniques for postmortem investigation allowing the automatic generation of results (i.e., potential scenarios). In this context, Ellouze et al. (2014) proposed a postmortem investigation system of lethal security incidents on cardiac IMDs. Such a system allows the generation of potential attack scenarios source of the death of the patient carrying a cardiac IMD. It reconciles in the same framework the conclusions derived by forensic medical experts and technical investigators.

The proposed system defines two types of evidence: medical and technical. Medical evidence refers to the medical experts (e.g., pathologists) findings during a forensic analysis of the victim's body and IMD. Typically, medical evidence include:

1. The history of the electromyogram (EMG) of the patient over the period of time preceding the death;
2. The set of therapies (i.e., electric shocks) delivered by the IMD, as a series of time stamped reactions along with the value of electric shocks;
3. The clinical observations which are derived during autopsy; and
4. The information collected from the medical record of the victim.

Technical evidence present the set of sensitive events executed on the IMD. They are typically stored in IMD logs as a series of time stamped events. They include:

1. Access information which help differentiating between sessions of remote connection;
2. Evidential traces related to the updates of IMD configuration and therapy settings;
3. Evidential data showing the occurred sensitive actions (e.g., the update of the IMD firmware); and
4. Information of the traffic exchanged between the IMD and remote devices. Such information is useful for the identification of some security attacks (e.g., battery depletion).

As the results of postmortem investigation mainly rely on the correctness and the trustworthy of the provided evidence, Ellouze et al. (2014) proposed an in depth security solution, which allows securing cardiac IMDs against security attacks and protecting the provided evidence from tampering to ensure their integrity. The proposed solution implements two security layers. The first layer is responsible for the protection of the cardiac IMD against security attacks (e.g., unauthorized access). It implements a mutual authentication protocol together with a security protocol ensuring a secure encrypted exchange between the IMD and the authorized programmer. The second layer is responsible of the protection of IMD logs against tampering and removal. It can only be executed by remote users who have been successfully authenticated in the first layer. The second layer implements also a biometric authentication protocol (Ellouze et al., 2013) allowing the verification of the physical proximity of the remote user. In fact, only authorized physicians, who are able to provide the biometric key computed over the electrocardiogram collected from the patient body, can get access to modify or delete records in IMD logs.

The proposed postmortem investigation system implements a three-step methodology. The first step consists in the medical investigation, which is responsible of the automatic generation of potential medical scenarios source of the death of the victim based on an inference engine executed in backward chaining starting from the victim death. This step is conducted based on the medical evidence collected from the cardiac IMD under investigation and a library of inference rules, which describe the causal relations between the different types of arrhythmias and the reactions undertaken by the cardiac IMD. Typically, an inference rule of this library takes the following form to state that the successive occurrence of *Ev* for n times induces the successive occurrence of *Ev* m times within a period of time T, where n and m are positive non-zero integers, and *Ev* and *Ev'* are a conjunction and/or disjunction of simple events (e.g., *Ev* is conjunction of two simple events: an arrhythmias and an instantaneous reaction undertaken by the IMD; and *Ev'* is a subsequent arrhythmia). Events included in inference rules can be classified into: a) observable events, which are the events detected by the IMD and included in the provided medical evidence. Examples of observable events include the delivery of electric shocks and the occurrence of ventricular fibrillation; and b) unobservable events, which are the events that cannot be detected by the IMD, so that they are not included in the medical evidence. Starting from the last observed event in the medical evidence (i.e., death), inference rules are executed in backward chaining to reconstruct a tree of potential medical scenarios, whose root node is the death event.

In the second step, which refers to the technical investigation, investigators are in charge of reconstructing the potential attacks scenarios. Starting from the library of attacks, they combine elementary actions to construct attack scenarios that provide the same collected evidence when executed. Typically, an attack scenario, say *S*, takes the following form $S = \left\langle s_0, A_1, s_1, \ldots, A_n, s_n \right\rangle$, where s_0 is the initial system state, $A_i \left(i \in \left[1.n\right] \right)$ are the elementary actions of the scenarios, which can be legitimate or malicious, and $s_i \left(i \in \left[0..n\right] \right)$ represent the description of the intermediate system states. An intermediate system state s_i is generated unless an action A_i is enabled at state s_{i-1} and is executed from it. With respect to the monitoring and security supervision mechanism implemented on the IMD, an action or a state can be visible (i.e., its value is included in the available evidence) or invisible (i.e., none information regarding its occurrence can be determined from the evidence). To support the automatic reconstruction of potential attack scenarios, a Model Checking based algorithm is executed in forward chaining. Such an algorithm is in charge of executing possible actions from the library, to generate a graph of technical scenarios satisfying the provided evidence.

After the generation of potential medical scenarios and potential technical scenarios, a correlation between these two types of scenarios is performed during the third step. This correlation allows proving whether the malicious actions in the technical scenarios of attacks caused the absence of reactions or the execution of inappropriate reactions identified in the medical scenarios. Correlation of the generated scenarios is performed in three sub-steps. The first sub-step consists in the deeply analysis of the potential medical scenario to check whether there are suspicious IMD reactions (e.g., delivery of unsuitable therapy) in the potential medical scenarios, and identify their related parameters. In the second sub-step, malicious actions threatening the IMD security are identified through the examination of the generated potential technical scenarios. A correlation is conducted in the third sub-step to check whether there is a causal relation between one of the identified suspicious IMD reactions and the determined malicious actions.

An example of a lethal attack on cardiac IMD is described as follows. An attacker, who gained an unauthorized access to the IMD, altered the thresholds associated to the detection of some arrhythmias, so that the IMD becomes unable to appropriately detect and treat the occurred arrhythmias. This inadequate configuration of the IMD has led to the occurrence of fatal arrhythmias causing the victim death. To investigate this lethal attack, the three-step methodology is performed as follows. During the first step, pathologists generate the medical scenario leading to the victim death. For instance, starting from the available EMG history and the IMD response traces, pathologists prove that the occurrence of successive events of a fatal arrhythmia (e.g., ventricular fibrillation) has induced the death of the victim as follows. They demonstrate that:

1. The IMD inappropriately detected the occurred arrhythmia events, for example it detected Sinus-Tachycardia (ST) events as Ventricular Fibrillation (VF) events. To this end, it delivered the therapy suitable for VF rather than ST;
2. The delivery of successive inappropriate therapies have led to the occurrence of VF events whose intensity grew from an event to another; and
3. The IMD was unable to handle the occurrence of VF events and deliver the suitable therapy, since it reached the maximum number of electric shocks it can deliver.

In the second step, starting from the available technical evidence and the library, which contains simple attacks targeting IMDs, technical investigators reconstruct attack scenarios, which induced the inappropriate detection of arrhythmias. For instance, they prove that the inappropriate detection of the IMD occurred further a remote attack executed on the IMD, which altered the thresholds associated to the detection of some arrhythmias (e.g., Sinus-Tachycardia). In the third step, the correlation of two types of generated scenarios (medical and technical) showed that the alteration of IMD settings (i.e., thresholds associated to the detection of some arrhythmias) makes the IMD unable to deliver the therapy suitable to the occurred arrhythmias, which led to the victim death.

SECTION 5: COMPUTER AIDED PHYSICAL CRIMES INVESTIGATION

A set of research works were proposed in the literature took interest to the development of theoretical approaches for the investigation of physical health crime scenes. In the sequel, we detail the most important ones of these approaches.

Modeling Crime Scenarios Using Assumption Based Truth Maintenance System (ATMS)

In order to improve the criminal investigation process and assist investigators, a decision support system (DSS) was proposed in the work of Keppens and Schafer (2006). The proposed system implements a knowledge driven methodology together with an abductive diagnosis approach. The principal component of the proposed architecture is an Assumption based Truth Maintenance System (ATMS), which is an inference mechanism allowing the reconstruction of all possible scenarios that can provide a set of explanations for the available evidence and support some hypotheses. Possible scenarios are generated starting from an initial set of inputs (facts and evidence) using a knowledge base. The constructed possible scenarios are then grouped in the form of a data structure, namely the scenario space. In order to analyze the scenario space, users can generate a set of standard queries which are translated into a specification of ATMS nodes of interest through the query analyzer. Answers related to the received queries are computed through the extraction of the relevant parts from the scenario space, transformed in a user understandable format by the report generator, and then sent back to users.

According to the proposed DSS, a scenario consists of a set of events, states, and causal relations between these events and states. It is constructed using a knowledge base, which integrates the use of three principal constructs. The first construct is the property definitions, which allow describing the involved types of events and states. The second construct is a set of causal rules, called scenario fragments. An example of a causal rule is as follows.

```
if {
suffers(P, C),
cause-of-death(C, P),
medical-examiner(E)
} assuming {
determine(E,cause-of-death(P)),
correct-diagnosis(E,cause-of-death(P))
} then {
cod-report(E, P, C)
}
```

This rule states that: a) if there is a person *P* who suffers from ailment or injury (denoted by *C)*, *C* is the cause of death of the person *P*, and there exists a medical examiner, denoted by *E*; and b) assuming that *E* determines the cause of death of *P* and performs the correct diagnosis; then a piece of evidence is generated in the form of a report which indicates that according to *E*, *C* is the cause of death of *P*.

The third construct consists of a set of inconsistencies, which allows identifying the combination of events, and states that are impossible and inconsistent with one another. An example of inconsistency is as follows.

```
inconsistent {
suicide-action(hanging, P),
is-hanged(P)}
```

This inconsistency states that a person P cannot kill himself (i.e., suicide) and be hanged by another person in the same time.

The proposed decision support system (Keppens and Schafer, 2006) implements two types of inference mechanisms. The first type is a backward chaining inference mechanism. It infers plausible scenarios, which explains the available evidence, starting from the available evidence and until reaching the initial state of the system. The second type is a forward chaining inference mechanism. It is executed starting from the initial system state and until reaching the available evidence. It allows the generation of new plausible scenarios, in addition to those created during the backward chaining phase.

Modeling Crime Scenarios in a Bayesian Network (BN)

A Bayesian network (BN) is a probabilistic graphical model that encodes probabilistic relationships among a collection of relevant variables. For instance, in the medical field, BN may allow representing the relationships between the occurred cardiac arrhythmias and the death of a patient. It can be also used to compute the probabilities of the occurrence of the death event. In this context, the use of a Bayesian network (BN) can be a promising solution for the modeling plausible crime scenarios and the proof of the communication between investigators and judges in legal cases (e.g., crime on e-health system). Nevertheless, the identification of relevant variables, during the construction of such a network, is not always easily feasible. To this end, a formal foundation for evidential reasoning, which allows the automatic construction of a Bayesian network, can be used to enable the development of a software tool, which allows assisting investigators and judges during the investigation of crimes on healthcare systems.

Vlek et al. (2013) proposed a formal evidential reasoning approach, which allows modeling plausible crime scenarios for a legal case in a single Bayesian Network and connecting them to the provided evidence. The proposed approach integrates four main steps described as follows. The first step consists in formulating all the relevant scenarios and identifying the guilt hypotheses that could be supported by each specified scenario. It may exist relevant scenarios which do not support any guilt hypothesizes. Guilt hypothesis should be formulated in such a way they are either equal, or mutually exclusive. During the second step, a set of scenarios idiom are generated and represented in the graph under construction starting from the relevant scenarios (formulated in the first step). This can be achieved as follows. For every state or event in the formulated relevant scenario, a binary node is included in the graph under construction. Then, an arrow is drawn between dependent events or states, since the absence of an arrow between two nodes, representing events or/and states, means that they are independent from each other. After that, a set of binary scenario nodes are also included to represent every scenario formulated in the first step, and an arrow is drawn from each scenario node to all state and event nodes in that scenario. To represent the supported guilt hypothesis, a set of binary nodes are added, and a set of arrows are drawn from every scenario node to the guilt hypothesis it supports. In the third step, in order to merge the generated idiom scenarios in one Bayesian Network, the same guilt hypothesis nodes are replaced by one node, which will be connected to the different scenarios supporting this guilt hypothesis. After merging the scenarios idioms, a verification of the existence of other dependencies between nodes should be performed, in order to be modeled with arrows. Moreover, if there are nodes describing equal states, events or evidence, they are replaced by one node. Nevertheless, if there are nodes, in two different scenarios, describing conflicting states, events or evidence that cannot occur simultaneously, a constraint node is included to present the identified constraint. Finally, the fourth step consists in adding the relevant evidential nodes to the Bayesian network under construction. A binary evidential node representing each piece of evidence, collected during the investigation process, is included. These included evidential nodes are also connected to the event or state node in the scenario it supports. The resulting graph (i.e., the Bayesian network) will be connected, representing all idiom scenarios of a legal case.

Automated Inference of Past Criminal Action Instances in Digital Investigations

Because of the technological evolution, and the intensive use of digital equipment by persons to access to diverse types of services, the amount of digital evidence that should be handled during postmortem investigation is continuing to increase. In this context, James and Gladyshev (2015) proposed a signature analysis model allowing the automatic provision of data to knowledge acquisition for the involved digital investigators. The proposed model ensures the automated approximation and reconstruction of past action instances within a compromised digital system. It integrates the use of signature-based methods to provide a formal description of the different categories of signatures. In this work, a signature is expressed as follows $S = \left\{T_i, \theta, cm\right\}$, where: T_i represents the set of objects time stamps associated to an action instance, θ is the object update threshold related to the action instance, and *cm* defines the update consistency checking function which is specific to the category of object update patterns. Three principal time stamp-related update patterns are defined in the work of James and Gladyshev (2015). Below, we detail each pattern.

The first time stamp-update pattern, namely Core object update, defines the update pattern of Core object time stamps as follows. Core object time stamps represent the set of time stamps, denoted by Score, which are always updated to be equal to the value of the clock of the system each time a specific action is executed. This definition means that when observing a trace in a Core set, it can be noticed that an action instance might have occurred. In fact, an artifact observed in a Core set can be related to only single action. Moreover, due to the fact that time stamps belonging to Score are always updated, each time stamp should be within a certain time range of each other that is identified according to the object update threshold of the action, denoted by θ. Let us consider the example of a configuration file of a Program X that is modified each time the Program X is closed, thus the modification time stamp of this file is a Core trace for the action "Close Program X". Starting from the definition of the first pattern, an object time stamp update consistency function, namely CoreTest, was developed. Such a function is in charge of checking whether each object update conforms to the Core signature category based on the object update threshold and the TraceStates array that includes the values of time stamps of all objects specified in the signature. According to this function, if the difference between the recent timestamp value and the oldest time stamp value of the TraceStates array is lower than the object update threshold, the Core traces are considered as consistent, otherwise, they are inconsistent.

The second time stamp-update pattern, namely Supporting object update, defines the update pattern of Supporting object time stamps as follows. The supporting object time stamps represent the set of time stamps, denoted by $S_{support}$, which are irregularly (i.e., not always) updated each time a single particular action instance is executed, and they can only be updated by a single specific action. Similarly, to Core signatures, the detection of a trace in a supporting signature means that an action instance must have occurred, since an artifact observed in a supporting signature can be related to a single action. For example, an irregular update of time stamp may be figured when a file is cached in memory after the first execution of the first action instance. In fact, it may happen that the subsequent action instances accessed the file data cached in memory rather than the file disk, so that the trace related to this update would be unobservable on the disk, since the original file's meta-data on disk was not updated. Starting from the definition of the second pattern, an object time stamp update consistency function, called SupportTest, was derived. Such a function is in charge of testing whether each object update conforms to the supporting signature category based on the object update threshold θ and the TraceStates array that includes the values of time stamps of all objects specified in the signature. If an object update conforms to the supporting update category, and if each trace has been updated within the threshold θ, the action execution time can be defined to be approximately equal or shortly lower than the oldest time stamp in the TraceStates array. In the case where there exists a time stamp updated outside of θ from another related object time stamp, then it can be noticed that a separate instance of the same action must have happened.

The third time stamp-update pattern, namely Shared object update, defines the update pattern of Shared object time stamps as follows. Shared object time stamps represent the set of time stamps, denoted by Shared, which may be always or irregularly updated on the occurrence of each execution of multiple actions. Differently to the Core signatures and the Supporting signatures, more than one action can be associated to a trace in a Shared signature, so that the only information that can be derived from the observation of a trace in a Shared signature is that at least one of the actions associated to this trace must be executed. The access time stamp of a .dll file (.dll represents the file extension of a Dynamic-link library) can be considered as an example of a Shared object time stamp, since more than one action may induce the .dll file to be accessed. The conclusion that may be derived when only analyzing this file (without any additional information) is that each action, which is able to induce the .dll file to be accessed, has the same occurrence likelihood. An object time stamp update consistency function, called SharedTest, was derived from the definition of the Shared object update pattern. This function allows testing whether each object update conforms to the Shared object update category, and determining the actions associated to the trace. If an object update conforms to the Shared update category, and if each trace has been updated within the threshold θ, then the action execution time can be defined to be approximately equal or shortly lower than the oldest time stamp in the TraceStates array. In the case when there exists a time stamp updated outside θ from another object time stamp, then it can be noticed that a separate instance of the same action must have happened, because objects are irregularly updated. Since multiple actions can be associated to a trace, additional information are also required to enable the identification of the action causing the trace.

SECTION 6: ADVANCED ISSUES

Several approaches were developed in the literature to conduct a digital investigation on compromised digital system. Several issues were addressed by these ranging from the need to generate provable results, address scalability, and provide resilience to anti-forensic attack. However, the whole majority of these approaches are not directly applicable to investigate healthcare attacks. In fact, contrary to general types of digital attacks which affect only the target system, crimes on e-health systems could firstly affect the medical devices, and then spread to the patient. A healthcare investigation would therefore require the cooperation between at least two types of experts: forensic pathologists and digital security investigators. Moreover, a healthcare attack can be conducted with a long-term interest (a modification of electronic healthcare records could lead to an unsuitable medication that will be prescribed a long time after), Techniques for the long-term secure storage of evidence need to be developed. As a medical attack on a healthcare system can affect people, its impact will vary from a patient to another, introducing an uncertainty in the attack consequence. Such an uncertainty needs to be handled by the existing investigation techniques.

Despite some advances in the development of frameworks for the forensic investigation of digital crimes in healthcare applications, several issues remain unsolved.

The first issue is related to the development of forensic readiness. We have shown in the previous sections of this chapter the importance of the risk associated to attacks on wireless medical systems, and their consequence on the patients and practitioners' safety, privacy, and legal liability. To make attacks on medical systems investigable, the complete healthcare system should be made forensically ready so that a complete and successful investigation can be conducted, or a root cause analysis can be performed when the security incident occurs. Developing the forensic readiness aspects in healthcare requires setting technical and non-technical measures to maximize the ability of collecting and securing evidences. These measures include, but are not limited to:

1. The collection of evidence legally while minimizing at the maximal possible any interference with the business process of the healthcare system;
2. The definition of the healthcare system usage scenarios that require a collection of evidence;
3. The identification of the potential sources of digital evidence, including the different wireless access networks used by patients and healthcare professionals, the various used cloud infrastructures and services, and the diverse access equipment;
4. The maximization of the capabilities of collecting evidence from the healthcare system in a way that keeps them authentic, secure, and admissible in courts of laws;
5. Training the technical staff to conduct future digital investigation; and
6. Developing the procedures to facilitate the postmortem analysis.

All of these mechanisms should be made possible, and capable to cope with the voluminous aspects of the collected medical data, the huge number of intervening persons, the diversity of the access equipment, the distributed aspects of healthcare systems and applications, the heterogeneity of the evidence to be collected, and the complexity of healthcare investigation.

The second aspect is related to the need to maximize the ability of a healthcare crime investigation system to cope with anti-forensic attacks. These attacks target the availability and usefulness of digital evidences to the healthcare forensic investigation process. The evidence can be compromised by hiding, destroying, or forging them. An attacker can conduct a successful crime and later alter the generated traces to make it non investigable. Aware of these types of attacks, the developed frameworks for the investigation of healthcare crimes should develop new techniques to first detect anti-forensic attacks, and also to conceal their effect on the compromised evidence. Once the anti-forensic attacks are identified, it becomes possible to proceed with the scenarios reconstruction, and the crime identification. Several issues make these actions challenging. First, the anti-forensic attacks are difficult to detect as most of them do not leave traces on their execution. Wiping an evidence file to completely hide the original content, for example, is not only difficult to detect, but also impossible to recover. Second, several classes of ant-forensic attacks exist (e.g., address anonymization, multimedia steganography, data hiding in slack space), making it necessary to develop the required formalism to model them within libraries of attacks, useable during an investigation. Third, the protection from anti-forensic attacks requires the development of novel tamper-evident technologies to make unauthorized access to the device storing the evidence easily detected. Additional levels of protection are also required to identify the potential tampers and their gained level of knowledge, determine the techniques and methods used to attempt to gain access, control access to the evidence, and reduce to the maximum possible the cost associated to the tamper evident features and the detection of tampering.

The third issue is related to the need to cope with the resources scarcity of the wireless healthcare systems, especially as they are showing an extensive use of small and tiny devices for the purpose of sensing, monitoring, identification, and on-demand information exchange. While several approaches attempted to overcome the limitation of resources and the transient unavailability of the collection devices, by using virtualization and cloud computing technologies, an extensive work still needs to be developed. The aim is not only to virtualize the storage space and the processing resources, but also to virtualize all the types of sensors used by the healthcare solution, in order to decrease the number of required sensors, increase the accuracy of the sensed data by taking profit from the redundancy of sensors, increase the network lifetime and the continuous delivery and availability of services, collect complex data starting from diverse physical sensors, and decouple the physical sensors resources from the developed sensing application. The new expected types of cloud sensors for healthcare applications should also meet the requirements in terms of quality of service, security, and energy preservation.

The last issue is related to the need to cope with the increasing need of energy. In fact, the prominent need to make investigation in healthcare be proactive instead of postmortem, makes it necessary to develop novel techniques for the continuous collection and delivery of evidence, and the instantaneous reaction to potential digital crimes. These techniques will certainly increase the consumption of energy from the battery of medical equipment (wearable or mobile sensors), making it necessary to optimize the used algorithms to reduce their consumption of energy, or to find alternative sources of power. One of the potential used solutions is to use highly sophisticated batteries and power management systems, which will certainly increase the cost of the healthcare solution. Another, alternative and highly cheaper solution consists in using power harvesting or energy scavenging techniques to power the different tiny and autonomous sensors from many external sources such as solar power, thermal energy, and Radio Frequency energy. The ongoing and future research development should work on eliminating the battery from the energy-sensitive medical equipment and get rid of the weakest component in these devices. In some devices, such as pacemakers, the use of energy harvesting techniques would avoid doing surgical intervention by physicians to replace the patient's pacemaker each time its battery is depleted.

CONCLUSION

In this chapter, we took interest in the postmortem investigation of digital crimes on healthcare applications. Firstly, we provided an overview of healthcare systems' architectures together with a detailed description of the involved components and their functions. We also reviewed and classified the most important types of healthcare applications proposed in the literature. Then, we identified and described a representative set of digital healthcare crimes. These crimes have been organized into four classes based on their goals and their impact on the patients' safety and privacy. We also discussed the impact of these crimes on the availability and the accuracy of the provided healthcare services. After identifying digital crimes on healthcare applications, we discussed the main requirements that should be fulfilled during the design of a postmortem investigation system tailored to these applications. A literature review of research works related to the use of theoretical techniques for the investigation of digital crimes on healthcare applications, and also the investigation of physical health crime scenes, was provided. Finally, we discussed a set of advanced issues that should be addressed during the design of an efficient postmortem investigation system capable of providing accurate results.

REFERENCES

Al-Qurishi, M., Al-Rakhami, M., Al-Qershi, F., Hassan, M. M., Alamri, A., Khan, H. U., & Xiang, Y. (2015). A Framework for Cloud-Based Healthcare Services to Monitor Noncommunicable Diseases Patient. *International Journal of Distributed Sensor Networks*, 2015.

Almadani, B., Bin-Yahya, M., & Shakshuki, E. M. (2015). E-AMBULANCE: Real-Time Integration Platform for Heterogeneous Medical Telemetry System. *Procedia Computer Science*, *63*, 400–407. doi:10.1016/j.procs.2015.08.359

Aquino-Santos, R., Martinez-Castro, D., Edwards-Block, A., & Murillo-Piedrahita, A. F. (2013). Wireless sensor networks for ambient assisted living. *Sensors (Basel, Switzerland)*, *13*(12), 16384–16405. doi:10.3390/s131216384 PMID:24351665

Astorga, J., Astorga, J. C., Jacob, E., Toledo, N., & Higuero, M. (2014). Securing access to next generation IP-enabled pacemakers and ICDs using Ladon. *Journal of Ambient Intelligence and Smart Environments, 6*(2), 157-177.

Carrier, B. D., & Spafford, E. H. (2006). Categories of digital investigation analysis techniques based on the computer history model. *Digital Investigation*, *3*, 121–130. doi:10.1016/j.diin.2006.06.011

Chen, H., Cheng, B. C., Liao, G. T., & Kuo, T. C. (2014). Hybrid classification engine for cardiac arrhythmia cloud service in elderly healthcare management. *Journal of Visual Languages and Computing*, *25*(6), 745–753. doi:10.1016/j.jvlc.2014.09.012

Cusack, B., & Kyaw, A. K. (2012). Forensic readiness for wireless medical systems. In *Proceedings of the 10th Australian Digital Forensics Conference* (pp. 21-32).

Dmitrienko, A., Hadzic, Z., Löhr, H., Sadeghi, A. R., & Winandy, M. (2013).Securing the access to electronic health records on mobile phones. *Biomedical Engineering Systems and Technologies*, *273*, 365–379.

Ellouze, N., Allouche, M., Ben Ahmed, H., Rekhis, S., & Boudriga, N. (2013). Securing implantable cardiac medical devices: use of radio frequency energy harvesting. In *Proceedings of the third international workshop on Trustworthy embedded devices* (pp. 35-42). doi:10.1145/2517300.2517307

Ellouze, N., Rekhis, S., Allouche, M., & Boudriga, N. (2014). Digital Investigation of Security Attacks on Cardiac Implantable Medical Devices. In *Proceedings of the Advanced Intrusion and Prevention Workshop in conjunction with the International Information Security and Privacy Conference* (pp. 15-30). doi:10.4204/EPTCS.165.2

Felisberto, F., Laza, R., Fdez-Riverola, F., & Pereira, A. (2015). A Distributed Multiagent System Architecture for Body Area Networks Applied to Healthcare Monitoring. *BioMed Research International, 2015*(2015).

Hei, X., Du, X., Wu, J., & Hu, F. (2010). Defending resource depletion attacks on implantable medical devices. In *Proceedings of the Global Telecommunications Conference* (pp. 1-5). doi:10.1109/GLOCOM.2010.5685228

Hu, F., Jiang, M., Celentano, L., & Xiao, Y. (2008). Robust medical ad hoc sensor networks (MASN) with wavelet-based ECG data mining. *Ad Hoc Networks*, *6*(7), 986–1012. doi:10.1016/j.adhoc.2007.09.002

Hui, J. W., & Culler, D. E. (2008). Extending IP to low-power, wireless personal area networks. *IEEE Internet Computing*, *12*(4), 37–45. doi:10.1109/MIC.2008.79

James, J. I., & Gladyshev, P. (2015). Automated inference of past action instances in digital investigations. *International Journal of Information Security*, *14*(3), 249–261. doi:10.1007/s10207-014-0249-6

Kaur, P. D., & Chana, I. (2014). Cloud based intelligent system for delivering health care as a service. *Computer Methods and Programs in Biomedicine*, *113*(1), 346–359. doi:10.1016/j.cmpb.2013.09.013 PMID:24139021

Keppens, J., & Schafer, B. (2006). Knowledge based crime scenario modelling. *Expert Systems with Applications*, *30*(2), 203–222. doi:10.1016/j.eswa.2005.07.011

Ko, J., Lim, J. H., Chen, Y., Musvaloiu-E, R., Terzis, A., Masson, G. M., & Dutton, R. P. et al. (2010). MEDiSN: Medical emergency detection in sensor networks. *ACM Transactions on Embedded Computing Systems*, *10*(1), 1–29. doi:10.1145/1814539.1814550

Kumar, P., & Lee, H. J. (2011). Security issues in healthcare applications using wireless medical sensor networks: A survey. *Sensors (Basel, Switzerland)*, *12*(1), 55–91. doi:10.3390/s120100055 PMID:22368458

Li, C., Raghunathan, A., & Jha, N. K. (2011). Hijacking an insulin pump: Security attacks and defenses for a diabetes therapy system. In *Proceedings of the 13th IEEE International Conference on e-Health Networking Applications and Services* (pp. 150-156).

Magaña-Espinoza, P., Aquino-Santos, R., Cárdenas-Benítez, N., Aguilar-Velasco, J., Buenrostro-Segura, C., Edwards-Block, A., & Medina-Cass, A. (2014). WiSPH: A Wireless Sensor Network-Based Home Care Monitoring System. *Sensors (Basel, Switzerland)*, *14*(4), 7096–7119. doi:10.3390/s140407096 PMID:24759112

Maia, P., Batista, T., Cavalcante, E., Baffa, A., Delicato, F. C., Pires, P. F., & Zomaya, A. (2014). A Web platform for interconnecting body sensors and improving health care. *Procedia Computer Science, 40*, 135-142.

Mashima, D., & Ahamad, M. (2012). Enabling robust information accountability in e-healthcare systems. In *Proceedings of the third USENIX Workshop on Health Security and Privacy* (pp. 14-14).

Oh, S. E., Chun, J. Y., Jia, L., Garg, D., Gunter, C. A., & Datta, A. (2014). Privacy-preserving audit for broker-based health information exchange. In *Proceedings of the fourth ACM conference on Data and application security and privacy* (pp. 313-320). doi:10.1145/2557547.2557576

Rekhis, S., & Boudriga, N. (2011). Formal reconstruction of attack scenarios in mobile ad hoc and sensor networks. *EURASIP Journal on Wireless Communications and Networking*, (1): 1–17.

Savci, H. S., Sula, A., Wang, Z., Dogan, N. S., & Arvas, E. (2005, April). MICS transceivers: regulatory standards and applications [medical implant communications service]. In *Proceedings of the IEEE SoutheastCon* (pp. 179-182).

Srinivasan, V., Stankovic, J., & Whitehouse, K. (2008). Protecting your daily in-home activity information from a wireless snooping attack. In *Proceedings of the 10th international conference on Ubiquitous computing* (pp. 202-211). doi:10.1145/1409635.1409663

Steinfeld, R., Bull, L., Wang, H., & Pieprzyk, J. (2003). Universal designated-verifier signatures. Advances in Cryptology-Asiacrypt, 2894(2003), 523-542. doi: doi:10.1007/978-3-540-40061-5_33 doi:10.1007/978-3-540-40061-5_33

Tan, H., Hu, W., & Jha, S. (2011). A TPM-enabled remote attestation protocol (TRAP) in wireless sensor networks. In *Proceedings of the sixth ACM workshop on Performance monitoring and measurement of heterogeneous wireless and wired networks* (pp. 9-16). doi:10.1145/2069087.2069090

Vlek, C., Prakken, H., Renooij, S., & Verheij, B. (2013). Modeling crime scenarios in a Bayesian network. In *Proceedings of the Fourteenth International Conference on Artificial Intelligence and Law* (pp. 150-159). doi:10.1145/2514601.2514618

KEY TERMS AND DEFINITIONS

Attack Scenario: A series of malicious and legitimate actions executed on a digital system to harm its security. At some step in the scenario, a malicious action is executed to transform the system state from safe to unsafe (these states are already defined in a security policy).

Digital Crimes: Encompass all offences against the secrecy, integrity, and availability of electronic data and digital systems. When executed, they could lead to a set of serious threats ranging from economic to life threats.

Digital Forensic Investigation: The process of a postmortem analysis of a compromised system, to identify and retrieve digital evidence, understand the incident, identify attackers, and reconstruct potential attack. To conduct a forensic investigation, scientific methods can be used to prove/disapprove a claim about the incident in a court of law.

E-Health Systems: Healthcare systems which integrate the use of information and communications technologies to provide medical services to patients. Thanks to the integration of these technologies, a wide set of e-health applications, which improve the quality of life of high risk patients, were developed.

Implantable Medical Devices: A specific class of digital devices (e.g., pacemakers, defibrillators, insulin pumps), which are surgically implanted into a human's body, and used to treat chronic ailments (cardiac arrhythmia, diabetes, Parkinson).

Lethal Attacks: Security attacks that generally target medical devices and e-health systems. When executed, these attacks seriously harm the health status of the victim patient and lead to its death.

Physical Healthcare Crimes: Encompass all violations against the person's bodies. They generally cause serious physical damage (e.g., abuse, homicide) to the bodies of victim persons.

Section 4
Denial of Service, Cyber-Crime, and Intrusion Detection Management

Chapter 8
Data Mining Analytics for Crime Security Investigation and Intrusion Detection

Boutheina Fessi
CN&S, University of Carthage, Tunisia

Yacine Djemaiel
CN&S, University of Carthage, Tunisia

Noureddine Boudriga
CN&S, University of Carthage, Tunisia

ABSTRACT

This chapter provides a review about the usefulness of applying data mining techniques to detect intrusion within dynamic environments and its contribution in digital investigation. Numerous applications and models are described based on data mining analytics. The chapter addresses also different requirements that should be fulfilled to efficiently perform cyber-crime investigation based on data mining analytics. It states, at the end, future research directions related to cyber-crime investigation that could be investigated and presents new trends of data mining techniques that deal with big data to detect attacks.

DOI: 10.4018/978-1-5225-0463-4.ch008

INTRODUCTION

The continuous increase of the information streams and the dynamic feature of the environment, where the enterprise operates, could led to the emergence of new kinds of attacks that threat its information system. In fact, distributed and cyber attacks may be launched from different locations and targeted many sources, creating consequently a need to perform network data analysis from several networks locations.

A set of techniques and models are applied to mitigate these attacks but unfortunately they do not provide accurate protection. Therefore, novel measures and tools should be set up to prevent and secure these systems considering the high performance of computers, the newly smart attacks and the rising of vulnerabilities from inside and outside the information systems. Furthermore, tracing back the attack is an important task to perform since it determines the intruder identity and source, and provides then the appropriate response to counter the detected attack.

Data mining techniques are a set of techniques that prove their effectiveness to cope with the cited issues. They are applied in several fields and implement different tasks. They could be performed in concert to make better detection and their principal aim is the extraction of knowledge from data which is tightly necessary when performing data collection and detection.

As it is mentioned in Figure 1, these techniques are used during the security investigation process that is performed within the enterprise. This latter is subjected to several factors that could affect its security, despite the existing policies and security tools. The investigation process is thus performed to efficiently detect and track the attacks that could harm its safety. It is based on data mining analytics, which deal with huge amounts of data and could perform several tasks related to cleaning, classifying and examining collected data.

The proposed chapter aims at presenting the harnessing of data mining analytics to crime security investigation and intrusion detection in company's communication networks. Numerous applications and models are described based on these analytics. The chapter also provides a review about the usefulness of applying data mining techniques to detect intrusion within dynamic environments, where the management of huge amounts of data is unavoidable. A set of challenges are thus identified when dealing with big data, including the detection and the tracing back of the attack if the information system is flooded by real time data. In addition, two cases studies related to medical and crime investigation are detailed showing the use of data mining techniques for the identification of attack scenarios.

Moreover, the chapter addresses different requirements that should be fulfilled to efficiently perform cyber-crime investigation based on data mining analytics. These requirements are mainly associated to defining attack environment and characteristics for the investigation process on one hand, and the appropriateness and

Figure 1. Deployment of data mining techniques into enterprise investigation process

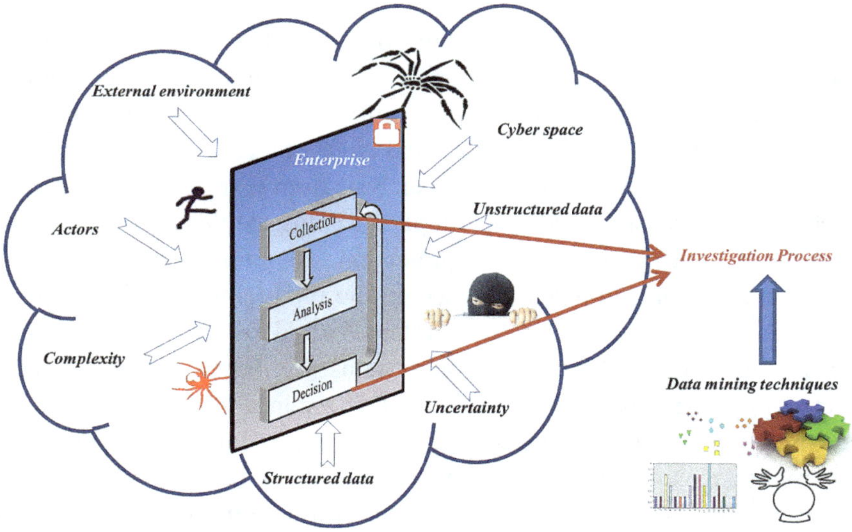

the need of using data mining techniques on the other hand. Finally, the chapter states future research directions related to cyber-crime investigation that could be investigated and presents new trends of data mining techniques that deal with big data to detect attacks.

INVESTIGATION OF SECURITY ATTACKS

This section defines the investigation of security attacks and provides the defined process to reconstruct attack scenarios. A set of available applications that deal with security or criminal investigation are also presented. They show the importance of conducting such investigation since it allows the identification of the source of attacks and provides consequently the appropriate response.

In 1999, McKemmish defined forensic computing as "the process of identifying, preserving, analyzing and presenting digital evidence in a manner that is legally acceptable" (McKemmish, 1999).

Digital Investigation Process

The investigation process comprises a set of steps that should be followed by investigators to identify the potential attack scenario. This process focuses on the investigation of an incident after it has happened and it helps investigators to find responses to a set of aspects related to the investigated attack including:

1. The followed strategy to break into the system;
2. The occurrence time of the attack;
3. The used tools to compromise the system;
4. The data that has been accessed, modified, or altered during the attack;
5. The vulnerability exploited by the intruder.

In this context, a digital evidence should be collected from the system to support the decision made by the investigator regarding the incident. A digital evidence is defined as "Any data stored or transmitted using a computer that support or refute a theory of how an offence occurred or that address critical elements of the alibi such as intent or alibi" (Casey, 2011).

This process may cover the study of the attackers' trends and motivations behind the system compromise. As a consequence, the investigator may discover new tools (e.g. Trojans, backdoor) and techniques that are used by the intruders during the attack.

Digital investigation is not limited only to incident response but it can be used by law enforcement for the analysis of incidents that makes use of computers to perform a set of malicious activities such as the stealing of credit card numbers or the tampering with online transactions. Another application of digital investigation is related to the diagnosis of unreliable and faulty systems. In this context, this activity helps to identify the problems, diagnosis them and propose an effective solution.

The most common steps for the investigation process are detailed as follows (Casey, 2011):

- **Preparation:** The aim of this step is to make the investigator ready for performing a digital investigation by preparing a specific investigation policy and a set of forensic toolkits that are needed to conduct the investigation tasks. The investigation policy defines the set of requirements that clarifies the approach to be taken and indicates the features of the system to be investigated.
- **Survey/Identification:** During this step, evidences are collected and are classified into three categories: volatile, temporary and persistent. Volatile data, such as the memory content, registers, caches, etc., are highly sensitive to system usage and may be lost. As a consequence, these data should be collected first to minimize their lost. Temporary data are related to running processes, network connections, listening servers. They should be also collected as quickly as possible before they disappear but the collection should be performed after the volatile data. The persistent data comprises file systems, log files and users' data that are located in most cases on storage devices.
- **Preservation:** The aim of this step is to prevent changes that may happen to collected evidences by implementing several security measures including the isolation of the system on the network and securing relevant log files. During

this step, evidence management activities are performed which include storing in addition to maintaining digital evidence and provenance.

- **Examination and Analysis:** This phase is considered as the most complex compared to the previous ones. It aims to examine all relevant information and correctly determine the causes and the effects of the occurred incident. Two processes are conducted within this step. The former extracts and views information from the evidence, and making it available for analysis. The latter is the forensic analysis that consists on the application of the scientific method to provide responses to questions related to the investigated attack: who, what, where, when, how and why.
- **Presentation:** The examination step is followed by the reporting of the investigation process results in a manner which satisfies the context of the investigation, whether it is corporate, military or any other.

Use of Scientific Methods in Digital Investigation

In order to deal with the major issues related to the realization of an investigation process, there is a need to bridge digital investigation practices and computer science theory to demonstrate the role of the scientific method within a digital investigation. In this context, Carrier has proposed in (Carrier, 2006) an initial model, denoted Hypothesis Based approach to digital forensic investigations. The approach introduces a model of computer history based on a finite state machine view of computing and storage, describing the history of the state of a digital device in terms of low-level computations and storage operations and of user perceivable events and storage operations. This model has initiated the application of scientific methods but it is required to show in this section how the scientific methods are applied for each step of a digital investigation process. Starting by the collected observations, digital investigators will form a theory of what may have occurred. Based on the hypothesis, the investigator may identify missing actions and possible locations of evidences. At a next step, investigator should analyze the available evidences to test the hypothesis.

A Hierarchical Visibility Theory for Formal Digital Investigation of Anti-Forensic Attacks

Several research works have been conducted to define formal models for the investigation of security attacks. In addition, the research community has taken interest to the anti-forensic attacks that may be performed by an intruder to prevent the investigation of attacks by determining the intruder's identity and the exploited vulnerability that have leaded to the success of the attack.

In (Rekhis, 2012), a formal approach based on a theory of hierarchical visibility has been proposed enabling the investigation of security attacks that has targeted complex systems and integrating anti-forensic attacks. This theory provides the way to reason on anti-forensic attacks over complex systems, gives situations under which they are provable and proves their occurrence starting from incomplete evidences. Two forms of known anti forensic attacks are modeled starting by the simple forms of anti-forensic attack scenarios obtained by the execution of recurrent series of events that are issued by the intruder to compromise some security properties (e.g. availability, confidentiality). The advanced forms of anti-forensic attacks are also modeled. These attacks aim in most cases to overwrite metadata and log files, hide data that are in most cases generated or altered by an intruder in addition to the used techniques that ensure the injection of malicious codes in memory.

In order to achieve this objective, a formal logic-based model is developed to enable the representation of complex systems and attack scenarios under different levels of abstractions in addition to the identification and selection of the security solutions deployed to protect the investigated system. This model represents also the generated evidences by the security solutions that are needed during the investigation steps.

The visibility theory has been integrated in the preparation and analysis phases of an investigation process. During the preparation phase, investigators generate all potential threats that target their systems based on their formal description and the content of the library of attacks. Next, the investigator selects the adequate security solutions that make these properties provable from the evidences that are collected after the occurrence of the security attack. During the analysis phase, the proposed model enables the investigator to prove the occurrence of anti-forensic attacks and identify the hidden or inserted traces of executed actions based on the collected evidences.

Digital Investigation for IPv6-Based Wireless Sensor Networks

In (Kumar, 2014), an approach is proposed for the analysis of extracted data and the retrieval of network-related information, such as routing table and Neighbor Discovery (ND) cache contents. Moreover, it enables the correlation of the information gathered from multiple devices in order to reconstruct the network topology. The proposed approach follows three step process consisting of retrieving, analyzing and correlation. The first step aims to retrieve the content of the considered devices holding volatile and/or persistent information. Then, the extracted content is analyzed to determine the events and factors related to the performed security attack targeting the investigated devices (e.g. identifying the node's networking state). The last step is performed when several devices are considered during the investigation process.

This stage ensures the correlation of data collected from those devices to obtain supplementary information that may be of interest for the previous achieved results. Through the use of the proposed approach, it is possible to partially reconstruct the network's layers (2 and 3) topologies, by correlating information extracted by only a subset of the nodes forming the network.

The processing of the proposed approach may be prevented due to a set of restrictions that may be implemented by the solicited interfaces for the investigated devices. For example, the extraction of flash contents may not be achieved when the lock bits are enabled. Moreover, the proposed approach could not support divers' operating systems since it is operational with a specific investigated system.

DATA MINING: PRINCIPLES AND APPLICATIONS

This section deals with the data mining definition, goals and benefits. It also describes the different techniques and applications that adopt data mining.

Definition and Principles

Several definitions of data mining have been developed and cited in the literature. Many researchers and practitioners used data mining and knowledge discovery interchangeably. Others consider data mining as one step of the knowledge discovery process and named it differently, such as knowledge extraction, information discovery, information harvesting, data archeology, and data pattern processing (Cios, 2007).

Despite this variation, they all agreed that the core aim of the data mining is to make sense of large amounts of data. The proposed definition of Fayyad et al. (1996) is among the most popular and insightful definitions, where the data mining is defined as a "process of identifying valid, novel, potentially useful, and ultimately comprehensive knowledge from database that is used to make crucial business decisions" (Fayyad, 1996).

Data mining ensures two fundamental tasks: prediction and description. The former involves using some variables or fields in the data set to predict unknown or future values of other variables of interest. In this case predictive data mining produces the model of the system described by the given data set; whereas the latter objective (i.e. description) focuses on finding patterns describing the data that can be interpreted by humans. Therefore, descriptive data mining produces new, nontrivial information based on the available data set.

Data mining is considered as a step of the knowledge discovery process, which consists of six steps (Cios, 2005):

1. Problem understanding;
2. Data understanding;
3. Data cleaning and preprocessing;
4. Data mining;
5. Evaluation; and
6. Deployment.

The purpose of the data mining stage is to find new and potentially useful patterns from data in a particular representational form or a set of such representations, through applying various techniques such as classification, rules or trees, regression, sequence modeling, dependency, and line analysis.

Considerable benefits could be obtained from applying data mining approaches. They are related essentially to processing huge amounts of data, discovering hidden values in the handled data that could be used for competitive advantage, finding out complex relationships that could not be determined using traditional database queries, and building patterns that are automatically extracted from data.

Data Mining Techniques and Applications

Data mining is of interest to researchers in the fields of artificial intelligence, statistics, machine learning, knowledge acquisition, pattern recognition, databases, and information retrieval. Much of the techniques are issued from these fields, and include, but are not limited to, markov process, classification tree, association rule, neural networks, genetic algorithms, sequence analysis, clustering techniques (Wu, 2009; Singhal, 2006).

Different taxonomies are proposed on the literature. A number of researchers classify data mining techniques according to two categories: supervised learning and unsupervised learning methods (Maimon, 2011). Others classify these techniques according to the kind of the required analysis. These tasks are commonly defined as follows (Padhy, 2012):

- **Class Description:** Provides concise and succinct summarization of a collection of data and distinguishes it from others.
- **Classification:** Analyzes a set of training data and constructs a model for each class based on the features in the data. Then, the new data are mapped into one of the several predefined categorical classes. Examples of techniques include: decision tree, neural networks, Bayesian classification, support vector machines, etc.

- **Clustering:** Identifies clusters embedded in the data using automatic techniques and does not require a learning set in advance. A cluster is defined as a collection of data objects that are discovered by natural groupings of data items based on similarity metrics or probability density models. A good clustering method produces high quality clusters. Examples of techniques include: partitioning methods, grid-based methods, model-based methods, hierarchical agglomerative methods, etc.
- **Association:** The discovery of association relationships or correlations among a set of items. They are often expressed in the rule form showing attribute-value conditions. Examples of techniques include: a priori search, mining multiple level, constraint based mining, mining correlations, mining associations for numerical, etc.
- **Prediction:** Predicts the possible values of some missing data or the value distribution of certain attributes in a set of objects. The core objective of this class of techniques is to discover the different kind of relationships between variables: dependent and/or independent variables. Examples of techniques include: regression analysis, generalized linear model, genetic algorithms, neural networks, etc.
- **Time Series (or Sequence) Analysis:** Analyzes large set of time series data to find certain regularities and interesting characteristics. The goal is to model the states of the process generating the sequence or to extract and report deviation and trends over time. Examples of techniques include: search for similar sequences or subsequences, mining sequential patterns, periodicities, trends and deviations, etc.

Different models, based on data mining techniques, have been developed and succeeded to resolve issues in several fields (Padhy, 2012; Bhatnagar, 2014). The following domains present some samples where data mining has important implications and proves its efficiency in managing, analyzing and making appropriate decisions.

- **Healthcare:** The application of data mining to this area has arisen for several years. It was first applied to help practitioners and physicians to reduce possible errors when diagnosing diseases. Different works have been developed using specifically predictive data mining techniques as it is described in (Mousavirad, 2014). This work analyzes and compares various predictive data mining techniques for the medical diagnosis, such as decision trees, neural networks, support vector machine, and lazy modeling. In (Tomar, 2013), a survey on data mining approaches is stated. The paper also shows the utility of different techniques in health domain. It is noted that descriptive techniques are associated with predictive ones to provide better results (e.g. using association rules with classification techniques to enhance the analysis capability). Furthermore, the work described in (Kharya, 2012) underlines the effectiveness of applying data mining techniques to detect several kinds of tumor, like cancer disease. The presented paper focuses mainly on classification techniques that can be used for breast cancer prognosis and diagnosis.

- **Banking and Finance:** Data mining techniques solve important issues in these fields since credit industry faces a noticeable growth and an increase of consumers' credit data number. It is noted that the most applied techniques are those that belong to classification, where a credit analysis is considered as a pattern classification task that involves the estimation of credit application's reliability and profitability. Therefore, the support vector machine is approved to be the best technique for the credit risk evaluation problem and is the widely used technique. Whereas, for credit scoring problem, developed models describe the use of classification methods and even provide comparison of their related performance. These techniques include neural networks, decision trees, bayesian networks methods, etc. (Koh, 2006; Yeh, 2009; Carvalho, 2009). The data mining techniques prove their efficiency to help credit providers quantify and manage the financial risk involved in providing credit by performing careful analysis and thus making better decisions.
- **Marketing:** Data mining techniques are applied according to the kind of the required objectives/tasks to achieve, i.e. customer profiling and retention, identifying potential customers, market segmentation, customer relationship management. In Berry et al. book (2004), a review of different data mining techniques applied to marketing, sales, and customer relationship management is presented. In fact, among these techniques, predictive methods are used for example to forecast future behavior of customers and to locate people who will be valuable customers in the future. They could be also applied to determine the different alternatives to perform for each market situation in case of emergency problem. For customer segmentation, classification methods and clustering techniques are used. The former are applied to perform a segmentation of the customer to preliminary defined segments, whereas the later are adopted to identify patterns (customers) in the data that correspond to the new segments. These latter are built with respect to a marketing goal (Berry, 2004).
- **Fraud Detection:** It is related to any illegal activities performed to damage system resources (i.e. hardware, software, physical access, and data). In this case, the employed techniques aim to avoid, detect, or even response to these actions. For instance, the works described in (Kirkos, 2007; Gupta, 2012) aim to detect and prevent fraudulent financial statements. The former examines the usefulness of data mining classification techniques (decision trees, neural

networks, and bayesian networks) to identify and estimate the likelihood of fraudulent statements of various fields, based on financial factors. The latter proposes a data mining framework that prevents and detects fraudulent financial statements. The framework implements five stages process to manage financial data, detect fraud by using predictive data mining technique (classification), and perform prevention via descriptive data mining (association rules). Another example that deals with computer system security is the intrusion detection systems. In fact, many works are conducted from decade using all kinds of data mining techniques. The works of (Kalarani, 2014; Patond, 2014; Ruth, 2014) are samples of reviews that describe the usage of these techniques to perform and enhance intrusion detection. Further details are cited in the following sections.

In this chapter, the reviewed data mining approaches and models are directed towards crime investigation and intrusion detection. Moreover, the significance of their application to resolve the identified issues, consisted in handling and managing huge amounts of data, is examined.

DATA MINING APPROACHES FOR FORENSIC CONDUCTING

As highlighted previously, investigation is a significant process to perform in order to detect, track, and respond to attacks. These tasks are critical since they have great impacts on the system security. In addition, information systems are increasingly facing new attacks as they are hosted in dynamic, complex, and uncertain environment. Thus, the used techniques should consider this issue and provide accurate investigation.

In this section, a review of the data mining techniques and analytics for conducting investigation process is presented. The usefulness of these approaches is also examined in supporting the law enforcement and security agencies to better conduct crime investigation.

Data Mining Techniques

The use of data mining techniques to crime investigation show that basic works are directed to matching crimes through applying combination of techniques.

In Keyvanpour et al.'s paper (2011), a general crime matching framework to detect and investigate crime is developed (Keyvanpour, 2011). This framework is based on the application of data mining techniques and consists of three main components: entity extraction, crime data clustering, and crime matching components.

The proposed model exploited the capabilities of data mining techniques especially for clustering and classifying crime data through using SOM (Self-Organizing Map) and MLP (Multi-Layer Perceptron) neural networks methods. The resulted knowledge gained from data mining techniques represents a help and support for police forces.

In the same way, Tseng et al. (2012) presented a term-relationship mining method for crime investigation to explore and build a general term network based on the term similarity (Tseng, 2012). The developed method investigates the huge crime news or official criminal records and proposed an evidence-based relation exploration for the term network. The resulted network serves as a knowledge model that helps to mine, link, and aggregate pieces of information from individual documents and then reveals the knowledge that is implicit in the relation path.

Another approach, described in Sindhu et al.'s work (2012), aims to minimize the system vulnerability through designing a system that performs crime investigation using data mining techniques. The system discovers pattern of cyber attacks and determines the number of attacks types happened during a period (Sindhu, 2012). The proposed model collects evidence from system resources than apply a crime data mining algorithm to identify attack patterns. This latter is based on association rules to determine relationships between collected items such as the maximum frequent item sets, finding signs of evidences correlation, contingences.

Data Mining Analytics for Investigation

In the last decades, a number of models were developed to support cyber-crime investigation based on applying intelligent analysis methods, such as neural networks, supervised and unsupervised learning methods, bayesian networks, and genetic algorithms (Oatley, 2004; Adderley, 2007; Gayathri, 2013). A significant project, named COPLINK, was also developed to perform complex crime analysis based on data mining and artificial intelligence (Chen,2003; Hauck, 2002; Garfinkel, 2012). It deals with preprocessing and gathering data and then extracting patterns out of large volumes of crime data by applying classification and clustering methods.

The effective investigation of crime is also examined in research by enhancing cyber security measures. A number of works have been proposed in this context dealing with different data mining techniques. In fact, to reduce crime incidences in the police stations jurisdiction, Renushe et al. (2012) design proactive services based on using data mining tools, called Clementine (Renushe, 2012). This latter includes a number of machine learning and modeling tools grouped according to the types of problems they are intended to solve. Clementine tool allows also facilities to manipulate, display and visualize the data.

In the same context, Nath (2006) presented a data mining framework based on clustering technique and used along with a geo-spatial plot of crime (Nath, 2006). The used technique succeeded to discover and classify crime patterns based on the identified attributes for the different crimes types. The resulted patterns are then plotted on the geo-spatial plot and a detailed description of each pattern is provided illustrating the total number of crimes incidents including in each group with the significant attributes that characterize the group. The developed framework formulates crime patterns detection as a machine learning task that improves and supports detectives and law enforcement officers to identify and solve crimes.

The next sub-section shows the significance of applying data mining techniques to help and support law enforcement and policy agencies.

Data Mining Techniques for Law Enforcement

The adoption of data mining techniques by the investigation process allows the enhancement of the analysis and the detection of (cyber) attacks and contributes to improved cyber security practices. In fact, various approaches are developed to help security agencies when conducting crime investigation.

Nigerian researchers have focused on getting active solutions on crime investigation. The work of Uddin (2014) highlights the significance of data mining techniques to help security authority in analyzing large volume of data and in providing automatic timely solution prevention, arrest, and investigation of crimes (Uddin, 2014).

In the same line of research, Yamuna et al. (Yamuna, 2012), Krishnamurthy et al. (Krishnamurthy, 2012), and Bharathi et al. (Bharathi, 2014) show the importance of data mining techniques in the context of law enforcement and intelligence analysis. The proposed approaches model and alleviate the crime detection problems by discovering useful information necessary for matching crimes. Then, they classify that information into crime groups and anticipate their trends to help the police system catching intruders.

Memon et al. (2005) proposed an Investigative Data Mining (IDM) approach to counter terrorism and organized crime using semantic link analysis and visualization of findings (Memon, 2005). The developed IDM allows the discovering of hidden instances of patterns of interest related for example to organized crime activity. It performs advanced filtering and mining in information streams and intelligence, and finds the relationships between individuals and organizations. Furthermore, the described approach supported the law enforcement agencies by destabilizing the terrorist network.

Recent works (Varghese, 2010; Dhakshinamoorthy, 2013; Jani, 2014) show that clustering techniques represent the most used data mining techniques for crimes patterns detection since they could deal with enormous amounts of data and with noisy or missing data about the crime incidents. The different works stress on the benefits of applying such technique to help security and criminal investigators identify and solve the crime faster and easier.

DATA MINING TECHNIQUES FOR EVIDENCE COLLECTION

This section examines the application of data mining techniques for intrusion detection to observe and analyze the network data in order to collect evidences related to the performed attack. First, a presentation of data mining techniques objectives and their classification in intrusion detection are described. Then, a number of developed intrusion detection models based on data mining techniques are examined.

Data Mining Techniques for Intrusion Detection

Data mining techniques are performed in intrusion detection to achieve different aims, such as description, classification, clustering, association, prediction, and time-series analysis. Moreover, they could enhance the performance of existing systems for various functions, including analysis of massive stream of data, the visualization and querying tools, association, correlation, and discriminative pattern analysis (Sitaram, 2013).

The choice of the technique to be used depends on the type of the analysis to perform, i.e. misuse or anomaly detections, since the functioning and the required parameters for these approaches are different. In fact, misuse detection is based on known attacks signatures, where it analyzes system activity and audit data stream to look for (sets of) events that have a perfect matching with a predefined pattern of events that describe a known attack; whereas anomaly detection approach deals with establishing profiles for normal behavior of a system and any action that significantly deviates from this profile is considered intrusive. The main benefit from using data mining is related to the discovery and the extraction of useful and interesting patterns from huge amount of data.

The developed researches for intrusion detection based on data mining techniques make different taxonomies for those techniques, some are based on learning approaches (supervised and unsupervised) and others categorized them into a number of classes that detect both known and unknown attacks (classification, clustering, association rules, etc.) (Youssef, 2011; Sitaram, 2013; Singh, 2014). Furthermore, several models have been developed considering issues regarding enhancing the performance of the intrusion detection system (Kumar, 1995; Lee, 2001; Helmer, 2002; Dickerson, 2000; Honig, 2002).

Data Mining Models for Intrusion Detection

The developed work described in (Dokas,2002) shows the successful use of data mining techniques to automatically identify several novel unknown types of intrusions that could not be detected using traditional tools (such as SNORT). The proposed model, named MINDS for Minnesota Intrusion Detection System, implements an anomaly detection approach based on classification algorithms that build predictive models for learning from rare classes. The presented model also performs association pattern analysis that is used to summarize and characterize anomalous network connections.

The work of Nadiammai et al. (2014) portrayed an intrusion detection system (IDS) that integrates data mining techniques to detect anomalies and attacks in the network (Nadiammai, 2014). The proposed model is based on a decision tree algorithm that classifies data using hybrid PSO and C4.5 techniques. The efficiency of this approach has been proved since it shows better accuracy and reduced false alarm rate compared to other existing algorithms.

In Oh et al. (2009), an anomaly detection approach based on unsupervised learning technique, SOM (Self-Organizing Map), to detect intrusion for medical sensor network is presented (Oh, 2009). The proposed system created firstly a map based on the preprocessed and normalized data using SOM. Then, it classified them into clusters based on the traffic feature correlations. And finally, real-time detection is performed and the system is trained to be adapted to new data. The developed model succeeded to reach reasonable misclassification rates through several experiments with KDD Cup 1999 data set.

Another useful IDS is proposed in (Sitaram, 2013). The developed system handles a high volume and velocity network traffic as input and is based on clustering techniques. These techniques are used as a learning approach to train the IDS, using a subset of the streamed data, to further detect anomalous behavior. Furthermore, the authors intend to develop a novel intrusion detection model that should capture, inspect, and analyze huge data using big data analytics technologies, like Hadoop, in addition to clustering algorithm and machine learning techniques. The envisaged model will be able to be performed in an evolving environment where the traffic volumes are very high, the enterprise boundaries are blurred, and the likelihood of malicious attacks is extremely high.

CASE STUDIES

This section discusses the use of data mining techniques to determine attack scenarios in medical and crime investigations.

Case 1: Medical Investigation

This case deals with the description of digital investigation of security attacks on cardiac Implantable Medical Devices (IMD)[1] that has been detailed in (Ellouze, 2014), since they are subject to a set of lethal attacks, which may cause death, due to lacks of 1) communications protocols and 2) used security mechanisms deployed on these devices.

The model describes a system for postmortem analysis of lethal attack scenarios targeting cardiac IMDs. It aims to automatically identify and reconstruct potential attack scenarios, by first collecting evidences from IMDs, and then proving the causality between the death of a patient carrying an IMD and an identified potential attack scenario on such implanted device. To perform such investigation, the proposed model implements an inference system and a formal technique for model checking. The former comprises a set of inference rules describing causal relations between the different types of arrhythmia and IMD reactions. They are used to automatically infer potential medical scenarios that could have led to the death of a patient through examining a set of medical rules. These rules are stored in a library that is detailed in (Ellouze, 2014). A medical rule has the following expression: $\left(Ev\right)^n \rightarrow_T \left(Ev'\right)^m$ where *n* and *m* are positive non-zero integers. This rule means that the occurrence of *Ev* for *n* times successively leads to the occurrence of *Ev' m* times successively within a period of time *T*. An example of rules, $ST, IR \rightarrow_T ST$, defined in the library, states that the occurrence of a Sinus-Tachycardia (*ST*), followed by an inappropriate response (*IR*) of the IMD, leads to the occurrence of another episode of *ST*, within the following period of time of length *T*.

The formal technique for model checking allows the reconstruction of potential technical attack scenarios on the IMD after collecting required evidences based on an investigation library. This library includes a description of all simple attacks on IMDs and the actions executed by the IMD in response to remote users' actions or detected arrhythmia. A correlation is then conducted between the results obtained by the two techniques to prove whether a potential attack scenario is the source of the patient's death. The developed system reconciles conclusions derived by technical investigators and deductions generated by pathologists.

Despite the efficiency of the proposed model, it is noted that it requires a minimum of expertise due to the use of formal approaches. To overcome this shortcoming, the use of data mining tools seem to be more appropriate to conduct such investigation thanks to its capabilities to provide more comprehensible and visualized results than formal tools. In fact, the use of data mining techniques for investigation of security attacks targets critical environments. In this case, Figure 2 shows the use of data mining techniques for the investigation of lethal attacks targeting IMD.

Figure 2. Investigation process using DM for attacks targeting IMD

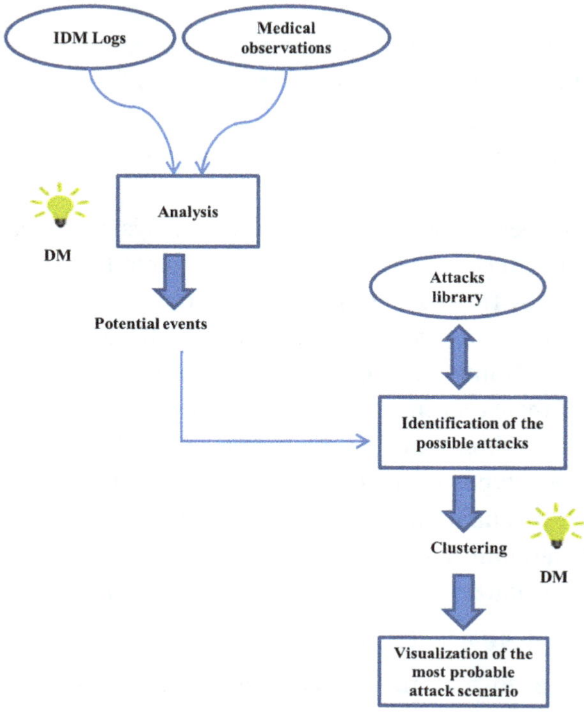

According to the described investigation process, the first step consists in the collection of evidences which includes the set of access and system log files that hold sensitive actions related to access and configuration. In addition, the evidences are collected by the IMD, from the medical observations which includes, for example, the patient's electromyogram (EMG) recorded by the IMD over a period of time before death and set of clinical observations collected during autopsy, among others.

In order to perform the investigation, an inference system defining a set of medical rules is needed to identify the potential medical scenarios that may lead to the death of the victim carrying an IMD. These scenarios are determined through a backward execution of these rules. At this level, a data mining technique is applied to extract the events related to the performed attack leading to the patient's death. The extraction of events may be performed using a keyword-based fetching technique that analyzes the stored logs and checks the occurrence of a set of keywords characterizing the performed malicious activity. After identifying the set of potential events, the next step aims to identify the potential attacks, which is performed in a forward chaining and based on the library of attacks used to support the reconstruction. A set of missing events are identified and added to the events that are collected in the previous step by conducting a correlation based on several techniques such as the similarity based approaches, the input/output dependencies, etc. Another data mining techniques that may allow the prediction of missing events such as genetic algorithms, neural networks, etc. A clustering approach is then applied to order events and to determine the different possible attack scenarios. This technique allows the identification of new attack scenarios and could deal with huge set of data. The last step of this process ensures the selection and visualization of the most probable attack scenario among the set of predetermined ones using for example statistical techniques.

According to the aforementioned steps, a set of medical and technical evidences are collected from the IMD, including session opening further to a successful authentication, modification of therapy settings, and session closing. A set of events that are related to important arrhythmia and IMD responses, are identified such as six successive episodes of *ST* where each one of them is immediately followed by a delivery of a therapy suitable for *VF*, several episodes of *VF* whose intensity grew from an episode to another, and heart death. Applying the presented data mining techniques, different attack scenarios are generated based on the possible attacks and the defined inference system. Finally, the most probable attack scenario is selected.

Case 2: Crime Investigation

The proposed case study examines the modeling of crime scenarios in a Bayesian network based on narrative and probabilistic reasoning (Vlek, 2013). The established model handles evidences and shows the interaction of the variables in a case via numerical computations. It does not intend to make a decision, it is rather considered as a mean to advise and assist a judge or jury in making the decision through observing and determining insights into the variables connections of the considered network.

The proposed Bayesian network design follows a four-steps process. First, relevant scenarios and supported guilty hypothesis are identified. Next, each scenario is represented through a set of nodes, characterizing states and events. These latter are connected to describe the different followed crime sequences. After that, a Bayesian network is built through merging the different established scenarios. In this context, additional nodes could be added to the network to avoid overlapping and conflicting states/events. Finally, a set of evidences is added to extend the structure of the Bayesian network.

The accuracy of the proposed model is tested through a real case concerning a burglary in which a number of items were stolen, two suspects were identified and several evidences were collected from the crime scene (the case is registered as JLN BO 4007 and detailed in (Vlek, 2013)). In this context, the design method is applied to construct a Bayesian network that describes this burglary case. In the first step of the design process and from the examined events and the collected evidences from the crime scene, four possible scenarios are identified as well as the hypotheses they support. These scenarios are detailed thoroughly based on the interpretation of the presented case.

For each scenario, a description of the potential states/events and their relationships are then illustrated through using a Bayesian network. The structure includes a set of nodes depicting scenario node, hypotheses, states/events and constraint nodes. In addition, probability tables for all states/events in the identified scenarios are expressed to evaluate their degree of involvement into their related scenarios. The next step allows the merge of the different scenarios into a single network while respecting the hypotheses and the events sequences. The resulted network structure could show the addition of a number of constraints nodes to express the mutually exclusive relation between states/events. Moreover, some nodes could be merged into a single node if they appear in different scenarios, and therefore the nodes connections are updated accordingly. Finally, the collected evidences are integrated into the network to extend the Bayesian network structure and to add more strengthens and clarification to the different crime scenarios.

The presented Bayesian network could be adapted and extended as new scenarios or evidences are turned up since they have an effect on the probability of the other nodes of the network. In addition, the designed Bayesian network prevents tunnel vision among investigators or judges as it presents a comparative view of the various modeled scenarios and evaluates the most probable one. Thus, the use of this data mining technique, Bayesian network, is appropriate to model the crime scenarios during the crime investigation process.

DATA MINING TRENDS FOR ATTACKS USING BIG DATA

Several challenges are identified when dealing with big data, including the detection and the tracing back of the attack if the information system is flooded by real time data. It is noted that the managing of the huge volume of data, named also big data, could affect the efficiency of the existing analysis components and could lead to high false alarms. Therefore, it is necessary to cope with these issues and integrate new functionalities to perform efficient attack detection and identification.

This section examines the application of data mining techniques in analyzing attacks through the related collected massive data and describes the developed models that deal with it.

Big Data Analytics Framework for Peer-to-Peer Botnet Detection

The arising attacks are usually originated from multiple nodes at a lower speed, such as the Peer-to-Peer Botnets. Machine learning is among the techniques used to detect such kind of attacks. In (Singh, 2014), a distributed framework using Hive for sniffing and handling network traces, in order to extract dynamic network features, is introduced. Moreover, the parallel processing powers of Mahout are exploited to generate a random forest based decision tree model which is applied to the Peer-to-Peer Botnet detection. The proposed framework is composed of the following components:

1. Traffic sniffer module for pre-processing packets,
2. Feature extraction module for generating features set, and
3. Machine learning module for learning and detecting the malicious traffic.

The decision tree presents some drawbacks related to the low prediction accuracy when compared to other machine learning algorithms. This limitation is resolved using ensembles of trees (Dietterich, 2002). Furthermore, low frequency communications are difficult in most cases to be detected since the majority of IDS systems generate alerts only if some thresholds are exceeded.

Using an Adaptive Detection Approach for Big Network Traffic

In (Zhang, 2014), a novel technique, called Adaptive Stream Projected Outlier detector (A-SPOT), has been proposed to detect anomalies from big data streams collected through networking environments. This technique generates Sparse Subspace Template (SST) representing a set of subspaces that are considered as a location where anomalies may be detected with high probability. The identification of these subspaces is performed based on the use of multiple criteria, called Projected Cell Summaries (PCS). The SST is composed of three groups of subspaces: Fixed SST Subspaces (FS), Unsupervised SST Subspaces (US) and Supervised SST Subspaces (SS). FS is a compulsory component of SST while US and SS are optional.

Furthermore, three effective measures are used to represent the overall data sparsity of each projected cell from different perspectives. These measures are Relative Density (RD), Inverse Relative Standard Deviation (IRSD), and Inverse k-Relative Distance (IkRD). These measures are used together in A-SPOT to obtain a good measurement of data outlierness. This latter (A-SPOT) is performed according to two stages: the learning and detection stages. The learning stage uses either the unlabeled training data, such as stored historic data, and/or the labeled anomaly examples provided by domain experts to generate SST subspaces. During the detection stage, A-SPOT performs anomaly detection for continuously incoming network data and assigns labels to anomalies that indicate their anomaly class membership.

The proposed approach proves its efficiency in large and high-dimensional network data streams. It allows the detection of anomalies subspaces and produces a significantly lower level of false positives than the existing anomaly detection methods.

Hybrid Data Mining Approach for the Assessment of Phishing Attacks

The number of reported phishing incidents grew exponentially these last days. It is among the major security threats that aim to collect the personal information and financial credentials for online consumers. The assessment of the severity of phishing attacks in terms of their risk levels and the potential loss in market values is among the studied issues by the research communities. Moreover, data mining techniques are among the tools that can improve the assessment of such kind of attacks.

In (Chen, 2011), a hybrid approach is detailed. It enables the collection, the preparation and the analysis of alerts to assess the severity of phishing attacks in addition to the identification of important antecedents that influence the classification. Several approaches are used to classify the risk levels including: the neural network (NN), decision tree (DT) and support vector machine (SVM). The NN is efficient at learning non-linear relationships between input data and output data. Using SVM, the classification is performed by constructing a hyperplane that maximizes the separation in order to divide the vectors into different classes. Data sets are viewed as vector spaces. The DT ensures a minimum effort for data preprocessing. In order to convert the free text of the phishing alerts to structural data, text mining techniques are used. In this context, the text mining module of the SPSS Clementine is used to extract the key semantic concepts from the phishing alerts.

The proposed approach enables the estimation of the financial loss resulting from phishing attacks. It is based on a hybrid text and data mining model. This latter uses a key phrase extraction technique to discover important semantic categories from the textual content of the phishing alerts. The proposed scheme combines then those discovered categories with financial data of the targeted companies in order to ensure the classification of risk level of the attack and the loss in market value.

Detection of Unknown Attacks Based on the Analysis of Big Data

The detection of recent unknown attacks that can easily bypass existing security solutions by using encryption and obfuscation is among the issues that are handled by the research community. In this context, Suthaharan (2014) proposed a new model based on big data analysis techniques that enable the extraction of information from multiple sources to detect unknown attacks (Suthaharan, 2014). The kind of studied attacks is commonly known as APT (Advanced Persistent Threat) that targets a specific system and analyses vulnerabilities of the system for a long time period.

As mentioned in (White, 2012), it is hard to prevent and detect APT attacks, compared to traditional attacks, which could lead to considerable damage. These attacks use social engineering, zero day vulnerabilities and additional techniques to gain access to the victims and to collect valuable information. Since unknown attacks have not yet a set of known signatures that are available for intrusion detection systems, it is needed to perform an analysis for collected big data in order to extract useful information related to the performed malicious activity.

The big data analysis is performed by focusing on four techniques: prediction, classification, relation rule and atypical data-mining that are useful to detect unknown attacks. The prediction of attacks behaviors may be performed using regressing analysis that can predict similar behaviors from collected attack logs or collected users' activities. Classification predicts the group of new attack from huge data. Relation rule is used to discover hidden relations among data which can help to determine abnormal behavior by analyzing user and process behaviors. The atypical data-mining techniques (e.g. text-mining, web-mining and social-mining) process particular types of data such as pictures, video, audio, etc.

REQUIREMENTS FOR EFFICIENT INVESTIGATION BASED ON DATA MINING

In this section, the different requirements that should be fulfilled to efficiently perform cyber-crime investigation based on data mining analytics are addressed. These requirements are mainly associated to defining attack environment and characteristics for the investigation process on one hand, and the appropriateness and the need of using data mining techniques on the other hand.

Requirements for Investigation Process

The applied techniques within the investigation process should cope with the growing volume of data. In fact, the investigation process should consider the constraints related to the handled big data and by considering the 5V. Based on these constraints, the classical investigation process is not appropriate to reconstruct the attack scenario and should be adapted. For example, the traditional investigation schemes consider the collection of data and evidences before starting the analysis. Since big data may vary through the time, it is needed in this case, to initiate the analysis and ensuring the continuity of the collection phase. Moreover, the great size of the collected data requires the use of extensive processing and storage resources in order to prevent the processing and storage overhead due to the investigation activity. Therefore, performing the investigation process in a distributed manner is among the solutions to fulfill this need.

In addition, the use of heterogeneous devices by intruders is another issue that need a specific attention since they implement various protocols to conduct security attacks. To deal with this feature, a generic investigation technique is required to enable the interaction with these devices during the different steps using a generic interface.

Need of Application of Data Mining Techniques

DM techniques should be adapted to be able to deal with and resolve Big Data issues, such as the increased volume of data and the variety and veracity of data. The reconstruction of the attack scenario requires the collection of the needed evidences from a huge volumes of data. These evidences may be related to different activities performed by the intruder at different locations such as log files stored in public servers, buffer contents for routers located at the provider's level or even stored in mobile devices. As a consequence, it is needed to process these huge volumes of data in order to extract the needed evidences or even to locate the potential data sources that should be considered to collect the information which may enrich the set of needed evidences for the conducted digital investigation process.

In this context, the following example illustrates an attack performed by multiple agents located at remote networks and using several techniques that may change through the time or when a set of conditions are verified (e.g. the target service is filtered by the victim). The performed malicious activity generates huge volumes of data in addition to a set of evidences that may help investigators to reconstruct the attack scenario. The former should be processed in order to extract evidences. As an example, the huge volumes of data include the set of packets that are generated by the malicious agents in the case of a SYN flooding attack or the packets that hold the malicious commands that are executed on the victims (e.g. the command "service syslog stop" that disables the processing of the logging service on a server). These data should be processed in order to extract knowledge that represent the evidences related to the reconstructed attack scenario. The evidences in this case are related to the agent's identities, the performed malicious commands and the attacked services extracted from the collected network traffic that is available at different networks and at the victim. In order to extract such evidences, data mining techniques, based on artificial intelligence and statistical techniques, should be employed.

Securing Data

The efficiency of the investigation process is threatened by the possible attacks that may be performed on the collected data and evidences in relation with the investigated attacks. These attacks aim in most cases to alter evidences for example by spoofing the intruder's IP address or by removing the log entries related to the performed malicious activity and that may be available at different locations (servers, routers, firewalls, etc.). In order to prevent the realization of such threats, it is required that a set of security mechanisms are implemented to ensure the major security services. The confidentiality is the most important security service to be ensured in this case to prevent the sniffing of the related attack data that can be in next step modified by the intruder to prevent the reconstruction of the attack scenario or to generate an erroneous scenario. Facing this threat, a set of security mechanisms including the digital signature should be implemented to ensure the integrity for the exchanged forensic data. This security service should be also ensured for the stored data and evidences that are available for investigators and needed for investigation applications. Moreover, the authenticity should be verified either for the investigators that process the collected forensic data or even for the used modules that interact during the different investigation steps to prevent an intruder or malicious module to interfere within this critical process. The physical security of investigation frameworks should also be deployed to prevent a set of physical attacks from happening, such as: unauthorized physical access to the processing units and storage devices used to hold evidences and collected data.

FUTURE RESEARCH DIRECTIONS

This section presents a number of future research directions related to cyber-crime investigation. It also examines new trends of data mining techniques dealing with big data to detect attack.

The major challenge to digital investigation is the increasing growth of the volume and the diversity of the data that should be analyzed in addition to the nature of the storage environments used to store related attack data, such as public cloud storage systems. As consequence, several issues still be studied related to the enhancement of data mining techniques, the data reduction, the reducing of the processing overhead by reinforcing distributed processing, etc.

According to Quick et al. (2014), there are many issues that should be well investigated such as the study of the enhancements that are required to apply data mining to forensic datasets (Quick, 2014). At this level, there is a need to develop novel data mining techniques that are well adapted to the big data based attack constraints. Moreover, the decision made during the investigation process is usually affected by the accuracy of the extracted knowledge from the conducted analysis process. As a consequence, the validation of the generated evidences is among the issues that should be studied in the future in order to ensure that the evidences are accurate and therefore the investigation process is efficient.

The data reduction is a preliminary step that precedes data mining. This step should be well investigated since it prevents the loss of valuable data needed during the investigation process. The adopted strategy should be performed in a dynamic manner by considering the nature of handled data in addition to the activity/the service that generates the huge volume of data to be investigated.

Another issue needing deep investigation is the heterogeneity of devices generating different format of data to be investigated. These data could not be analyzed by some investigation frameworks that do not support such format, such as system files related to mobile devices. In this case, it is needed to provide a common format that may be used as repository for heterogeneous processed data. A work has been conducted by Garfinkel (2012) in this context, where a digital forensic XML method is proposed to store common forensic information as a generic data store for a range of tools, enabling parsed data to be stored in a common format (Garfinkel, 2012).

File carvers are among the tools that are used to recover deleted files but they are unable to find overwritten files as well as temporarily cached files. This feature is available for attacks using big data and that overwrites frequently such kind of data. As a consequence, it is needed to analyze carving techniques and propose novel approaches to support big data constraints that prevent current carving techniques to be used.

Moreover, imaging is among the first technique used in digital investigation in order to image, or copy the media to be examined. Due to the evolution of storing devices and the great increase in the size of images, it is required to use cloud infrastructures to perform storage and processing of such images while considering the integrity and the confidentiality of their contents. Therefore, storing and securing images in such environments are among the issues that should be well investigated.

CONCLUSION

The management of dynamic environment and the increasing amounts of data represent huge challenges to resolve in order to efficiently deal with the accurate data for further analysis. The deployment of data mining analytics has proved its usefulness and have been widely used for different types of applications in several areas. It is noted that these techniques are widely applied in intrusion detection and proved promising results in crime investigation and law enforcement. However, remaining issues, related mainly to the kind and size of data, should be considered and resolved to provide efficient outcomes. Based on the current constraints related to the handled data, several research projects are being conducted to provide efficient investigation techniques that are able to deal with big data features within the support of enhanced data mining techniques.

This chapter reviews the usability and efficiency of data mining analytics. It details the investigation of security attacks and describes a set of applications that deal with it. In addition, the chapter focuses on the significance of data mining approaches in enhancing evidence detection and law enforcement and examines the requirements and future directions for efficient investigation based on data mining.

REFERENCES

Adderley, R. W. (2007). *The use of data mining techniques in crime trend analysis and offender profiling*. (Unpublished doctoral dissertation). University of Wolverhampton.

Berry, M. J. A., & Linoff, G. S. (2004, April). *Data Mining Techniques. For Marketing, Sales, and Customer Relationship Management* (2nd ed.). Indianapolis, IN: Wiley Publishing, Inc.

Bharathi, A., & Shilpa, R. (2014, August). A Survey on Crime Data Analysis of Data Mining Using Clustering Techniques. *International Journal of Advance Research in Computer Science and Management Studies*, *2*(8), 9–13.

Bhatnagar, V. (2014). *Data Mining and Analysis in the Engineering Field. Ambedkar Institute of Advanced Communication Technologies and Research*. IGI Global.

Carrier, B. D. (2006). *A hypothesis-based approach to digital forensic investigations*. (Unpublished doctoral dissertation). Purdue University.

Carvalho, A. C. P. L. F., Gama, J. M. P., & Ludermir, T. B. (2009). Credit Risk Assessment and Data Mining. In *Encyclopedia of Information Science and Technology* (pp. 800–805). IGI Global. doi:10.4018/978-1-60566-026-4.ch130

Casey, E. (2011). *Digital Evidence and Computer Crime*. Baltimore, MD: Academic Press.

Chen, H., Atabakhsh, H., Petersen, T., Schroeder, J., Buetow, T., Chaboya, L., & Huang, Z. et al. (2003). COPLINK: Visualization for Crime Analysis. In *Proceedings of the 2003 annual national conference on digital government research* (pp. 1-6). Boston: Digital Government Society of North America.

Chen, H., Chung, W., Qin, Y., Chau, M., Xu, J. J., Wang, G., . . . Atabakhsh, H. (2003). Crime data mining: an overview and case studies. In *Proceedings of the 2003 annual national conference on Digital government research* (dg.o '03). Boston, MA: Digital Government Society of North America.

Chen, X., Bose, I., Leung, A. C. M., & Guo, C. (2011, March). Assessing the severity of phishing attacks: A hybrid data mining approach. *Decision Support Systems, 50*(4), 662–672. doi:10.1016/j.dss.2010.08.020

Cios, K. J., & Kurgan, L. A. (2005). Trends in Data Mining and Knowledge Discovery. In Advanced Techniques in Knowledge Discovery and Data Mining (pp. 1-26). London: Springer-Verlag. doi:10.1007/1-84628-183-0_1

Cios, K. J., Pedrycz, W., Swiniarski, R. W., & Kurgan, L. A. (2007). The Knowledge Discovery Process. In Data Mining- A Knowledge Discovery Approach (pp. 9-24). Springer Science & Business Media. doi:10.1007/978-0-387-36795-8_2

Dhakshinamoorthy, P., & Kalaiselvan, T. (2013, July). Crime Pattern Detection Using Data Mining. *International Journal of Advanced Research in Computer Science and Applications, 1*(1), 46–50.

Dickerson, J. E., & Dickerson, J. A. (2000). Fuzzy network profiling for intrusion detection. In *Proc. of NAFIPS 19th International Conference of the North American Fuzzy Information Processing Society* (pp. 301-306). Atlanta, GA: IEEE.

Dietterich, T. G. (2002, September). Ensemble Learning. In M. A. Arbib (Ed.), *Brain Theory and Neural Networks*. Cambridge, MA: MIT Press.

Dokas, P., Ertoz, L., Kumar, V., Lazarevic, A., Srivastava, J., & Tan, P.-N. (2002, November). Data mining for network intrusion detection. In *Proc. NSF Workshop on Next Generation Data Mining*, (p. 21-30). Baltimore, MD: AAAI/MIT Press.

Ellouze, N., Rekhis, S., Allouche, M., & Boudriga, N. (2014, June). Digital Investigation of Security Attacks on Cardiac Implantable Medical Devices. In *Proceedings of Advanced Intrusion and Prevention Workshop 2014 (AIDP 2014)* (pp. 15–30). doi:10.4204/EPTCS.165.2

Fayyad, U. M., Piatetsky-Shapiro, G., & Smyth, P. (1996). From data mining to knowledge discovery: an overview. In U. M. Fayyad, G. Piatetsky-Shapiro, P. Smyth, & R. Uthurusamy (Eds.), *Advances in Knowledge Discovery and Data Mining* (pp. 1–34). USA: AAAI-Press.

Garfinkel, S. (2012, February). Digital forensics XML and the DFXML toolset. *Digital Investigation, 8*(3-4), 161–174. doi:10.1016/j.diin.2011.11.002

Gayathri, R., & Malathi, A. (2013, November). Investigation of Data Mining Techniques in Fraud Detection: Credit Card. *International Journal of Computers and Applications*, *82*(9), 12–15. doi:10.5120/14143-1560

Gupta, R., & Gill, N. S. (2012, July). A Data Mining Framework for Prevention and Detection of Financial Statement Fraud. *International Journal of Computers and Applications*, *50*(8), 7–14. doi:10.5120/7789-0889

Hauck, R. V., Atabakhsh, H., Ongvasith, P., Gupta, H., & Chen, H. (2002, March). Using Coplink to Analyze Criminal-Justice Data. Computer, 35(3), 30-37.

Helmer, G., Wong, J. S. K., Honavar, V., & Miller, L. (2002, February). Automated discovery of concise predictive rules for intrusion detection. *Journal of Systems and Software*, *60*(3), 165–175. doi:10.1016/S0164-1212(01)00088-7

Honig, A., Howard, A., Eskin, E., & Stolfo, S. (2002). Adaptive model generation: An architecture for the deployment of data mining based intrusion. In Applications of data mining in computer security, (pp. 153-194). Boston: Kluwer.

Jani, V. H. (2014). Survey of Identifying Criminal Pattern using Data Mining Algorithm. *IJIRT*, *1*(7), 5–7.

Kalarani, P., & Brunda, S. S. (2014, September). A Survey on Efficient Data Mining Techniques for Network Intrusion Detection System (IDS). *International Journal of Advanced Research in Computer and Communication Engineering*, *3*(9), 8028–8031.

Keyvanpour, M. R., Javideh, M., & Ebrahimi, M. R. (2011). Detecting and investigating crime by means of data mining: A general crime matching framework. *Procedia Computer Science*, *3*, 872–880. doi:10.1016/j.procs.2010.12.143

Kharya, S. (2012, April). Using data mining techniques for diagnosis and prognosis of cancer disease. *International Journal of Computer Science Engineering and Information Technology*, *2*(2), 55–66.

Kirkos, E., Spathis, C., & Manolopoulos, Y. (2007, May). Data Mining techniques for the detection of fraudulent financial statements. *An International Journal Expert Systems with Applications*, *32*(4), 995–1003. doi:10.1016/j.eswa.2006.02.016

Koh, H. C., Tan, W. C., & Goh, C. P. (2006). Two-step Method to Construct Credit Scoring Models with Data Mining Techniques. *International Journal of Business and Information*, *1*(1), 96–118.

Krishnamurthy, R., & Kumar, J. S. (2012, August). Survey of Data Mining Techniques on Crime Data Analysis. *International Journal of Data Mining Techniques and Applications*, *1*(2), 117–120.

Kumar, S. (1995). *Classification and Detection of Computer Intrusion.* West Lafayette, IN: Purdue Univ.

Kumar, V., Oikonomou, G., Tryfonas, T., Page, D., & Phillips, I. (2014). Digital investigations for IPv6-based Wireless Sensor Networks. *Digital Investigation, 11*, S66–S75.

Lee, W., & Xiang, D. (2001). Information-theoretic measures for anomaly detection. *InProc. of the 2001 IEEE Symp. on Security and Privacy* (pp. 130-143). Oakland, CA: IEEE Computer Society Press.

Maimon, O., & Rokach, L. (2010). Introduction to Knowledge Discovery and Data Mining. In O. Maimon & L. Rokach (Eds.), *Data Mining and Knowledge Discovery Handbook* (pp. 1–15). Springer. doi:10.1007/978-0-387-09823-4

McKemmish, R. (1999, June). What is Forensic Computing?. *Australian Institute of Criminology trends and issues in crime and criminal justice, 118*, 1-6.

Memon, N., & Qureshi, A. R. (2005, September). Investigative Data Mining and its Application in Counterterrorism. In *Proceedings of the 5th WSEAS Int. Conf. on Applied Informatics and Communications*, (pp. 397-403).

Mousavirad, S. J., & Ebrahimpour-Komleh, H. (2014). A Comparative Study on Medical Diagnosis Using Predictive Data Mining: A Case Study. In Data Mining and Analysis in the Engineering Field (pp. 327-360). IGI Global. doi:10.4018/978-1-4666-6086-1.ch017

Nadiammai, G. V., & Hemalatha, M. (2014). Effective approach toward Intrusion Dection System using data mining techniques. *Egyptian Informatics Journal, 15*(1), 37–50. doi:10.1016/j.eij.2013.10.003

Nath, S. V. (2006, December). Crime Pattern Detection Using Data Mining.*2006 IEEE/WIC/ACM International Conference on Web Intelligence and Intelligent Agent Technology Workshops, 2006. WI-IAT 2006 Workshops.*, (pp. 41 - 44). Hong Kong: IEEE. doi:10.1109/WI-IATW.2006.55

Oatley, G. C., Zeleznikow, J., & Ewart, B. W. (2004). Matching and Predicting Crimes. In R. E. Ann Macintosh (Ed.), *Proceedings of the Twenty-fourth SGAI International Conference on Knowledge Based Systems and Applications of Artificial Intelligence (AI2004)* (pp. 19-32). London: Springer.

Oh, H., Doh, I., & Chae, K. (2009). Attack Classification Based on Data Mining Technique and its Application for Reliable Medical Sensor Communication. *International Journal of Computer Science and Applications*, *6*(3), 20–32.

Padhy, N., Mishra, P., & Panigrahi, R. (2012, June). The Survey of Data Mining Applications and Feature Scope. *International Journal of Computer Science Engineering and Information Technology*, *2*(3), 43–58.

Patond, K., & Deshmukh, P. (2014, April). Survey on Data Mining Techniques for Intrusion Detection System. *International Journal of Research Studies in Science Engineering and Technology*, *1*(1), 93–97.

Quick, D., & Choo, K.-K. R. (2014). Impacts of increasing volume of digital forensic data: A survey and future research challenges. *Digital Investigation*, *11*(4), 273–294. doi:10.1016/j.diin.2014.09.002

Rekhis, S., & Boudriga, N. (2012). A Hierarchical Visibility theory for formal digital investigation of anti-forensic attacks. *Computers & Security*, *31*(8), 967–982. doi:10.1016/j.cose.2012.06.009

Renushe, H. N., Rasal, P. R., & Desai, A. S. (2012, May-June). Data Mining Practices for Effective Investigation of Crime. *Int.J. Computer Technology & Applications*, *3*(3), 865–870.

Ruth, D., & Lovelin Ponn Felciah, M. (2014, May). A Survey on Intrusion Detection System with Data Mining Techniques. *International Journal of Innovative Science. Engineering & Technology*, *1*(3), 271–275.

Sindhu, K. K., & Meshram, B. B. (2012). Digital Forensics and Cyber Crime Datamining. *Journal of Information Security*, *3*(3), 196–201. doi:10.4236/jis.2012.33024

Singh, K., Guntuku, S. C., Thakur, A., & Hota, C. (2014, September). Big Data Analytics framework for Peer-to-Peer Botnet detection using Random Forests. *Information Sciences*, *278*, 488–497. doi:10.1016/j.ins.2014.03.066

Singh, N. & Khare, N. (2014, July-August). Efficient Data Mining Techniques to Enhance Intrusion Detection System. *International Journal of Latest Research in Science and Technology, 3*(4), 122-125.

Singhal, A., & Jajodia, S. (2006, September). Data warehousing and data mining techniques for intrusion detection systems. *Journal Distributed and Parallel Databases*, *20*(2), 149–166. doi:10.1007/s10619-006-9496-5

Sitaram, D., Sharma, M., Zain, M., Sastry, A., & Todi, R. (2013, October). Intrusion Detection System for High Volume and High Velocity Packet Streams: A Clustering Approach. *International Journal of Innovation. Management and Technology*, *4*(5), 480–485.

Suthaharan, S. (2014, March-April). Big Data Classification: Problems and Challenges in Network Intrusion Prediction with Machine Learning. SIGMETRICS Perform. Eval. Rev., 41(4), 70-73.

Tomar, D., & Agarwal, S. (2013). A survey on Data Mining approaches for Healthcare. *International Journal of Bio-Science and Bio-Technology*, *5*(5), 241–266. doi:10.14257/ijbsbt.2013.5.5.25

Tseng, Y.-H., Ho, Z.-P., Yang, K.-S., & Chen, C.-C. (2012, September). Mining term networks from text collections for crime investigation. *Expert Systems with Applications*, *39*(11), 10082–10090. doi:10.1016/j.eswa.2012.02.052

Uddin, O. O., & Uddin, P. S. O. (2014, March). Data Mining: An Active Solution for Crime Investigation. *International Journal of Computer Science and Technology*, *5*(1), 28–32.

Varghese, B. M., Unnikrishnan, A., Jacob, P., & Jacob, J. (2010, December). Correlation Clustering Model for Crime Pattern Detection. *International Journal of Advancements in Computing Technology*, *2*(5), 125–128. doi:10.4156/ijact.vol2.issue5.14

Vlek, C., Prakken, H., Renooij, S., & Verheij, B. (2013, June). Modeling crime scenarios in a Bayesian network. In *Proceedings of the Fourteenth International Conference on Artificial Intelligence and Law (ICAIL'13)* (pp. 150–159). New York: ACM. doi:10.1145/2514601.2514618

White, T. (2012). *Hadoop - The Definitive Guide* (3rd ed.). O'Reilly Media / Yahoo Press.

Wu, S.-Y., & Yen, E. (2009, April). Data mining-based intrusion detectors. *Expert Systems with Applications*, *36*(3), 5605–5612. doi:10.1016/j.eswa.2008.06.138

Yamuna, S., & Bhuvaneswari, N. S. (2012). Datamining Techniques to Analyze and Predict Crimes.[IJES]. *International Journal of Engineering Science*, *1*(2), 243–247.

Yeh, I.-C., & Lien, C.-H. (2009, March). The comparisons of data mining techniques for the predictive accuracy of probability of default of credit card clients. *An International Journal Expert Systems with Applications*, *36*(2), 2473–2480. doi:10.1016/j.eswa.2007.12.020

Youssef, A., & Emam, A. (2011, December). Network Intrusion Detection Using Data Mining and Network Behaviour Analysis.[IJCSIT]. *International Journal of Computer Science & Information Technology*, *3*(6), 87–98. doi:10.5121/ijcsit.2011.3607

Zhang, J., Li, H., Gao, Q., Wang, H., & Luo, Y. (2014, October). Detecting anomalies from big network traffic data using an adaptive detection approach. *Information Sciences*, *318*, 91–110. doi:10.1016/j.ins.2014.07.044

ADDITIONAL READING

Carrier, B. D., & Spafford, E. H. (2004, August). An Event-based Digital Forensic Investigation framework. *InProceedings of the 2004 Digital Forensic Research Workshop* (pp. 1-12). Baltimore, Maryland: CERIAS, Purdue University.

Islam, S., Aziz, B., & Blackwell, C. (2013, April). A Framework for Digital Forensics and Investigations: The Goal-Driven Approach. *International Journal of Digital Crime and Forensics*, *5*(2), 1–22. doi:10.4018/jdcf.2013040101

Meena, D., & Gupta, H. (2013, April). Digital Crime Investigation using Various Logs and Fuzzy Rules: A Review. *International Journal of Advanced Research in Computer and Communication Engineering*, 2(4), 1785–1788.

Nirkhi, S. M., Dharaskar, R. V., & Thakre, V. M. (2012, November). Data mining: A prospective approach for digital forensics. *International Journal of Data Mining & Knowledge Management Process*, 2(6), 41–48. doi:10.5121/ijdkp.2012.2604

KEY TERMS AND DEFINITIONS

Big Data: A general term describing huge volumes of data. It includes heterogeneous kinds of data from structured to unstructured and it is characterized by 5V (Volume, Velocity, Variety, Value and Veracity).

Clustering Techniques: A set of data mining techniques classified as unsupervised learning techniques. This set aims to partition a given set of data objects into meaningful sub-classes, called clusters, such that similar objects are grouped into a cluster and dissimilar objects are grouped into other clusters.

Crime: A set of actions that describe an offense, serious wrongdoing or a sin. They are legally prohibited and the law punishes the person who commits it.

Cyber Security: The set of security activities and measures designed and applied to protect information system resources (i.e. networks, computers, programs, data, etc.) from attack, damage, or unauthorized access or use. This discipline covers application security, information security, network security, disaster recovery / business continuity planning, and end-user education.

Cybercrime: May be defined as malicious activity that engender a damage to information system resources.

Data Mining: A process based on a set of techniques used to explore huge amounts of data, using automated approaches, in order to reveal meaningful and relevant patterns, and/or systematic relationships between variables.

Evidence Collection: Related to the collection of relevant information associated to the occurred security incident. If the collection is well performed, these evidences allow to reconstruct the underlying attack scenario and even identify the intruder.

Forensic Computing: Also named investigation process. It is a process of identifying a crime, surveying it, and performing its analysis by providing related approved evidences.

Intrusion Detection: A process that aims to detect malicious activity performed by intruders having as target computing and networking resources. The detection is performed according to two approaches: misuse detection and anomaly detection. The former is based on known attacks signatures and the latter is based on the detection of deviations from normal behaviors.

Pattern Detection: The discovery of hidden knowledge from large and complex data sets and modeling them for further evaluation. This process could be performed through various methods, such as statistical modeling, clustering, graph theory, advanced mathematics, etc.

Security Attack: A set of interrelated malicious actions performed by one or several actors targeting information system resources.

ENDNOTE

1 A Cardiac Implantable Medical device is a tool implanted surgically into a patient's body to perform medical therapeutic functions. It is configured by an external programmer using wireless communication channel and respecting the prescription of physicians and doctors.

Chapter 9
Automated Identification of Child Abuse in Chat Rooms by Using Data Mining

Mohammadreza Keyvanpour
Alzahra University, Iran

Mohammadreza Ebrahimi
Concordia University, Canada

Necmiye Genc Nayebi
École de Technologie Supérieure (ÉTS), Canada

Olga Ormandjieva
Concordia University, Canada

Ching Y. Suen
Concordia University, Canada

ABSTRACT

Providing a safe environment for juveniles and children in online social networks is considered as one of the major factors of improving public safety. Due to the prevalence of the online conversations, mitigating the undesirable effects of child abuse in cyber space has become inevitable. Using automatic ways to combat this kind of crime is challenging and demands efficient and scalable data mining techniques. The problem can be casted as a combination of textual preprocessing in data/text mining and pattern classification in machine learning. This chapter covers different data mining methods including preprocessing, feature extraction and the popular ways of feature enrichment through extracting sentiments and emotional features. A brief tutorial on classification algorithms in the domain of automated predator identification is also presented through the chapter. Finally, the discussion is summarized and the challenges and open issues in this application domain are discussed.

DOI: 10.4018/978-1-5225-0463-4.ch009

1. INTRODUCTION

The ease of access and anonymity of the Internet users facilitate child exploitation, online bullying and cyber sexual abuse. This has been a major concern in developed countries with a high rate of Internet access in which children are basically the most vulnerable Internet stakeholders. Automated Online Predator Identification (OPI) is a proactive way to counteract the undesirable effects causing by aforementioned crimes. Recently in the literature, this is also known as Sexual Predator Identification (SPI) or Sexual Predator Detection (SPD). Although practical OPI problem involves dealing with textual data and images, textual data are considerably more convenient to be used for automation purposes rather than the imagery data. Accordingly, dealing with textual data is meant throughout the chapter, wherever the OPI is mentioned in general. This part highlights the importance of Online Predator Identification as an effective action toward improving public safety in society. The target audience of this chapter is the researchers working in the area of crime data mining and readers who want to have an overall grasp of the OPI field. In sections 1-1 and 1-2, we present the key concepts about public safety, OPI domain and the domain related aspects, whereas Section 1-3 will provide further information in regards to the relationship between data mining and OPI.

1.1 Public Safety and OPI

The ease of access and anonymity of the Internet users has made child abuse easier than the past. According to Kierkegaard (2008), sexual solicitations of 89% of youth are made in chat rooms. This implies the vital need for mining large volumes of anonymous chat logs in order to combat this kind of social crime. Providing a safe environment for juveniles and children in online social networks is considered as one of the major factors of improving public safety. Due to the prevalence of the online conversations, mitigating the undesirable effects of juvenile abuse in cyber space has become critical.

1.2 Domain Concepts

This part contains the essential information about legal and psychological aspects of online predator identification.

1.2.1 Legal Aspects

Although all of the legislative and regulatory provisions regarding online child sexual abuse aim to combat and mitigate the impact of this threat, they may vary in different countries or even for different jurisdictions in the same country. According to Kierkegaard (2008), while virtual child porn using avatars is generally considered illegal in the European Union, it might not necessarily be treated as such in the United States *(p. 44)*. Similarly, *images which are illegal to view in the USA may not be illegal to view in Germany* (p. 41). The same situation exists in the concept of age disparity between the adult and minor. Hence, there have been countless writings on legal aspects of child sexual abuse in online environment which go beyond the scope of this chapter.

1.2.2 Psychological Aspects

The most effective and also naïve psychological aspects of "predatorhood" might be those defined by Morris in his master of science thesis (Morris, 2013). The author defined predatorhood as having two major components: *age disparity* and *inappropriate intimacy*. The former relates to the psychological immaturity of the victim compared to that of predator (adult) which may differ in various countries by law. The latter corresponds to the attempt of adult to establish an intimate conversation that usually involves implicit or explicit sexual comments.

One of the most practical psychological theories which is widely used in online predator identification is known as *luring communication theory* (Olson, Daggs, Ellevold, & Rogers, 2007). The theory comprises three main phases needed for committing a predatory act:

1. Gaining access to the victim.
2. Entrapping and grooming until the victim accepts sexual advances.
3. Initiating and maintaining the abusive relationship.

On the Internet, the most common way for gaining access to the victim is through online conversations in chat rooms. The second stage can be distinguished by observation of the predator's attempt to desensitize the child to inappropriate intimacy. Finally, the third step involves explicit sexual exploitation of the minor. When an explicit exploitation is about to occur, a reliable OPI system can flag the conversation for the attention of law enforcement in order to prevent the predator from approaching the victim.

1.3 Data Mining and OPI

During the past decade, automated Online Predator Identification (OPI) has become tractable by using data/text mining algorithms. These algorithms are capable of identifying likely predators for the attention of law enforcement. Using automatic ways to combat this kind of crime is challenging and demands efficient and scalable

Figure 1. The relationship of OPI with text mining, pattern classification and criminal psychology

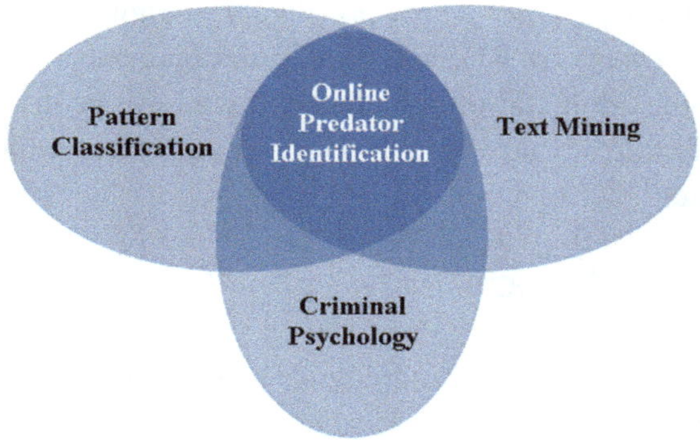

data mining techniques that are able to handle large volumes of chat logs. Since huge amounts of text data (e.g. chat logs, web sites, and forums) are required to be processed, the automated predator identification task relies on scalable data mining algorithms. There are two major OPI problems in which data mining plays an important role:

1. Detecting predators.
2. Visualizing and analyzing predator criminal networks.

The solution to these problems can be casted as a combination of textual preprocessing in data/text mining and pattern classification in machine learning and also criminal psychology (Figure 1).

As it has been illustrated in this figure, text mining and pattern classification techniques form the algorithmic foundations of OPI. A comprehensive but concise survey of text mining which incorporates the gist of text mining algorithms has been provided by Aggarwal (2015). Pattern classification (also known as pattern recognition) encompasses the classification algorithms used in predator identification and it goes hand in hand with machine learning techniques (Duda, Hart, & Stork, 2012).

More specifically, the solution to the second OPI problem is provided by extracting the underlying relationships and using graph mining techniques to analyze the resultant social networks. This topic will be discussed briefly in section 2. Figure 2 illustrates the main data mining techniques used in OPI along with their relationships. The details of each part will be given in sections 3, 4 and 5.

Figure 2. Major data mining techniques which are used in OPI and their relationships with each other

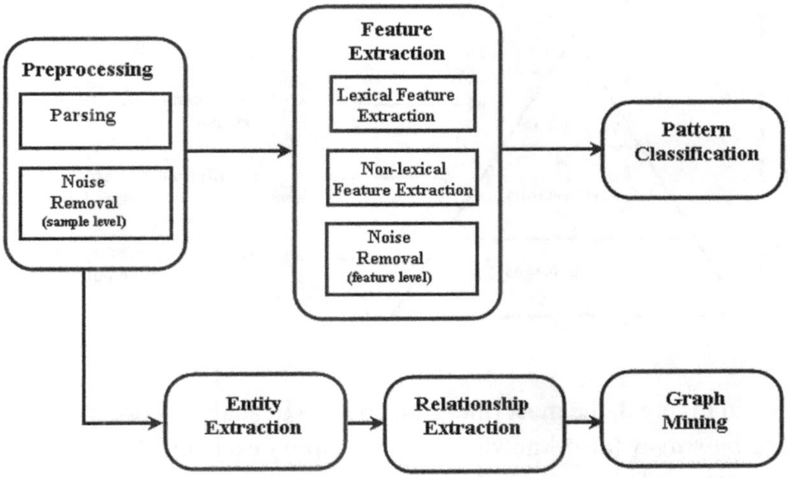

There has been a dedicated competition for Sexual Predator Identification in PAN-2012 as part of the CLEF 2012 competition ("PAN-2012," n.d.) that expedited the movement of applying data mining techniques on chat logs in order to identify the likely predators. Several competitors from all over the world applied their data mining techniques on a relatively huge volume of chat logs. The chapter covers the gist of this competition with a focus on data mining techniques. The competition encompasses the following two tasks (Inches & Crestani, 2012):

1. Distinguishing the predators and victims.
2. Specifying predatory messages in predatory conversation.

Accomplishing the first task is of greater help to law enforcement in terms of narrowing down their search space significantly. According to Villatoro-Tello et al. (2012), this task can be performed in two consecutive steps:

1. Identifying the predatory conversations among all conversations.
2. Distinguishing the sexual predator and victim among participants of predatory conversations.

We propose an abstract taxonomy which encompasses the different classification techniques which are used in the OPI field. There are three main different granularity levels of analysis in dealing with online predator identification. These levels are shown in Figure 3.

Figure 3. Classification granularity levels and their corresponding classification problem in OPI

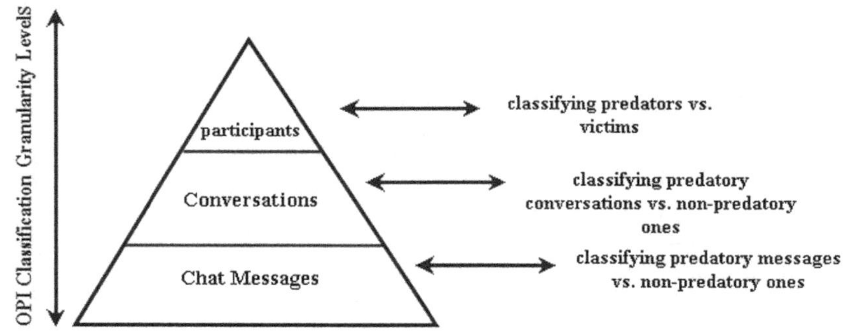

As seen in Figure 3, the most fine-grained level of analysis corresponds to direct analysis of *messages* (also known as *interventions*) exchanged by participants in their conversation. This kind of analysis corresponds to the task of distinguishing the sexual predators. The next level of granularity relates to the task of identifying online predatory conversations. Finally, distinguishing the predators among all of the participants in the entire corpus can be considered as the highest level of abstraction which might be the ultimate goal. These analyses are accomplished by utilizing the proper data mining classification methods which are discussed in the very last sections of this chapter.

This chapter aims to cover the state-of-the-art methods and results of domain-specific papers in the field. In this regard, the usage of data mining techniques including preprocessing, feature extraction and classification have been discussed in various aspects of an OPI problem. The chapter starts with a brief introduction of terminology and a discussion on the necessity of OPI in online safety. Next, different methods of preprocessing, which have been found to be quite useful for filtering the noise and unnecessary data and improving the overall performance, are discussed. These methods include the most popular data formats, noise removal procedure and dimensionality reduction. Then feature extraction and the popular ways of feature enrichment in this domain of application are described. After discussing related feature extraction techniques, a brief basic tutorial about classification algorithms in the domain of automated predator identification is presented. These algorithms cover a wide range of classification algorithms such as Entropy-based classification, Naïve Bayes, Support Vector Machine, and Neural Networks (see section 5 for a discussion on these algorithms). Dissecting the unnecessary technical details about the internal mechanism of machine learning algorithms has been avoided. Instead, we have tried to refer the keen readers to the related resources about the fully-detailed theories behind these algorithms. Finally, we compare the performance of these methods and introduce the most successful ones based on the outcome of CLEF 2012 conference. Finally, in the final part of the chapter we describe the open issues and remaining challenges in this field. Particularly, we address the usage of Web-based Dynamic Social Networks (WDSN) and its relationship to the online predator identification. In addition, the most likely future trends in this field and its connection with natural language processing are discussed at the end of this chapter.

2. BACKGROUND

As mentioned in the previous section, OPI has its root in text mining and pattern classification. With the rapid increase of available textual data in different domains including news, social media, and web pages, text mining has drawn the attention of researchers during the last decade. There has been a variety of algorithms and approaches including text clustering and classification, text summarization, topic modeling, and opinion mining. Opinion mining or sentiment analysis is an important discipline in Natural Language Processing (NLP) that extracts people's opinion, attitudes and emotions toward entities, other people, events, and their attributes. The reader may refer to (Aggarwal, 2015; Irfan et al., 2015; Liu & Zhang, 2012) for comprehensive explanations of these algorithms and approaches. Here, we narrow down the focus of the chapter to the usage of these techniques in OPI and describe the related background.

One of the very first successful attempts for using data mining in OPI problem was accomplished by Pendar (2007) who used weighted K-NN classifier to distinguish predators from underage victims. In addition to this, the first empirical system with capability of determining predatory messages in chat logs is ChatCoder1 (Kontostathis, 2009). Afterwards, ChatCoder2 (see section 2) was implemented and evolved on top of the previous version to improve its performance (Mcghee et al., 2011). The system used a rule based approach in conjunction with decision trees and instance-based learning methods (K-NN).

Michalopoulos and Mavridis (2011), and Escalante et al. (2013) have utilized Luring Communication Theory which was described in the previous section, to combine psychological aspects of predation phenomenon with computer science and machine learning.

Recently, the PAN-2012 conference has acted as a boost for applying machine learning techniques to this area. Several machine learning algorithms have been used to solve OPI problem in this competition. These algorithms cover a wide range of classification algorithms such as Entropy-based Classification (Eriksson & Karlgren, 2012), K-Nearest Neighbor (Kang, Kim, Kang, & Na, 2012), Support Vector Machine (Morris, 2013) and Neural Networks (Villatoro-Tello et al., 2012).

Eventually, one team has been announced as the winner based on their classification accuracy and an augmented F-measure. The winner team (Villatoro-Tello et al., 2012) used a two-step binary classification approach called SCI (Suspicious Conversation Identification) and VFP (Victim From Predator Disclosure) using SVM and Neural Networks.

As one of the most recent works, Escalante et al. (2013) proposed a novel method using the chained-classifiers based on adapting a psychological hypothesis that underscores three stages employed by predators to approach the victim. Although this method could not outperform the approach used by Villatoro-Tello et.al, it revealed that adopting psycho-linguistic hypotheses could improve the accuracy.

Due to the inadequacy of bag-of-words models in reflecting deep semantic notions hidden in the conversations, Bogdanova et al. (2012b) tried to enrich the features by introducing sentiments and emotions to the original feature set. In another research (Bogdanova, Rosso, & Solorio, 2014) they improved their feature set by adding more high level features such as neuroticism and psychological aspects. We will cover these studies in more detail through the chapter.

Deeper linguistic attempts in this field were started by Forsyth & Martell (2007) in a research for creating an annotated chat corpus with both lexical and semantic tags to facilitate application of data mining in this domain. As another linguistic analysis example, Bogdanova et al. (2012a) have worked on identifying fixated discourse on chat logs. Fixated discourse associates to the strong intention of the predator to keep the focus of the conversation on sexual topics. Finally, a holistic approach has been presented by Cano et al. (2014) based on leveraging lexical features, sentiment features, content and psycho-linguistic features and discourse patterns. They have used semantic frames, which incorporate the general aspects of a discourse, and added them as additional features to the original bag-of-word model.

In the remainder of the chapter, we discuss the methods mentioned above in greater detail and highlight their strengths and weaknesses. Table 1 shows a mapping between data mining techniques and their applications in predator identification problem as well as the reference to corresponding works which have been done in the domain.

2.1 Criminal Network Analysis and Visualization

Another aspect of OPI deals with pedophile covert network analysis and visualization. Iqbal et al. (2012) have used the concept of criminal clique mining on chat logs to reveal the hidden relationship among criminals. Figure 4 depicts the main components of their framework.

Table 1. Mapping of applications in OPI and corresponding data mining techniques

Application Area in OPI	Data Mining Technique(s)	Previous Works
Predator Detection	Statistical Binary classification	• Approaches in PAN-2012 • (Morris, 2013) • (Cano et al., 2014) • (Pendar, 2007)
	Latent Semantic Indexing	• (Kontostathis et al, 2013)
	Rule-based approach	• (Mcghee et al., 2011)
• Criminal Network Analysis • Criminal Network Visualization	Graph Mining	• (Iqbal et al., 2012) • (Carley, 2015)

Figure 4. Overview of the framework for mining criminal networks in chat logs
Iqbal et al., 2012.

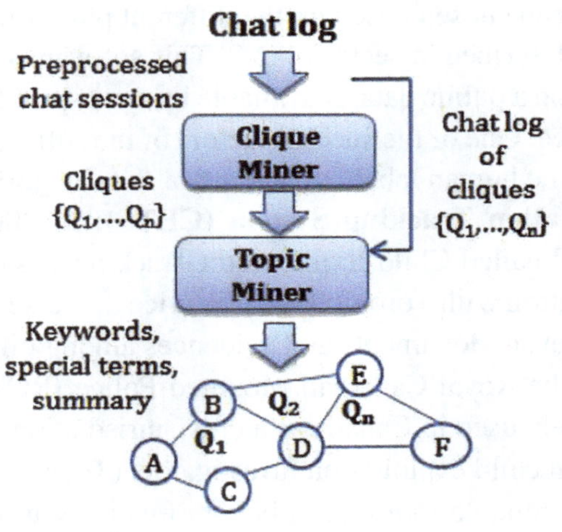

To analyze a criminal social network we need to explore the communication structure and the patterns by which network communications evolve. Based on the work of Klerks (2003), criminal network investigation approaches can be categorized into three types:

1. Manual approach,
2. Graphic-based approach, and
3. Social network analysis.

Since the focus of this chapter is on the identification aspects rather than network visualization and analysis, we focus on the predator detection through the remaining sections.

2.2 Successful Sample Tools

In order to introduce successful examples of automated online predator identification we briefly describe two software tools in which data mining techniques have been applied to this domain in a practical environment.

- **ChatCoder 2:** This tool was implemented at Mathematics and Computer Science Department of Ursinus College in Pennsylvania in 2011(Mcghee et al., 2011). The software leveraged a rule-based approach to classify the messages in forums into several categories including 'exchange of personal information', 'grooming', 'approach', and 'none of the categories'. These categories have been chosen based on the different phases defined in communication theory described in section 1-2-2. This software system could provide 68% accuracy on a public dataset available by a non-profit organization called perverted justice. One of the success factors of the software is that the system outperformed the human labeling in some of the categories.
- **Child Exploitation Tracking System (CETS):** In 2003, Microsoft initiated a new tool called Child Exploitation Tracking System (CETS) through close collaboration with Toronto Police Service to create an infrastructure for sharing the relevant documents and evidences among different investigators. According to the Royal Canadian Mounted Police (RCMP) the tool is still being extensively used in Canada as a cross-jurisdiction information sharing system between child exploitation investigators (Toews, 2013). CETS can be construed as a reliable tool that is being effectively utilized for combating child exploitation.

In the remainder of this chapter, we will describe the data mining methods used for preprocessing textual data and common algorithms for predator identification.

3. PREPROCESSING METHODS FOR CHAT LOGS

All data mining processes require a domain specific data preprocessing task which is often a tedious and time consuming task. Preprocessing of chat logs includes different subtasks ranging from parsing the raw textual log files to removing noise and reducing dimensionality.

3.1 Chat log's Data Format

Since analyzing textual data is less expensive and more efficient than analyzing other media such as image and video, currently almost all of the approaches for OPI use solely textual data. The logs format strongly depends on the software tool which is used for logging the conversations on the chat server. Although it can be any log format depending on the logging tool, usually the raw chat log data is gathered in a semi-structured textual format such as XML or Jason file. Various items can be stored in these logs among which the following three elements are essential for OPI analysis:

- **Authors:** Participants who are usually identified by unique identifiers.
- **Message Text:** The textual transferred message.
- **Time Stamps:** The date and time corresponding to each exchanged message.

Figure 5 shows a sample template for a chat log in XML format.

3.2 Noise Removal

Noise removal procedure is done for the purpose of improving the performance of learning (in terms of precision, recall, and accuracy) and also reducing the training time. In OPI problems, the noise removal procedure falls into one of the following categories or a combination of both:

Figure 5. A simple chat log in XML format with essential items for OPI

```
<Log date=May 05,2015>
    <message id=1>
            <participant id= Q12445678D></participant>
            <text> hi </text>
            <time>May 05,2015-16:45:20</time>
    </message>
    <message id=2>
            <participant id= Q12445678D></participant>
            <text> r u there? </text>
            <time>May 05,2015-16:45:26</time>
    </message>
    <message id=3>
            <participant id= F11445E211></participant>
            <text> hi </text>
            <time>May 05,2015-16:45:20</time>
    </message>
</Log>
```

1. **Removing Noisy Conversations:** This category of noise removal procedure includes identifying and eliminating useless samples that do not affect the learning process. This includes removing the following items:
    a. **Non-Textual Samples:** Real-world chat logs may contain conversations with only non-textual data or a very tiny amount of textual information. These samples can be safely ignored.
    b. **Conversations which Include Only One Participant:** This kind of conversations usually exists in a chat log corpus due to the fact that a participant may be unsuccessful in having a conversation with another participant.
    c. **Extremely Short Messages:** E.g. those which only contain a normal short greeting between two or more participants.
2. **Removing Noisy Features:** This category includes removal procedures for eliminating noise from features obtained during the feature extraction procedure (see section 4). Feature extraction and its corresponding methods in OPI will be discussed in the next section. For now, features can be considered as the set of important terms in a conversation. Noisy features may include the followings:
    a. Terms which are not in the proper encoding (This happens especially when there are multiple languages involved in the training corpus or there are other encodings than Unicode Transformation Format (UTF).)
    b. Small images or emoticons transferred among a whole bunch of textual conversations are construed as noisy features depending on the approach. It should be noted that emoticons are considered as a valuable source of information especially for extracting sentiment features. In such cases, emoticons should not be treated as noise.
    c. Unintentional Misspelled words throughout the conversation. It is worth mentioning that *intentional* misspelled words often play an important role in this application domain. As Villatoro-Tello Villatoro-Tello et al. (2012) state: For example in the grooming phase the perpetrator may amend the relationship by an emphasized "soryyyyyyyyy" when the child felt threatening by any obtrusive language *(p. 4). On the other hand, differentiation of intentional from unintentional spelling errors is not an easy task. Therefore, some researchers avoid the entire spell checking in the hope of gaining quality improvement.*

3.3 Feature Selection and Dimensionality Reduction

Feature selection involves a procedure to select a smaller subset of terms from a large set of candidate terms. The process is applied in order to increase the accuracy and/or decrease the training time (see section 5).

Let *D* be a data set with set of *n* terms denoted by *N*, and also let *f* be the function which maps the conversations into $l \in \{p, np\}$ in which *P* and *NP* represent the predatory instances and non-predatory instances respectively. Feature selection can be defined as the process of finding $N^* \subseteq N$ so that the performance of classifier *f* is maximized. Performance of classifier is typically defined by accuracy, precision, recall, and f-measure. Forman describes a holistic introduction of feature selection techniques used in text classification (Forman, 2003). Two common feature selection techniques are widely used in OPI domain. One of them falls into the category of supervised feature selection techniques and the other one is an unsupervised technique:

- **Unsupervised Feature Selection:**
  - **Document Frequency Thresholding:** Let *d*(*t*) be the number of documents in which term *t* occurs. Subset N^* contains ***t*** if and only if $d(t) \geq l$, in which $l \in \mathbb{N}$ is an arbitrary threshold. As Yang and Pedersen (1997) state, Document frequency thresholding is the simplest technique which scales well to large corpora.
- **Supervised Feature Selection:**
  - **Information Gain:** Supervised feature selection techniques measure each feature based on its contribution to identification of the correct category (i.e. predatory or non-predatory). Among numerous supervised techniques for feature selection in text classification task, information gain can be considered as the most successful technique in the domain of OPI. The notation used by Forman (2003) for calculating information gain in binary classification problem suits well in OPI. According to this notation, information gain for a specific term (feature) is defined as:

$$IG(t) = e(pos, neg) - \left[P(t)e(tp, fp) + P'(t)e(fn, tn)\right]$$

where:

$$e(x, y) = -\frac{x}{x+y}\log_2\left(\frac{x}{x+y}\right) - \frac{y}{x+y}\log_2\left(\frac{y}{x+y}\right)$$

In addition, *pos* and *neg* represent the number of predatory and non-predatory cases respectively. Also *tp* represents the number of predatory cases containing the term, *fp* is the number of non-predatory cases containing the term, *fn* is the number of predatory cases not containing the term and *tn* represents the number of negative cases not containing the term. $P(t)$ is calculated as follows:

$$p(t) = \frac{no.\ of\ cases\ containing\ term\ t}{total\ no.\ of\ cases}; p'(t) = 1 - p(t)$$

There is a large variety of dimensionality reduction techniques used in data mining but there is a text-specific dimensionality reduction technique called stemming which is widely used in text mining. The purpose of doing this preprocessing step is to reduce the terms 'work', 'works', 'worker' and 'working' into one dimension as 'work'. This process usually has a desirable effect on the performance of text categorization both in terms of quality and time efficiency. However, unfortunately this technique may not provide the same desirable effect for the OPI problem domain due to the fact that it will distort the information pertaining to the writing style of predators in chat logs. Accordingly, the best results have been reported while stemming has been avoided.

4. FEATURE EXTRACTION

Table 2 categorizes the features which are used in mining OPI problems along with corresponding previous works that have utilized these features.

In the remaining part of this section, the above categories are dissected in greater detail.

4.1 Lexical Features

Lexical features are word-related features that are directly extracted from the sentence. These words are used as candidate features in classification algorithms in order to determine the category to which chat logs belong. One of the simplest approaches used in OPI problem to extract features is the *bag-of-words approach* that treats a chat log as a set of words. Each word that exists in a chat log is considered as a candidate feature and then these features are weighted in terms of their frequency of occurrence. Typically, the initial candidate feature set is built by extracting n-grams (unigrams, bigrams, and trigrams) from the training data. Usually words that have insubstantial lexical meaning or known as stop words are filtered out during pre-

Table 2. Categorization of features which are used in OPI problem

Feature Category	Description	Application Examples
Lexical Features	Bag-of-word representations including: • Unigrams • Bigrams • Trigrams and other N-grams	• (Villatoro-Tello et al., 2012) • (Morris, 2013) • (Pendar, 2007)
Behavioral Features	• The number of times this author initiates a conversation • The number of times the author asks a question • Response Time • Conversation Dominance • Number of turn-takings	• (Morris, 2013)
Psychological and Linguistic Features	• Fixated Discourse (see below) • Writing Style (see below) • Emoticons (see below) • Tendency to change conversation to sexual discourse • Awareness of doing an illegal and non-moral action that may cause prosecution • Mimicking children language	• (Bogdanova et al., 2012a) • (Mcghee et al., 2011) • (Hogenboom et al., 2013)
Sentiment-oriented Features	Fear, Anger, Anticipation, Joy, Sadness, Disgust, Surprise, etc.	• (Bogdanova et al., 2012b)

processing in standard text categorization and Information Retrieval (IR) studies, but because of the fact that chat logs have their own vocabulary and rules, which makes general stop word list non-functional, researchers usually create their own list of stop words. As an example, the stop word list used by Pendar (2007) contained specifically 79 most frequent words in the corpus. After filtering out the entire stop words successfully, the *n*-grams and their corresponding frequencies for each chat log (or for each chat participant) are extracted.

Standard bag-of-words model has been shown to be robust in a wide variety of text classification problems. *Term Frequency-Inverse Document Frequency (TF-IDF),* is the most common weighting approach that is extensively used for weighting the candidate features before performing any feature selection procedure. In this weighting scheme, the most important words tend to have higher weights. This is implicitly achieved by multiplying the frequency of term *t* by a magnitude which is inversely proportional to the occurrence of term *t* in the whole corpus. Generally speaking, building unigrams and bigrams (pairs of consecutive words) produce better results than higher *n*-grams. Depending on the training corpus, the use of bigrams may increase the performance at the expense of increasing the size of the feature-space. However, for a training problem it may turn out that unigram model produces a better performance. Regardless of the classification performance, the size of the feature set for bigram representation is typically much bigger than that of unigram model. The resultant feature set can also be enriched by adding *domain-specific* features.

As an instance, in the work of Morris (2013), special tokens such as \SMILEY, \MALE.name, \FEMALE.name, \NUM and \PHONE.name were added to the lexical features in order to enrich the initial feature set. However, it was mentioned that these enhancements seemed to add a non-remarkable improvement.

Considering the inadequacy of bag-of-words models in reflecting deep semantic notions hidden in the conversations, one can also enrich the feature set with behavioral features which would be explained in detail below.

4.2 Behavioral Features

In this part, we list the high-level behavioral features and their applicability in the detection of online predators. Behavioral features are characterized as features that capture the actions of a user within a conversation. Morris (2013) has classified behavioral features as: 'Initiative', 'Attentiveness' and 'Conversation dominance' for which the details are given accordingly:

- **Initiative:** This can be measured by *number of initiations* (i.e. number of times a specified participant starts the conversation), *initiation rate* (i.e. the ratio of number of initiations to the whole number of conversations), questions and question rate in order to understand the author's tendency during the conversation.
- **Attentiveness:** This feature corresponds to the mean, median, and max response times for each author.
- **Conversation Dominance:** A set of features such as 'Message Ratio', 'Word Count Ratio' that reflect the degree to which the focal author dominates the conversation.

In order to successfully distinguish predators from victims, the above mentioned features are critical for *'symmetry-breaking'* (Morris, 2013). That is, given the fact that two authors in a chat conversation use very similar languages, behavioral features are one of the significant identifiers or non-lexical aspects of the conversation which are able to differentiate predators from victims.

4.3 Psychological and Linguistic Features

Psycho-linguistic features form another important aspect of feature extraction in OPI domain. 'Fixated discourse' is one of the most prominent psychological features used in OPI. Bogdanova et al. (2012a) defined fixated discourse as the unwillingness of the predator to change the topic. For instance, predators always ignore the question or interruptions of pseudo-victim and has the tendency to go back to the sex-related conversation. According to them, chat logs might include implicit and explicit sexual content as predators gradually alter the direction of conversation to sex by starting with some ordinary compliments. On the other hand, predators often are aware of the fact that what they do on chat rooms is not moral and they try to transfer the responsibility of the victim and they often behave as children by copying the children's linguistic style (Bogdanova et al., 2014).

The following analysis of chat logs identifies the important characteristics of predators' psychological and linguistic features (Bogdanova et al., 2014):

- ***Implicit/Explicit Content:*** *Typically, pedophiles shift gradually to the sexual conversation, starting with ordinary compliments and then they shift the conversation to make it overtly related to sex. They do not hide their intentions.*
- ***Fixated Discourse:*** *Pedophiles are reluctant to step aside from the sexual conversation. In other words, pedophiles try to come back to the sex-related conversation when the victim steps outside of the topic.*
- *Offenders often understand that what they are doing is not moral.*
- *They transfer responsibility to the victim.*
- *Offenders often behave as children, copying their linguistic style. Colloquialisms appear often in their messages.*

Mcghee et al. (2011) have proposed the following linguistic features which were denoted as 'Writing Style' in Table 2: Total number of words in a line, number of first-person pronouns, second-person pronouns or third-person pronouns, number of personal information nouns *(e.g., age, pic)*, number of relationship nouns *(e.g., boyfriend, date)*, number of family nouns *(e.g., mom, sibling)*, number of communicative desensitization words *(e.g., kiss, bra)*, number of approach verbs *(e.g., meet, see, hotel)*.

Hogenboom et al. (2013) mentioned that their research had shown that people were influenced by the nonverbal cues and emoticons. These are widely used to express sentiments such as happiness, sadness, joy or anger, therefore emoticons could also be used to reveal the predators' sentiments and their tendencies in order to be dominant in the conversation and also to copy children's' behavior as explained above. Table 3 shows the typical examples of emoticons and their sentimental interpretations (Hogenboom et al., 2013).

Table 3. Typical examples of emoticon synsets

Emoticon Synset	Emoticons
Happiness	:-D, =D, xD, (^_^)
Sadness	:-(, =(
Crying	:'(, ='(, (;_;)
Boredom	-_-, -.-, (>_<)
Love	<3, (L)
Embarrassment	:-$, =$, >///<

Hogenboom et al., 2013.

4.4 Sentiment-Oriented Features

In addition to the emoticons explained earlier, sentiment of chat logs can provide significant markers in terms of predator identification and unveil other important semantic dimensions. According to Bogdanova et al, in general, predatory conversations contain more positive and less negative words. The sentiments and emotional markers shown in Table 4 were used as features in their experiments.

5. LEARNING PREDATORY PATTERNS

First, we formally introduce the notion of binary classification which is used in OPI problem. Let data set *D* be defined as $D \subset X \times Y$ where $X = \{X_1, X_2, \ldots, X_m\}$ is the set of *m* observation vectors $X_i; i \in \{1, 2, \ldots, m\}$, so that $X_i = (x_1, x_2, \ldots, x_n)^T$

Table 4. Sentiment features

Feature	Example
Positive words	Cute, pretty
Negative words	Dangerous, annoying
JOY words	Happy, cheer
SADNESS words	Bored, sad
ANGER words	Annoying, furious
SURPRISE words	Astonished, wonder
DISGUST words	Yucky, nausea
FEAR words	Scared, panic

Bogdanova et al., 2014.

is the corresponding vector of ith observation containing *n* feature values $X_j; j \in \{1,\ldots,n\}$. Also $Y = \{p, np\}$ is the set of two class labels corresponding to predatory and non-predatory instances respectively. The classification task is defined as finding a mapping function $f: X \rightarrow Y$ such that $f(X)$ is able to predict $y \in Y$ as accurately as possible.

As a typical approach, the data is split into training and testing sets and the classification model learns from the training set and then applies to the test set to evaluate the performance of classification. A wide variety of learning algorithms for learning function *f* have been proposed and utilized in data mining. In the following parts of this section, we introduce the most common algorithms that have been used for solving OPI problems.

5.1 OPI Standard Classification Methods

This part is dedicated to introducing concrete data mining classification algorithms which have been used in OPI problems. First, we describe a highly-standard probabilistic algorithm called Naïve Bayes which has been used for text classification since long time ago. Then we discuss the most intuitive algorithm which is usually used in information retrieval called K-NN. Then we proceed to more advanced algorithms such as Entropy-based classification, Support Vector Machines and Artificial Neural Networks.

5.1.1 Naive Bayes

This algorithm is used extensively as the baseline in text classification studies. This means that researchers accept it as an efficient algorithm and aim to improve its performance through other novel algorithms. Although the reader can refer to Duda et al. (2012) for a thorough explanation of the algorithm, we present a simple description here. Let *D* be a data set defined in the previous section. Assuming that all discrete-valued features are conditionally independent given the class label **y** (known as '*Naive Bayes assumption*') we can simplify $P(X \mid y)$ that is the conditional probability of observation vector *X* given *y* as follows:

$$P(X \mid y) = P(x_1, x_2, \ldots, x_n \mid y) = P(x_1 \mid y) P(x_2 \mid x_1, y) \ldots P(x_n \mid y, x_1, x_2, \ldots, x_{n-1})$$
$$= P(x_1 \mid y) P(x_2 \mid y) \ldots P(x_n \mid y) = \prod_i P(x_i \mid y);\ by\ Naive\ Bayes\ assumption$$

Having $P(X \mid y)$ calculated as above, one can predict the most likely class label (y^*) by using the Bayes rule as follows:

$$y^* = \arg\max_y P(y)P(X \mid y) = \arg\max_y P(y)\prod_i P(x_i \mid y)$$

Specifically in OPI problems, we deal with labels *p* and *np* and accordingly we can rewrite the above as:

$$y^* = \max\left(P(y = p)\right)\prod_i P(x_i \mid y = p), P(y = np)\prod_i P(x_i \mid y = np)\right)$$

5.1.2 K-Nearest Neighbor

Kang et al. (2012) have used K-Nearest Neighbor (also known as KNN) for online predator identification. They have used a weighted modification of classic KNN. Although their result is not comparable with other methods, their approach is worth mentioning due to the rational justification behind it. The simplest version of the algorithm can be outlined as shown in Algorithm 1, where majority function simply calculates the majority of class labels among neighbors. A more sophisticated explanation can be found in Duda et al. (2012).

There are also weighted versions of KNN which assigns different weights to the neighbors based on its distance to the query point (i.e. the instance that might be whether predatory or non-predatory). The authors of Kang et al. (2012) state that choosing a good number of *k* which can provide good results both on training set and testing set still remains as a challenge.

5.1.3 Maximum Entropy Classification

The conditional independence assumption of Naive Bayes is not realistic at least in dealing with textual documents. Therefore, we may need statistical models that can consider the notion of dependent random variables. Maximum Entropy Classifier is a *discriminative* approach which tries to build a statistical model of conditional probability distribution $P(y \mid X)$. There is an infinite number of such models, but based on the maximum entropy principle, the best model is the one which maximizes entropy of $H(P)$. Berger et al. (1996) formally state this as follows:

$$H(P) \equiv -\sum_{x,y} \tilde{P}(x)P(y \mid X)\log P(y \mid X)$$

Algorithm 1. KNN (D, x, k, m)

```
    Input:
        D ← Training data set
         χ ← Query vector
        m ← Distance measure (e.g. Euclidean Distance)
    Output:
        y: predicted class label 'p' or 'np' (i.e. deciding
whether the sample χ is predatory or not)
begin
1.          N, L ← Ø
2.          Find k nearest neighbors to x based on the distance
measure m and add them to neighbors set N.
3.          Add the corresponding class labels of found neigh-
bors in N to Labels set L.
4.          y ← Majority (L)
end
```

In order to choose the best model P^* from set C (the set of valid probability distributions), based on the maximum entropy selection, we have to solve the following optimization problem:

$$P^* = \arg\max_{P \in C} H\left(P\right)$$

Note that in Berger's notation the probability distributions are denoted by *p* instead of P. However, we use *P* for denoting the distributions since we have already reserved symbol *p* for representing the 'predatory' class label.

Also note that the above optimization problem is a constrained one. Nevertheless, describing the complete theoretical background of Maximum Entropy Classifier is beyond the scope of this chapter. A keen reader may like to refer to Berger's et al. (1996) seminal paper about introducing max entropy on natural language processing.

Eriksson and Karlgren (2012), and Kern et al. (2012) used Maximum Entropy Classifier in the OPI domain on PAN-2012 data set. Their obtained results are comparable with the winner's approach of PAN-2012 and can be considered as a successful approach for solving OPI problems.

5.1.4 Support Vector Machines

Currently, Support Vector Machines (SVMs) have shown the best results among all different classification algorithms which have been used for OPI problems. SVM was explicitly introduced by Vapnik, (1995) in his book entitled *'The Nature of Statistical Learning Theory'*. The goal of SVM algorithm is to obtain a hyperplane which maximizes the margins between positive and negative instances (predatory and non-predatory samples in our case). The margin is defined as two times the distance from the decision hyperplane. Figure 6 illustrates the idea of SVM.

Instances which are located on the margins are called 'support vectors'. The main result of training an SVM model is to obtain these support vectors also known as *supports*. These instances are the only ones that take into considerations when a new instance is supposed to be classified by the trained model. The training procedure contains solving a constrained optimization problem which is usually solved by out-of-the-shelf quadratic programming tools. SVM has been used by Morris (2013), and Villatoro-Tello et al. (2012) and as already mentioned, SVM has the highest performance among algorithms used in PAN-2012. The reader may refer to Bishop (2006) for the mathematical background of support vector machines. Note that besides the classification algorithm, preprocessing methods and feature extraction methods, described in previous part, have also drastic impact on the final performance.

5.1.5 Neural Networks

Even though there are a large variety of neural network algorithms, the one that has been successfully utilized in OPI is the Multi Layer Perceptron (MLP). In a pioneering work, the researchers tested MLP for identifying predatory conversations and also

Figure 6. A toy example showing the output of SVM for a binary classification as well as the margin and three support vectors. Squares and circles represent predatory and non-predatory samples respectively

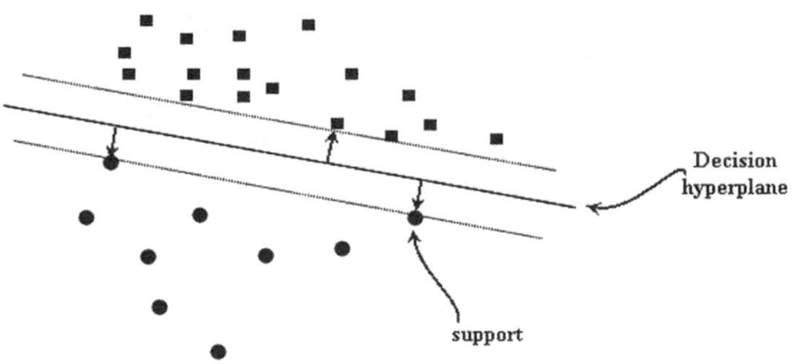

identifying the likely predators and then compared the obtained performance with that of Support Vector Machines (Villatoro-Tello et al., 2012). The results showed that the performance of neural network and SVM are so close to each other. More specifically, the neural network outperformed SVM in identifying predators versus victims and on the contrary, SVM performed better in identifying the predatory conversations. Here, we introduce the key concepts of MLPs without a detailed description of algorithm.

Units are considered as building blocks of MLPs. Each unit resembles a neuron that has a specific 'activation function' which generates the final output of a neuron. In a higher level of abstraction, the network contains several layers of units including input, output and one or more hidden units. The units in a layer are not connected to each other, while usually all of the units in a previous layer are connected to the units in the next layer. There is a real number assigned to each connection called 'weights'. The final output z_j of a neuron located in the first hidden layer with M units is calculated as follows (Bishop, 2006):

$$z_j = h\left(\sum_{i=1}^{D} w_{ji}^{(1)} x_i + w_{j0}^{(1)}\right)$$

where h is the activation function for neurons in the hidden layer which is usually chosen to be a sigmoidal function. Also D is the number of features in the input sample. Finally, superscript (1) denotes the layer in which neuron is located. This process of linear transformations continues in a cascading manner from previous layers to the last hidden layer and eventually the output layer in which the final output of the network is generated.

The learning algorithm of an MLP with a specified structure is an algorithm which finds the relatively optimal network weights. The learning procedure encompasses a technique called 'backpropagation' and also an optimization technique called 'gradient descent'. For a complete description about Neural Networks, user could refer to Bishop's book (2006). Similar to SVM, there are out-of-the-shelf libraries and tools for building and training neural networks.

To summarize this section, we mention the outstanding algorithms among the above-mentioned methods. In terms of accuracy, precision, and recall rate, Support Vector Machines and Neural Networks (Multi-layer Perceptron) outperform other classification methods. However, it is suggested to always apply a simple approach such as Naïve Bayes to obtain a performance baseline so that if there is a problem with parameter tuning of the two mentioned algorithms, it will be revealed at the first stages of the analysis.

6. FUTURE RESEARCH DIRECTIONS

In spite of the considerable achievements mentioned in this chapter, there are still prominent challenges which researchers need to tackle in the field of OPI. Accordingly, we describe the potential future research lines based on our anticipation of the problem domain. In the following, we demonstrate the necessity for deeper linguistic analysis as well as the related challenges are discussed and then the newly emerged field of Web-based Dynamic Social Networks is introduced.

6.1 Performing Deeper Linguistic Analysis on Chat logs

Mining chat logs is strongly correlated to challenging problems in the domain of NLP including Word Sense Disambiguation (identifying the sense for a polysemic part of speech), Discourse Analysis (Discovering the conversation concepts and psychological characteristics of the writer), and also Named Entity Recognition (Extraction of role-playing entities such as locations, people and organizations).

On top of these linguistic challenges, there is another important issue related to the nature of chat logs: Conversational (i.e non-official) writing style of participants. Consider the following predatory conversation:

```
<text>i'm bored</text>
<text>Awww babe</text>
<text>I'm sorwy</text>
<text>where u at</text>
<text>Vegas</text>
<text>5-6 hours away</text>
<text>dude y cant u come then!?</text>
<text>I'm n vegas lol</text>
<text>I'm n another state</text>
<text>I'm not n california</text>
<text>i thought u wanted 2 come c me</text>
<text>I do</text>
<text>But how can I went I'm n another state</text>
<text>when do u leave?</text>
<text>Dis mornin</text>
<text>well i guess u aint really my bf then cuz u lied</text>
```

This writing style requires some additional considerations that make it different from normal text mining. A common issue which arises in such a context is the existence of non-grammatical sentences which makes the typical parsing algorithms inefficient. For instance, 'But how can I went I'm n another state'. Another issue is regarding the use of drastically misspelled words such as in 'Dis mornin'. Even using the sophisticated spell checkers or stemmers on such a data as a preprocessing phase would not be so efficient. Having too many different forms of writing for a single word causes the problem which is known as 'curse of dimensionality' which makes the learning algorithms significantly inefficient.

Another important issue which might not be so related to the linguistic aspects of OPI is the imbalanced nature of chat logs data. This means usually there are too many non-predatory instances compared to predatory ones. This problem makes the learning process more challenging since it requires specific algorithms to deal with this type of imbalanced data.

6.2 Learning Deep Architectures

Recently there has been a hot trend among researchers in the field of artificial intelligence and machine learning about a new paradigm of learning which can mimic the behavior of human brain or human visual system in a more accurate way (Bengio, 2009; Schmidhuber, 2015). The new learning way is called deep learning because of the fact that there is a hierarchy of numerous layers in the main model and each layer encodes a level of abstraction in the training data. Using these models has been proven to be more efficient than the simple data mining and machine learning models mentioned above. Accordingly, we anticipate that these models will be utilized in the field of OPI in the near future.

6.3 Web-Based Dynamic Social Networks

Criminal social network analysis and visualization was briefly mentioned previously. Unlike the traditional criminal networks which have a strictly hierarchical structure, online pedophile networks naturally have a cellular and distributed structure and usually do not have obvious leaders. These special types of networks demand the usage of approaches specifically designed for tackling with the cellular distributed crime networks. These approaches should be able to analyze smaller crime networks that do not necessarily have a specific powerful leader. A new tool for analyzing this sort of networks has been developed by Carley (2015) at Carnegie Mellon University which might be useful for analyzing pedophile covert networks. In addition to the approaches identified by Klerks in section 1, a new branch of social network analysis called Web-based Dynamic Social Network has been revealed recently to address the mentioned requirement. In this point of view, WDSN differs from traditional social networks in the sense that they are cellular, distributed, web-based, dynamic, and may contain varying levels of uncertainty. According to Berger-Wolf and Saia

(2006), dynamic network analysis enables probabilistic reasoning about changes in dynamic networked web-based communities and how such networks evolve, adapt to changes, and how they can be destabilized. Leveraging WDSN to identify pedophile covert networks and analyze their evolving network communication structure can be considered as one of the most significant directions in the field.

According to the above-mentioned challenges, we anticipate the future of this field spin around the following issues:

- Achieving a deeper understanding of text, or more generally natural language, to uncover the semantics behind the chat logs and improve the accuracy of classification models.
- Leveraging deep learning as a new trend in artificial intelligence for building more sophisticated language models from chat logs.
- Using the concepts of WDSN introduced above to identify pedophile covert networks and analyze their evolving network communication structure.

7. CONCLUSION

Rapidly growing penetration of online communications in juveniles' daily lives makes it vital to leverage data mining techniques for automatic identification of online predators. Automated investigation of chat logs is one of the most proactive and effective approaches that can be used to avoid the consequences of related crimes. The most popular preprocessing techniques including noise removal, feature selection, and dimensionality reduction were introduced. Also, different aspects of suitable feature extraction procedure for this problem domain were discussed and finally the most common data mining classification algorithms which are frequently used in OPI were introduced. We predict that the future of this research line in the next decade will spin around Social Network Analysis featured by deeper linguistic analysis to understand the semantics of messages.

ACKNOWLEDGMENT

This research was supported by grants from the Natural Science and Engineering Research Council of Canada and Concordia University.

REFERENCES

Aggarwal, C. C. (2015). Mining Text Data. In *Data Mining* (pp. 429–455). Springer International Publishing.

Bengio, Y. (2009). Learning Deep Architectures for AI. *Found. Trends Mach. Learn.*, *2*(1), 1–127. doi:10.1561/2200000006

Berger, A. L., Pietra, V. J. D., & Pietra, S. A. D. (1996). A Maximum Entropy Approach to Natural Language Processing. *Computational Linguistics*, *22*(1), 39–71.

Berger-Wolf, T. Y., & Saia, J. (2006). A Framework for Analysis of Dynamic Social Networks. In *Proceedings of the 12th ACM SIGKDD International Conference on Knowledge Discovery and Data Mining* (pp. 523–528). New York, NY: ACM. doi:10.1145/1150402.1150462

Bishop, C. (2006). *Pattern Recognition and Machine Learning*. New York: Springer-Verlag.

Bogdanova, D., Rosso, P., & Solorio, T. (2012a). Modelling Fixated Discourse in Chats with Cyberpedophiles. In *Proceedings of the Workshop on Computational Approaches to Deception Detection* (pp. 86–90). Stroudsburg, PA: Association for Computational Linguistics.

Bogdanova, D., Rosso, P., & Solorio, T. (2012b). On the Impact of Sentiment and Emotion Based Features in Detecting Online Sexual Predators. In *Proceedings of the 3rd Workshop in Computational Approaches to Subjectivity and Sentiment Analysis* (pp. 110–118). Stroudsburg, PA: Association for Computational Linguistics.

Bogdanova, D., Rosso, P., & Solorio, T. (2014). Exploring high-level features for detecting cyberpedophilia. *Computer Speech & Language*, *28*(1), 108–120. doi:10.1016/j.csl.2013.04.007

Cano, A., Fernandez, M., & Alani, H. (2014). Detecting Child Grooming Behaviour Patterns on Social Media. In L. Aiello & D. McFarland (Eds.), *Social Informatics* (Vol. 8851, pp. 412–427). Springer International Publishing. doi:10.1007/978-3-319-13734-6_30

Carley, K. M. (2015, May 8). *DyNet*. Retrieved from http://www.casos.cs.cmu.edu/projects/DyNet/dynet_info.html

Duda, R. O., Hart, P. E., & Stork, D. G. (2012). *Pattern Classification*. Wiley-Interscience.

Eriksson, G., & Karlgren, J. (2012). *Features for modelling characteristics of conversations*. Presented at the Notebook for PAN at CLEF 2012, Rome, Italy.

Escalante, H. J., Villatoro-Tello, E., Juárez, A., Montes-y-Gómez, M., & Villaseñor, L. (2013). Sexual predator detection in chats with chained classifiers. In *Proceedings of the 4th Workshop on Computational Approaches to Subjectivity, Sentiment and Social Media Analysis* (pp. 46–54). Atlanta, GA: Association for Computational Linguistics.

Forman, G. (2003). An Extensive Empirical Study of Feature Selection Metrics for Text Classification. *Journal of Machine Learning Research, 3*, 1289–1305.

Forsyth, E. N., & Martell, C. H. (2007). Lexical and Discourse Analysis of Online Chat Dialog. In *Semantic Computing, 2007. ICSC 2007. International Conference on* (pp. 19–26).

Hogenboom, A., Bal, D., Frasincar, F., Bal, M., de Jong, F., & Kaymak, U. (2013). Exploiting Emoticons in Sentiment Analysis. In *Proceedings of the 28th Annual ACM Symposium on Applied Computing* (pp. 703–710). New York, NY: ACM. doi:10.1145/2480362.2480498

Inches, G., & Crestani, F. (2012). *Overview of the International Sexual Predator Identification Competition at PAN-2012*. CLEF (working notes).

Iqbal, F., Fung, B. C. M., & Debbabi, M. (2012). Mining Criminal Networks from Chat Log. In *Web Intelligence and Intelligent Agent Technology (WI-IAT), 2012 IEEE/WIC/ACM International Conferences on* (Vol. 1, pp. 332–337). doi:10.1109/WI-IAT.2012.68

Irfan, R., King, C. K., Grages, D., Ewen, S., Khan, S. U., Madani, S. A., … Li, H. (2015). A survey on text mining in social networks. *The Knowledge Engineering Review, 30*(2), 157–170.

Kang, I.-S., Kim, C.-K., Kang, S.-J., & Na, S.-H. (2012). *IR-based k-Nearest Neighbor Approach for Identifying Abnormal Chat Users.* Presented at the Notebook for PAN at CLEF 2012, Rome, Italy.

Kern, R., Klampfl, S., & Zechner, M. (2012). *Vote/Veto Classification, Ensemble Clustering and Sequence Classification for Author Identification.* Presented at the Notebook for PAN at CLEF 2012, Rome, Italy.

Kierkegaard, S. (2008). Cybering, online grooming and ageplay. *Computer Law & Security Report, 24*(1), 41–55. doi:10.1016/j.clsr.2007.11.004

Klerks, P. (2003). The network paradigm applied to criminal organizations: Theoretical nitpicking or a relevant doctrine for investigators? Recent developments in the Netherlands. In *Transnational Organised Crime Perspectives on Global Security*. London: Routledge.

Kontostathis, A. (2009). Toward the tracking and categorization of internet predators. In *Proceeding of Text Mining Workshop 2009 held in conjunction with Ninth Siam International Conference Data Mining*.

Kontostathis, A., Reynolds, K., Garron, A., & Edwards, L. (2013). Detecting Cyberbullying: Query Terms and Techniques. In *Proceedings of the 5th Annual ACM Web Science Conference* (pp. 195–204). New York, NY: ACM. doi:10.1145/2464464.2464499

Liu, B., & Zhang, L. (2012). A Survey of Opinion Mining and Sentiment Analysis. In C. C. Aggarwal & C. Zhai (Eds.), *Mining Text Data* (pp. 415–463). Springer, US. doi:10.1007/978-1-4614-3223-4_13

Mcghee, I., Bayzick, J., Kontostathis, A., Edwards, L., Mcbride, A., & Jakubowski, E. (2011). Learning to Identify Internet Sexual Predation. *International Journal of Electronic Commerce*, *15*(3), 103–122. doi:10.2753/JEC1086-4415150305

Michalopoulos, D., & Mavridis, I. (2011). Utilizing document classification for grooming attack recognition. In *Computers and Communications (ISCC), 2011 IEEE Symposium on* (pp. 864–869). doi:10.1109/ISCC.2011.5983950

Morris, C. (2013, January 30). *Identifying Online Sexual Predators by SVM Classification with Lexical and Behavioral Features* (Master of Science Thesis). University of Toronto, Canada. Retrieved from ftp.cs.toronto.edu/pub/gh/Morris,Colin-MSc-thesis-2013.pdf

Olson, L. N., Daggs, J. L., Ellevold, B. L., & Rogers, T. K. K. (2007). Entrapping the Innocent: Toward a Theory of Child Sexual Predators' Luring Communication. *Communication Theory*, *17*(3), 231–251. doi:10.1111/j.1468-2885.2007.00294.x

PAN-2012. (n.d.). Retrieved from http://pan.webis.de

Pendar, N. (2007). *Toward spotting the pedophile telling victim from predator in text chats*. Washington, DC: IEEE. doi:10.1109/ICSC.2007.32

Schmidhuber, J. (2015). Deep learning in neural networks: An overview. *Neural Networks*, *61*, 85–117. doi:10.1016/j.neunet.2014.09.003 PMID:25462637

Toews, V. (2013). *Royal Canadian Mounted Police Report on Plans and Priorities 2013-2014*. Canada: RCMP. Retrieved from http://www.rcmp-grc.gc.ca/rpp/2013-2014/rpp-eng.htm

Vapnik, V. N. (1995). *The Nature of Statistical Learning Theory*. New York, NY: Springer-Verlag New York, Inc. doi:10.1007/978-1-4757-2440-0

Villatoro-Tello, E., Juárez-González, A., Escalante, H. J., Montes-y-Gómez, M., & Villaseñor-Pineda, L. (2012). *A Two-step Approach for Effective detection of Misbehaving Users in Chats*. Presented at the Notebook for PAN at CLEF'12, Rome, Italy.

Yang, Y., & Pedersen, J. O. (1997). A Comparative Study on Feature Selection in Text Categorization. In *Proceedings of the Fourteenth International Conference on Machine Learning* (pp. 412–420). San Francisco, CA: Morgan Kaufmann Publishers Inc.

KEY TERMS AND DEFINITIONS

Age Disparity: The significant difference between the age of predator adult and that of minor (i.e. victim).

Conversation: A chat session that encompasses the messages exchanged between participants.

Clique: In the context of graph theory, a clique is a set of vertices which their corresponding subgraph is complete (i.e. fully connected). While, in the context of mining criminal networks this definition can be manipulated to less mathematical definitions. Specifically, in the context of chat logs, a clique might be defined as a set of persons who participate in a minimum number of chat sessions.

Luring Communication Theory: A communication theory that models the behavior of predator for approaching, entrapping, and establishing the predatory relationship with minor.

Maximum Entropy Principle: The principle that states the best probability distribution for a statistical model is the one that has the maximum entropy.

Minor: A Person under the age of 18 who is considered as the potential victim of predatory attacks in cyber space.

Vector Space Model: The algebraic representation of documents based on their terms and the frequency of occurrence of each term.

Chapter 10
Data Mining Techniques for Distributed Denial of Service Attacks Detection in the Internet of Things:
A Research Survey

Pheeha Machaka
Decision Sciences Department, University of South Africa, South Africa

Fulufhelo Nelwamondo
Modelling and Digital Science, Council for Scientific and Industrial Research, South Africa

ABSTRACT

This chapter reviews the evolution of the traditional internet into the Internet of Things (IoT). The characteristics and application of the IoT are also reviewed, together with its security concerns in terms of distributed denial of service attacks. The chapter further investigates the state-of-the-art in data mining techniques for Distributed Denial of Service (DDoS) attacks targeting the various infrastructures. The chapter explores the characteristics and pervasiveness of DDoS attacks. It also explores the motives, mechanisms and techniques used to execute a DDoS attack. The chapter further investigates the current data mining techniques that are used to combat and detect these attacks, their advantages and disadvantages are explored. Future direction of the research is also provided.

DOI: 10.4018/978-1-5225-0463-4.ch010

INTRODUCTION

We are living in a rapidly changing information age, were information is available at our fingertips. The use of Information Communications Technology (ICT) has made access to information-on-demand relatively easy and cheaper. Computing has now moved away from the era of the traditional desktop computer to the paradigm of the Internet of Things (IoT). In the IoT, many of the objects that surround us will be on the internet network in one form or another. The use of the technology in the IoT has resulted in the generation of enormous amounts of data which have to be stored, processed and presented in a seamless, efficient, and easily interpretable form. However, having so many devices connected to the internet brings about interesting internet security challenges.

The proliferate use of internet and network technologies has led to significant dependence of society on ICT systems. Consequently, any malfunction and disruption to the services provided by these systems directly affects major aspects of society. This interruption may be sharply felt even if it is momentary. For example, an interruption in a business organisation or government's ICT infrastructure may have a substantial impact on their day-to-day activities. This may lead to significant financial losses (business and law suits) and increased operational costs from fraudulent activities.

The resulting disruptions may be due to a hacker's attempt to disrupt services using Denial of Service (DoS) attacks. A DoS attack is a malicious attempt by an attacker to disrupt the online services of a service provider to make it unavailable to its legitimate users. A large scale variant of DoS is the Distributed Denial of Service (DDoS). This kind of attack on an organisation may have catastrophic results. This may lead to disgruntled service consumers and major financial losses; it may also lead to losses in an organisation's intellectual property which in turn affects the long term competitiveness of businesses and governments in industrial and military espionage incidents (Choo, 2011). It is therefore important that organisations and governments deploy methods and techniques that will help them to accurately and reliably detect the onset and occurrence of the DDoS attacks.

This chapter studies the IoT phenomena. It provides a background overview and how the internet and evolved into the Internet of Things. The chapter also explores the characteristics of an IoT system. The current use of IoT applications in homes and business is also investigated.

The research further investigates the security concerns of the Internet of things, together with how the technology can be used as a platform to perpetrate and even inject threats and attacks. The research further investigates the landscape of distributed denial-of-service attacks by attempting to answer the following questions:

- What are DDoS attacks? How pervasive are these attacks?
- Why are DDoS attacks executed? How are DDoS executed?
- What is the attack targeting? Which DDoS attacks are common?
- What strategies and mechanisms are used for a successful DDoS attack? Which tools are used to conduct a DDoS attack?
- What defense mechanisms are currently used to combat DDoS attacks? What are their advantages and disadvantages?

The sections that follow will give a background of how the internet evolved into the IoT. It will explore the characteristics and current applications of the IoT paradigm. The security concerns that are present with the IoT are also discussed. The chapter further introduces the concept of DDoS; the various attack types and its background. The rationale and motives, together with methods and tools used to conduct a large scale DDoS are also presented in this chapter. The various defense mechanisms that are currently implemented in industry are explored together with their advantages and disadvantages. The chapter further presents the state of the art literature review of detection algorithms that are integrated in the defense mechanisms and network intrusion detection systems. The challenges of defending a network against a DDoS in an IoT environment is also heighted, while giving future direction and research questions that can be explored.

THE INTERNET OF THINGS

To understand the paradigm of the he Internet of Things (IoT), it is important for one to look at the evolution of the internet.

Evolution of the Internet

Communication technology began with the invention of the telegraph, telephone, radio, and the electronic computer. In the 1960's the US Department of Defense awarded contracts for the development for the ARPANET (Advanced Research Projects Agency Network). The ARPANET was the early packet switching network and the first to implement the TCP/IP protocol suite. This technology became the technical foundation of the Internet. In the early 1990's the technology was commercialised and became what is known as the World Wide Web (WWW).

The WWW became popular and experienced enormous use and rapid growth. Mobile devices developed to have internet connection capabilities and together they formed the mobile internet. This technology allowed devices and people to be connected from remote locations, and there emerged social networking platforms.

This allowed more and more devices to be connected and to communicate to each other over the internet. This was the dawn of the internet of things (IoT).

What Is the Internet of Things (IoT)?

"Internet of Things" was first mentioned by Kevin Ashton in 1998 (Ashton, 2009); and the term was formally introduced by the ITU (International Telecommunications Union) in their internet report of 2005 (Strategy & Unit, 2005). Since then there have been several debates on the precise definition of the IoT. This is due to the influence of several contributing fields, from information technology engineering, academia and marketing. For the purposes of this work we will define IoT as (Vermesan et al., 2011):

The Internet of Things allows people and things (or objects) to be connected Anytime, Anyplace, with anything and anyone; ideally using any path/network and any service.

The Figure 1 provides an example to better clarify the definition of IoT. In the past decade, there has been tremendous growth in the number of devices that humans use to produce and consume information. It has been reported that in 2003, there were 500 million devices, and this increased to 12.5 billion internet-enabled devices in the year 2010 (Evans, 2011). It is estimated that the year 2020 will see between 50 billion to 100 billion such devices connected to the internet (Sundmaeker, Guillemin, Friess, & Woelfflé, 2010).

Figure 1. Definition of internet of things with examples

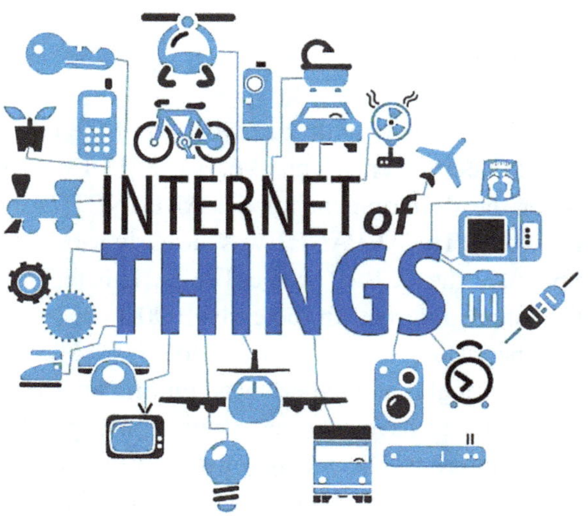

CHARACTERISTICS OF IoT

In this section of the work the major characteristics of the IoT are explored. Even though this may not be a comprehensive enumeration of the characteristics of IoT, those characteristics that are pertinent to internet and network security are identified as: size and population; complexity and intelligence; heterogeneity and interoperability.

Size and Population

The numbers of devices or entities involved in IoT are growing at a rapid rate. It is predicted that by the year 2020 there will be 50-100 billion devices connected to the internet (Sundmaeker et al., 2010). These are devices that are embedded with information and have the capabilities of transmitting the data using a particular method or channel of transmission, which a prone to abuse by an attacker. The increased size and population of devices that are connected to the internet provides a sea of available option that an attacker may use across the internet in addition to that specific domain application, to instigate an attack.

Complexity and Intelligence

IoT devices interact autonomously amongst each other. This interaction differs from one domain application to another based on the complexity and intelligence capabilities of the device. A device may have limited capabilities such as storage and processing power. This makes the device a low-complexity device with a small attack space. On the other hand, a device may have large storage and processing power, making it a highly intelligent device with a large attack space. The population of these intelligent devices is on the rise and they are becoming cheaper to acquire, therefore posing a threat to the internet and the domain in which these devices are deployed.

Heterogeneity and Interoperability

The demand and population of complexity intelligent devices is expected to grow rapidly; this is due to their ubiquitous and pervasive nature. They have the ability to operate in heterogeneous environments and also provide opportunities for interoperability between entities within an environment and across the IoT platform. There are advocacies for the need for universal interoperability and open standards in the IoT; however, progress has been halted by the reluctance of industries to cooperate. This is because universal interoperability is coupled with the challenge of accountability and management of security issues. This leaves industries and stakeholders in a situation where they are solely accountable and responsible to identify, prevent and resolve security issues in a distributed manner.

IoT APPLICATIONS DOMAIN

The vision and concept of IoT presents diverse capabilities to enable ICT innovation in various application domains. IoT may enhance competitiveness between different application domains and boost new venture possibilities by traversing a wide range of business segments. Therefore, IoT technologies impacts various application domains, and these application domains may be classified based on the type of network available, coverage, scale, heterogeneity, repeatability, user involvement and impact (Gluhak et al., 2011). The work of authors in (Gubbi, Buyya, Marusic, & Palaniswami, 2013; Miorandi, Sicari, De Pellegrini, & Chlamtac, 2012; Perera, Zaslavsky, Christen, & Georgakopoulos, 2014) has made attempts to classify IoT application domains and all their classification has common elements; and therefore the classification below will be adopted for the purpose of our work:

- Personal and Home Applications.
- Utilities and Environment applications.
- Smart Business and Smart Cities Applications.

The subsections that follow will explain the various application domains and provide a few examples.

Home and Personal Applications

The IoT platform also allows for user to build smart homes using IoT technologies. IoT can be used for home applications like those that allow users to gain control of home equipment such as refrigerators, air conditioners, washing machines and many more. This allows the user to better manage the home and energy consumption. A prototype design and framework of an internet based application that automates functional home devices has been developed by authors in (Alkar & Buhur, 2005).

Home applications like Ubiquitous Health and e-Health can use IoT technologies to help develop assisted-living solutions. These applications allow doctors to monitor the elderly and patients in their own homes; this in turn helps reduce the costs of in-hospital monitoring and again it allows for early treatment and intervention. For instance, the elderly and patients will carry medical sensors to monitor health parameters like blood pressure, body temperature and breathing activities and movement. Smartphones and other wearable technologies are equipped with accelerometer sensors, location and proximity sensors, and gyroscopes sensors that can be used to gather data about their patient's activities in their homes. The monitored data is used by local medical personnel for decision making about the patient health and rapid response when it is needed (Baig, Gholamhosseini, & Connolly, 2013).

A more popular example of IoT personal application is that of wearable technology and personal body area networks. These sensor technologies are connected to smartphones through Wi-Fi or Bluetooth technology to track daily activities like performance on exercise routines, distance ran, steps walked and calories burned. This data can be used to monitor a patient or user against set goals in order to enhance their lifestyle or to prevent health problems (Latré, Braem, Moerman, Blondia, & Demeester, 2011).

Utilities and Environment Applications

IoT provides a suitable platform for utilities and environmental monitoring applications. Some of these applications are implemented by municipalities and utility companies in the form of smart metering for water and electricity supplies. These applications are made up of large networks of sensors, usually on a regional and national scale. These applications are used to monitor consumer consumption in order to better manage resources and optimise services (Yun & Yuxin, 2010).

The same technology can be extended and applied towards monitoring drinking water and irrigation. Sensors are placed at strategic locations to monitor critical water and soil parameters. This can help avoid water and soil contamination and allow for better decision making concerning drinking water and agriculture (Liqiang, Shouyi, Leibo, Zhen, & Shaojun., 2011).

IoT technologies allows the distributed placement of sensors at various strategic location, in a seamless and self-managing manner. Sensor technologies allow communication amongst them and report on real-time events. These sensors can be placed in critical areas were human presences can be harmful (examples: volcanic areas and oceanic abysses). This can help monitor and detect anomalies in the environment (like wildfires (Oppermann, Boano, & Römer, 2014)) that can endanger human and animal life.

Smart Business and Smart Cities Applications

IoT technologies can provide a number of novel and diverse applications in smart cities scenarios. Sensors technologies can be deployed and used to provide advanced traffic control systems; this monitors vehicle traffic in big cities and highways so that in cases of congestion, alternative traffic routing advice can be provided.

This application can further be extended such that sensors monitor wear and tear on highway and road network infrastructures. In a city scenario, sensors can be deployed to further monitor and detect pollution levels in the air. They can do this by monitoring for levels of carbon dioxide, nitrogen oxide, ammonia and other pollutants (Miorandi et al., 2012).

Businesses can also benefit from the use of IoT technologies; they have used RFID and sensor technologies for inventory management in the supply and delivery sectors. These provide the ability for businesses to track the movement of goods and products throughout the various phases of its life-cycle. In the retail environment RFID has been used to reduce theft and counterfeiting of goods. In the food industry, bio sensor technologies have been used to monitor the production process of products. The sensors can help to ensure that the production process of the food products meets the set quality standards and can therefore determine the deterioration or shelf-life of the products (Gubbi et al., 2013).

Another important application of IoT technologies that benefits both government and businesses is security surveillance. Security surveillance is one of the most widely used camera network technology in business buildings, shopping malls, airports, road intersections, car parks and other public places. When IoT technologies like ambient sensors, infrared and sophisticated video analytics are combined, organizations will be able to track targets, distinguish suspicious behavior and detect left luggage and prevent unauthorized access (Gubbi et al., 2013; Miorandi et al., 2012).

IoT SECURITY CONCERNS

Security is a major concern for the widespread adoption of IoT technologies and applications. Industries and stakeholders are unlikely to adopt IoT technologies and applications if there is no guarantee for system and data confidentiality, privacy and trust. In light of the advocacy for an open IoT platform, there rise several security concerns. In this work we focus on security concerns in terms of cyber-attacks and their implication to the IoT platform.

Data Confidentiality

In many IoT application domains data is an important asset that needs to be protected. For example, in a business application domain, data is an asset that is used for an organization's competitiveness in the market. In this case, data confidentiality remains the most important because it assures that only those stakeholders and entities with authorization can access and modify the data generated by the application. The nature of IoT allows for entities to be mobile and interoperable across the application domain. This complicates authentication and access control to the application system and information. This amplifies the threat to the IoT application by providing an opportunity for attackers with access to the system to compromise its entities and carry out an attack to the environment.

Privacy

Another important security concern for the IoT platform is Privacy. Data privacy is concerned with defining rules for access to data; what kind of data can be accessed by which user or entity in the application domain. This is particularly important to an application domain like Ubiquitous-Healthcare; where these applications carry personal and sensitive information. It is therefore important to implement appropriate mechanisms for data privacy. The IoT platform allows for the use of ubiquitous wireless communication channels. However, if implemented incorrectly, the use of these communication channels may present risks and potential violation of the data privacy rules. This may be due to remote access capabilities that are vulnerable to eavesdropping, masquerade attacks and denial of service attacks.

Trust

Trust in information systems refers to security policies regulating access to resources and credentials that are required to satisfy the policies (Blaze, Feigenbaum, & Lacy, 1996). Trust negotiation mechanisms are used to exchange credentials. This is in order to allow individuals or devices requesting services or resources from the device or entities providing those services or resources. This approach to trust negotiation and management is a classic decentralized and static approach. It may not work well in an IoT environment where various individuals, entities and devices are heterogeneous, mobile and broadly distributed in physical space. This dynamic and distributed nature of the IoT makes trustworthiness extremely challenging because an attacker may design a masquerading attack in order to gain access and control of the physical and logical system and consequently gain access and control of the data generated by the system.

Summary

The Internet of Things is a new era of internet computing that is experiencing accelerated growth. This continuous advancement in IoT technologies will be integrated in our lives and change the way we live and the way organizations conduct business. However, the growth of networked and computing devices is also accompanied with an increased potential risk and attack space. A large number of these computing devices are increasingly becoming more mobile and distributed in their design, which means that current security processes and tools may need to be changed considerably.

The characteristics and nature of IoT also present attackers with increased opportunities and a broad spectrum of target systems to exploit. This will in turn give rise to more sophisticated tools and attacks that will be available for attackers so that they may perpetrate an attack. This will make the provision of data confidentiality, privacy and trust a challenging task. Therefore, new security approaches on information systems would needs to be continuously researched and developed so to strengthen and ensure safety and security for the IoT environment.

The attacks and threats that are important to this research are those that disrupt, degrade, deny and destroy the services rendered by the IoT application. The commonly used suite of attacks for the purpose of disruption and degradation of services are the Denial-of-Service (DoS) attacks. Given the distributed nature of the IoT platform, this provides the attacker with an opportunity to use the platform to carry out and even inject a distributed denial-of-service (DDoS) attack in the IoT application. The section that follows will give a detailed analysis of the nature of the DDoS attacks and their defense mechanisms.

INTRODUCTION TO DDoS ATTACKS

Recently, Forrester Consulting conducted a survey (Forrester Consulting, 2009) to study DDoS threats and protection in the US and Europe. Four hundred IT decision-makers and security professionals took part in the survey. These respondents were from various industries organisations that conduct business online or have a significant investment in their online brand and reputation. This included online financial services (eBanking), e-commerce services, online multimedia (news, video and audio services) and entertainment (online gaming). It was found that DDoS attacks have become a common occurrence such that it has become a top IT security threat. Nearly 75% of respondent reported that they have experienced one or more 'targeted' DDoS attack on their organisations in the past 12 months.

The first DoS attack on the public Internet occurred in August 1999 (Garber, 2000). In February 2000, a year after the first DoS incident, a group of commercial websites: Yahoo, CNN and eBay encountered their first DDoS attacks. A large number of requests flooded the websites; this forced the company's services offline, and therefore resulting in significant financial losses. A popular example of a DDoS attack is the July 4 2009 cyber-attack (Zargar, Joshi, & Tipper, 2013). A series of cyber-attacks were launched against major government, news media and financial websites in South Korea and the United States. These attacks resulted in service disruptions and in some cases millions of dollars per hour were lost while the organizations struggled to reinstate their online services.

The Forrester survey (Forrester Consulting, 2009) further revealed that many organizations are concerned about the threat of DDoS attacks. In the survey, only few organizations have specific DDoS protection mechanisms in place. Those that addressed the DDoS threat found that the mechanisms in place lack the capacity and agility to mitigate attacks rapidly before they reach the entire network. The failure of traditional DDoS defense mechanisms to adequately and rapidly defend networks may be attributed to the extraordinary and rapid changes in the DDoS terrain.

The nature of DDoS keeps changing over time as intruders adapt their attack methods to evade existing intrusion detection mechanisms. DDoS attacks have become larger, stealthier, more targeted and more sophisticated than ever. Almost every day sees a launch of new and sophisticated DDoS attacks with unknown motives (for social, political or criminal motives). The challenging task is therefore to develop adaptive DDoS defense mechanisms that have the ability to detect large scale attacks adequately and rapidly. It is therefore important to develop defense mechanisms that are able to detect DDoS attacks accurately (with low false alarm rate) and reliably (with low detection delay).

DDoS ATTACKS BACKGROUND

A DoS attack can be described as an attack designed to leave a computer or network incapable of providing normal services to its legitimate users. It is the result of malicious action taken by an attacker with the intention of blocking or degrading the services of a computer or network. The section that follows looks at characteristics of DoS attacks, tools used to coordinate these attacks.

Denial of Service (DoS) Attacks

A DoS attack is a malicious attempt by an attacker to disrupt the online services of a service provider to make it unavailable to its legitimate users (Douligeris & Mitrokotsa, 2004; Zargar et al., 2013; Zhou, Leckie, & Karunasekera, 2010). These attacks are one of the major threats against the availability of internet services. The attack makes particular network services unavailable (such as internet and emails) by consuming resources extensively such that the intended service is no longer accessible to its authorised users. The DoS attack may target computational resources like the CPU, or a network resource such as bandwidth.

The first documented DoS attack occurred during the week of 1 February 2000(Garber, 2000). This was a series of orchestrated attacks against e-commerce sites that included Amazon.com and eBay.com. These attacks used computers at multiple locations to overwhelm the vendors' computers and shut down their websites to legitimate commercial traffic. The impact of a DoS attack can range from a minor increase in the service response time to complete inaccessibility, and at times having financial implications on organisations heavily reliant on the availability of their internet services.

Distributed Denial of Service (DDoS) Attacks

A variant of the DoS attack is the Distributed Denial of Service (DDoS) attack. In a DDoS, the attacker uses a network of compromised machine (bots, zombies, slaves or agents) to attack a single target-victim to cause a large scale DoS. The compromised machines will be infected with a Trojan or backdoor program (without owner's knowledge) that allows the attacker (bot-master) to take control of them. The master-bot will instruct all bots to simultaneously and repeatedly flood the target system with a large number of factitious requests. This will eventually cause a DDoS for the legitimate users of the targeted victim's system. This is illustrated by the Figure 2 that illustrates a typical architecture of a DDoS attack.

Figure 2. A typical DDoS architecture

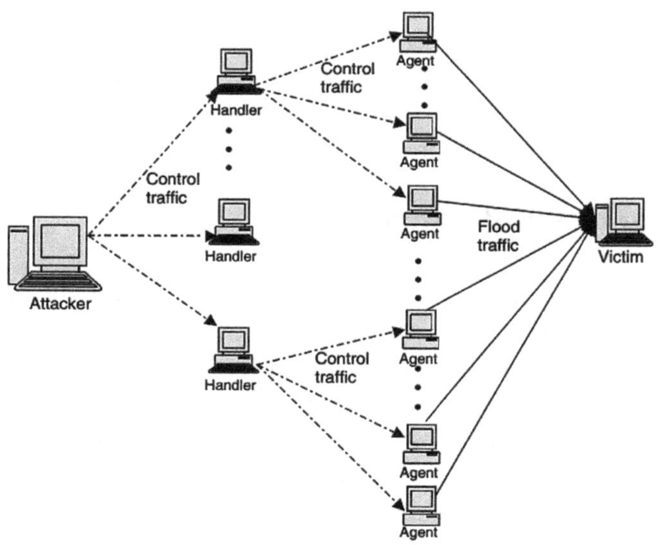

A DDoS attack consumes available critical resources on the victim. The method of achieving this is by launching a high-rate flooding (HRF) attack towards the victim with a large number of packets and thus exhausting its available network or computing resources. There are several types of HRF attacks; the most common are buffer overflow, ping of death (PoD), TCP SYN floods, UDP floods, smurf, Neptune, teardrop and land. For instance, in February of 2000, Yahoo incurred a significant advertising revenue loss due to a major DDoS attack that lasted for about two hours. In December of 2000, financial organisations like PayPal, Visa.com and MasterCard.com experienced a DDoS flooding attack. While in another instance, 9 major U.S banks were continuously experiencing a series of DDoS flooding attacks since September of 2012 (Zargar et al., 2013).

Hackers have been using DDos attacks for a long time, and they have changed their attack profiles considerably in efforts to evade current defense mechanisms (Forrester Consulting, 2009). DDos attacks have become more sophisticated, disparate and unrelated; therefore, making them an even greater threat.

The Prevalence of DDoS Attacks

A Q4 2012 report on Global DDoS attacks by Prolexic Technologies (Prolexic Technologies, 2012) revealed that there has been a general increase in DDos tools and attacks. Most attacks were targeted against key infrastructure service that had a large online service rendering. These are clients in industries such as financial sector, e-Commerce, software-as-a-Service (SaaS), and energy sector as well as government organisations. In the year 2012, the total number of new DDoS attacks increased by 19% when compared to Q4 2011. The average duration of attack for DDoS has increased from 19.2 hours to 32.2 hours when compared to Q3 of the same year.

The capability and prevalence of a DDoS attacks is in the fact that DDoS attacks mainly take advantage of the Internet architecture. The Internet was designed with functionality in mind, and not security. The Internet is a simple network that is4 optimized for packet forwarding. The design of the Internet follows the *end-to-end paradigm*. This design leaves the responsibility to establish security features to the sender and receiver (end-users) of the two-way communication. And this has led to several security issues that have been utilized by attackers for DDoS attacks. The work of authors in (Mirkovic & Reiher, 2004) and (Douligeris & Mitrokotsa, 2004) argue that the following design issues make the internet prone to DDoS attacks:

- **Internet Security Is Highly Interdependent:** In spite of how secure the victim's system may be, it is still prone to a DDoS attack because it is dependent on the state of security in rest of the global Internet.

- **Internet Resources Are Limited:** Each internet system is limited resources that can be consumed by sufficient number of users.
- **Accountability Is Not Enforced:** IP spoofing gives attackers the mean to execute attacks and be able to escape from accountability of their actions.
- **Intelligence and Resources Are Not Collocated:** The end-to-end communication design of the Internet has limited the amount of processing in the intermediate network so that packets could be forwarded efficiently at minimum cost. The intelligence for service guarantee was left to the end host. Meanwhile, research and the demand for large throughput have led to the design of high bandwidth pathways in the intermediate network. In this way, attackers are presented with an opportunity to exploit the abundant resources on an innocent network in order to flood a victim with malicious messages.

Attackers Motives

The motives for a DDoS attacks vary and few researchers (P. Liu, Zang, & Yu, 2005) have attempted to model and infer attacker motives in such a way that decision-making, risk-assessment and proactive cyber defense could be strengthened. The attacker's motive to launch a DDoS attacks can then be classified into the following five categories (Douligeris & Mitrokotsa, 2004):

- **Financial/Economic Gain:** These types of attacks are a major concern to companies that conduct their business online or have a significant investment in their online brands. Mainly because the attacker that launches this type of attack is the most technical and experienced. These attacks are dangerous, hard to detect and hard to stop.
- **Revenge:** The source of this attack is normally frustration. Attackers in this category are possibly individuals with novice technical skills and carry out the attack in reaction to a supposed suppression.
- **Ideological Belief:** Some attackers are motivated by their ideological beliefs. For example, the political motives that led to DDoS attack sabotages to the WikiLeaks website.
- **Intellectual Challenge:** This group of attackers are young hacking enthusiast that are experimenting and learning how to execute various types of attacks.
- **Cyber Warfare:** Cyber warfare attackers are considered to be very dangerous, well trained and have plenty of resources. They are usually politically motivated, and belong to a military or terrorist organisation. They attack telecommunications service providers, energy infrastructures and financial organisations. These types of attackers spend most of their time and resource towards the disruption of services. This may disrupt critical services to a country and therefore the organization may suffer substantial economic loses.

DDoS Attack Classifications and Targets

DDoS attacks target different points in a network and have diverse consequences; however, they all intend to interrupt and discontinue a service of their targets. DDoS attacks may differ based on their target. A DDoS attack that targets a network differs to an attack that targets an application. There have been various classifications of DDoS attacks in the literature (Anand, 2014; Bhattacharyya & Kalita, 2013; Douligeris & Mitrokotsa, 2004; Kumar, 2015; Lazarevic, Kumar, & Srivastava, 2005; Mirkovic & Reiher, 2004; Nagpal, Sharma, Chauhan, & Panesar, 2015; Prathibha, 2014; Zargar et al., 2013; Zhou et al., 2010); the surveys categorise DDoS attacks according to their target; degree of automation; exploited weakness; attack rate dynamics; and impact on the victim (Mirkovic & Reiher, 2004). The different classifications are examined in the subsections that follow.

- **Classification Based on DDoS Attack Targets:** DDoS attacks may target different points in the OSI model of the communication channel. At each point the attack may produce varied effects, however the overall effect of an attack is to degrade and disrupt services to their intended users. DDoS targets can be divided into network-transport layer targets and application level targets.
- **Network-Transport Level Targeting DDoS Attacks:** The primary target of Network/Transport layer DDoS attacks is on the volume of traffic being sent to the victim, rather than the actual content of the packets. They target Network Layer (Layer 3) and Transport Layer (Layer 4) of the OSI model. The aim of these attacks is to consume incoming network bandwidth of the target victim by sending large volumes of packets. An attacker may also evade detection by using IP address spoofing techniques. Example of this type of attacks includes: TCP SYN, UDP and ICMP flooding attacks (discussed in a section that follows).
- **Application Level Targeting DDoS Attacks:** Application level DDoS attacks exploit the vulnerability in the design and implementation of the application running on the target victim machine. They are not 'volume-based' attacks and they generally consume less bandwidth. They use low rate attacks mechanisms to prevent legitimate users from accessing the services provided by the target victim machine. They use 'superficially legitimate' attack packets and are difficult to detect. Examples of these attacks include the HTTP request attack and the DNS Amplification attack.

This research study will explore the most common DDoS flooding attacks in which the attacker attempts to disrupt a legitimate user's connectivity by exhausting bandwidth, router processing capacity or network resources (network and transport layer flooding attacks); attacks that exhaust the server resources like sockets, memory and database bandwidth (application layer flooding attacks) are not a focus of this study.

- **Classification Based on Degree of Automation:** Attacks can also be classified based on their degree of automation. There are various strategies available to launch an HRF DDoS attack, they can be launched manually through human coordination, or they can be automated through the use of botnets (Mirkovic & Reiher, 2004).
- **Attack Coordination:**
    - **Manual Attacks:** The early DDoS attacks employed a manual launch strategy. This type of attacks requires significant human coordination in order to result into an effective attack on the victim. The attacker will manually scan for vulnerable and compromised remote machines; break into them to install an attack code/program which will control the onset of the attack. Depending on the number of machines involved in the attack, their computational capacity and the sophistication of the attack tool being used, the total volume of traffic sent to the victim may crush its online services. This attack strategy belonged to early DDoS attacks. However, the availability of fast computers and fast internet connections has made this coordination strategy obsolete.
    - **Semi-Automated and Automated Attacks:** These types of attack launch strategies consist of a master machine and agents (slave, daemon, and zombie) machines. The onset of the attack, duration, attack type and victim are pre-programmed in the installed attack code. This attack strategy offers minimal exposure to the attacker as he is only involved at the start of the recruitment process. The most popular automated mechanisms that are used to launch attacks are amplification and reflection based attacks (Zargar et al., 2013).
- **Attack Strategy:**
    - **Amplification-Based Attacks:** Attackers exploit network services to allow them to generate multiple messages, for every message sent (Internet Control Message Protocol-ICMP Echo request), in order to amplify traffic towards the victim. In this attack mechanism, the amplification network is a network of host machines that enable IP broadcast messages. The broadcast message is sent using a spoofed IP address, and it triggers a response from every host machine in the amplification network directed towards the victim. This is depicted by Figure 3.

  - **Reflection-Based Attacks:** In order to initiate this attack, a set of hosts (reflector network) is used. A reflector is one that is capable of responding to an incoming message (e.g. SYN) by sending a reply message (SYN+ACK) to the packet's spoofed source IP address (of the intended victim). Web-server and DNS servers are usually used as reflectors. The reflection attack will result in a large volume of traffic towards the intended victim. This is depicted by Figure 4.
- **Attack Components:** In order to coordinate a large scale DDoS attack, reflection and amplification attack mechanisms may be used simultaneously. Botnets have been constantly used to assist with both reflection and amplification attacks. Botnets consist of masters, handlers and bots (Douligeris & Mitrokotsa, 2004; Mirkovic & Reiher, 2004; Peng, Leckie, & Ramamohanarao, 2007). The Figure 5 depicts the elements of a Botnet-based attack.
  - **Masters (Attackers):** These are attackers that sent command and control instructions to both handlers and the bots in order to initiate and execute an attack.
  - **Handlers:** Handlers are malicious programs that are installed on compromised host machines. Attackers (the master) use handlers as a method to indirectly communicate and send instructions to the bots. Attackers use various methods to communicate with the handlers and bots, and lately they have been using Instant Messaging (IM) and Internet Relay Chat (IRC).

Figure 3. Amplification-based attack mechanism

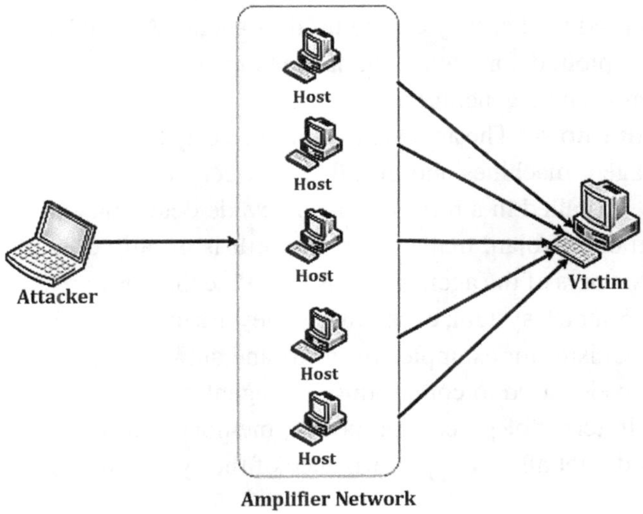

Figure 4. Reflection-based DDoS attack mechanism

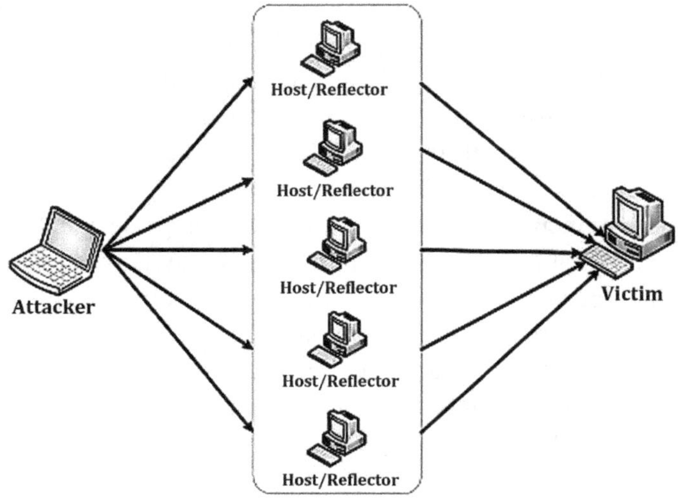

- ◦ **Bots:** These are compromised host machines that have the malicious handler program installed on them. They are the machines that will be used to carry out the large scale distributed attack.

- **DDoS Attack Process:** There are several steps involved in coordinating and launching a DDoS attack (Bhuyan, Kashyap, Bhattacharyya, & Kalita, 2013; Douligeris & Mitrokotsa, 2004).
    - ◦ **Recruitment and Selection of Agents:** In this step the attacker selects the agents that will perform the attack. This selection is based on the nature of the machine's present vulnerabilities. These machines are compromised so that they can be used as agents. Normally, these machines are exploited for their abundant resources, so that a powerful attack stream can be generated.
    - ◦ **Compromise:** The attacker exploits security flaws and vulnerabilities of the agent machines and installs the attack code. The attack code needs to be installed in a form that it can evade detection and removal (in the form of a Trojan, malware or virus). It is usually difficult for the users and owners of the agent systems to realize that they are participating in a DDoS attack system, except when they are using a sophisticated defense mechanism (for example anti-virus and anti-malware software). The attack codes used to compromise the agent machines are very cost effective in terms of processing power, memory and bandwidth. Therefore, they do not affect the performance of the system notably.

Figure 5. Elements of a Botnet
Zargar et al., 2013.

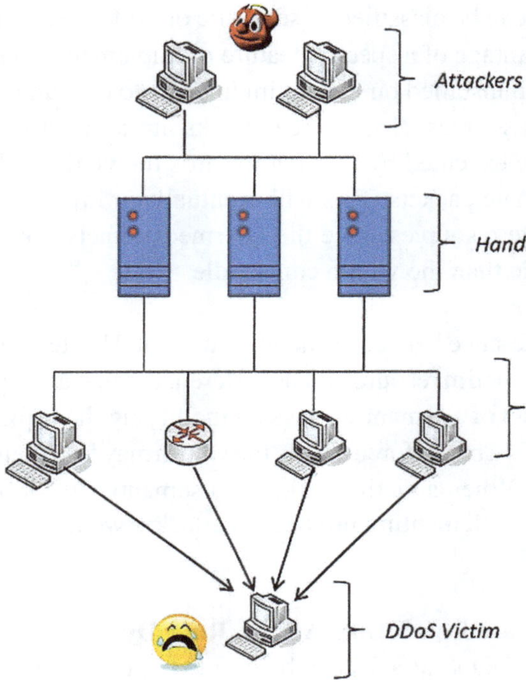

- **Communication:** The attacker communicates with a large number of handlers through various protocols such as ICMP, TCP, or UDP. In this communication, the attacker would like to identify which agents are up and running; when to schedule attacks; or when to upgrade the handlers. In recent years, an on-line, multi-user chatting system known as the Internet Relay Chat (IRC) channels have been used for communication between the attacker and the agents. The use of the IRC channels for launching a DDoS attack has become popular largely due to three main benefits: It offers a high degree of anonymity; it is difficult to detect; and it provides a strong, guaranteed delivery system.
- **Attack:** The attacker sends a command to initiate the attack. The victim, the duration of the attack as well as special features of the attack such as the type, length, TTL, and port numbers can be adjusted. If there are substantial variations in the properties of attack packets, it is beneficial to the attacker, since it hardens detection.

- **Classification Based on Exploited Vulnerability:** DDoS attacks exploit numerous weaknesses in a system; however classification according to exploited vulnerability can be classified as semantic or brute-force attacks. Semantic attacks take advantage of a specific feature or implementation bug of a protocol or application installed on the victim in order to consume excess amounts of is available resources. Brute-force attacks are an alternative to semantic attacks. They are executed by sending towards the victim, a large amount of supposed legitimate packets. This will eventually or immediately exhaust the victim's available resources since the intermediate network can deliver high volumes of traffic than the victim can handle.

There is subtle difference between semantic attack and brute-force attacks. They both exhaust available victim resources. The difference is that a victim can considerably mitigate the impact of a semantic attack by modifying the exploited protocol or by deploying proxies. In a brute-force attack, the victim may find themselves helpless to mitigate the attack. When a victim mitigates a semantic attack by modifying an exploited protocol or implementing proxies, an attacker would normally resolve to use a brute-force strategy.

- **Classification Based on DDoS Attack Rate Dynamics:** Based on attack rate dynamics, a DDoS attacks can be divided into constant rate attacks and variable rate attacks. This classification is described below.
- **Constant Rate Attacks:** A large number of attacks assume this format. In this form of attack and from the onset of the attack, attack packets from the attack agents are sent at a steady and constant rate. The agent machines generate attack packets using all available resources at once, without a break or variation in the rate of attack. The impact of such an attack on a victim is quick, continuous and sudden.
- **Variable Rate Attacks:** Variable rate attacks are not immediate in their attack strategy. Their attack strategy has a variable rate. In this way they are able to avoid detection. Variable rate attacks have the ability to manipulate a defense mechanisms training model in such a way that it evades detection. Variable rate attacks can further be divided in to *increasing rate* attacks and *fluctuating rate* attacks.

Increasing rate attacks have a low rate attack strategy and gradually increases until all resources are exhausted. This strategy delays the detection of the attack by slowly degrading the victim's services over an extended period of time. Fluctuating rate attacks adjust their attack rate based on the victim's behaviour and response to the attack. In this form of attack, the victim will experience a periodic service disruption because attack will occasionally relieve the attack effect from the victims in order to evade detection.

- **Classification Based on DDoS Attack Impact on Victim:** A DDoS attack can have one of two impacts on a victim. The Impact may be disruptive or degrading. A disruptive attack is one that leads to a complete depletion of victim resources and therefore denying the service to the victim's clients. A majority of attacks belong to this category. A degrading attack is one that consumes a portion of the victim's resources. The attack will slow down the victim's services in order to prevent access for legitimate users. For the reason that the attack does not cause a complete service disruption, it can therefore remain undetected for a long period of time.

Common Types of DDoS Attacks

In a 2015 first quarter report by Kaspersky Lab (Kaspersky Labs, 2015) it was revealed that the TCP SYN flood; HTTP flood; UDP flood; and the ICMP flood attacks were the most common. The sub-sections that follow discuss the various types of HRF DDoS attacks.

In the subsections that follow, the most common types of flooding attacks are discussed.

- **TCP SYN Flooding Attacks:** A TCP SYN flooding attack is an example of a network layer flooding attack, and it is one of the most common and powerful flooding methods. It exploits the vulnerabilities of the TCP three-way

Figure 6. TCP three-way handshake

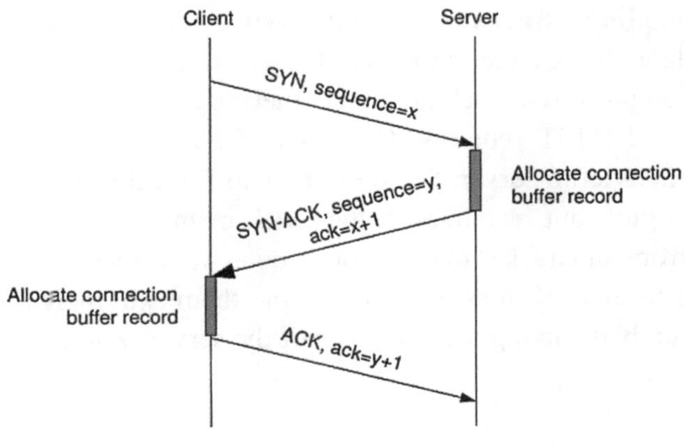

handshake; this is depicted by the Figure 6. In a normal TCP connection, the client initiates the connection by sending a SYN packet to the server, as a way of requesting a connection. Upon receiving the connection request, the server will open a connection session and respond with a SYN_ACK packet; by doing this the server stores details of the requested TCP connection in the memory stack and allocates resources to this open session (Douligeris & Mitrokotsa, 2004).

The connection remains in a half-open state, i.e. the SYN_RECVD state. To complete the three-way handshake with the server, the client will need to confirm the connection and respond with an ACK packet. The server will then check the memory stack for an existing connection request, and the TCP connection will be moved from the SYN_RECVD state to ESTABLISHED state. If there is no ACK packet sent within a specific period of time, the connection will timeout and therefore releasing the allocated resources (Bhuyan et al., 2013).

In a TCP SYN flooding attack, the attacker streams large volumes of SYN packets towards the victim server. These packets normally contain spoofed IP addresses, i.e. IP addresses that are non-existent or are not utilised. TCP SYN floods can also be launched using compromised machines with legitimate IP addresses, however the machines need to be configured in such a way that it does not respond or acknowledge a SYN_ACK packet from the victim server. In this way the server will not receive any ACK packet from the clients for the 'half-open' connection request.

During the high rate flooding attack, and for a period of time, the server will maintain a large volume of incomplete three-way handshake and allocates resource towards the fictitious connection requests. The server will gather more fictitious requests and eventually exhaust its resources. This will prevent new requests, plus legitimate client requests, from being further processed by the server (Mirkovic & Reiher, 2005).

- **HTTP Flooding Attacks:** An HTTP flooding attack is an example of a high rate flooding attack targeting the application layer. The attacker uses a large army of compromised machines and botnets to stream a large volume of supposedly valid HTTP requests (GET and POST) for a web-page or a large file from the victim server. For the server to fulfil this request, it sometime allocates significant recourses in the CPU, memory and bandwidth. HTTP requests from an attacker may masquerade as valid requests. This will cause the server to treat them as normal, making them extremely difficult to filter and eventually depleting the resources of the server (Zargar et al., 2013).

- **UDP Flooding Attacks:** During a UDP Flood attack, the victim system is sent a large number of UDP packets. The attacker uses a large number of bots and agents to saturate the victim system's network and exhaust its available bandwidth for legitimate service requests. The attacker normally uses bots and agents with spoofed IP addresses to send UDP packet to the victim.

When the victim system receives the packet, it will determine the application that is supposed to be waiting on the destination port. When it realizes that there is no application that is waiting on the port, it will generate a "destination unreachable" packet to the forged source address. With an army of bots and a large UDP packets delivered to ports of the victim, the system will saturate (Mirkovic & Reiher, 2005).

- **ICMP Flooding Attack:** This type of flooding attacks takes advantage of the Internet Control Message Protocol (ICMP). The protocol permits a user machine to send an ICMP_ECHO_REPLY packet (known as a "ping" message) to a target host or remote server. This is in efforts of testing the reachability of the host and to measure the roundtrip time of the message sent back to the user machine. If the target host is reachable, a response will be sent back to the user machine. Response packets will include statistical information like the minimum, maximum, mean and standard deviation of the packet rountrip. For the target host to generate a response packet, it utilizes its CPU (Central Processing Unit) and network resources (Mirkovic & Reiher, 2005).

In an ICMP flooding attack, the attacker uses an army of bots and agents with spoofed IP addresses. The bots will repeatedly and simultaneously send ICMP_ECHO_REPLY packets to the target victim. The packet request reply from the victim (to a spoofed IP address) has the consequence of saturating the victim CPU and network resources (Douligeris & Mitrokotsa, 2004).

Commonly Used DDoS Tools

There are several known DDoS tools available for attackers. A comprehensive list of DDoS tools can be found in literature (Alomari, Manickam, Gupta, Karuppayah, & Alfaris, 2012; Bhuyan et al., 2013; Z. Chen, Chen, & Delis, 2007; Douligeris & Mitrokotsa, 2004; Gupta, Joshi, & Misra, 2009; Mishra, Gupta, & Joshi, 2011; Somal & Virk, 2014). These tools are, to a certain degree, similar in architecture and design. Some tools are modifications and improvements by hackers on previous attack tools. In this subsection we analyse the popular DDoS tools used by hackers.

- **Trinoo:** Trinoo (Criscuolo, 2000; Dittrich, 1999c) is a widely distributed and used tacking tool by hackers. It is a bandwidth depletion tool used to launch coordinated UDP flood attacks against one or many IP addresses. The tool uses fixed-size UDP packets that are randomly sent to the victim machine's ports. It provides encryption and password protection for the communication channel. Trinoo does not support source IP address spoofing, but it can be modified such that it can support source IP spoofing.
- **Tribe Flood Network (TFN):** Tribe Flood Network (TFN) (Dittrich, 1999b) is another widely distributed and used DDoS attack tool. It is used to launch coordinated UDP flood; TCP SYN flood; ICMP echo request flood; directed ICMP flooding attacks. TFN can generate attacks directed to one or more target IP addresses. It is not capable of encrypting the communication channel between attack components, making it possible to detect. It is capable of generating spoofed source IP addresses.
- **TFN2K:** The TFN2K (Barlow & Thrower, 2000) is a more advanced variant of the TFN. It is built based on the TFN architecture. The TFN2K has improved from TFN with features designed specifically to make it possible that its traffic is difficult to recognize and filter. It enables remote command execution, and conceals the true source of the attack using IP address spoofing. TFN2K traffic is transported over multiple transport protocols including UDP, TCP, and ICMP. Attacks involve flooding the victim's system and crashing or introducing instabilities into systems by sending malformed or invalid packets, such as those found in the Teardrop and Land attacks. TFN2K uses the master-agent architecture to communicate, and all of the communications between the master and the agent are encrypted.
- **Stacheldraht:** Stacheldraht (Dittrich, 1999a) (a German term for 'barbed wire') is an attack tool based on a feature combination of the TFN and Trinoo attack tools. It eliminates some of the TFN weak points and combines the handler/agent feature of the Trinoo. It has the capability of performing updates on agents automatically. Stacheldraht also has a secure telnet connection through symmetric key encryption between the attacker and the handler systems. This helps with avoiding detection. The attack tools is able to launch attacks like the UDP flood, TCP SYN flood and ICMP echo request flood.
- **Mstream:** Mstream (Dittrich, Weaver, Dietrich, & Long, 2000) is a simple point-to-point attack tool used to launch TCP ACK Floods towards its victim. It uses spoofed TCP packets with the ACK flag set to attack the target. It uses UDP/TCP packets for communication between the master and agent, through an unencrypted telnet communication channel.

- **Shaft:** Shaft (Dietrich, Long, & Dittrich, 2000) it is derived from the Trinoo attack tool and it has similar architecture (agent/handler architecture). The handler communicates with the agent using an unencrypted telnet connection. It uses spoofed source IP addresses, and has the ability to change IP addresses during an attack in real time. It has additional features of providing the attacker with statistical information of the launched flood attack. These statistics are useful to the attacker to know when the victim's system has saturated. It has capabilities of launching UDP, ICMP, and TCP flooding attacks.
- **Trinity v3:** Trinity v3 (Hancock, 2000) is a sophisticated attack tool that is capable of launching various types of flooding attacks towards a victim machine. Flood attacks that can be launched include UDP, TCP SYN and other floods. It uses the IRC communication channel to establish a connection between the handler and the agent.
- **Knight:** The Knight (Center,) is a very lightweight yet powerful IRC-based DDoS attack tool. The tool is capable of launching TCP SYN attacks, UDP Flood attacks. It is designed to run on Windows operating systems and it is typically installed using a Trojan horse program called Back Orifice.
- **Low Orbit Ion Cannon (LOIC):** The Low Orbit Ion Cannon (LOIC) (Batishchev, 2012) is an IRC based attack tool. It is capable of launching the UDP flood, TCP flood and the HTTP flood. It is available as a binary and web-based application.

DDoS DEFENSE MECHANISMS

The nature of DDoS keeps changing over time as intruders adapt their attack methods to evade existing intrusion detection mechanisms. DDoS attacks have become larger, stealthier, more targeted and more sophisticated than ever. Almost every day sees a launch of new and sophisticated DDoS attacks with unknown motives (be it social, political or criminal motives). The challenging task is therefore to develop adaptive DDoS defense mechanisms that have the ability to detect large scale attacks adequately and rapidly. To achieve this, one needs to discover how a technique is designed and deployed. In this section we ask the following questions:

- Where is the attack detected?
- What is the response mechanism?
- How is the attack detected?

Classification Based on Defense Points (or Defense Location)

It is important to understand and know the point or location where a defense mechanism is implemented. A defense mechanism can be deployed at the victim-end, the source-end or the intermediate network. Each deployment location has its advantages and disadvantages. Detection of DDoS attacks can take place along the path between the destination (attack victim) and the source of the attack. Detecting a DDoS attack can be comparatively easier at the victim, because all traffic packets can be observed at the victim. Conversely, it is complicated for a single source network to detect an attack except if most or all attacks are launched from that source network. One would preferably want to detect an attack closer to its source; however, there is a trade-off between detection accuracy and the detection mechanism's proximity to the attack source. The subsection that follows discusses the advantages and disadvantages of the three points of defense.

- **Victim-End Defense Mechanism:** Victim-end defense mechanisms perform detection at the destination of the attack. Historically, most defense mechanisms were designed to work at the victim-end since the victim experiences the undesirable effects of the attack. These mechanisms are installed either at the edge outer or at the access router of the victim ISP. They have the ability to model victim's network traffic behaviour and they are therefore able to discriminate attack traffic from legitimate traffic. In (Ferguson, 2000; Geng & Whinston, 2000; Jin, Wang, & Shin, 2003; K. Park & Lee, 2001; Peng, Leckie, & Ramamohanarao, 2003; Wang, Jin, & Shin, 2007; Ye, Vilbert, & Chen, 2003) the authors proposed architectures and systems that can be used for victim-end defense mechanisms.
- **Source-End Defense Mechanism:** Source-end defense mechanisms perform detection near the source of the attack in order to prevent an ISP's clients from taking part in a large scale DDoS attack. These mechanisms can be installed at the source network's routers or at the ISP's access and edge routers. The source-end defense point is the best point of defense because they are near to the source of the attack; the mechanisms can simplify a traceback in an investigation of the attack and minimize the damage caused by the attack. Detecting attacks at their source has advantages; however, discriminating legitimate traffic from attack traffic at the source can be a serious challenge due to a number of reasons (Zargar et al., 2013):
    - Since sources are distributed among different domains, it is difficult for a single source to accurately detect an attack.
    - Since the volume of traffic at the source is not large enough, it may be difficult to differentiate between legitimate traffic and attack traffic.

- Source-end defense mechanisms prevent the source network from participating in a DDoS attack, and therefore the benefit is for the potential victim and not entirely for the source network. Therefore, there is low motivation to deploy these mechanisms since they are expensive to deploy.

Several source-end defense mechanisms have been proposed in literature (Burch & Cheswick, 2000; Ferguson, 2000; Mirkovic & Reiher, 2005; Mirković, Prier, & Reiher, 2002).

- **Intermediate Network Defense Mechanism**: Intermediate network defense mechanisms are normally installed at an ISP's core routers. They are more effective than victim-end defense mechanisms because they can minimize the effect of the attack at the victim. The core routers independently filter and rate-limit the traffic passing through it. However, core routers process highly aggregated and large volumes of traffic, therefore they are not able to detect and filter for each possible victim. To be able to discriminate between attack in the intermediate network, core routers will require high storage and processing power since large volumes of packets are processed at these routers. Therefore, intermediate network defense mechanisms face the challenge of accurately discriminating attack traffic from legitimate traffic. In (Zhang & Parashar, 2006) Zhang et al. proposed an architecture that can be used for attack detection in the intermediate network.

Defense Approaches and Strategies (Point in Time Defense)

These are based on reaction time, defense approaches can be broadly classified into three types, namely: Prevention Approaches, Survival Approaches and Responsive Approaches; which are discussed in the subsection that follows.

The best way of defending against a DDoS attack is to prevent the attack from taking place. It is therefore the aim of these types of approaches to detect attacks and to impede attackers' attempts earlier before it could reach the victim machine. With this approach, the victim is not aware that they were under an attack. Routers perform an important task in these approaches by detecting and filtering attack traffic before it could reach the victim. These are routers that are placed closer to the traffic (attack) source, core routers, or end-routers closer to the victim machine. The routers apply techniques that attempt to distinguish and filter malicious from legitimate traffic. Some of the specific approaches are discussed below:

- **Ingress/Egress Filtering (Ferguson, 2000):** This is a filtering approach used to stop attack packets before the attack extends to the victim machine. Ingress filtering is a mechanism that is concerned with preventing inbound-incoming packets from illegitimate and spoofed IP address sources from entering the network. This approach can reduce DDoS attacks significantly by dropping packets coming from suspicious IP addresses. However, sometimes it can drop legitimate packets. Egress filtering is also a mechanism similar to Ingress; however, it is concerned with outgoing-outbound packets. It ensures that traffic packet is only coming from IP address space that is already allocated. The Egress filtering technique does not particularly protect the network from attacks, however, it protects the domain network from participating in a DDoS attack against other domains.
- **Route-Based Distributed Packet Filtering (K. Park & Lee, 2001):** This filtering mechanism is an extension of the Ingress filtering mechanism to core routers of the internet. The approach uses routing information to filter spoofed IP packets. This approach has the capabilities of filtering a large number of spoofed IP packets at the border router before it could reach the victim network.
- **Disabling Unused Services (Geng & Whinston, 2000):** Attackers may use unused services to conduct a complete DDoS attack. For example: UDP echo, ping and IP broadcast services. Therefore, it is important that a service that is not needed should be disabled from the network.
- **History-Based Filtering:** Peng et al., (2003) proposed this approach towards prevention of DDoS attacks. In this approach, the edge router keeps a database of IP addresses based on previous connection history. The approach will permit incoming packets whose source address corresponds to an IP address in the database.
- **Secure Overlay Services (SOS) (Keromytis, Misra, & Rubenstein, 2002):** This approach is a distributed system that requires target systems to modify their architecture in order to offer prevention against DDoS. In this architecture, in order for a client to gain access the client needs to be authenticated with one of the SOAP (Service Overlay Access Points) nodes. This allows the client to also gain access to the overlay network which filters out all other unauthenticated traffic packets. The overlay network uses servlets to filter legitimate traffic and the target system will only accept traffic packets coming from the small number of nodes called servlets.
- **Responsive Techniques (Reactive Strategies):** During the attack: In a responsive technique, the ISP experiences a DDoS attack on its services and will implement (invoke) a detection and mitigation procedure. The invoked procedure is meant to help control the attack traffic flow by tracing and locat-

Table 1. Advantages and disadvantages of prevention approaches

Advantages	Disadvantages
• Effective in a way that the victims do not notice that they are under attack. • They are lightweight to implements because the ISP has knowledge of the address space that is assigned to each customer. • Filtering can be done based on various criteria, e.g. IP address, protocol type, port number etc. • It helps reduce spoofed IP addresses significantly before they reach the target victim. • Filtering approaches have the ability of preventing attack traffic at their source network. • With collaboration amongst ISP, more accurate attack signatures can be generated. This will therefore reduce the false positive rate.	• Most of the techniques can be effective with universal deployment and collaboration with other ISP. • Attackers use tools that allow them to use non-spoofed IP addresses to generate attacks. • Some implementation may benefit the ISP at the cost of network performance. • Some approaches have no benefit to the ISP deployed, but may prevent them from participating in a DDoS attack. • Most of these approaches suffer from high false positive rate, where legitimate traffic packets are dropped from the network. • It is possible for an attacker to learn the prevention approach and develop methods to circumvent them.

ing the origin of the attack and filter traffic based on the identified source. Most DDoS defense techniques belong to this category (Beitollahi & Deconinck, 2012), and the most popular are analysed below.

- **Pushback Technique:** At the router level, a local Aggregate Congestion Control (ACC) detects congestion and develops an attack signature that can be used for router filtering. The signature delineates a traffic aggregate for a group of traffic flows with similar properties. Given the developed signature, an appropriate rate limit is also defined for the ACC which is shared amongst adjacent routers. Should a router become congested, a rate limit request is sent to the neighbouring router to rate limit traffic that matches the ACC's signature, this request is also further broadcast to other upstream neighbouring routers (Mahajan et al., 2002).
- **Hop Count Packet Filtering (HCF):** This technique was proposed in (Jin et al., 2003; Wang et al., 2007) and is based on discovering the time-to-live (TTL) value of packets. A packet is launched with a TTL value from the sender (normal values: 30, 32, 60, 64, 128 and 255) when sent to the target. The victim estimates the initial TTL value of the packet when it was launched. The hop count is determined by difference between initial TTL value and the current value. When the victim is not under attack, a table is created of the most frequent legitimate users and their associated hop count. However, during an attack, spoofed packets are those that are not stored in the table and their hop count do not match with their respective launch address. With this technique, it is difficult for an attacker to estimate the TTL value of a forged packet in order to bypass the filtering technique.

- **K-Max-Min:** This is a technique proposed by (Hosaagrahara & Sethu, 2008; Yau, Lui, Liang, & Yam, 2005) wherein a DDoS attack is viewed as a resource management problem. This is an improved version of the Pushback technique. The proposed solution is to distribute the victim's congested bandwidth resources amongst the level-k routers. Level-k routers are routers that are directly connected to the host but are either k-hops away from the target or less than k-hops away from the target. Various techniques are used to distribute the congested bandwidth among the level-k routers.
- **IP Traceback:** These techniques trace the true source of the attack (Bellovin, Leech, & Taylor, 2003; Sung & Xu, 2003). Since an attack is made up of a significant number of zombie machines with spoofed IP addresses, using IP addresses to track the true location of the attacker machine may not be helpful. Therefore, various traceback techniques have been proposed such as link testing (Burch & Cheswick, 2000; Stone, 2000); Probabilistic Packet Marking (PPM) (Adler, 2005; Song & Perrig, 2001); Algebraic based traceback techniques (Dean, Franklin, & Stubblefield, 2002).
- **Survival Techniques (Survival Strategies) after the Attack:** An ISP that uses survival techniques will procure and implement devices and systems to expand their resources in order to cope in a DDoS attack (Mirkovic & Reiher, 2004). In this technique, more resources like CPU power, memory and bandwidth are procured statically or dynamically, so that services may be replicated.

The enlarged resource pool enables the ISP to have sufficient resources to serve both legitimate and malicious packet requests during an attack. This ensures that service is still available to legitimate users even when the ISP is under attack. With the replication procedure, the ISP can successfully protect static services; but cannot

Table 2. Advantages and disadvantages of responsive techniques

Advantages	Disadvantages
• The technique work with routers that are close to the victim server. Therefore they can accurately filter attack packets. • They can effectively determine the edge network containing the DDoS sources. • They can effectively mitigate a DDoS attacks when attacker machines are gathered within close proximity. • They are simple, lightweight and cheap to implement for protection of a network against DDoS.	• During an attack, rate limiting techniques may have a severe impact on legitimate traffic. • For these techniques to be highly effective, they need universal deployment on the internet and collaboration amongst ISP's. This leads to the high costs of implementation. • An attacker can use a large number of zombie machines with spoofed IP address; or a reflector attack with real IP addresses. This renders the traceback technique ineffective because the real attack source cannot be found.

Table 3. Advantages and disadvantages of survival approaches

Advantages	Disadvantages
• More resources are made available to cope with a DDoS attack. • Service is still available to legitimate users, even when the service is under attack. • Enhances resistance to DDoS attacks. • Offers successful DDoS protection and load balancing to static internet content.	• Not all services are replicable • Replication for some service may require a great deal of effort and investment. • It is costly to implement the technique. • They protect victims against small scale attack, but they cannot deflect large scale. • May be ineffective when an attacker produces traffic volume greater than the expanded capacity of the resources.

protect dynamic services from an attack. However, dynamic services are targets for attackers, therefore making the replication procedure obsolete for defense against DDoS.

The effectiveness of this technique is dependent on whether the expanded resources are greater than the attack traffic volume. This may be hard to achieve because an attacker can recruit thousands of zombie machines to help them perpetuate the attack and possibly deplete the enlarged victim resources.

Given that procuring more devices to expand network resources may be ineffective in a large scale DDoS attack, the victim may need to deploy augmenting defense mechanisms. These defense mechanisms should accurately detect and identify the source of the attack and implement response strategies. Today, most of the DDoS response techniques are designed to minimize the impact of the attack on the victim, since the DDoS attack cannot completely be prevented or stopped. After detecting an attack, there are two further steps in the defense process. These steps are attack source identification and attack defense response and they are explained below.

Attack Source Identification techniques have been proposed in literature (Adler, 2005; Al-Duwairi & Govindarasu, 2006; Bellovin et al., 2003; R. Chen, Park, & Marchany, 2006a; Dean et al., 2002; John & Sivakumar, 2009; Savage, Wetherall, Karlin, & Anderson, 2000; Savage, Wetherall, Karlin, & Anderson, 2001; Song & Perrig, 2001; Sung & Xu, 2003). They attempt to traceback the source of the attack. Some of techniques attempt to solve the problem of using spoofed ip-addresses. These traceback techniques identify the attack source by traversing all routers from the victim to the source in reverse order, differentiating between legitimate paths and packets from the illegitimate ones.

Attack Defense Response is a step in the defense against DDoS attacks that is meant for launching an appropriate response to the attack upon its source identification. The most common response methods are throttling (rate limiting) and packet filtering. In literature there are various throttling or rate-limiting techniques (R. Chen & Park, 2005; R. Chen, Park, & Marchany, 2006b; X. Liu, Yang, & Lu, 2008; Peng et al., 2003; Wang et al., 2007; Yaar, Perrig, & Song, 2003), and packet filtering techniques (Argyraki & Cheriton, 2009; R. Chen & Park, 2005; Mahajan et al., 2002; Mirkovic, Robinson, & Reiher, 2003; Yau et al., 2005) that have been proposed.

The section that follows describes the various detection techniques and algorithms that have been successfully implemented and integrated into the network intrusion detection systems (NIDS). The section also reviews the relevant literature that pertains to the techniques and algorithms. These are detection techniques and algorithms that are based on change-point detection; wavelet-transforms; artificial neural networks; and artificial immune systems.

INTRUSION DETECTION TECHNIQUES (STATE-OF-THE-ART DETECTION)

A Network Intrusion Detection System (NIDS) is a device or software application that is used to monitor abnormal network traffic patterns or those patterns that violate network policies. Intrusion detection techniques have been integrated into several Network Intrusion Detection Systems (NIDS) (Cabrera, Lewis, Qin, Lee, & Mehra, 2002; J. Park & Kim, 2008; Qin, Lee, Lewis, & Cabrera, 2002; Streilein, Fried, & Cunningham, 2003; Yu, Lee, Kim, & Park, 2008). There exist two types of NIDS classifications, signature-based and anomaly-based NIDS. Signature-based detection systems attempt to define a set of templates (signatures or policies) that can be used to decide that a given network traffic pattern is that of an intruder. If the attack belongs to a class of attacks listed in the database, then it can be successfully detected or identified. As a result, signature-based systems are capable of attaining high levels of accuracy and minimal number of false positives in identifying intrusions. However, signature-based detection fails to detect unknown attacks or variation of known attacks (Liao, Richard Lin, Lin, & Tung, 2013).

The limitations of the signature-based intrusion detection were therefore the motivation for developing anomaly-based NIDS. Anomaly-based intrusion detection systems (ABIDS) are interested with identifying events that appear to be anomalous with respect to 'normal' system behaviour. An attack is declared once a deviation from normal traffic behaviour is observed.

Signature-based NIDS and anomaly-based NIDS are complementary in their use; because signature-based NIDS search for known intrusion while anomaly-based NIDS search for unusual or suspicious patterns in network performance and behaviour. In recent years, the intrusion detection research community has concentrated on improving performance (i.e. detection rate and detection delay) of anomaly-based NIDS, since they can detect both known and unknown attacks (Bhattacharyya & Kalita, 2013). For this reason, ABIDS are of interest in this proposed study.

Anomaly-based network intrusion detection systems are interested in distinguishing between normal network activities and anomalous activities. This is done by creating the system's normal profile, learned from historical data, and monitoring for significant deviations from normal profile activities.

In the event of a DDoS attack, abrupt changes in network traffic can be observed. Similarly, an abrupt change in statistical properties of detection parameters can be observed. Thus, the problem of anomaly detection can be constructed as change point detection problem (Tartakovsky, Rozovskii, Blazek, & Kim, 2006; Tartakovsky, Polunchenko, & Sokolov, 2013). The section that follows will review some of the most pertinent literature in the field of change point detection for network anomaly detection.

In the past decade there have been several techniques proposed for defense of DDoS attacks, however the early and accurate detection of DDoS attacks has remained a tough challenge. As a result, the development of techniques for efficient and timely detection of DDoS attacks remains an active area of research. It is important to develop techniques that can accurately detect an attack earlier, so that remedying actions can be implemented before a serious damage is caused.

The defense techniques developed thus far are based on data mining and artificial intelligence techniques for accurate detection. These techniques monitor features in traffic flow. They learn the normal behaviour of the network or application in order to develop a normal-behaviour model. Based on the monitored information, an attack is detected if there is a deviation from the normal behaviour model. This is a concept know as Network Intrusion Detection (NID), and it is further discussed in the subsection that follows.

Most well-known defense mechanisms that are currently employed can be further classified into Change-point Detection Techniques, Wavelet-based Signal Analysis, Artificial Neural Networks, and Artificial Immune Systems.

Change Point Detection Techniques

The aim of change detection techniques is to help detect a change in statistical properties of observed parameters with minimal detection delay and false positive rate (Basseville & Nikiforov, 1993). The approach first starts by applying filter to the traffic data according to desired parameters and arraigning the data into a time series data. For change detection, if there was a DDoS attack at time λ, the time series will show a significant statistical change around or at a time greater than λ (Poor & Hadjiliadis, 2009).

Detecting changes in statistical properties of observed parameters has been studied extensively and applied in various fields like image processing, network traffic and financial analysis. There are a number of techniques that are used for change detection and amongst them the most common techniques used for the detection of DDoS attacks are Cumulative Sum (CUSUM) and Exponentially Weighted Moving Average (EWMA) (Carl, Kesidis, Brooks, & Rai, 2006).

Cumulative Sum (CUSUM) Technique

The CUSUM algorithm was first introduced by Page in (Page, 1954). The CUSUM algorithm is based on hypothesis testing and was developed for independent and identically distributed random variables $\{y_i\}$. In the approach, an abrupt change occurring at any time can be modelled using two hypothesis, θ_1 and θ_2. The first hypothesis θ_1 represents the statistical distribution before the abrupt change occurring; and the second hypothesis θ_2 represents the statistical distribution after the abrupt change has occurred. The test for signalling a change is based on the log-likelihood ratio S_n.

$$S_n = \sum s_i$$

where,

$$s_i = \ln \frac{P_{\theta_1(y_i)}}{P_{\theta_2(y_i)}}$$

According to Siris et. al. (Siris & Papagalou, 2006), the typical behaviour of the log-likelihood ratio S_n includes a negative divergence before an abrupt change and a positive divergence after the change. Therefore, the relevant information for detecting a change lies in the difference between the value of the log-likelihood ratio and its current minimum value (Basseville & Nikiforov, 1993). The alarm condition for the CUSUM algorithm takes the form:

If $g_n \geq h$ (h is a threshold parameter) then signal alarm at time n, where

$$g_n = S_n - m_n \tag{1}$$

and

$$m_n = \min_{1 \leq j \leq n} S_j . \tag{2}$$

In the above equations, it is assumed that $\{y_i\}$ are independent Gaussian random variables with known variance σ^2 and mean μ_0 and μ_1 represents the mean before and after the abrupt change, respectively. Accordingly, $\theta_0 = N(\mu_0, \sigma^2)$ and $\theta_1 = N(\mu_1, \sigma^2)$. Following an application of various calculations, Basseville et al (Basseville & Nikiforov, 1993) implemented the following CUSUM algorithm:

$$g_n = \left[g_{n-1} + \frac{\mu_0 - \mu_1}{\sigma^2} \left(y_n - \frac{\mu_1 + \mu_0}{2} \right) \right]^+ \quad (3)$$

The above algorithm was adapted and applied to the problem of detecting SYN flooding attacks. This algorithm was applied as follows:

$$\tilde{x}_n = x_n - \bar{\mu}_{n-1} \quad (4)$$

where x_n represents the number of SYN packets in the n-th time interval, and $\bar{\mu}_n$ represents the estimated mean rate at time n. The estimates mean rate is computed using an exponentially weighted moving average as follows:

$$\bar{\mu}_n = \beta \bar{\mu}_{n-1} + (1 - \beta) x_n \quad (5)$$

where β is the exponentially weighted moving average (EWMA) factor.

The mean value of $\tilde{x}_n$ prior to a change is zero, therefore the mean in (3) is $\mu_0 = 0$. The mean traffic rate after a change cannot be known in advance. It can therefore be estimated with $\alpha \bar{\mu}_n$, were α is an amplitude percentage parameter. The parameter equates to the most likely percentage increase of the mean rate after an attack has occurred. For purposes of detecting SYN flood attacks, the algorithm in (3) has been adapted to:

$$g_n = \left[g_{n-1} + \frac{\alpha \bar{\mu}_{n-1}}{\sigma^2} \left(x_n - \bar{\mu}_{n-1} - \frac{\alpha \bar{\mu}_{n-1}}{2} \right) \right]^+ \quad (6)$$

In the CUSUM algorithm, the tuning parameters are the amplitude factor, α, the EWMA factor, β, and the CUSUM algorithm threshold, *h*.

The CUSUM technique has been applied to various problems including DDoS detection. It calculates the cumulative sum of difference between actual and expected values of a sequence, the CUSUM value. This value is compared to a threshold value (an upper bound). A CUSUM value greater than the upper bound indicates a change in statistical properties of the parameter time series values.

There are a number of variations of the CUSUM technique, and Tartakovsky et al. (Tartakovsky et al., 2006) proposed fully-sequential and batch-sequential algorithms. They are both non-parametric variations of the CUSUM techniques adapted to detecting changes in multiple bins. The algorithms were found to be self-learning, which enables them to adapt to various network loads and usage patterns. They also allow for the detection of attacks with a small average delay for a given false-alarm rate and they are computationally feasible and thus can be implemented online.

Bo et al. (Bo, Fang, & Yun, 2005) also used an algorithm which was a variation of the CUSUM technique to help with quick detection of worm attack incidents. In their experiments they observed the computer's degree of connection to estimate the CUSUM score. It was concluded that the algorithm could detect new attacks fast and effectively.

Siris et al. (Siris & Papagalou, 2006) proposed and investigated a change point detection algorithm, which is also based on the CUSUM technique. The algorithm revealed robust performance over various attack types, it was computationally feasible and not costly to implement. Wang et al. (Haining Wang, Danlu Zhang, & Shin, 2002) also proposed an algorithm which is a variation of the CUSUM technique on an application for detecting DDoS attacks. Protocol behaviours of TCP SYN – FIN (RST) pairs where used to make detections. The experiment results revealed that the algorithm had a low detection delays and high detection accuracy.

Exponentially Weighted Moving Average (EWMA) Technique

EWMA was first introduced by Roberts (Roberts, 1959), it analyses whether the value of the parameters being observed, in a given time interval, exceeds a particular threshold value. The algorithm adaptively calculates the threshold value (the parameter mean value of recent observations in each sampling interval) instead of using a predefined threshold value.

$$\text{If } X_n \geq (\alpha + 1)\bar{\mu}_{n-1}, \tag{7}$$

then an alarm is signalled at time n, where the tuning parameter $0 < \alpha \leq 1$ indicates the amplitude factor, a percentage above the mean value that is considered to be an indication of anomalous behaviour. This amplitude factor parameter is used for computing the alarm threshold. The mean $\overline{\mu}n$ can be computed over some past time window or using an exponential weighted moving average of previous measurements.

$$\overline{\mu}n = \beta\overline{\mu}_{n-1} + \left(1-\beta\right)Xn\,, \tag{8}$$

where the tuning parameter $0 < \beta \leq 1$, is the weighting factor parameter. The parameter β determines the rate at which "older" data enter into the calculation of the EWMA statistic. A value of $\beta = 1$ implies that only the most recent measurement influences the EWMA. Thus, a large value of $\beta = 1$ gives more weight to recent data and less weight to older data; a small value of β gives more weight to older data.

However, if the algorithm is applied in its original format, it will yield a higher rate of false alarms. To improve the performance a modification to the algorithm was to raise an alarm after a minimum number of successive violations of the threshold. Therefore,

$$\text{If } \sum_{i-n-k+1}^{n} 1_{x_i \geq (\alpha+1)\overline{\mu}_{i-1}} \geq k \tag{9}$$

Then an alarm is raised at time n, where $k > 1$ is a tuning parameter that indicates the number of successive intervals the threshold must be violated before an alarm is signalled.

The tuning parameters for the EWMA algorithm are the threshold value (amplitude factor) α, the EWMA factor β, and k which signifies the number of successive threshold violations before raising an alarm.

There have been a number of variations of the EWMA algorithm that was used for intrusion detection and flooding attacks.

Siris et al (Siris & Papagalou, 2006) proposed an adaptive threshold algorithm, which is a variation of the EWMA technique. They used real traffic traces to analyse and compare the performance based on detection delay, false alarm rate and detection accuracy. The algorithm adaptively learns the normal behaviour of the network traffic. The algorithm revealed satisfactory results for high intensity attacks, however the performance declined for low intensity attacks. However, it is of paramount importance to detect the onset of an attack whose intensity increases slowly.

Ye et al. (Ye, Borror, & Zhang, 2002; Ye et al., 2003) investigated and applied EWMA techniques to help detect anomalous changes in the events intensity for intrusion detections. The techniques were applied on the large DARPA datasets.

Their findings revealed that the EWMA techniques can work well for detecting abrupt changes in event intensity, and also small mean shifts through the gradually increased or decreased event intensity.

Münz et al. (Münz & Carle, 2008) investigated and evaluated the network traffic anomaly detection capabilities of the CUSUM and EWMA techniques. In order to cope with seasonal variation and serial variation, a time series of prediction errors was used instead of using direct time-series of the traffic data. The traffic data was collected from an Internet Service Provider (ISP). From their experiments it was found that CUSUM does not perform better than Shewart and EWMA when applied to time-series of prediction errors.

Wavelet-Based Detection Techniques

Wavelet analyses have recently attracted a lot of attention. It has been successfully applied to signal processing, image analysis and telecommunications. This is due to its ability to analyse rapidly changing and transitory signals. They are useful in processing and analysing nonstationary signals.

They decompose a time series into time frequency space, and they are therefore able to establish the recurrent trend of variability and how these trends vary with time (Dainotti, Pescapé, & Ventre, 2006).

Wavelet analyses deals with the development of new functions in terms of a set of underlying foundational functions. These functions are expressed and developed in terms of translations and dilations of a fixed function called the mother wavelet. These wavelet functions have specific scaling properties and they are delimited in time and frequency. Therefore a wavelet analysis is concerned with the derivation of these foundational functions and their efficient methods of computation (Goswami & Chan, 2011).

Wavelet Transform Background

The concept of wavelets is not a new theory because most of the underlying techniques involved in wavelet analyses have been developed separately. However, a merger of these techniques has brought about good results in the subject of wavelet analyses framework. There have been independent developments in the analysis on nonstationary signals, specifically in the form of short-term Fourier transforms. This was progressed further by the discovery, in wavelet theory, of smooth mother wavelets. Mother wavelets have a set of discrete translations and dilations forms an orthogonal basis for L2(R), where R is the real numbers. L2 is the set of all functions, f, that have bounded energy for which the following conditions are satisfied:

$$\int_{-\infty}^{\infty} \left|\psi\left(t\right)\right|^2 dt < \infty \tag{10}$$

$$c_\psi = 2\pi \int_{-\infty}^{\infty} \frac{\left|\Psi\left(\omega\right)\right|^2}{\omega} d\omega < \infty \tag{11}$$

where Ψ is the Fourier transform of ψ. The first condition implies finite energy for the function ψ, and the second condition is the admissibility condition, which implies that if $\Psi(\omega)$ is smooth then $\Psi(0) = 0$. The function ψ is the mother wavelet. Wavelet transforms can be regarded as the continuous wavelet transform or the discrete wavelet transform.

In the *Continuous Wavelet Transform* (CWT), if ψ satisfies the admissibility condition in Equation (10), then the wavelet transform is a real signal $s(t)$ with respect to the wavelet function $\psi\left(t\right)$ can be defined as:

$$S\left(b,a\right) = \frac{1}{\sqrt{a}} \int_{-\infty}^{\infty} \psi'\left(\frac{t-b}{a}\right) s\left(t\right) dt \tag{12}$$

where ψ' represents the complex conjugate of ψ, and this is defined on the open (b,a) half-plane ($b \, \varepsilon \, R$, $a > 0$). The parameter b corresponds to the time shift and the parameter a corresponds to the scale of the analysing wavelet.

If we define

$$\psi_{a,b}\left(t\right) = a^{\frac{-1}{2}} \psi\left(\frac{t-b}{a}\right), \tag{13}$$

Which means rescaling by a and shifting by b, then Equation 11 above can be written as a scalar or inner product of the real signal $s(t)$ with the function $\psi_{a,b}\left(t\right)$:

$$S\left(b,a\right) = \int_{-\infty}^{\infty} \psi_{a,b}\left(t\right) s\left(t\right) dt \tag{14}$$

When function $\psi(t)$ satisfies the admissibility condition, the original signal *s*(*t*) can be obtained from the wavelet transform *S*(*b*,*a*) by the following inverse formula:

$$s(t) = \frac{1}{C_{\psi}} \int_{-\infty}^{\infty} \int_{-\infty}^{\infty} S(b,a) \psi_{a,b}(t) \frac{da db}{a^2} \tag{15}$$

In the *Discrete Wavelet Transform* (DWT), the scale and shift parameters are discretised as $a = a_0^m$ and $b = nb_0$, and the analysing wavelets are also discretised as follows:

$$\psi_{m,n}(t) = a_0^{\frac{-m}{2}} \psi\left(\frac{t - nb_0}{a_0^m}\right), \tag{16}$$

where *m* and *n* are integer values. The discrete wavelet transform and its inverse transform are defined as follows:

$$S_{m,n} = \int_{-\infty}^{\infty} \psi'_{m,n} s(t) dt, \tag{17}$$

$$s(t) = k_{\psi} \sum_{m} \sum_{n} S_{m,n} \psi_{m,n}(t) \tag{18}$$

where k_{ψ} is a constant value for normalisation.

The function $\psi_{m,n}(t)$ provides sampling points on the scale-time plane: linear sampling in the time (b-axis) direction but logarithmic in the scale (a-axis) direction.

In most cases, a_0 is chosen as:

$$a_0 = 2^{\frac{1}{v}}, \tag{19}$$

where v is an integer value, and that v pieces of $\psi_{m,n}(t)$ are processed as one group, which is called the voice. The integer v is the number of voices per octave; it defines a well-tempered scale in the sense of music. This is analogous to the use of a set of narrowband filters in conventional Fourier analysis.

The CWT and the DWT differ in that the CWT calculates a number of coefficients that decreases with the scaling factor (a). The CWT also differs from the DWT because the same number of coefficients is always acquired at each scale; whereas with the DWT, the number of coefficients declines as the value of the scaling factor increases. Additionally, the DWT is mainly used for signal decomposition avoiding redundancy, while the CWT can easily be interpreted as a cross-correlation function at several scales (Dainotti, Pescapé, & Ventre, 2009). There are several variations the CWT and DWT functions available, however their applications differ (Goswami & Chan, 2011).

In recent literature, wavelets have also been widely used for network intrusion detection problems. This is due to its inherent time-frequency property that enables a single signal to be decomposed into several signals that represent different frequencies.

The work of Li et. al. (Li & Lee, 2005) discovered that aggregated network traffic is bursty across a wide range of time scales; therefore, they applied a wavelet analysis to capture complex temporal correlations across multiple time scales with very low computational complexity. Wavelet analysis provided energy distribution data for complete information of traffic behaviour. With normal traffic, it was observed that normal traffic exhibit remarkably stationery energy distribution. However, when a DDoS attack is synthetically injected into the traffic data, a significant variance change is observed.

The work of authors in (Ramanathan, 2002) presented an approach called WADeS (Wavelet-based Attack Detection Signatures) used for detection of DDoS attacks. In this approach, wavelets transform is applied on traffic signals and the variance of corresponding wavelet coefficients is used to estimate attack points. The authors in (Li & Lee, 2005) also applied a wavelet analysis to detect DDoS attacks in network traffic. In the research they discovered that normal traffic exhibits a remarkably stationary energy distribution; however, when a DDoS attack is introduced, a spike is caused in the energy distribution.

In Barford et al. (Barford, Kline, Plonka, & Ron, 2002) a wavelet transform is applied for analyzing and characterizing the flow-based traffic behaviors. SNMP and IP Flow signals are split into three different components ranges of frequencies, and a wavelet transform is applied for characterising and analysing network traffic behaviours. The three components frequencies range are: low, mid and long frequency components. Each component frequency had a representative deviation algorithm that identified network traffic anomalies by setting a threshold (deviation score) for the signal composed from the wavelet coefficients at different frequency levels. Their evaluation results revealed that some form of DDoS is detected within the mid and high component frequencies due to their inherent traffic pattern activities. However, it is not clear what type of attacks and DDoS were detected by the algorithms; and the results do not reveal the detection rate and the false positive rate for the algorithms.

Wavelet–based techniques for anomaly detection had limitations due to the high computational complexity of a wavelet transform and the scale sensitivity during detection. To overcome the limitations, authors in (Gao, Hu, Yao, & Chang, 2006) proposed a detection method based on wavelet transformation, the fast wavelet packet algorithm. The detection method had the capability to adaptively adjust the decomposition process, therefore improving the detection accuracy in the middle and high frequency anomalies that could not be detected in the multi-resolution analysis. The proposed method was found to be efficient and fast in detecting network anomalies.

The authors in (Dainotti et al., 2009) used wavelet transform to monitor anomalies caused by DDoS attacks in high volume network traffic. In this multistage approach the authors used traditional detection approaches like adaptive thresholds and cumulative sum as the underlying technique and augmented this with a continuous wavelet transform (CWT) for further detection. In their experiments, the detection approach was able to estimate start and end time of a DDoS attacks; the approach also showed improved trade-off between detection rate and false detection rate. However, the proposed approach was evaluated on an offline dataset under special delimited conditions. The evaluations conditions may need to be improved I such a way that they represent a real network environment.

Artificial Neural Networks

The human brain is a highly interconnected network of about 100 billion biological neurons. This network of biological neurons facilitates important vital human body functions like reading, breathing, motion and thinking. Some parts of the neural structures are present in the human body since birth, while others are established by experience (Lee & Stolfo, 1998).

All biological neural features, including memory, are stored in the neurons and in their connections between them. Learning is viewed as a new connection between the neurons or the modification of existing neurons. This continues to change throughout life (Catania & Garino, 2012).

Figure 7 represents a schematic drawing of the biological neuron. For the purposes of this research and for simplicity, the biological neuron is made up of three main components: the dendrite, the cell body, and the axon.The dendrite is a tree-like network of nerve fibres that carry electrochemical signals from other neural cells, into the cell body of the dendrite. (The point of contact between the neurons is a synapse).

Figure 7. A schematic drawing of the biological neuron
Catania & Garino, 2012.

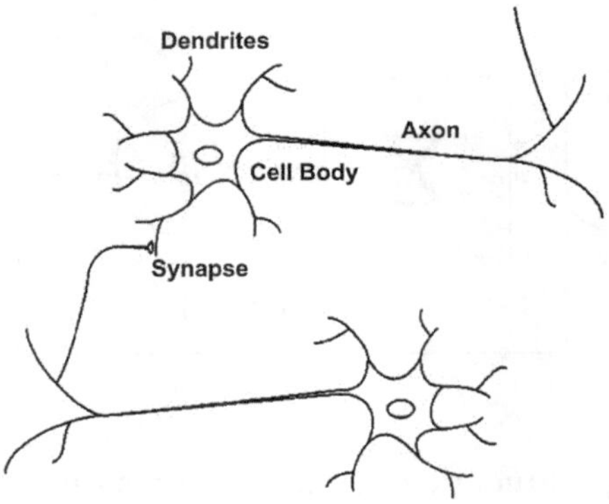

The cell body receives incoming electrochemical stimulation/signal from other dendrites and will effectively sum up and threshold these signals, and determines the extent to which action potentials are produced by the neuron. The axon is a single long fibre of a nerve cell that carries electrochemical signals from the cell body out of the other neurons; and this is conducted by the synapse, which is a point of contact between the axon of one cell and the dendrite of another cell, and sometimes contacts with muscles or gland cell.The neural structure/network continues to develop throughout life and consists mainly of strengthening or weakening of synaptic junctions.

There has been significant research for understanding the functioning of the brain and biological neurons, and scientists have long had the desire to understand the brain and emulate its behaviour. This has led researchers to build mathematical models for the biological neurons such that the brain's working model can be simulated. Researchers therefore came up with the idea of the biologically inspired Artificial Neural Networks (ANN) (Kruegel, Mutz, Robertson, & Valeur, 2003; Lee & Stolfo, 1998).

ANNs (sometimes referred to as neural networks) are mathematical or computational models that get their inspiration from biological neural systems. They are information-processing systems with certain computational properties that are analogous to those that are learned from the biological neural network. The simplified biological neuron basically receives electrochemical signals from another neuron, for processing by allowing a specific action to be fired when a certain threshold is reached. In this way an artificial neuron can be seen as computational units that receive signals from other units (Kruegel et al., 2003) .The ANN is made up of large networks of simple processing units called neurons or nodes along with their connections (synapse) in the network. The connection from one neuron to another has an associated weight, which encodes the knowledge of the network.

Figure 8. The artificial neuron

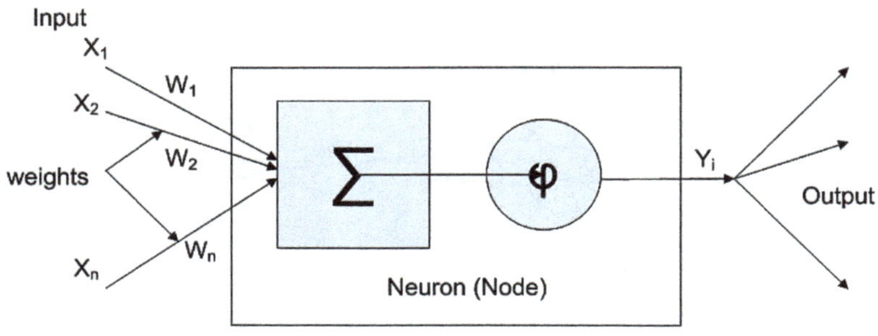

Figure 8 displays the structure of an artificial neuron. The nodes (or neurons) can be seen as computational units that receive input to process and produce an output. The processing might be simple (as in addition, subtraction, etc.) or it can be a complex computation (involving another network). The processing is computed using a simple or complex mathematical function, the activation function. The activation function is computed using the input from other neurons (nodes) to give the output, and may involve a certain threshold depending on the problem domain. The connection (synapse) between the neurons indicates an association between them (pointing from one neuron to the other). Each connection has a set of weights which encode the knowledge in the network.

ANNs have been used by scientists across a variety of research fields. This includes aerospace, banking, medicine and speech recognition, to mention just a few. Across most of the fields, different ANN models were used for problem solving and in such cases the problem can become complex. There exist several ANN architectures including fully connected networks, acyclic neural networks, modular neural networks and feed-forward neural networks. It is widely recognised that for complex tasks, ANN models with feed-forward multiple layers of neurons are necessary. This ANN model is generally referred to as the Multiple Layer Perceptron (or simply MLP) (Portnoy, Eskin, & Stolfo, 2001).

The essential structure of the MLP is that of perceptron (or nodes) interconnected in layers with the output from one layer forming the input to the next layer. Generally, the model is made up of three layers (this may differ from one textbook/author to the next): The input layer, hidden layer and the output layer.

- **The Input Layers:** The nodes at this layer are input nodes; they encode and prepare the raw network data for further processing.

- **The Hidden Layers:** This layer is not directly visible to the input and output layers. The nodes or neurons at this layer compute an internal representation of the data. With the use of MLP algorithms like the back propagation, the values of the connections (or weights) are adjusted accordingly, and algorithms may add non-linearity features, as opposed to linear best-fit algorithms that try to minimize the distance between the misclassified or the incorrectly predicted.
- **The Output Layers:** The neurons at this layer encode data representations from the results obtained by the computations at the hidden layer (Portnoy et al., 2001).

In Li et al (2012 DDoS-neural) a Leaning Vector Quantization (LVQ) neural network was used to detect DDoS attacks. LQV is a supervised version of the vector quantisation; it uses known target output classifications for each input pattern. It has been applied to pattern recognition, multi-class classification and data compression tasks. In their simulations the dataset was pre-processed into numerical format so that it can be fed to the neural network for training and testing. The LVQ neural network achieved a 99.7% detection rate while Back Propagation (BP) neural network achieved 89.9% detection rate. However, the data collected was simulated using a small number of simulation PC; and this may not be represented of a real DDoS attack. The pre-processing detail of the data was not clarified.

The work of authors in (Akilandeswari & Shalinie, 2012) proposed an attack traffic classification method that is based on Probabilistic Neural Network; a feed-forward network that is used for non-linear pattern classification. In this method, the network uses the Bayesian decision rule for Bayes inference; this was coupled with the Radial Basis Function Neural Network (RBFNN) because it is suitable for attack traffic classification problems. The proposed method was used to effectively classify attack traffic patterns from legitimate traffic using single and joint distributions of various packet attributes. It successfully classified TCP SYN, UDP and ICMP flooding attacks. In their experiments the average detection rate was below 80% with an average false alarm rate of 1%. However, there is room for improvements in order to achieve a higher detection rate.

The work of Siatelris et al. in (Siaterlis & Maglaris, 2005) presented DDoS detection as a classification problem and they proposed a Multilayer Perceptron Neural Network as a data fusion algorithm. Current DDoS research attempts to identify a single detection metric that can reliably detect DDoS attacks, however in their research a multiple set of passive network measurements are used as input and fused with the MLP algorithm to successfully detect a DDoS attack. The proposed method was found to have detection rate greater than 74% and false alarm rate less than 3%. However, the authors used a self-generated dataset of traffic using DDoS tools, and it was not clear how the data was generated and what were the configuration details of the data generation tools.

The work by Chung-Lung et al. (Tsai, Chang, & Ming-Szu, 2010) presented an early warning system for DDoS attack detection was developed for integration into traditional IDS. The system developed was based on a Time Delay Neural Network (TDNN). TDNN is a kind of neural network that has the time delay factor integrated and implicitly represented inside the signal. In their experiments the TDNN was implemented in a two-layer structure; this enables the system to take proactive action against a DDoS attack like initiating an integrated IPS. In their implementation, nodes were dispatched at the demilitarized zone or between the first and second layer of the firewall. Each node's activities are monitored by neighbouring nodes and attack data is conveyed to the expert module for further analysis. The approach was found to have an 82.7% detection rate; however, the information about the false alarm rate was not available.

Artificial Immune System

The Human Immune System (HIS) is a robust, complex network of specialized cells and organs that defend the human body against a sea of harmful microorganisms called antigens. Building upon its capability of differentiating the cells and molecules of the body into self (what belongs) and non-self (what does not belong) (Kelly, 2007; Schindler, 1991), the HIS has led to the development of the Artificial Immune System (AIS) computational paradigm that may solve complex computational problems.

As depicted by Figure 9, once the body recognizes an invasion by antigens (I-III), the immunological response (IV-VI) consists of neutralizing or destroying the invading antigens through the release and use of B-cells and T-cells (lymphocytes that originate from the bone marrow and play an important role in the immunological response). The B and T-cells will then destroy the invading antigens and remove them from the body.

A biologically inspired computational technique, called Artificial Immune System (AIS) has emerged from the HIS metaphor. The HIS features that are of particularly relevant to AIS includes matching, diversity and distributed control. These features have been implemented in many AIS mechanisms such as the immune system's Immune Network Theory, Negative Selection mechanism and Clonal Selection Principle to solve real world science and engineering problems.

The HIS mechanism provides tolerance for self-cells, and reacts against unknown antigens. The HIS generates antibodies through a pseudo random rearrangement process and undergoes a censoring process in the thymus as described by (Kelly,

Figure 9. A pictorial representation of the acquired immune system mechanism
Taken from (De Castro & Timmis, 2002).

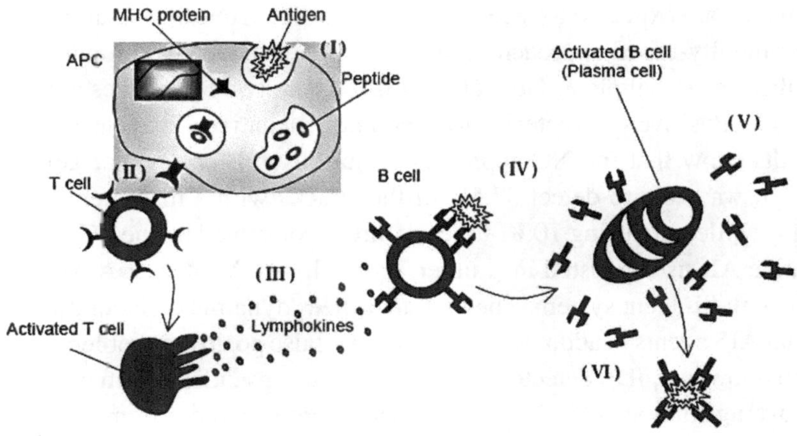

2007; Schindler, 1991). Only those antibodies that do not bind to the self-protein are allowed to leave the thymus to circulate throughout the body to perform immunological functions and protect the body against foreign antigens.

The AIS framework has been used in several applications to detection intrusions that deviate from normal operations of a network. However, little attention has been given towards detection of DDoS attacks. The authors in (Shafiq & Farooq, 2007) used the AIS framework to defend against a DoS attack on wireless network access points. It was found that the security framework could counter de-authentication and disassociation attacks (similar to TCP-SYN attacks). For their experiments, the AIS framework shows an impressive low false positive that was below 0.001% for both attack types; and a 100% detection rate after varying the threshold values for both attack types. In (Ali, Aib, & Boutaba, 2009), the authors proposed a peer-to-peer architecture that allowed peers to exchange intrusion detection experience in order to enhance attack detection and mitigation.

LISYS (Hofmeyr & Forrest, 2000) is an example of how HIS can be applied to computer security. It uses negative selection (Esponda, Forrest, & Helman, 2004) mechanisms in order to differentiate between self (normal) behavior and non-self (abnormal) behavior. LISYS was successful in identifying unauthorized TCP connections in a broadcast network. However, there are several characteristics of LISYS that limits its usage in anomaly detection. First, it only monitors TCP connections so any intrusions done using other protocols will evade the detection mechanism. In addition, it assumes that the monitored network is a broadcast network. Therefore, it will not be useful for switched networks like Local Area Networks (LANs). Moreover, LYSIS characterizes normal behavior as TCP datapaths (Hofmeyr & Forrest, 2000) which will not be suitable to detect attacks against some systems like web servers which are expected to receive connections from multiple changing sources.

An immunity-based approach to characterize intrusions in computer networks is described in (Dasgupta & González, 2002) where two techniques are explained in the work: Positive Characterization (PC) and Negative Characterization (NC). The results show that the NC approach is more useful for detector generation in AISes as it was able to detect 87.5% of the attacks with a maximum false alarm rate of 1% while only using 10% of the resources consumed by the PC technique. A cooperative AIS is suggested in (Luther, Bye, Alpcan, Muller, & Albayrak, 2007) based on a multi-agent system. The system utilizes dynamic collaboration between individual AIS agents to address the well-known false positives problem in anomaly detection. However, IDS detectors are generated in a pseudorandom way leading to a poor coverage of non-self (abnormal) space. Moreover, the system has a high false positives rate of 18%. Other cooperative approaches were suggested like multi-agent systems (Dasgupta, Gonzalez, Yallapu, Gomez, & Yarramsettii, 2005), (Juszczyszyn et al., 2006) and p2p approaches (Duma, Karresand, Shahmehri, & Caronni, 2006), (Janakiraman, Waldvogel, & Zhang, 2003). However, those techniques are not capable of defending the network against novel attacks as opposed to AISes.

SUMMARY AND FUTURE RESEARCH DIRECTION

The sections above reviewed scholarly work on existing methods for DDoS attack instigation and defense. It presented a comprehensive classification of various DDoS attack types and their targets; DDoS degree of automation and rate dynamics. Defense techniques were presented based on their defense location and defense strategies. The advantages and disadvantages of each defense strategy were also presented. A literature review of the most well-known and currently employed defense techniques was also presented.

As it stands, exact comparison of these detection techniques is not viable. This is due to the fact that some of the surveyed papers report good results while some results are not clearly reported. Some papers do not clearly report about the methods used to attain their results. Again, the evaluation of these detection schemes use different datasets and different testing parameters. It is therefore important for researchers to decide on a benchmark of evaluation methods, datasets and testing parameters. Therefore, our future work will investigate methods that can be used to evaluate DDoS attack detection techniques, benchmark datasets and testing parameters. Furthermore, the dissertation will address some of the research challenges that were identified below:

1. **Existing DDoS Attack Datasets Have Limitations:** There are legal and privacy issues that accompany sharing of captured datasets. This has therefore led to a lack of real datasets that may be used to model DDoS attacks and to evaluate new DDoS attack detection techniques. Research questions that arise from this challenge are:
    a. What are the essential characteristics of a DDoS attack?
    b. How can we model DDoS attack behaviour so that we can synthetically generate realistic DDoS attack traffic data?
2. In order to evaluate and develop new detection techniques for DDoS attacks, it is important that these techniques are evaluated on the most recent and realistic traffic datasets. However, there are only a limited number of DDoS attack datasets and those datasets that are available in the public domain are outdated. This gives rise to the next research question:
    a. How can we design and implement a DDoS detection testbed framework using available network traffic generators and emulators?
3. There is a number of detection techniques developed so far, but they each have their shortfalls. This leads to the next research question:
    a. Which of these detection techniques perform better?
    b. How do they perform for low-rate attacks and high rate attacks?
4. The nature of DDoS attacks keeps changing over time as intruders adapt their attack methods to evade existing intrusion detection techniques. Signature-based detection techniques work well for known DDoS attacks patterns; however, they do not work well for unknown DDoS attack patterns. Anomaly-based detection techniques are designed to detect unknown attack patterns, but these detection techniques may not be suitable for real-time detection due to the heavy resource consumption. Detection of new attacks becomes a challenge for existing defense mechanisms. This leads to the next research question:
    a. How can we extend current work on DDoS attack detection techniques to help detect zero-day and unknown DDoS attacks?
    b. How can we best develop an ensemble-based DDoS attack detection technique that can detect known and unknown DDoS attacks accurately and in a timely manner?

REFERENCES

Adler, M. (2005). Trade-offs in probabilistic packet marking for IP traceback. *Journal of the ACM*, *52*(2), 217–244. doi:10.1145/1059513.1059517

Akilandeswari, V., & Shalinie, S. M. (2012). *Probabilistic neural network based attack traffic classification*. Paper presented at the Advanced Computing (ICoAC), 2012 Fourth International Conference On. doi:10.1109/ICoAC.2012.6416848

Al-Duwairi, B., & Govindarasu, M. (2006). Novel hybrid schemes employing packet marking and logging for IP traceback. *Parallel and Distributed Systems. IEEE Transactions On*, *17*(5), 403–418.

Ali, K., Aib, I., & Boutaba, R. (2009). *P2P-AIS: A P2P artificial immune systems architecture for detecting DDoS flooding attacks*. Paper presented at the Information Infrastructure Symposium.

Alkar, A. Z., & Buhur, U. (2005). An internet based wireless home automation system for multifunctional devices. *Consumer Electronics. IEEE Transactions On*, *51*(4), 1169–1174.

Alomari, E., Manickam, S., Gupta, B., Karuppayah, S., & Alfaris, R. (2012). *Botnet-based distributed denial of service (DDoS) attacks on web servers: Classification and art*. arXiv Preprint arXiv:1208.0403

Anand, V. (2014). *Intrusion detection: Tools, techniques and strategies*. Paper presented at the 2014 ACM SIGUCCS Annual Conference on User Services Conference.

Argyraki, K., & Cheriton, D. R. (2009). Scalable network-layer defense against internet bandwidth-flooding attacks. *IEEE/ACM Transactions on Networking*, *17*(4), 1284-1297.

Ashton, K. (2009). That 'internet of things' thing. *RFiD Journal*, *22*(7), 97–114.

Baig, M. M., Gholamhosseini, H., & Connolly, M. J. (2013). A comprehensive survey of wearable and wireless ECG monitoring systems for older adults. *Medical & Biological Engineering & Computing*, *51*(5), 485–495. doi:10.1007/s11517-012-1021-6 PMID:23334714

Barford, P., Kline, J., Plonka, D., & Ron, A. (2002). *A signal analysis of network traffic anomalies*. Paper presented at the 2nd ACM SIGCOMM Workshop on Internet Measurment. doi:10.1145/637201.637210

Barlow, J., & Thrower, W. (2000). *TFN2K–an analysis*. Axent Security Team.

Basseville, M., & Nikiforov, I. V. (1993). *Detection of abrupt changes: Theory and application*. Prentice Hall.

Batishchev, A. (2012). *Low orbit ion cannon (loic)*. Retrieved from http://Sourceforge.Net/Projects/Loic/

Beitollahi, H., & Deconinck, G. (2012). Analyzing well-known countermeasures against distributed denial of service attacks. *Computer Communications*, *35*(11), 1312–1332. doi:10.1016/j.comcom.2012.04.008

Bellovin, S. M., Leech, M., & Taylor, T. (2003). *ICMP traceback messages*. Academic Press.

Bhattacharyya, D. K., & Kalita, J. K. (2013). *Network anomaly detection: A machine learning perspective*. CRC Press.

Bhuyan, M. H., Kashyap, H. J., Bhattacharyya, D. K., & Kalita, J. K. (2013). Detecting distributed denial of service attacks: Methods, tools and future directions. *The Computer Journal*, bxt031.

Blaze, M., Feigenbaum, J., & Lacy, J. (1996). *Decentralized trust management*. Paper presented at the Security and Privacy, 1996.

Bo, C., Fang, B., & Yun, X. (2005). *A new approach for early detection of internet worms based on connection degree*. Paper presented at the Machine Learning and Cybernetics, 2005.

Burch, H., & Cheswick, B. (2000). *Tracing anonymous packets to their approximate source*. Paper presented at the LISA.

Cabrera, J. B., Lewis, L., Qin, X., Lee, W., & Mehra, R. K. (2002). Proactive intrusion detection and distributed denial of service attacks—a case study in security management. *Journal of Network and Systems Management*, *10*(2), 225–254. doi:10.1023/A:1015910917349

Carl, G., Kesidis, G., Brooks, R. R., & Rai, S. (2006). Denial-of-service attack-detection techniques. *IEEE Internet Computing*, *10*(1), 82–89. doi:10.1109/MIC.2006.5

Catania, C. A., & Garino, C. G. (2012). Automatic network intrusion detection: Current techniques and open issues. *Computers & Electrical Engineering*, *38*(5), 1062–1072. doi:10.1016/j.compeleceng.2012.05.013

Center, C. C. (2001). *Carnegie Mellon Software Engineering Institute, CERT Advisory CA-2001-20 Continuing Threats to Home Users*. Carnegie Mellon.

Chen, R., & Park, J. (2005). *Attack diagnosis: Throttling distributed denial-of-service attacks close to the attack sources*. Paper presented at the Computer Communications and Networks, 2005.

Chen, R., Park, J., & Marchany, R. (2006a). *NISp1-05: RIM: Router interface marking for IP traceback*. Paper presented at the Global Telecommunications Conference, 2006.

Chen, R., Park, J., & Marchany, R. (2006b). *TRACK: A novel approach for defending against distributed denial-of-service attacks. Technical P~ Eport TR ECE—O6-02. Dept.of Electrical and Computer Engineering*. Virginia Tech.

Chen, Z., Chen, Z., & Delis, A. (2007). An inline detection and prevention framework for distributed denial of service attacks. *The Computer Journal*, *50*(1), 7–40. doi:10.1093/comjnl/bxl042

Choo, K. R. (2011). The cyber threat landscape: Challenges and future research directions. *Computers & Security*, *30*(8), 719–731. doi:10.1016/j.cose.2011.08.004

Forrester Consulting. (2009). *The trends and changing landscape of DDoS threats and protection*. Author.

Criscuolo, P. J. (2000). *Distributed Denial of Service: Trin00*. Tribe Flood Network, Tribe Flood Network 2000, and Stacheldraht CIAC-2319.

Dainotti, A., Pescapé, A., & Ventre, G. (2006). *Wavelet-based detection of DoS attacks*. Paper presented at the Global Telecommunications Conference, 2006.

Dainotti, A., Pescapé, A., & Ventre, G. (2009). A cascade architecture for DoS attacks detection based on the wavelet transform. *Journal of Computer Security*, *17*(6), 945–968.

Dasgupta, D., & González, F. (2002). An immunity-based technique to characterize intrusions in computer networks. Evolutionary Computation. *IEEE Transactions On*, *6*(3), 281–291.

Dasgupta, D., Gonzalez, F., Yallapu, K., Gomez, J., & Yarramsettii, R. (2005). CIDS: An agent-based intrusion detection system. *Computers & Security*, *24*(5), 387–398. doi:10.1016/j.cose.2005.01.004

De Castro, L. N., & Timmis, J. (2002). *Artificial immune systems: A new computational intelligence approach*. Springer Science & Business Media.

Dean, D., Franklin, M., & Stubblefield, A. (2002). An algebraic approach to IP traceback. *ACM Transactions on Information and System Security*, *5*(2), 119–137. doi:10.1145/505586.505588

Dietrich, S., Long, N., & Dittrich, D. (2000). *Analyzing distributed denial of service tools: The shaft case*. Paper presented at the LISA.

Dittrich, D. (1999a). *The 'stacheldraht'distributed denial of service attack tool.* Academic Press.

Dittrich, D. (1999b). The "Tribe flood network" distributed denial of service attack tool. University of Washington.

Dittrich, D. (1999c). *The DoS project's 'trinoo' distributed denial of service attack tool.* Academic Press.

Dittrich, D., Weaver, G., Dietrich, S., & Long, N. (2000). *The ''mstream''distributed denial of service attack tool.* Retrieved from Http://Staff.Washington.Edu/Dittrich/Misc/Mstream.Analysis.Txt

Douligeris, C., & Mitrokotsa, A. (2004). DDoS attacks and defense mechanisms: Classification and state-of-the-art. *Computer Networks, 44*(5), 643–666. doi:10.1016/j.comnet.2003.10.003

Duma, C., Karresand, M., Shahmehri, N., & Caronni, G. (2006). *A trust-aware, p2p-based overlay for intrusion detection.* Paper presented at the Database and Expert Systems Applications.

Esponda, F., Forrest, S., & Helman, P. (2004). A formal framework for positive and negative detection schemes. *Systems, Man, and Cybernetics, Part B: Cybernetics. IEEE Transactions On, 34*(1), 357–373.

Evans, D. (2011). *The internet of things: How the next evolution of the internet is changing everything*. CISCO White Paper.

Ferguson, P. (2000). *Network ingress filtering: Defeating denial of service attacks which employ IP source address spoofing*. Academic Press.

Gao, J., Hu, G., Yao, X., & Chang, R. K. (2006). *Anomaly detection of network traffic based on wavelet packet.* Paper presented at the Communications, 2006. APCC'06. Asia-Pacific Conference On. doi:10.1109/APCC.2006.255840

Garber, L. (2000). Denial-of-service attacks rip the internet. *Computer, 33*(4), 12–17. doi:10.1109/MC.2000.839316

Geng, X., & Whinston, A. B. (2000). Defeating distributed denial of service attacks. *IT Professional, 2*(4), 36–42. doi:10.1109/6294.869381

Gluhak, A., Krco, S., Nati, M., Pfisterer, D., Mitton, N., & Razafindralambo, T. (2011). A survey on facilities for experimental internet of things research. *Communications Magazine, IEEE, 49*(11), 58–67. doi:10.1109/MCOM.2011.6069710

Goswami, J. C., & Chan, A. K. (2011). *Fundamentals of wavelets: Theory, algorithms, and applications*. John Wiley & Sons.

Gubbi, J., Buyya, R., Marusic, S., & Palaniswami, M. (2013). Internet of things (IoT): A vision, architectural elements, and future directions. *Future Generation Computer Systems, 29*(7), 1645–1660. doi:10.1016/j.future.2013.01.010

Gupta, B., Joshi, R. C., & Misra, M. (2009). Defending against distributed denial of service attacks: Issues and challenges. *Information Security Journal: A Global Perspective, 18*(5), 224-247.

Hancock, B. (2000). Trinity v3, a DDoS tool, hits the streets. *Computers & Security, 19*(7), 574.

Hofmeyr, S. A., & Forrest, S. (2000). Architecture for an artificial immune system. *Evolutionary Computation, 8*(4), 443–473. doi:10.1162/106365600568257 PMID:11130924

Hosaagrahara, M., & Sethu, H. (2008). Max-min fair scheduling in input-queued switches. *Parallel and Distributed Systems. IEEE Transactions On, 19*(4), 462–475.

Janakiraman, R., Waldvogel, M., & Zhang, Q. (2003). *Indra: A peer-to-peer approach to network intrusion detection and prevention*. Paper presented at the Enabling Technologies: Infrastructure for Collaborative Enterprises. doi:10.1109/ENABL.2003.1231412

Jin, C., Wang, H., & Shin, K. G. (2003). *Hop-count filtering: An effective defense against spoofed DDoS traffic.* Paper presented at the 10th ACM Conference on Computer and Communications Security. doi:10.1145/948109.948116

John, A., & Sivakumar, T. (2009). Ddos: Survey of traceback methods. *International Journal of Recent Trends in Engineering, 1*(2), 241–245.

Juszczyszyn, K., Nguyen, N. T., Kolaczek, G., Grzech, A., Pieczynska, A., & Katarzyniak, R. (2006). Agent-based approach for distributed intrusion detection system design. *Computational Science–ICCS, 2006*, 224–231.

Kelly, J. (2007). *Understanding the immune system-how it works*. National Institute of Allergy and Infectious Diseases Science Education.

Keromytis, A. D., Misra, V., & Rubenstein, D. (2002). SOS: Secure overlay services. Paper presented at the ACM SIGCOMM. *Computer Communication Review, 32*(4), 61–72. doi:10.1145/964725.633032

Kruegel, C., Mutz, D., Robertson, W., & Valeur, F. (2003). *Bayesian event classification for intrusion detection.* Paper presented at the Computer Security Applications Conference. doi:10.1109/CSAC.2003.1254306

Kumar, K. V. (2015). Distributed denial of service (DDOS) attack, networks, tools and DEFENSE. *International Journal of Applied Engineering Research*, *10*(8).

Labs, K. (2015). *Statistics on botnet-assisted DDoS attacks in Q1 2015*. Retrieved from www.kaspersky.com

Latré, B., Braem, B., Moerman, I., Blondia, C., & Demeester, P. (2011). A survey on wireless body area networks. *Wireless Networks*, *17*(1), 1–18. doi:10.1007/s11276-010-0252-4

Lazarevic, A., Kumar, V., & Srivastava, J. (2005). *Intrusion detection: A survey. Managing cyber threats*. Springer. doi:10.1007/0-387-24230-9_2

Lee, W., & Stolfo, S. J. (1998). *Data mining approaches for intrusion detection.* Paper presented at the Usenix Security.

Li, L., & Lee, G. (2005). DDoS attack detection and wavelets. *Telecommunication Systems*, *28*(3-4), 435–451.

Liao, H., Richard Lin, C., Lin, Y., & Tung, K. (2013). Intrusion detection system: A comprehensive review. *Journal of Network and Computer Applications*, *36*(1), 16–24. doi:10.1016/j.jnca.2012.09.004

Liqiang, Z., Shouyi, Y., Leibo, L., Zhen, Z., & Shaojun., W. (2011). A crop monitoring system based on wireless sensor network. *Procedia Environmental Sciences, 11*(Part B), 558-565. doi:10.1016/j.proenv.2011.12.088

Liu, P., Zang, W., & Yu, M. (2005). Incentive-based modeling and inference of attacker intent, objectives, and strategies. *ACM Transactions on Information and System Security*, *8*(1), 78–118. doi:10.1145/1053283.1053288

Liu, X., Yang, X., & Lu, Y. (2008). To filter or to authorize: Network-layer DoS defense against multimillion-node botnets. *Computer Communication Review*, *38*(4), 195–206. doi:10.1145/1402946.1402981

Luther, K., Bye, R., Alpcan, T., Muller, A., & Albayrak, S. (2007). *A cooperative AIS framework for intrusion detection*. Paper presented at the Communications, 2007. doi:10.1109/ICC.2007.237

Mahajan, R., Bellovin, S. M., Floyd, S., Ioannidis, J., Paxson, V., & Shenker, S. (2002). Controlling high bandwidth aggregates in the network. *Computer Communication Review*, *32*(3), 62–73. doi:10.1145/571697.571724

Miorandi, D., Sicari, S., De Pellegrini, F., & Chlamtac, I. (2012). Internet of things: Vision, applications and research challenges. *Ad Hoc Networks*, *10*(7), 1497–1516. doi:10.1016/j.adhoc.2012.02.016

Mirković, J., Prier, G., & Reiher, P. (2002). *Attacking DDoS at the source*. Paper presented at the Network Protocols.

Mirkovic, J., & Reiher, P. (2004). A taxonomy of DDoS attack and DDoS defense mechanisms. *Computer Communication Review*, *34*(2), 39–53. doi:10.1145/997150.997156

Mirkovic, J., & Reiher, P. (2005). D-WARD: A source-end defense against flooding denial-of-service attacks. *Dependable and Secure Computing. IEEE Transactions On*, *2*(3), 216–232.

Mirkovic, J., Robinson, M., & Reiher, P. (2003). *Alliance formation for DDoS defense*. Paper presented at the 2003 Workshop on New Security Paradigms. doi:10.1145/986655.986658

Mishra, A., Gupta, B., & Joshi, R. C. (2011). *A comparative study of distributed denial of service attacks, intrusion tolerance and mitigation techniques*. Paper presented at the Intelligence and Security Informatics Conference (EISIC). doi:10.1109/EISIC.2011.15

Münz, G., & Carle, G. (2008). *Application of forecasting techniques and control charts for traffic anomaly detection*. Paper presented at the ITC Specialist Seminar on Network Usage and Traffic, Berlin, Germany.

Nagpal, B., Sharma, P., Chauhan, N., & Panesar, A. (2015). *DDoS tools: Classification, analysis and comparison*. Paper presented at the Computing for Sustainable Global Development (INDIACom).

Oppermann, F. J., Boano, C. A., & Römer, K. (2014). *A decade of wireless sensing applications: Survey and taxonomy. The art of wireless sensor networks*. Springer.

Page, E. (1954). Continuous inspection schemes. *Biometrika*, *41*(1-2), 100–115. doi:10.1093/biomet/41.1-2.100

Park, J., & Kim, M. (2008). *Design and implementation of an SNMP-based traffic flooding attack detection system. In Challenges for next generation network operations and service management* (pp. 380–389). Springer.

Park, K., & Lee, H. (2001). On the effectiveness of route-based packet filtering for distributed DoS attack prevention in power-law internets. *Computer Communication Review*, *31*(4), 15–26. doi:10.1145/964723.383061

Peng, T., Leckie, C., & Ramamohanarao, K. (2003). *Protection from distributed denial of service attacks using history-based IP filtering*. Paper presented at the Communications.

Peng, T., Leckie, C., & Ramamohanarao, K. (2007). Survey of network-based defense mechanisms countering the DoS and DDoS problems. *ACM Computing Surveys*, *39*(1), 3, es. doi:10.1145/1216370.1216373

Perera, C., Zaslavsky, A., Christen, P., & Georgakopoulos, D. (2014). Context aware computing for the internet of things: A survey. *IEEE Communications Surveys and Tutorials*, *16*(1), 414–454. doi:10.1109/SURV.2013.042313.00197

Poor, H. V., & Hadjiliadis, O. (2009). *Quickest detection*. Cambridge University Press.

Portnoy, L., Eskin, E., & Stolfo, S. (2001). *Intrusion detection with unlabeled data using clustering*. Paper presented at the ACM CSS Workshop on Data Mining Applied to Security (DMSA-2001).

Prathibha, R. (2014). A comparative study of defense mechanisms against SYN flooding attack. *International Journal of Computers and Applications*, *98*(18).

Prolexic Technologies, I. (2012). *Prolexic quarterly global DDoS attack report (Q4 2012)*. doi:knowledge-center-ddos-attack-report-2012-q4.html

Qin, X., Lee, W., Lewis, L., & Cabrera, J. B. (2002). *Integrating intrusion detection and network management*. Paper presented at the Network Operations and Management Symposium.

Ramanathan, A. (2002). *WADeS: A tool for distributed denial of service attack detection*. (Doctoral Thesis).

Roberts, S. (1959). Control chart tests based on geometric moving averages. *Technometrics*, *1*(3), 239–250. doi:10.1080/00401706.1959.10489860

Savage, S., Wetherall, D., Karlin, A., & Anderson, T. (2000). Practical network support for IP traceback. *Computer Communication Review*, *30*(4), 295–306. doi:10.1145/347057.347560

Savage, S., Wetherall, D., Karlin, A., & Anderson, T. (2001). Network support for IP traceback. *IEEE/ACM Transactions on Networking, 9*(3), 226-237.

Schindler, L. W. (1991). *Understanding the immune system*. DIANE Publishing.

Shafiq, M. Z., & Farooq, M. (2007). *Defense against 802.11 dos attacks using artificial immune system. In Artificial immune systems* (pp. 95–106). Springer.

Siaterlis, C., & Maglaris, V. (2005). *Detecting incoming and outgoing DDoS attacks at the edge using a single set of network characteristics*. Paper presented at the Computers and Communications. doi:10.1109/ISCC.2005.50

Siris, V. A., & Papagalou, F. (2006). Application of anomaly detection algorithms for detecting SYN flooding attacks. *Computer Communications*, *29*(9), 1433–1442. doi:10.1016/j.comcom.2005.09.008

Somal, I. K., & Virk, S. (2014). *Classification of distributed denial of service Attacks–Architecture, taxonomy and tools*. Academic Press.

Song, D. X., & Perrig, A. (2001). Advanced and authenticated marking schemes for IP traceback. *Proceedings of the IEEE*, *2*, 878–886.

Stone, R. (2000). *CenterTrack: An IP overlay network for tracking DoS floods*. Paper presented at the USENIX Security Symposium.

Strategy, I., & Unit, P. (2005). ITU internet reports 2005: The internet of things. Geneva: International Telecommunication Union (ITU).

Streilein, W. W., Fried, D. J., & Cunningham, R. K. (2003). *Detecting flood-based denial-of-service attacks with snmp/rmon*. Paper presented at the Workshop on Statistical and Machine Learning Techniques in Computer Intrusion Detection, Fairfax, VA.

Sundmaeker, H., Guillemin, P., Friess, P., & Woelfflé, S. (2010). *Vision and challenges for realising the internet of things*. Academic Press.

Sung, M., & Xu, J. (2003). IP traceback-based intelligent packet filtering: A novel technique for defending against internet DDoS attacks. *Parallel and Distributed Systems. IEEE Transactions On*, *14*(9), 861–872.

Tartakovsky, A. G., Polunchenko, A. S., & Sokolov, G. (2013). Efficient computer network anomaly detection by changepoint detection methods. *Selected Topics in Signal Processing. IEEE Journal Of*, *7*(1), 4–11.

Tartakovsky, A. G., Rozovskii, B. L., Blazek, R. B., & Kim, H. (2006). A novel approach to detection of intrusions in computer networks via adaptive sequential and batch-sequential change-point detection methods. *Signal Processing. IEEE Transactions On*, *54*(9), 3372–3382. doi:10.1109/TSP.2006.879308

Tsai, C., Chang, A. Y., & Ming-Szu, H. (2010). *Early warning system for DDoS attacking based on multilayer deployment of time delay neural network.* Paper presented at the Intelligent Information Hiding and Multimedia Signal Processing (IIH-MSP). doi:10.1109/IIHMSP.2010.178

Vermesan, O., Friess, P., Guillemin, P., Gusmeroli, S., Sundmaeker, H., Bassi, A., & Eisenhauer, M. et al. (2011). Internet of things strategic research roadmap. *Global Technological and Societal Trends*, *1*, 9-52.

Wang, , & Zhang, , & Shin. (2002). Detecting SYN flooding attacks. Paper presented at the INFOCOM 2002. Twenty-First Annual Joint Conference of the IEEE Computer and Communications Societies. *Proceedings of the IEEE*, *3*, 1530–1539. doi:10.1109/INFCOM.2002.1019404

Wang, H., Jin, C., & Shin, K. G. (2007). Defense against spoofed IP traffic using hop-count filtering. *IEEE/ACM Transactions on Networking, 15*(1), 40-53.

Yaar, A., Perrig, A., & Song, D. (2003). *Pi: A path identification mechanism to defend against DDoS attacks*. Paper presented at the Security and Privacy. doi:10.1109/SECPRI.2003.1199330

Yau, D. K., Lui, J., Liang, F., & Yam, Y. (2005). Defending against distributed denial-of-service attacks with max-min fair server-centric router throttles. *IEEE/ACM Transactions on Networking, 13*(1), 29-42.

Ye, N., Borror, C., & Zhang, Y. (2002). EWMA techniques for computer intrusion detection through anomalous changes in event intensity. *Quality and Reliability Engineering International*, *18*(6), 443–451. doi:10.1002/qre.493

Ye, N., Vilbert, S., & Chen, Q. (2003). Computer intrusion detection through EWMA for autocorrelated and uncorrelated data. *Reliability. IEEE Transactions On*, *52*(1), 75–82.

Yu, J., Lee, H., Kim, M., & Park, D. (2008). Traffic flooding attack detection with SNMP MIB using SVM. *Computer Communications*, *31*(17), 4212–4219. doi:10.1016/j.comcom.2008.09.018

Yun, M., & Yuxin, B. (2010). *Research on the architecture and key technology of internet of things (IoT) applied on smart grid*. Paper presented at the Advances in Energy Engineering (ICAEE).

Zargar, S. T., Joshi, J., & Tipper, D. (2013). A survey of defense mechanisms against distributed denial of service (DDoS) flooding attacks. *IEEE Communications Surveys and Tutorials*, *15*(4), 2046–2069. doi:10.1109/SURV.2013.031413.00127

Zhang, G., & Parashar, M. (2006). Cooperative defense against ddos attacks. *Journal of Research and Practice in Information Technology*, *38*(1), 69–84.

Zhou, C. V., Leckie, C., & Karunasekera, S. (2010). A survey of coordinated attacks and collaborative intrusion detection. *Computers & Security*, *29*(1), 124–140. doi:10.1016/j.cose.2009.06.008

Conclusion

THOUGHTFUL DISCUSSION ON DATA MINING TRENDS AND APPLICATIONS IN CRIMINAL SCIENCE AND INVESTIGATIONS

This chapter provides an overview of the various topics discussed in the chapters presented in this edited book, considering the fact that achieving crime reduction and criminal apprehension targets in resource-constrained settings require a paradigm shift in the minds of crime data mining researchers. Current trends indicate that several challenges, such as developing scalable programming models, as well as efficient and effective hybrid approaches for strategic or tactical crime analysis, persist in this domain and need to be addressed. Such challenges necessitate the development of more intuitive intelligence investigation techniques for crime pattern and situation recognition, in order to foster proactive safety solutions by the security agencies, public safety and law enforcement authorities.

The aim of producing an edited book on data mining trends and applications in criminal science and investigations is motivated by the need to understand the nature, scope and limitations of existing crime mining solutions across different domains and suggest new intervention strategies for a more inclusive solution for public safety improvement. This is particularly important for resource-constrained environments as it is noted, from observational evidence, that the ever growing population and assets, often times, tend to overshadow the available security and public safety agencies. In addition, the advancement in information and communication technology has led to the emergence of a wide set of applications, in order to meet up with daily operational needs across different domains. For example health-care applications, which sometimes exhibit significant security weaknesses as rightly pointed out by the authors, Ellouze et al., In Chapter 8. These applications also give room for offenders to perpetuate different kinds of crime such as cyber-crime, Denial of Service (DoS) and intrusion related offences. These developments have necessitated the need to develop more intuitive solutions for deterring crime across domains. Furthermore, empowering future criminal justice systems requires better insight into the Modus Operandi of criminals, as well as the dynamic mode of offenders behaviour as explained by Ghaziasgar et al. in Chapter 5. The authors investigate the automatic detection of micro-expressions from a video feed, which have been reported to be strong indicators of deception, in order to empower the future criminal justice system.

More generally, applying data mining techniques in the field of criminal science and investigation has culminated into a field known as crime data mining. The crime data encompass textual, image, and multimedia data. The goal of crime data mining is to discover interesting, non-trivial and potentially useful information, which can assist in decision support, crime investigation, prediction and control across different domains of life. The ultimate safety goal is to reduce and/or deter criminal activities. There are two fundamental theories in environmental criminology, crime pattern theory and routine activity theory, which try to explain the motivation for perpetrating crime. However, it is crucial to further investigate other intrinsic factors that contribute to the different crimes committed, for actionable solutions. Therefore, this book presents solutions that take all of these important factors into consideration, in order to empower the future criminal justice system and promote the realisation of public safety targets. Effective interventions to promote public safety in resource constrained environments can be realised through rather unconventional approaches to public safety solution model.

In some scenarios depicted by some of the solutions presented in this book, one might note that actionable and viable solutions require slight modifications to some of the parameters in the solution model, while certain other instances require a completely different intervention strategy. More generally, a user's application requirements and preferences determine the choice of appropriate methods or techniques to adopt in solving a crime problem. While actionable solutions could be derived from crime data information, it is important to recognise that in certain cases, a high level of missing data values may drastically affect crime prediction accuracy or the solution model. In other cases, the non-disclosure agreement constraint on releasing crime information to crime analysts or researchers makes it impractical to gain full access to real crime data. This has an implication of making the adoption of advanced, automated and computerised approaches of analysis to facilitate crime investigation and prediction in resource constrained settings conservative.

In public safety modeling and predictive policing, we note that there are several advantages to be derived in spatio-temporal related analysis, such as hotspots detection, for Knowledge support. This is noted in various related chapters such as in Chapter 3, where Ku et al. provide an insightful discussion on how the combination of visualization techniques with text and data mining tends to offer added benefits in crime data analysis. Moreover in Chapter 4, Eftelioglu et al. report on a computational perspective to crime hotspot analysis and detection using spatial scan statistics, with a focus on statistically significant hotspot detection techniques that aim to remove chance patterns. We observe that while several research have investigated hotspot and spatio-temporal related problems, there is still room for exploring crime spree and/or series-like detection, which is a set of crime thought to be committed by the same set of offender. This type of analysis takes a deeper and more careful look into the modus operandi of offenders. Isafiade et al. gave some insights into such an analysis in Chapter 6, through their discussion on the use of Bayesian Network (BN) in crime suspect modeling and legal decision support. Identifying an ongoing spree or series is of significant importance for predictive policing and crime control.

In conclusion, we investigate intrusion detection challenges within dynamic environments and its contribution in digital investigation, as well as distributed denial of service (DDoS) attack detection. These sought of challenges are prominent due to the emergence and wide acceptance of Internet-of-things (IoT). In today's world, the IoT is of practical significance in the daily human activities and engagements. The downside is that IoT has also created opportunities for offenders to perpetuate related crimes. Authors in Chapter 9, Keyvanpour etal., note that the prevalence of the online conversations have motivated the need for mitigating the undesirable effects of child abuse in cyber space. Therefore they present a system for the automatic identification of online predators in social networks, and further identified:

1. Detecting predators, and
2. Visualising and analysing predator criminal networks as two major predator identification problems in which data mining plays an important role.

Machaka et al., in Chapter 10, provide a discussion on data ming techniques for DDoS attack detection. They focus on the characteristics and pervasiveness of DDoS attacks, as well as motives, mechanisms and techniques used to execute a DDoS attack.

Current state-of-the-art approaches to crime data mining are generally amenable to scalable and efficient computational implementations, which researchers can further explore. In public safety modeling, predictive policing and crime data mining, the need to develop scalable solutions for massive geographical data coincides with the need to develop solutions for incomplete, noisy or heterogeneous sources of data, for crime situation recognition.

Potential avenues for future research in the domain of applying data mining techniques in criminal science and investigations include the following:

1. Reassessing existing solutions for suitability and possible extensions to suit emerging dynamic scenarios.
2. Deriving more intuitive intelligence investigation solutions and framework, in order to gain insight into dynamic crime trends and promote the realisation of safety targets across different domains.
3. Developing scalable, effective and efficient solutions for strategic and/or tactical crime analysis.

Omowunmi E. Isafiade
University of Cape Town, South Africa

Antoine B. Bagula
University of the Western Cape, South Africa

Compilation of References

Adderley, R. W. (2007). *The use of data mining techniques in crime trend analysis and offender profiling*. (Unpublished doctoral dissertation). University of Wolverhampton.

Adler, M. (2005). Trade-offs in probabilistic packet marking for IP traceback. *Journal of the ACM*, *52*(2), 217–244. doi:10.1145/1059513.1059517

Agarwal, D., McGregor, A., Phillips, J. M., Venkatasubramanian, S., & Zhu, Z. (2006). Spatial scan statistics. In *Proceedings of the 12th ACM SIGKDD international conference on Knowledge discovery and data mining - KDD '06* (p. 24). http://doi.org/ doi:10.1145/1150402.1150410

Aggarwal, C. C. (2015). Mining Text Data. In *Data Mining* (pp. 429–455). Springer International Publishing.

Akilandeswari, V., & Shalinie, S. M. (2012). *Probabilistic neural network based attack traffic classification*. Paper presented at the Advanced Computing (ICoAC), 2012 Fourth International Conference On. doi:doi:10.1109/ICoAC.2012.6416848 doi:10.1109/ICoAC.2012.6416848

Al-Duwairi, B., & Govindarasu, M. (2006). Novel hybrid schemes employing packet marking and logging for IP traceback. *Parallel and Distributed Systems. IEEE Transactions On*, *17*(5), 403–418.

Ali, K., Aib, I., & Boutaba, R. (2009). *P2P-AIS: A P2P artificial immune systems architecture for detecting DDoS flooding attacks*. Paper presented at the Information Infrastructure Symposium.

Alkar, A. Z., & Buhur, U. (2005). An internet based wireless home automation system for multifunctional devices. *Consumer Electronics. IEEE Transactions On*, *51*(4), 1169–1174.

Almadani, B., Bin-Yahya, M., & Shakshuki, E. M. (2015). E-AMBULANCE: Real-Time Integration Platform for Heterogeneous Medical Telemetry System. *Procedia Computer Science*, *63*, 400–407. doi:10.1016/j.procs.2015.08.359

Almeida, C. S. d. B., & Júnior, A. L. A. (2012). *OpenedEyes: Developing an Information Visualization Framework Using Web Standards and Open Web Technologies*. Academic Press.

Alomari, E., Manickam, S., Gupta, B., Karuppayah, S., & Alfaris, R. (2012). *Botnet-based distributed denial of service (DDoS) attacks on web servers: Classification and art*. arXiv Preprint arXiv:1208.0403

Al-Qurishi, M., Al-Rakhami, M., Al-Qershi, F., Hassan, M. M., Alamri, A., Khan, H. U., & Xiang, Y. (2015). A Framework for Cloud-Based Healthcare Services to Monitor Noncommunicable Diseases Patient. *International Journal of Distributed Sensor Networks*, 2015.

Anand, V. (2014). *Intrusion detection: Tools, techniques and strategies*. Paper presented at the 2014 ACM SIGUCCS Annual Conference on User Services Conference.

Andrews, C., Endert, A., Yost, B., & North, C. (2011). Information Visualization on Large, High-Resolution Displays: Issues, Challenges, and Opportunities. *Information Visualization, 10*(4), 341-355. Retrieved from http://ivi.sagepub.com/content/10/4/341.abstract

Ankerst, M., Breunig, M., Kriegel, H., & Sander, J. (1999). OPTICS: Ordering Points To Identify the Clustering Structure. In *ACM International conference on Management of Data* (pp. 49-60). ACM Press.

Anselin, L., Syabri, I., & Kho, Y. (2006). GeoDa: An introduction to spatial data analysis. *Geographical Analysis, 38*(1), 5–22. doi:10.1111/j.0016-7363.2005.00671.x

Aquino-Santos, R., Martinez-Castro, D., Edwards-Block, A., & Murillo-Piedrahita, A. F. (2013). Wireless sensor networks for ambient assisted living. *Sensors (Basel, Switzerland), 13*(12), 16384–16405. doi:10.3390/s131216384 PMID:24351665

Argyraki, K., & Cheriton, D. R. (2009). Scalable network-layer defense against internet bandwidth-flooding attacks. *IEEE/ACM Transactions on Networking, 17*(4), 1284-1297.

Ashby, M., & Bowers, J. (2013). A comparison of methods for temporal analysis of aoristic crime. *Springer Open Journal of Crime Science, 2(1)*, 1–16. doi:10.1186/2193-7680-2-1

Ashton, K. (2009). That 'internet of things' thing. *RFiD Journal, 22*(7), 97–114.

Astorga, J., Astorga, J. C., Jacob, E., Toledo, N., & Higuero, M. (2014). Securing access to next generation IP-enabled pacemakers and ICDs using Ladon. *Journal of Ambient Intelligence and Smart Environments, 6*(2), 157-177.

Axelrad, E. T., Sticha, P. J., Brdiczka, O., & Shen, J. (2013). A Bayesian Network Model for Predicting Insider Threats. In *Proceedings of Security and Privacy Workshops* (pp. 82–89). IEEE. doi:10.1109/SPW.2013.35

Bagula, A. (2006). Hybrid routing in next generation IP networks. *Elsevier Computer Communicationsg, 29*(7), 879–892. doi:10.1016/j.comcom.2005.08.009

Bagula, A. (2007). On achieveing bandwidth-aware LSP/lambdaSP multiplexing/separation in multi-layer networks. *IEEE Selected Areas in Communications, 25*(5), 987–1000. doi:10.1109/JSAC.2007.070611

Bagula, A. (2010). Modelling and implementation of QoS in wireless sensor networks: A multiconstrained traffic engineering model. *EURASIP Journal on Wireless Communications and Networking, 2010*(1), 468737. doi:10.1155/2010/468737

Compilation of References

Bagula, A., & Krzesinski, A. E. (2001). Traffic engineering label switched paths in IP networks using a pre-planned flow optimization model.*Proceedings of the IEEE Ninth International Symposium on Modeling, Analysis and Simulation of Computer and Telecommunication Systems*, (pp. 70-77). doi:10.1109/MASCOT.2001.948855

Baig, M. M., Gholamhosseini, H., & Connolly, M. J. (2013). A comprehensive survey of wearable and wireless ECG monitoring systems for older adults. *Medical & Biological Engineering & Computing*, *51*(5), 485–495. doi:10.1007/s11517-012-1021-6 PMID:23334714

Bansal, D., & Bhambhu, L. (2013a). Usage of Apriori Algorithm of Data Mining as an Application to Grievous Crimes against Women. *International Journal of Computer Trends and Technology*, *4*(9), 3194–3199.

Bansal, D., & Bhambhu, L. (2013b). Execution of APRIORI Algorithm of Data Mining Directed Towards Tumultuous Crimes Concerning Women. *International Journal of Advanced Research in Computer Science and Software Engineering*, *3*(9), 54–62.

Barford, P., Kline, J., Plonka, D., & Ron, A. (2002). *A signal analysis of network traffic anomalies*. Paper presented at the 2nd ACM SIGCOMM Workshop on Internet Measurment. doi:doi:10.1145/637201.637210 doi:10.1145/637201.637210

Barlow, J., & Thrower, W. (2000). *TFN2K–an analysis*. Axent Security Team.

Basseville, M., & Nikiforov, I. V. (1993). *Detection of abrupt changes: Theory and application*. Prentice Hall.

Batishchev, A. (2012). *Low orbit ion cannon (loic)*. Retrieved from http://Sourceforge.Net/Projects/Loic/

Baumgartner, K., Ferrari, S., & Palermo, G. (2008). Constructing Bayesian Networks for Criminal Profiling from Limited Data. Journal of Knowledge-Based Systems. doi:10.1016/j.knosys.2008.03.019

Baumgartner, K., Ferrari, S., & Salfati, C. (2005). Bayesian Network Modeling of Offender Behavior for Criminal Profiling. In *Proceedings of the 44th IEEE Conference on Decision and Control*, (pp. 2702-2709). doi:10.1109/CDC.2005.1582571

Beauregard, E., Proulx, J., & Rossmo, D. K. (2005). Spatial patterns of sex offenders: Theoretical, empirical, and practical issues. *Aggression and Violent Behavior*, *10*(5), 579–603. doi:10.1016/j.avb.2004.12.003

Beitollahi, H., & Deconinck, G. (2012). Analyzing well-known countermeasures against distributed denial of service attacks. *Computer Communications*, *35*(11), 1312–1332. doi:10.1016/j.comcom.2012.04.008

Belenko, S. R., & Spohn, C. (2015). *Drugs, crime, and justice*. Academic Press.

Bellovin, S. M., Leech, M., & Taylor, T. (2003). *ICMP traceback messages*. Academic Press.

Bengio, Y. (2009). Learning Deep Architectures for AI. *Found. Trends Mach. Learn.*, *2*(1), 1–127. doi:10.1561/2200000006

Berger, A. L., Pietra, V. J. D., & Pietra, S. A. D. (1996). A Maximum Entropy Approach to Natural Language Processing. *Computational Linguistics*, *22*(1), 39–71.

Berger-Wolf, T. Y., & Saia, J. (2006). A Framework for Analysis of Dynamic Social Networks. In *Proceedings of the 12th ACM SIGKDD International Conference on Knowledge Discovery and Data Mining* (pp. 523–528). New York, NY: ACM. doi:10.1145/1150402.1150462

Berry, M. J. A., & Linoff, G. S. (2004, April). *Data Mining Techniques. For Marketing, Sales, and Customer Relationship Management* (2nd ed.). Indianapolis, IN: Wiley Publishing, Inc.

Bharathi, A., & Shilpa, R. (2014, August). A Survey on Crime Data Analysis of Data Mining Using Clustering Techniques. *International Journal of Advance Research in Computer Science and Management Studies*, *2*(8), 9–13.

Bhatnagar, V. (2014). *Data Mining and Analysis in the Engineering Field. Ambedkar Institute of Advanced Communication Technologies and Research*. IGI Global.

Bhattacharyya, D. K., & Kalita, J. K. (2013). *Network anomaly detection: A machine learning perspective*. CRC Press.

Bhuyan, M. H., Kashyap, H. J., Bhattacharyya, D. K., & Kalita, J. K. (2013). Detecting distributed denial of service attacks: Methods, tools and future directions. *The Computer Journal*, bxt031.

Bishop, C. (2006). *Pattern Recognition and Machine Learning*. New York: Springer-Verlag.

Blaze, M., Feigenbaum, J., & Lacy, J. (1996). *Decentralized trust management*. Paper presented at the Security and Privacy, 1996.

Bo, C., Fang, B., & Yun, X. (2005). *A new approach for early detection of internet worms based on connection degree*. Paper presented at the Machine Learning and Cybernetics, 2005.

Bogahawatte, K., & Adikari, S. (2013). Intelligent criminal identification system. In *Computer Science & Education (ICCSE), 8th International Conference on* (pp. 633-638). doi:doi:10.1109/ICCSE.2013.6553986 doi:10.1109/ICCSE.2013.6553986

Bogdanova, D., Rosso, P., & Solorio, T. (2012a). Modelling Fixated Discourse in Chats with Cyberpedophiles. In *Proceedings of the Workshop on Computational Approaches to Deception Detection* (pp. 86–90). Stroudsburg, PA: Association for Computational Linguistics.

Bogdanova, D., Rosso, P., & Solorio, T. (2012b). On the Impact of Sentiment and Emotion Based Features in Detecting Online Sexual Predators. In *Proceedings of the 3rd Workshop in Computational Approaches to Subjectivity and Sentiment Analysis* (pp. 110–118). Stroudsburg, PA: Association for Computational Linguistics.

Bogdanova, D., Rosso, P., & Solorio, T. (2014). Exploring high-level features for detecting cyberpedophilia. *Computer Speech & Language*, *28*(1), 108–120. doi:10.1016/j.csl.2013.04.007

Borg, A., Boldt, M., Lavesson, N., Melander, U., & Boeva, V. (2014). Detecting Serial Residential Burglaries Using Clustering. *Expert Systems with Applications*, *41*(11), 5252–5266. doi:10.1016/j.eswa.2014.02.035

Bostock, M., & Heer, J. (2009). Protovis: A Graphical Toolkit for Visualization. *IEEE Transactions on Visualization and Computer Graphics*, *15*(6), 1121–1128. doi:10.1109/TVCG.2009.174 PMID:19834180

Bostock, M., Ogievetsky, V., & Heer, J. (2011). D^3 Data-Driven Documents. *IEEE Transactions on Visualization and Computer Graphics*, *17*(12), 2301–2309. doi:10.1109/TVCG.2011.185 PMID:22034350

Brantingham, P. L., & Brantingham, P. J. (1993). Environment, Routine, and Situation: Toward a Pattern Theory of Crime. *Routine Activity and Rational Choice: Advances in Criminological Theoy*, *5*, 259–294.

Brimicombe, A. J. (2005). *Cluster Detection in Point Event Data having Tendency Towards Spatially Repetitive Events*. Intl. Conf. on GeoComputation.

Buczak, A., & Gifford, C. (2010). Fuzzy Association Rule Mining for Community Crime Pattern Discovery. In *Proceedings of the ACM SIGKDD Workshop on Intelligence and Security Informatics*. doi:10.1145/1938606.1938608

Burch, H., & Cheswick, B. (2000). *Tracing anonymous packets to their approximate source*. Paper presented at the LISA.

Bureau of Justice Statistics (BJS). (n.d.). Retrieved from http://www.bjs.gov/

Burn, O. (1982). *Environmental criminology. Journal of Criminal Justice* (Vol. 10). Sage Publications. http://doi.org/<ALIGNMENT.qj></ALIGNMENT>10.1016/0047-2352(82)90028-9

Cabrera, J. B., Lewis, L., Qin, X., Lee, W., & Mehra, R. K. (2002). Proactive intrusion detection and distributed denial of service attacks—a case study in security management. *Journal of Network and Systems Management*, *10*(2), 225–254. doi:10.1023/A:1015910917349

Cano, A., Fernandez, M., & Alani, H. (2014). Detecting Child Grooming Behaviour Patterns on Social Media. In L. Aiello & D. McFarland (Eds.), *Social Informatics* (Vol. 8851, pp. 412–427). Springer International Publishing. doi:10.1007/978-3-319-13734-6_30

Carley, K. M. (2015, May 8). *DyNet*. Retrieved from http://www.casos.cs.cmu.edu/projects/DyNet/dynet_info.html

Carl, G., Kesidis, G., Brooks, R. R., & Rai, S. (2006). Denial-of-service attack-detection techniques. *IEEE Internet Computing*, *10*(1), 82–89. doi:10.1109/MIC.2006.5

Carrier, B. D. (2006). *A hypothesis-based approach to digital forensic investigations*. (Unpublished doctoral dissertation). Purdue University.

Carrier, B. D., & Spafford, E. H. (2006). Categories of digital investigation analysis techniques based on the computer history model. *Digital Investigation*, *3*, 121–130. doi:10.1016/j.diin.2006.06.011

Carvalho, A. C. P. L. F., Gama, J. M. P., & Ludermir, T. B. (2009). Credit Risk Assessment and Data Mining. In *Encyclopedia of Information Science and Technology* (pp. 800–805). IGI Global. doi:10.4018/978-1-60566-026-4.ch130

Casey, E. (2011). *Digital Evidence and Computer Crime*. Baltimore, MD: Academic Press.

Catania, C. A., & Garino, C. G. (2012). Automatic network intrusion detection: Current techniques and open issues. *Computers & Electrical Engineering*, *38*(5), 1062–1072. doi:10.1016/j.compeleceng.2012.05.013

Center, C. C. (2001). *Carnegie Mellon Software Engineering Institute, CERT Advisory CA-2001-20 Continuing Threats to Home Users*. Carnegie Mellon.

Chainey, S., Tompson, L., & Uhlig, S. (2008). *The Utility of Hotspot Mapping for Predicting Spatial Patterns of Crime*. http://doi.org/<ALIGNMENT.qj></ALIGNMENT>10.1057/sj.2008.6

Chainey, S., & Ratcliffe, J. (2005). *GIS and Crime Mapping. Mastering GIS: Technology, Applications and Management*. West Sussex, UK: John Wiley & Sons Ltd. doi:10.1002/9781118685181

Chang, C.-C., & Lin, C.-J. (2011). LIBSVM: A library for support vector machines. *ACM Transactions on Intelligent Systems and Technology*, *2*(3), 27. doi:10.1145/1961189.1961199

Chartered Financial Analyst Institute. (2013). *Urban Life: open-air computers*. Retrieved from http://www.economist.com/news/special-report

Chen, H., Chung, W., Qin, Y., Chau, M., Xu, J. J., Wang, G., . . . Atabakhsh, H. (2003). Crime data mining: an overview and case studies. In *Proceedings of the 2003 annual national conference on Digital government research* (dg.o '03). Boston, MA: Digital Government Society of North America.

Chen, R., & Park, J. (2005). *Attack diagnosis: Throttling distributed denial-of-service attacks close to the attack sources*. Paper presented at the Computer Communications and Networks, 2005.

Chen, R., Park, J., & Marchany, R. (2006a). *NISp1-05: RIM: Router interface marking for IP traceback*. Paper presented at the Global Telecommunications Conference, 2006.

Chen, H., Atabakhsh, H., Petersen, T., Schroeder, J., Buetow, T., Chaboya, L., & Huang, Z. et al. (2003). COPLINK: Visualization for Crime Analysis. In *Proceedings of the 2003 annual national conference on digital government research* (pp. 1-6). Boston: Digital Government Society of North America.

Chen, H., Cheng, B. C., Liao, G. T., & Kuo, T. C. (2014). Hybrid classification engine for cardiac arrhythmia cloud service in elderly healthcare management. *Journal of Visual Languages and Computing*, *25*(6), 745–753. doi:10.1016/j.jvlc.2014.09.012

Chen, H., Chung, W., Qin, Y., Chau, M., Xu, J., Wang, G., & Homa, A. et al. (2003). Crime Data Mining: An Overview and Case Studies. In *Proceedings of the Annual National Conference on Digital Government Research*.

Chen, H., Chung, W., Xu, J., Wang, G., Qin, Y., & Chau, M. (2004). Crime Data Mining: A General Framework and Some Examples. *Journal of IEEE Computer*, *37*(4), 50–56. doi:10.1109/MC.2004.1297301

Chen, R., Park, J , & Marchany, R. (2006b). *TRACK: A novel approach for defending against distributed denial-of-service attacks. Technical P~ Eport TR ECE—O6-02. Dept.of Electrical and Computer Engineering*. Virginia Tech.

Chen, X., Bose, I., Leung, A. C. M., & Guo, C. (2011, March). Assessing the severity of phishing attacks: A hybrid data mining approach. *Decision Support Systems*, *50*(4), 662–672. doi:10.1016/j.dss.2010.08.020

Chen, Z., Chen, Z. & Delis, A. (2007). An inline detection and prevention framework for distributed denial of service attacks. *The Computer Journal*, *50*(1), 7–40. doi:10.1093/comjnl/bxl042

Chiu, T., Fang, D., Chen, J., & Wang, Y. (2001). A Robust and Scalable Clustering Algorithm for Mixed Type Attributes in Large Database Environment. In *Proceedings of the seventh ACM SIGKDD international conference on Knowledge discovery and data mining*. . doi:10.1145/502512.502549

Choo, K. R. (2011). The cyber threat landscape: Challenges and future research directions. *Computers & Security*, *30*(8), 719–731. doi:10.1016/j.cose.2011.08.004

Chris, S. W., & Kevin, B. K. (1999). Learning Linear Causal Models by MML Sampling. In *Causal Models and Intelligent Data Management* (pp. 81–11). Springer-Verlag.

Cios, K. J., & Kurgan, L. A. (2005). Trends in Data Mining and Knowledge Discovery. In Advanced Techniques in Knowledge Discovery and Data Mining (pp. 1-26). London: Springer-Verlag. doi:10.1007/1-84628-183-0_1

Cios, K. J., Pedrycz, W., Swiniarski, R. W., & Kurgan, L. A. (2007). The Knowledge Discovery Process. In Data Mining- A Knowledge Discovery Approach (pp. 9-24). Springer Science & Business Media. doi:10.1007/978-0-387-36795-8_2

City of Chicago. (2013). *City of Chicago Data Portal*. Retrieved from https://data.cityofchicago.org/

City of Chicago. (2014). Methamphetamine Possession Cases Chicago 2013. Chicago.

City of Orlando, FL. (2014). *Orlando Crime Dataset*. Author.

Clarke, V. R., & Felson, M. M. (1993). Introduction: Criminology, Routine Activity, and Rational Choice. *Advances in Criminological Theory Routine Activity and Rational Choice*, *5*, 1–14.

Cohen, L. E., & Felson, M. (1979). Social Change and Crime Rate Trends: A Routine Activity Approach. *American Sociological Review*, *44*(4), 588. doi:10.2307/2094589

Coleman, M., Coleman, M., Mabuza, A. M., Kok, G., Coetzee, M., & Durrheim, D. N. (2009). Using the SaTScan method to detect local malaria clusters for guiding malaria control programmes. *Malaria Journal*, *8*(1), 68. doi:10.1186/1475-2875-8-68 PMID:19374738

Cook, K., Earnshaw, R., & Stasko, J. (2007). Guest Editors' Introduction: Discovering the Unexpected. *IEEE Computer Graphics and Applications*, *27*(5), 15–19. doi:10.1109/MCG.2007.126 PMID:17913020

Cooper, G. F. (1990). The computational complexity of probabilistic inference using Bayesian belief networks. *Artificial Intelligence*, *42*(2-3), 393–405. doi:10.1016/0004-3702(90)90060-D

Criscuolo, P. J. (2000). *Distributed Denial of Service: Trin00*. Tribe Flood Network, Tribe Flood Network 2000, and Stacheldraht CIAC-2319.

Cusack, B., & Kyaw, A. K. (2012). Forensic readiness for wireless medical systems. In *Proceedings of the 10th Australian Digital Forensics Conference* (pp. 21-32).

D3 Gallery. (n.d.). Retrieved from https://github.com/mbostock/d3/wiki/Gallery

D3. (n.d.). Retrieved from http://d3js.org/

Dagum, P., & Luby, M. (1993). Approximating probabilistic inference in Bayesian belief networks is NP-hard. *Artificial Intelligence*, *60*(1), 141–153. doi:10.1016/0004-3702(93)90036-B

Dainotti, A., Pescapé, A., & Ventre, G. (2006). *Wavelet-based detection of DoS attacks*. Paper presented at the Global Telecommunications Conference, 2006.

Dainotti, A., Pescapé, A., & Ventre, G. (2009). A cascade architecture for DoS attacks detection based on the wavelet transform. *Journal of Computer Security*, *17*(6), 945–968.

Dasgupta, D., & González, F. (2002). An immunity-based technique to characterize intrusions in computer networks. Evolutionary Computation. *IEEE Transactions On*, *6*(3), 281–291.

Dasgupta, D., Gonzalez, F., Yallapu, K., Gomez, J., & Yarramsettii, R. (2005). CIDS: An agent-based intrusion detection system. *Computers & Security*, *24*(5), 387–398. doi:10.1016/j.cose.2005.01.004

Datta, S., Bhaduri, K., Giannella, C., Wolff, R., & Kargupta, H. (2006). Distributed data mining in peer-to-peer networks. *IEEE Internet Computing*, *10*(4), 18–26. doi:10.1109/MIC.2006.74

De Castro, L. N., & Timmis, J. (2002). *Artificial immune systems: A new computational intelligence approach*. Springer Science & Business Media.

Dean, D., Franklin, M., & Stubblefield, A. (2002). An algebraic approach to IP traceback. *ACM Transactions on Information and System Security*, *5*(2), 119–137. doi:10.1145/505586.505588

Deshpande, S. & Thakare, V. (2010). Data Mining System and Applications: A Review. *International Journal of Distributed and Parallel systems, 1*(1), 32-44.

Devesh, B. (2012). Emerging Trends in Utilisation of Data Mining in Criminal Investigation: An Overview. *Journal of Environmental Science, Computer Science and Engineering & Technology, 1*(2), 124-131.

Devlin, K., & Lorden, G. (2007). *The Numbers Behind NUMB3RS: Solving Crime with Mathematics.* Academic Press.

Deylami, H., & Singh, Y. (2012). Adaboost and SVM based cybercrime detection and prevention model. *International Journal of Artificial Intelligence Research., 1*(2), 117–130.

Dhakshinamoorthy, P., & Kalaiselvan, T. (2013, July). Crime Pattern Detection Using Data Mining. *International Journal of Advanced Research in Computer Science and Applications, 1*(1), 46–50.

Dickerson, J. E., & Dickerson, J. A. (2000). Fuzzy network profiling for intrusion detection. In *Proc. of NAFIPS 19th International Conference of the North American Fuzzy Information Processing Society* (pp. 301-306). Atlanta, GA: IEEE.

Didimo, W., Liotta, G., & Montecchiani, F. (2014). Network Visualization for Financial Crime Detection. *Journal of Visual Languages and Computing, 25*(4), 433–451. doi:10.1016/j.jvlc.2014.01.002

Dietrich, S., Long, N., & Dittrich, D. (2000). *Analyzing distributed denial of service tools: The shaft case*. Paper presented at the LISA.

Dietterich, T. G. (2002, September). Ensemble Learning. In M. A. Arbib (Ed.), *Brain Theory and Neural Networks*. Cambridge, MA: MIT Press.

District of Columbia Crimespotting by Tableau. (n.d.). Retrieved from http://www.tableau.com/learn/gallery/crime-spotting

Dittrich, D. (1999a). *The 'stacheldraht'distributed denial of service attack tool.* Academic Press.

Dittrich, D. (1999b). The "Tribe flood network" distributed denial of service attack tool. University of Washington.

Dittrich, D. (1999c). *The DoS project's 'trinoo' distributed denial of service attack tool.* Academic Press.

Dittrich, D., Weaver, G., Dietrich, S., & Long, N. (2000). *The ''mstream''distributed denial of service attack tool*. Retrieved from Http://Staff.Washington.Edu/Dittrich/Misc/Mstream.Analysis.Txt

Dmitrienko, A., Hadzic, Z., Löhr, H., Sadeghi, A. R., & Winandy, M. (2013).Securing the access to electronic health records on mobile phones. *Biomedical Engineering Systems and Technologies, 273*, 365–379.

Dokas, P., Ertoz, L., Kumar, V., Lazarevic, A., Srivastava, J., & Tan, P.-N. (2002, November). Data mining for network intrusion detection. In *Proc. NSF Workshop on Next Generation Data Mining*, (p. 21-30). Baltimore, MD: AAAI/MIT Press.

Douligeris, C., & Mitrokotsa, A. (2004). DDoS attacks and defense mechanisms: Classification and state-of-the-art. *Computer Networks*, *44*(5), 643–666. doi:10.1016/j.comnet.2003.10.003

Duda, R. O., Hart, P. E., & Stork, D. G. (2012). *Pattern Classification*. Wiley-Interscience.

Duma, C., Karresand, M., Shahmehri, N., & Caronni, G. (2006). *A trust-aware, p2p-based overlay for intrusion detection*. Paper presented at the Database and Expert Systems Applications.

Eck, J., & others. (2005). *Mapping crime: Understanding hotspots*. Academic Press.

Eftelioglu, E., Shekhar, S., Oliver, D., Zhou, X., Evans, M. R., & Xie, Y., … Farah, C. (2014). Ring-Shaped Hotspot Detection: A Summary of Results. In *2014 IEEE International Conference on Data Mining* (pp. 815–820). doi:10.1109/ICDM.2014.13

Ekman, P. (2009). Lie catching and microexpressions. *The philosophy of deception*, 118-133.

Ekman, P., & Friesen, W. V. (1977). *Facial action coding system*. Academic Press.

Ekman, P., & Friesen, W. V. (1969). Nonverbal leakage and clues to deception. *Psychiatry*, *32*(1), 88–106. PMID:5779090

Ellouze, N., Allouche, M., Ben Ahmed, H., Rekhis, S., & Boudriga, N. (2013). Securing implantable cardiac medical devices: use of radio frequency energy harvesting. In *Proceedings of the third international workshop on Trustworthy embedded devices* (pp. 35-42). doi:10.1145/2517300.2517307

Ellouze, N., Rekhis, S., Allouche, M., & Boudriga, N. (2014). Digital Investigation of Security Attacks on Cardiac Implantable Medical Devices. In *Proceedings of the Advanced Intrusion and Prevention Workshop in conjunction with the International Information Security and Privacy Conference* (pp. 15-30). doi:10.4204/EPTCS.165.2

Endres, J., & Laidlaw, A. (2009). Micro-expression recognition training in medical students: A pilot study. *BMC Medical Education*, *9*(1), 47. doi:10.1186/1472-6920-9-47 PMID:19619307

Eriksson, G., & Karlgren, J. (2012). *Features for modelling characteristics of conversations*. Presented at the Notebook for PAN at CLEF 2012, Rome, Italy.

Escalante, H. J., Villatoro-Tello, E., Juárez, A., Montes-y-Gómez, M., & Villaseñor, L. (2013). Sexual predator detection in chats with chained classifiers. In *Proceedings of the 4th Workshop on Computational Approaches to Subjectivity, Sentiment and Social Media Analysis* (pp. 46–54). Atlanta, GA: Association for Computational Linguistics.

Esponda, F., Forrest, S., & Helman, P. (2004). A formal framework for positive and negative detection schemes. *Systems, Man, and Cybernetics, Part B: Cybernetics. IEEE Transactions On*, *34*(1), 357–373.

Estepp, I. (1987). Motived-based Offender profiles of arson and fire-related crimes. *FBI Law Enforcement Bulletin*, *56*(4), 17–23.

Ester, M. et al. (1996). *A density-based algorithm for discovering clusters in large spatial databases with noise* (pp. 226–231). AAAI Press.

Evans, D. (2011). *The internet of things: How the next evolution of the internet is changing everything*. CISCO White Paper.

Evett, L. W., Jackson, G., Lindley, D. V., & Meuwly, D. (2006). Logical Evaluation of Evidence When a Person is Suspected of Committing two Separate Offences. *Science & Justice*, *46*(1), 25–31. doi:10.1016/S1355-0306(06)71564-7 PMID:16878782

Fayyad, U. M., Piatetsky-Shapiro, G., & Smyth, P. (1996). From data mining to knowledge discovery: an overview. In U. M. Fayyad, G. Piatetsky-Shapiro, P. Smyth, & R. Uthurusamy (Eds.), *Advances in Knowledge Discovery and Data Mining* (pp. 1–34). USA: AAAI-Press.

Fei, B. K. L., Eloff, J. H. P., Olivier, M. S., & Venter, H. S. (2006). The use of self-organising maps for anomalous behaviour detection in a digital investigation. *Forensic Science International*, *162*(1-3), 33–37. doi:10.1016/j.forsciint.2006.06.046 PMID:16876359

Felisberto, F., Laza, R., Fdez-Riverola, F., & Pereira, A. (2015). A Distributed Multiagent System Architecture for Body Area Networks Applied to Healthcare Monitoring. *BioMed Research International, 2015*(2015).

Fenton, N. E., Neil, M., & Hsu, A. (2014). Calculating and understanding the value of any type of match evidence when there are potential testing errors. *Artificial Intelligence and Law*, *22*(1), 1–28. doi:10.1007/s10506-013-9147-x

Ferguson, P. (2000). *Network ingress filtering: Defeating denial of service attacks which employ IP source address spoofing*. Academic Press.

Forman, G. (2003). An Extensive Empirical Study of Feature Selection Metrics for Text Classification. *Journal of Machine Learning Research*, *3*, 1289–1305.

Forrester Consulting. (2009). *The trends and changing landscape of DDoS threats and protection*. Author.

Forsyth, E. N., & Martell, C. H. (2007). Lexical and Discourse Analysis of Online Chat Dialog. In *Semantic Computing, 2007. ICSC 2007. International Conference on* (pp. 19–26).

Frank, M., Herbasz, M., Sinuk, K., Keller, A., & Nolan, C. (2009*). I see how you feel: Training laypeople and professionals to recognize fleeting emotions.* The Annual Meeting of the International Communication Association, New York, NY.

Gao, J., Hu, G., Yao, X., & Chang, R. K. (2006). *Anomaly detection of network traffic based on wavelet packet.* Paper presented at the Communications, 2006. APCC'06. Asia-Pacific Conference On. doi:doi:10.1109/APCC.2006.255840 doi:10.1109/APCC.2006.255840

Garber, L. (2000). Denial-of-service attacks rip the internet. *Computer*, *33*(4), 12–17. doi:10.1109/MC.2000.839316

Garfinkel, S. (2012, February). Digital forensics XML and the DFXML toolset. *Digital Investigation*, *8*(3-4), 161–174. doi:10.1016/j.diin.2011.11.002

Gayathri, R., & Malathi, A. (2013, November). Investigation of Data Mining Techniques in Fraud Detection: Credit Card. *International Journal of Computers and Applications*, *82*(9), 12–15. doi:10.5120/14143-1560

Geng, X., & Whinston, A. B. (2000). Defeating distributed denial of service attacks. *IT Professional*, *2*(4), 36–42. doi:10.1109/6294.869381

Gephi. (n.d.). Retrieved from http://gephi.github.io/

Gera, P., & Vohra, R. (2014). City Crime Profiling Using Cluster Analysis. *International Journal of Computer Science & Information Technologies*, *5*(4), 5145–5148.

Giaccardi, E., & Fogli, D. (2008). *Affective Geographies: Toward a Richer Cartographic Semantics for the Geospatial Web*. Academic Press.

Giles, C. L., Bollacker, K. D., & Lawrence, S. (2004). *CiteSeer: An Automatic Citation Indexing System.* Paper presented at the third ACM conference on Digital libraries, Pittsburgh, PA.

Gluhak, A., Krco, S., Nati, M., Pfisterer, D., Mitton, N., & Razafindralambo, T. (2011). A survey on facilities for experimental internet of things research. *Communications Magazine, IEEE*, *49*(11), 58–67. doi:10.1109/MCOM.2011.6069710

Goetz, S. L. (n.d.). *ArcGIS Tool Implementation of Risk Terrain Modeling.*

Gonzales, A. R., Schofield, R. B., & Hart, S. V. (2005). Mapping Crime: Understanding Hot Spots. National Institute of Justice, 79.

González, P. C., & Velásquez, J. D. (2013). Characterization and detection of taxpayers with false invoices using data mining techniques. *Expert Systems with Applications*, *40*(5), 1427–1436. doi:10.1016/j.eswa.2012.08.051

Goswami, J. C., & Chan, A. K. (2011). *Fundamentals of wavelets: Theory, algorithms, and applications*. John Wiley & Sons.

Gray, G. L., & Debreceny, R. S. (2014). A taxonomy to guide research on the application of data mining to fraud detection in financial statement audits. *International Journal of Accounting Information Systems*, *15*(4), 357–380. doi:10.1016/j.accinf.2014.05.006

Gubbi, J., Buyya, R., Marusic, S., & Palaniswami, M. (2013). Internet of things (IoT): A vision, architectural elements, and future directions. *Future Generation Computer Systems*, *29*(7), 1645–1660. doi:10.1016/j.future.2013.01.010

Gupta, B., Joshi, R. C., & Misra, M. (2009). Defending against distributed denial of service attacks: Issues and challenges. *Information Security Journal: A Global Perspective, 18*(5), 224-247.

Gupta, R. (2014). Journey from Data Mining to Web Mining to Big Data. *International Journal of Computer Trends and Technology, 10*(1), 18-20. Retrieved from www.ijcttjournal.org

Gupta, R., & Gill, N. S. (2012, July). A Data Mining Framework for Prevention and Detection of Financial Statement Fraud. *International Journal of Computers and Applications*, *50*(8), 7–14. doi:10.5120/7789-0889

Hafedh, C., Ramon, G., Theresa, A., Taewoo, N., Sehl, M., Hans, J., . . . Karine, N. (2012). Understanding Smart Cities: An Integrative Framework. In *Proceedings of the Hawaii International conference on System Sciences (HICSS)*, (pp. 2289-2297).

Haggard, E. A., & Isaacs, K. S. (1966). Micromomentary facial expressions as indicators of ego mechanisms in psychotherapy. In *Methods of research in psychotherapy* (pp. 154–165). Springer. doi:10.1007/978-1-4684-6045-2_14

Haklay, M., & Weber, P. (2008). OpenStreetMap – User Generated Street Map. *IEEE Pervasive Computing / IEEE Computer Society [and] IEEE Communications Society*, *7*(4), 12–18. doi:10.1109/MPRV.2008.80

Hall, M., Frank, E., Holmes, G., Pfahringer, B., Reutemann, P., & Witten, I. H. (2009). "The WEKA data mining software: An update". In ACM Digital Library. *SIGKDD Explorations*, *11*(1), 10–18. doi:10.1145/1656274.1656278

Hammouda, K. M., & Kamel, M. S. (2009). Hierarchically distributed peer-to-peer document clustering and cluster summarization. *Knowledge and Data Engineering. IEEE Transactions on*, *21*(5), 681–698.

Hancock, B. (2000). Trinity v3, a DDoS tool, hits the streets. *Computers & Security*, *19*(7), 574.

Han, J., Pei, J., Yin, Y., & Mao, R. (2004). *Mining Frequent Patterns without Candidate Generation. ACM International Journal of Data Mining and Knowledge Discovery, 8(1)*, 53–87.

Harger, J. R., & Crossno, P. J. (2012). *Comparison of Open-Source Visual Analytics Toolkits*. Academic Press.

Hauck, R. V., Atabakhsh, H., Ongvasith, P., Gupta, H., & Chen, H. (2002, March). Using Coplink to Analyze Criminal-Justice Data. Computer, 35(3), 30-37.

Hearst, M. A. (2009). *Information Visualization for Search Interfaces Search User Interfaces*. Cambridge University Press. doi:10.1017/CBO9781139644082

Heer, J., Bostock, M., & Ogievetsky, V. (2010). A Tour Through the Visualization Zoo. *Communications of the ACM*, *53*(6), 59–67. doi:10.1145/1743546.1743567

Heer, J., & Shneiderman, B. (2012). Interactive Dynamics for Visual Analysis. *Communications of the ACM*, *55*(4), 45–54. doi:10.1145/2133806.2133821

Hei, X., Du, X., Wu, J., & Hu, F. (2010). Defending resource depletion attacks on implantable medical devices. In *Proceedings of the Global Telecommunications Conference* (pp. 1-5). doi:10.1109/GLOCOM.2010.5685228

Helbich, M., Hagenauer, J., Leitner, M., & Edwards, R. (2013). Exploration of unstructured narrative crime reports: an unsupervised neural network and point pattern analysis approach. Cartography and Geographic Information Science, 40(4).

Helmer, G., Wong, J. S. K., Honavar, V., & Miller, L. (2002, February). Automated discovery of concise predictive rules for intrusion detection. *Journal of Systems and Software*, *60*(3), 165–175. doi:10.1016/S0164-1212(01)00088-7

Hjortsjö, C.-H. (1969). *Man's face and mimic language*. Studentlitteratur.

Hofmeyr, S. A., & Forrest, S. (2000). Architecture for an artificial immune system. *Evolutionary Computation*, *8*(4), 443–473. doi:10.1162/106365600568257 PMID:11130924

Hogenboom, A., Bal, D., Frasincar, F., Bal, M., de Jong, F., & Kaymak, U. (2013). Exploiting Emoticons in Sentiment Analysis. In *Proceedings of the 28th Annual ACM Symposium on Applied Computing* (pp. 703–710). New York, NY: ACM. doi:10.1145/2480362.2480498

Holdener, A. T. (2011). HTML5 Geolocation. *Online*, 114. Retrieved from http://books.google.com/books?id=9aIA5P6dp2cC&pgis=1

Holzinger, A., Stocker, C., Ofner, B., Prohaska, G., Brabenetz, A., & Hofmann-Wellenhof, R. (2013). Combining HCI, Natural Language Processing, and Knowledge Discovery - Potential of IBM Content Analytics as an Assistive Technology in the Biomedical Field. In A. Holzinger & G. Pasi (Eds.), *Human-Computer Interaction and Knowledge Discovery in Complex, Unstructured, Big Data* (pp. 13–24). Springer Berlin Heidelberg.

Honig, A., Howard, A., Eskin, E., & Stolfo, S. (2002). Adaptive model generation: An architecture for the deployment of data mining based intrusion. In Applications of data mining in computer security, (pp. 153-194). Boston: Kluwer.

Hosaagrahara, M., & Sethu, H. (2008). Max-min fair scheduling in input-queued switches. *Parallel and Distributed Systems. IEEE Transactions On*, *19*(4), 462–475.

Hu, F., Jiang, M., Celentano, L., & Xiao, Y. (2008). Robust medical ad hoc sensor networks (MASN) with wavelet-based ECG data mining. *Ad Hoc Networks*, *6*(7), 986–1012. doi:10.1016/j.adhoc.2007.09.002

Hui, J. W., & Culler, D. E. (2008). Extending IP to low-power, wireless personal area networks. *IEEE Internet Computing*, *12*(4), 37–45. doi:10.1109/MIC.2008.79

Hussain, K. Z., Durairaj, M., & Farzana, G. (2012). Criminal behavior analysis by using data mining techniques. In *Advances in Engineering, Science and Management (ICAESM), International Conference on,* (pp. 656-658).

Ilango, M., & Mohan, V. (2010). A survey of grid based clustering algorithms. *International Journal of Engineering Science*, *2*(8), 3441–3446. Retrieved from http://www.ijest.info/docs/IJEST10-02-08-17.pdf

Inches, G., & Crestani, F. (2012). *Overview of the International Sexual Predator Identification Competition at PAN-2012*. CLEF (working notes).

International Association of Crime Analysts. (2011). *Crime Pattern Definitions for Tactical Analysis*. Standards, Methods, & Technology (SMT) Committee White Paper-2011-01. Retrieved from http://www iaca.net/Publications/Whitepapers/iacawp_2011_01_crime_patterns.pdf

Iqbal, F., Fung, B. C. M., & Debbabi, M. (2012). Mining Criminal Networks from Chat Log. In *Web Intelligence and Intelligent Agent Technology (WI-IAT), 2012 IEEE/WIC/ACM International Conferences on* (Vol. 1, pp. 332–337). doi:10.1109/WI-IAT.2012.68

Iqbal, F., Binsalleeh, H., Fung, B. C., & Debbabi, M. (2010). Mining writeprints from anonymous e-mails for forensic investigation. *Digital Investigation*, *7*(1), 56–64. doi:10.1016/j.diin.2010.03.003

Irfan, R., King, C. K., Grages, D., Ewen, S., Khan, S. U., Madani, S. A., ... Li, H. (2015). A survey on text mining in social networks. *The Knowledge Engineering Review, 30*(2), 157–170.

Isafiade, O. E., & Bagula, A. B. (2013). Citisafe: Adaptive spatial pattern knowledge using fp-growth algorithm for crime situation recognition. In *Ubiquitous Intelligence and Computing, IEEE 10th International Conference on and 10th International Conference on Autonomic and Trusted Computing (UIC/ATC)* (pp. 551-556).

Isafiade, O., Bagula, A., & Sonia, B. (2015). A Revised Frequent Pattern Model for Crime Situation Recognition Based on Floor-Ceil Quartile Function. In *Procedia Computer Science (PROCS5621).3rd ITQM Conference*, (*Vol. 55*, pp. 251-260). Elsevier. Doi:10.1016/j.procs.2015.07.042

Isafiade, O., & Bagula, A. (2013). CitiSafe: Adaptive Spatial Pattern Knowledge Using Fp- Growth Algorithm for Crime Situation Recognition. In *Proceedings of IEEE International Conference on Ubiquitous Intelligence and Computing*. doi:10.1109/UIC-ATC.2013.72

James, J. I., & Gladyshev, P. (2015). Automated inference of past action instances in digital investigations. *International Journal of Information Security*, *14*(3), 249–261. doi:10.1007/s10207-014-0249-6

Janakiraman, R., Waldvogel, M., & Zhang, Q. (2003). *Indra: A peer-to-peer approach to network intrusion detection and prevention.* Paper presented at the Enabling Technologies: Infrastructure for Collaborative Enterprises. doi:doi:10.1109/ENABL.2003.1231412 doi:10.1109/ENABL.2003.1231412

Janeja, V. P., & Atluri, V. (2005a). LS3: a Linear Semantic Scan Statistic technique for detecting anomalous windows. *Proceedings of the 2005 ACM Symposium on Applied Computing*, (pp. 493–497). http://doi.org/http://doi.acm.org/10.1145/1066677.1066790

Janeja, V. P., & Atluri, V. (2005b). LS3: a Linear Semantic Scan Statistic technique for detecting anomalous windows. In *Proceedings of the 2005 ACM symposium on Applied computing* (pp. 493–497). http://doi.org/http://doi.acm.org/10.1145/1066677.1066790

Jani, V. H. (2014). Survey of Identifying Criminal Pattern using Data Mining Algorithm. *IJIRT*, *1*(7), 5–7.

JavaScript InfoVis Toolkit. (n.d.). Retrieved from http://philogb.github.io/jit/

Jayech, K., & Mahjoub, M. A. (2010). New approach using Bayesian Network to improve content based image classification systems. *International Journal of Computer Science Issues.*, *7*(6), 53–62.

Jensen, F. V. (1996). *Introduction to Bayesian Networks*. New York: Springer.

Jiang, M. F., Tseng, S. S., & Liao, S. Y. (1999). Data types generalization for data mining algorithms. In *Systems, Man, and Cybernetics, 1999. IEEE SMC'99 Conference Proceedings. IEEE International Conference on,* (pp. 928-933).

Jiji, G., & Anantharadha, S. (2013). Automatic Tracking of Criminals using Data Mining Techniques. Journal of the Institution of Engineers (India): Series B, 93(4), 217-221.

Jin, C., Wang, H., & Shin, K. G. (2003). *Hop-count filtering: An effective defense against spoofed DDoS traffic*. Paper presented at the 10th ACM Conference on Computer and Communications Security. doi:doi:10.1145/948109.948116 doi:10.1145/948109.948116

John, E., Spencer, C., James, C., Michael, L., & Ronald, E. W. (2009). *Mapping Crime: Understanding Hot Spots*. Retrieved from https://www.ncjrs.gov/pdffiles1/nij/209393.pdf

John, A., & Sivakumar, T. (2009). Ddos: Survey of traceback methods. *International Journal of Recent Trends in Engineering*, *1*(2), 241–245.

Johnson, J. (2010). *Designing with the Mind in Mind: Simple Guide to Understanding User Interface Design Rules*. Morgan Kaufmann.

Jones, M., & Viola, P. (2003). Fast multi-view face detection. *Mitsubishi Electric Research Lab TR-20003-96, 3*, 14.

jQuery. (n.d.). Retrieved from https://jquery.com/

Juszczyszyn, K., Nguyen, N. T., Kolaczek, G., Grzech, A., Pieczynska, A., & Katarzyniak, R. (2006). Agent-based approach for distributed intrusion detection system design. *Computational Science–ICCS, 2006*, 224–231.

Kadam, A. S., & Pawar, S. S. (2013). Comparison of association rule mining with pruning and adaptive technique for classification of phishing dataset. In *Computational Intelligence and Information Technology, CIIT Third International Conference on,* (pp. 61-67). doi:doi:10.1049/cp.2013.2573 doi:10.1049/cp.2013.2573

Kadhim, B. (2011). A Proposed Framework for Analyzing Crime Data Set Using Decision Tree and Simple K-Means clustering Algorithms. *Journal of Kufa for Mathematics and Computer.*, *1*(3), 8–24.

Kalarani, P., & Brunda, S. S. (2014, September). A Survey on Efficient Data Mining Techniques for Network Intrusion Detection System (IDS). *International Journal of Advanced Research in Computer and Communication Engineering*, *3*(9), 8028–8031.

Kang, I.-S., Kim, C.-K., Kang, S.-J., & Na, S.-H. (2012). *IR-based k-Nearest Neighbor Approach for Identifying Abnormal Chat Users*. Presented at the Notebook for PAN at CLEF 2012, Rome, Italy.

Kangas, L. (2001). *Artificial Neural Network System for Classification of Offenders in Murder and Rape Cases*. National Criminal Justice Reference Service (NCJRS).

Kao, D.-Y., & Wang, S.-J. (2009). The IP address and time in cyber-crime investigation. *Policing: An International Journal of Police Strategies & Management*, *32*(2), 194–208. doi:10.1108/13639510910958136

Karypis, G., Han, E.-H. H. E.-H., & Kumar, V. (1999). Chameleon: Hierarchical clustering using dynamic modeling. *Computer*, *32*(8), 68–75. doi:10.1109/2.781637

Kaur, P. D., & Chana, I. (2014). Cloud based intelligent system for delivering health care as a service. *Computer Methods and Programs in Biomedicine*, *113*(1), 346–359. doi:10.1016/j.cmpb.2013.09.013 PMID:24139021

Keim, D. A., Mansmann, F., Schneidewind, J., Thomas, J., & Ziegler, H. (2008). Visual Analytics: Scope and Challenges. In S. J. Simoff, M. H. Böhlen, & A. Mazeika (Eds.), *Visual Data Mining* (pp. 76–90). Springer Berlin Heidelberg. doi:10.1007/978-3-540-71080-6_6

Keim, E. D., Kohlhammer, J., & Ellis, G. (2010). *Mastering the Information Age: Solving Problems with Visual Analytics*. Eurographics Association.

Kelly, J. (2007). *Understanding the immune system-how it works*. National Institute of Allergy and Infectious Diseases Science Education.

Keppens, J., & Schafer, B. (2006). Knowledge based crime scenario modelling. *Expert Systems with Applications*, *30*(2), 203–222. doi:10.1016/j.eswa.2005.07.011

Kern, R., Klampfl, S., & Zechner, M. (2012). *Vote/Veto Classification, Ensemble Clustering and Sequence Classification for Author Identification*. Presented at the Notebook for PAN at CLEF 2012, Rome, Italy.

Keromytis, A. D., Misra, V., & Rubenstein, D. (2002). SOS: Secure overlay services. Paper presented at the ACM SIGCOMM. *Computer Communication Review*, *32*(4), 61–72. doi:10.1145/964725.633032

Keyvanpour, M., Javideh, M., & Ebrahimi, M. (2010). Detecting and Investigating Crime by means of Data Mining: a general crime matching framework. *World Conference on Information Technology*, *3*, 872-880. doi:10.1016/j.procs.2010.12.143

Khan, N. & Bhagat, V. (2013). Effective Data Mining Approach for Crime-Terrorpattern Detection using Clustering Algorithm Technique. *International Journal of Engineering Research & Technology*, *2*(4), 2043-2048.

Kharya, S. (2012, April). Using data mining techniques for diagnosis and prognosis of cancer disease. *International Journal of Computer Science Engineering and Information Technology, 2*(2), 55–66.

Kienzle, W., Bakir, G. H., Franz, M. O., & Schölkopf, B. (2004). Face Detection-Efficient and Rank Deficient. *NIPS, 17*, 673–680.

Kierkegaard, S. (2008). Cybering, online grooming and ageplay. *Computer Law & Security Report, 24*(1), 41–55. doi:10.1016/j.clsr.2007.11.004

Kirkos, E., Spathis, C., & Manolopoulos, Y. (2007, May). Data Mining techniques for the detection of fraudulent financial statements. *An International Journal Expert Systems with Applications, 32*(4), 995–1003. doi:10.1016/j.eswa.2006.02.016

Klerks, P. (2003). The network paradigm applied to criminal organizations: Theoretical nitpicking or a relevant doctrine for investigators? Recent developments in the Netherlands. In *Transnational Organised Crime Perspectives on Global Security*. London: Routledge.

Koh, H. C., Tan, W. C., & Goh, C. P. (2006). Two-step Method to Construct Credit Scoring Models with Data Mining Techniques. *International Journal of Business and Information, 1*(1), 96–118.

Ko, J., Lim, J. H., Chen, Y., Musvaloiu-E, R., Terzis, A., Masson, G. M., & Dutton, R. P. et al. (2010). MEDiSN: Medical emergency detection in sensor networks. *ACM Transactions on Embedded Computing Systems, 10*(1), 1–29. doi:10.1145/1814539.1814550

Kontostathis, A. (2009). Toward the tracking and categorization of internet predators. In *Proceeding of Text Mining Workshop 2009 held in conjunction with Ninth Siam International Conference Data Mining*.

Kontostathis, A., Reynolds, K., Garron, A., & Edwards, L. (2013). Detecting Cyberbullying: Query Terms and Techniques. In *Proceedings of the 5th Annual ACM Web Science Conference* (pp. 195–204). New York, NY: ACM. doi:10.1145/2464464.2464499

Korb, K. B., & Nicholson, A. E. (2011). Bayesian Artificial Intelligence. Chapman & Hall/CRC.

Krishnamurthy, R., & Kumar, J. (2012). Survey of Data Mining Techniques on Crime Data Analysis. *International Journal of Data Mining Techniques and Applications, 1*(2), 117-120.

Krishnamurthy, R., & Kumar, J. S. (2012, August). Survey of Data Mining Techniques on Crime Data Analysis. *International Journal of Data Mining Techniques and Applications, 1*(2), 117–120.

Kruegel, C., Mutz, D., Robertson, W., & Valeur, F. (2003). *Bayesian event classification for intrusion detection.* Paper presented at the Computer Security Applications Conference. doi:doi:10.1109/CSAC.2003.1254306 doi:10.1109/CSAC.2003.1254306

Krug, S. (2005). *Don't Make Me Think: A Common Sense Approach to Web Usability* (2nd ed.). New Riders Press.

Ku, C. H., Nguyen, J. H., & Leroy, G. (2012). *TASC - Crime Report Visualization for Investigative Analysis: A Case Study.* Paper presented at the Information Reuse and Integration (IRI), 2012 IEEE 13th International Conference on. Retrieved from http://ieeexplore.ieee.org/ielx5/6294629/6302564/06303045.pdf?tp=&arnumber=6303045&isnumber=6302564

Ku, C., Iriberri, A., & Leroy, G. (2008). Crime Information Extraction from Police and Witness Narrative Reports. In *Proceedings of the IEEE International Conference on Technologies for Homeland Security*. doi:10.1109/THS.2008.4534448

Kulldorff, M. (2010). *SaTScan User Guide v. 9.0.* Academic Press.

Kulldorff, M. (1997). A spatial scan statistic. *Communications in Statistics. Theory and Methods*, *26*(6), 1481–1496. doi:10.1080/03610929708831995

Kulldorff, M., Huang, L., Pickle, L., & Duczmal, L. (2006). An elliptic spatial scan statistic. *Statistics in Medicine*, *25*(22), 3929–3943. doi:10.1002/sim.2490 PMID:16435334

Kulldorf, M. (1999). *Spatial Scan Statistics: Models, Calculations and Applications. Scan Statistics and Applications*. Springer; doi:10.1007/978-1-4612-1578-3_14

Kumar, K. V. (2015). Distributed denial of service (DDOS) attack, networks, tools and DEFENSE. *International Journal of Applied Engineering Research*, *10*(8).

Kumar, P., & Lee, H. J. (2011). Security issues in healthcare applications using wireless medical sensor networks: A survey. *Sensors (Basel, Switzerland)*, *12*(1), 55–91. doi:10.3390/s120100055 PMID:22368458

Kumar, S. (1995). *Classification and Detection of Computer Intrusion.* West Lafayette, IN: Purdue Univ.

Kumar, V., Oikonomou, G., Tryfonas, T., Page, D., & Phillips, I. (2014). Digital investigations for IPv6-based Wireless Sensor Networks. *Digital Investigation*, *11*, S66–S75.

Labs, K. (2015). *Statistics on botnet-assisted DDoS attacks in Q1 2015.* Retrieved from www.kaspersky.com

Latré, B., Braem, B., Moerman, I., Blondia, C., & Demeester, P. (2011). A survey on wireless body area networks. *Wireless Networks*, *17*(1), 1–18. doi:10.1007/s11276-010-0252-4

Laughlin, G. (2014) *Crime Over Time: Visualizing Crime Data in Chicago*. Retrieved from http://www.socrata.com/blog/crime-time-visualizing-crime-data-chicago/

LaValle, C. R., Haas, S. M., Turley, E., & Nolan, J. J. (2013). *Improving State Capacity for Crime Reporting: An Exploratory Analysis of Data Quality and Imputation Methods Using NIBRS Data*. Academic Press.

Lavine, N. (2013). *Introduction to CrimeStat IV (CrimeStat IV: A Spatial Statistics Program for the Analysis of Crime Incident Locations, Version 4.0)*. Academic Press.

Lazarevic, A., Kumar, V., & Srivastava, J. (2005). *Intrusion detection: A survey. Managing cyber threats*. Springer. doi:10.1007/0-387-24230-9_2

Le Khac, N. A., Markos, S., & Kechadi, M. (2010). A data mining-based solution for detecting suspicious money laundering cases in an investment bank. In *Advances in Databases Knowledge and Data Applications (DBKDA), Second International Conference on,* (pp. 235-240).

Lee, J., Brody, T. M., Zhang, R., Kim, H., & Bradac, M. (2002). *Simulating Urban Growth on the Web*. Academic Press.

Lee, W., & Stolfo, S. J. (1998). *Data mining approaches for intrusion detection*. Paper presented at the Usenix Security.

Lee, W., & Xiang, D. (2001). Information-theoretic measures for anomaly detection.*InProc. of the 2001 IEEE Symp. on Security and Privacy* (pp. 130-143). Oakland, CA: IEEE Computer Society Press.

Leong K, S. A. (2015). A review of spatio-temporal pattern analysis approaches on crime analysis. *International E-Journal of Criminal Sciences, 9.*

Levine, N. (2006). Crime mapping and the crimestat program. *Geographical Analysis*, *38*(1), 41–56. doi:10.1111/j.0016-7363.2005.00673.x

Li, X., Pfister, T., Huang, X., Zhao, G., & Pietikainen, M. (2013). A spontaneous micro-expression database: Inducement, collection and baseline. *Automatic Face and Gesture Recognition (FG), 2013 10th IEEE International Conference and Workshops on*, (pp. 1-6).

Liao, W., Liu, Y., & Choudhary, A. (2004). A grid-based clustering algorithm using adaptive mesh refinement. *Proc. of the 7th Workshop on Mining Scientific and Engineering Datasets.*

Liao, H., Richard Lin, C., Lin, Y., & Tung, K. (2013). Intrusion detection system: A comprehensive review. *Journal of Network and Computer Applications*, *36*(1), 16–24. doi:10.1016/j.jnca.2012.09.004

Li, C., Raghunathan, A., & Jha, N. K. (2011). Hijacking an insulin pump: Security attacks and defenses for a diabetes therapy system. In *Proceedings of the 13th IEEE International Conference on e-Health Networking Applications and Services* (pp. 150-156).

Li, L., & Lee, G. (2005). DDoS attack detection and wavelets. *Telecommunication Systems*, *28*(3-4), 435–451.

Liqiang, Z., Shouyi, Y., Leibo, L., Zhen, Z., & Shaojun., W. (2011). A crop monitoring system based on wireless sensor network. *Procedia Environmental Sciences, 11*(Part B), 558-565. doi:10.1016/j.proenv.2011.12.088

Li, S., Kuo, S., & Tsai, F. (2010). An Intelligent Decision-Support Model using FSOM and Rule Extraction for Crime Prevention. *International Journal of Expert Systems with Applications.*, *37*(10), 7108–7119. doi:10.1016/j.eswa.2010.03.004

Liu, B., & Zhang, L. (2012). A Survey of Opinion Mining and Sentiment Analysis. In C. C. Aggarwal & C. Zhai (Eds.), *Mining Text Data* (pp. 415–463). Springer, US. doi:10.1007/978-1-4614-3223-4_13

Liu, P., Zang, W., & Yu, M. (2005). Incentive-based modeling and inference of attacker intent, objectives, and strategies. *ACM Transactions on Information and System Security*, *8*(1), 78–118. doi:10.1145/1053283.1053288

Liu, X., Yang, X., & Lu, Y. (2008). To filter or to authorize: Network-layer DoS defense against multimillion-node botnets. *Computer Communication Review*, *38*(4), 195–206. doi:10.1145/1402946.1402981

Lodha, S. K., & Verma, A. (1999). Animations of Crime Maps Using Virtual Reality Modeling Language. *Western Criminology Review (now Criminology, Criminal Justice, Law & Society)*, *1*(2), 1-19.

Louis Engelbrecht, A. B. (2014). *Information Visualisation View Design: Principles and Guidelines*. doi:10.13140/2.1.1822.8808

Luo, W., & MacEachren, A. M. (2014). Geo-social visual analytics. *Journal of Spatial Information Science*, *8*, 27–66.

Luther, K., Bye, R., Alpcan, T., Muller, A., & Albayrak, S. (2007). *A cooperative AIS framework for intrusion detection*. Paper presented at the Communications, 2007. doi:doi:10.1109/ICC.2007.237 doi:10.1109/ICC.2007.237

Magaña-Espinoza, P., Aquino-Santos, R., Cárdenas-Benítez, N., Aguilar-Velasco, J., Buenrostro-Segura, C., Edwards-Block, A., & Medina-Cass, A. (2014). WiSPH: A Wireless Sensor Network-Based Home Care Monitoring System. *Sensors (Basel, Switzerland)*, *14*(4), 7096–7119. doi:10.3390/s140407096 PMID:24759112

Maguire, M. (2008). *Crime statistics*. Retrieved January 1, 2015, from https://www.fbi.gov/stats-services/crimestats/

Mahajan, R., Bellovin, S. M., Floyd, S., Ioannidis, J., Paxson, V., & Shenker, S. (2002). Controlling high bandwidth aggregates in the network. *Computer Communication Review*, *32*(3), 62–73. doi:10.1145/571697.571724

Maia, P., Batista, T., Cavalcante, E., Baffa, A., Delicato, F. C., Pires, P. F., & Zomaya, A. (2014). A Web platform for interconnecting body sensors and improving health care. *Procedia Computer Science, 40*, 135-142.

Maimon, O., & Rokach, L. (2010). Introduction to Knowledge Discovery and Data Mining. In O. Maimon & L. Rokach (Eds.), *Data Mining and Knowledge Discovery Handbook* (pp. 1–15). Springer. doi:10.1007/978-0-387-09823-4

Major Crimes from Overland Park. (n.d.). Retrieved from http://map.opkansas.org/crime-map/#

Maksymowicz, K., Tunikowski, W., & Kościuk, J. (2014). Crime Event 3D Reconstruction Based on Incomplete or Fragmentary Evidence Material – Case Report. *Forensic Science International, 242*, e6–e11. doi:10.1016/j.forsciint.2014.07.004 PMID:25132528

Malathi, A., & Baboo, S. (2011b). An Enhanced Algorithm to Predict a Future Crime using Data Mining. *International Journal of Computer Applications, 21*(1), 1-6. Retrieved from http://www.ijcaonline.org/archives/volume21/number1/2478-3335

Malathi, A., & Baboo, S. (2011a). Enhanced Algorithm to Identify Change in Crime Patterns. *International Journal of Combinatorial Optimization Problems and Informatics*, *2*(3), 32–38. Retrieved from http://ijcopi.org

Martin Kulldorff. (2014). *SaTScan User Guide for Version 9.3.* StatScan. Retrieved from http://www.satscan.org/

Martin, J. E., & Roland Andreas, P. (2014). Best of Both Worlds: Hybrid Knowledge Visualization in Police Crime Fighting and Military Operations. *Journal of Knowledge Management, 18*(4), 824–840. doi:10.1108/JKM-11-2013-0462

Mashima, D., & Ahamad, M. (2012). Enabling robust information accountability in e-healthcare systems. In *Proceedings of the third USENIX Workshop on Health Security and Privacy* (pp. 14-14).

McCullagh, M. (2006). Detecting hotspots in time and space. *Isg06*, 1–18. Retrieved from http://citeseerx.ist.psu.edu/viewdoc/download?doi=10.1.1.158.2442&rep=rep1&type=pdf

Mcghee, I., Bayzick, J., Kontostathis, A., Edwards, L., Mcbride, A., & Jakubowski, E. (2011). Learning to Identify Internet Sexual Predation. *International Journal of Electronic Commerce, 15*(3), 103–122. doi:10.2753/JEC1086-4415150305

McKemmish, R. (1999, June). What is Forensic Computing?. *Australian Institute of Criminology trends and issues in crime and criminal justice, 118*, 1-6.

Memon, N., & Qureshi, A. R. (2005, September). Investigative Data Mining and its Application in Counterterrorism. In *Proceedings of the 5th WSEAS Int. Conf. on Applied Informatics and Communications*, (pp. 397-403).

Michalak, K., & Korczak, J. (2011). Graph mining approach to suspicious transaction detection. In *Computer Science and Information Systems (FedCSIS), 2011 Federated Conference on,* (pp. 69-75).

Michalopoulos, D., & Mavridis, I. (2011). Utilizing document classification for grooming attack recognition. In *Computers and Communications (ISCC), 2011 IEEE Symposium on* (pp. 864–869). doi:10.1109/ISCC.2011.5983950

Milgram, A. (2013). Why smart statistics are the key to fighting crime. *TED Video*. Retrieved from https://www.ted.com/talks/anne_milgram_why_smart_statistics_are_the_key_to_fighting_crime

Milgram, A. (2013). Why smart statistics are the key to fighting crime. *TED-Talk video*. Retrieved from https://www.ted.com/talks/anne_milgram_why_smart_statistics_are_the_key_to_fighting_crime

Miorandi, D., Sicari, S., De Pellegrini, F., & Chlamtac, I. (2012). Internet of things: Vision, applications and research challenges. *Ad Hoc Networks*, *10*(7), 1497–1516. doi:10.1016/j.adhoc.2012.02.016

Mirković, J., Prier, G., & Reiher, P. (2002). *Attacking DDoS at the source*. Paper presented at the Network Protocols.

Mirkovic, J., Robinson, M., & Reiher, P. (2003). *Alliance formation for DDoS defense*. Paper presented at the 2003 Workshop on New Security Paradigms. doi:doi:10.1145/986655.986658 doi:10.1145/986655.986658

Mirkovic, J., & Reiher, P. (2004). A taxonomy of DDoS attack and DDoS defense mechanisms. *Computer Communication Review*, *34*(2), 39–53. doi:10.1145/997150.997156

Mirkovic, J., & Reiher, P. (2005). D-WARD: A source-end defense against flooding denial-of-service attacks. *Dependable and Secure Computing. IEEE Transactions On*, 2(3), 216–232.

Mishra, A., Gupta, B., & Joshi, R. C. (2011). *A comparative study of distributed denial of service attacks, intrusion tolerance and mitigation techniques*. Paper presented at the Intelligence and Security Informatics Conference (EISIC). doi:doi:10.1109/EISIC.2011.15 doi:10.1109/EISIC.2011.15

Mitchell, A. (1999). The ESRI guide to GIS analysis. Volume 1: Geographic patterns & relationships. *Annals of Physics*, *54*, 87–88. Retrieved from http://books.google.com/books?id=FOj8L-iDMq0C&pgis=1

Mohammad, A., Mohsen, J., Martin, E., Uwe, G., & Richard, F. (2011). CrimeWalker: A Recommendation Model for Suspect Investigation. In *Proceedings of the fifth ACM conference on Recommender systems*.

Moore, S., & Bowden, R. (2011). Local binary patterns for multi-view facial expression recognition. *Computer Vision and Image Understanding*, *115*(4), 541–558. doi:10.1016/j.cviu.2010.12.001

Morris, C. (2013, January 30). *Identifying Online Sexual Predators by SVM Classification with Lexical and Behavioral Features* (Master of Science Thesis). University of Toronto, Canada. Retrieved from ftp.cs.toronto.edu/pub/gh/Morris,Colin-MSc-thesis-2013.pdf

Mousavirad, S. J., & Ebrahimpour-Komleh, H. (2014). A Comparative Study on Medical Diagnosis Using Predictive Data Mining: A Case Study. In Data Mining and Analysis in the Engineering Field (pp. 327-360). IGI Global. doi:10.4018/978-1-4666-6086-1.ch017

Münz, G., & Carle, G. (2008). *Application of forecasting techniques and control charts for traffic anomaly detection*. Paper presented at the ITC Specialist Seminar on Network Usage and Traffic, Berlin, Germany.

Musdholifah, A., & Hashim, S. (2010). KNN-Kernel based Clustering for Spatio-Temporal Database. In *Proceedings of IEEE International Conference on Computer and Communication Engineering (ICCCE)*. doi:10.1109/ICCCE.2010.5556805

Mushfieldt, D., Ghaziasgar, M., & Connan, J. (2013). Robust facial expression recognition in the presence of rotation and partial occlusion.*Proceedings of the South African Institute for Computer Scientists and Information Technologists Conference*, (pp. 186-193). doi:10.1145/2513456.2513493

Nadiammai, G. V., & Hemalatha, M. (2014). Effective approach toward Intrusion Dection System using data mining techniques. *Egyptian Informatics Journal*, *15*(1), 37–50. doi:10.1016/j.eij.2013.10.003

Nagpal, B., Sharma, P., Chauhan, N., & Panesar, A. (2015). *DDoS tools: Classification, analysis and comparison.* Paper presented at the Computing for Sustainable Global Development (INDIACom).

Nair, V. V., Judith, J. E., & Jayakumari, J. (2011). Secured distributed document clustering & keyphrase extraction algorithm in structured Peer to Peer networks. In *Signal Processing, Communication, Computing and Networking Technologies (ICSCCN), International Conference on,* (pp. 151-156). doi:doi:10.1109/ICSCCN.2011.6024533 doi:10.1109/ICSCCN.2011.6024533

Nath, S. V. (2006, December). Crime Pattern Detection Using Data Mining.*2006 IEEE/WIC/ACM International Conference on Web Intelligence and Intelligent Agent Technology Workshops, 2006. WI-IAT 2006 Workshops.*, (pp. 41 - 44). Hong Kong: IEEE. doi:10.1109/WI-IATW.2006.55

National Crime Victimization Survey (NCVS). (n.d.). Retrieved from http://www.bjs.gov/index.cfm?ty=dcdetail&iid=245

Nazerfard, E., & Cook, D. J. (2013). Using Bayesian Networks for Daily Activity Prediction. Association for the Advancement of Artificial Intelligence. Retrieved from www.aaai.org

Nefian, A. V., Liang, L., Pi, X., Liu, X., & Murphy, K. (2002). Dynamic Bayesian Networks for Audio-Visual Speech Recognition. *EURASIP Journal on Applied Signal Processing*, *11*, 1–15.

Neill, D. B., & Moore, A. W. (2004). Rapid detection of significant spatial clusters. In *Proceedings of the 2004 ACM SIGKDD international conference on Knowledge discovery and data mining - KDD '04* (p. 256). http://doi.org/ doi:10.1145/1014052.1014082

Neill, D. B. (2009). An empirical comparison of spatial scan statistics for outbreak detection. *International Journal of Health Geographics*, *8*(1), 20. doi:10.1186/1476-072X-8-20 PMID:19371431

New York State Police. (n.d.). *Forensic Video/Multimedia Services Unit.* Retrieved from https://troopers.ny.gov/Academy/Multimedia_Services_Unit/

Ngai, E. W. T., Hu, Y., Wong, Y. H., Chen, Y., & Sun, X. (2011). The application of data mining techniques in financial fraud detection: A classification framework and an academic review of literature. *Decision Support Systems*, *50*(3), 559–569. doi:10.1016/j.dss.2010.08.006

Oatley, G. C., Zeleznikow, J., & Ewart, B. W. (2004). Matching and Predicting Crimes. In R. E. Ann Macintosh (Ed.), *Proceedings of the Twenty-fourth SGAI International Conference on Knowledge Based Systems and Applications of Artificial Intelligence (AI2004)* (pp. 19-32). London: Springer.

Oh, H., Doh, I., & Chae, K. (2009). Attack Classification Based on Data Mining Technique and its Application for Reliable Medical Sensor Communication. *International Journal of Computer Science and Applications*, *6*(3), 20–32.

Oh, S. E., Chun, J. Y., Jia, L., Garg, D., Gunter, C. A., & Datta, A. (2014). Privacy-preserving audit for broker-based health information exchange. In *Proceedings of the fourth ACM conference on Data and application security and privacy* (pp. 313-320). doi:10.1145/2557547.2557576

Ojala, T., Pietikäinen, M., & Mäenpää, T. (2000). Gray scale and rotation invariant texture classification with local binary patterns. In *Computer Vision-ECCV 2000* (pp. 404–420). Springer. doi:10.1007/3-540-45054-8_27

Oliver, D., Shekhar, S., Zhou, X., Eftelioglu, E., Evans, M. R., & Zhuang, Q. … Farah, C. (2014). Significant Route Discovery: A Summary of Results. In Proc. of GIScicence (pp. 284–300). Springer.

Olson, L. N., Daggs, J. L., Ellevold, B. L., & Rogers, T. K. K. (2007). Entrapping the Innocent: Toward a Theory of Child Sexual Predators' Luring Communication. *Communication Theory*, *17*(3), 231–251. doi:10.1111/j.1468-2885.2007.00294.x

Oppermann, F. J., Boano, C. A., & Römer, K. (2014). *A decade of wireless sensing applications: Survey and taxonomy. The art of wireless sensor networks*. Springer.

Ozgul, F., Atzenbeck, C., Celik, A., & Erdem, Z. (2011). Incorporating Data Sources and Methodologies for Crime Data Mining. In *Proceedings of IEEE International Conference on Intelligence and Security Informatics (ISI)*. doi:10.1109/ISI.2011.5983995

Padhy, N., Mishra, P., & Panigrahi, R. (2012, June). The Survey of Data Mining Applications and Feature Scope. *International Journal of Computer Science Engineering and Information Technology*, *2*(3), 43–58.

Page, E. (1954). Continuous inspection schemes. *Biometrika*, *41*(1-2), 100–115. doi:10.1093/biomet/41.1-2.100

Palshikar, G. K. (2002). The Hidden Truth -Frauds and Their Control: A Critical Application for Business Intelligence. *Intelligent Enterprise*, *5*(9), 46–51.

PAN-2012. (n.d.). Retrieved from http://pan.webis.de

Papoulis, A. (1984). Bayes' Theorem in Statistics and "Bayes' Theorem in Statistics (Reexamined). In Probability, Random Variables, and Stochastic Processes (2nd ed.). New York: McGraw-Hill.

Park, J., & Kim, M. (2008). *Design and implementation of an SNMP-based traffic flooding attack detection system. In Challenges for next generation network operations and service management* (pp. 380–389). Springer.

Park, K., & Lee, H. (2001). On the effectiveness of route-based packet filtering for distributed DoS attack prevention in power-law internets. *Computer Communication Review*, *31*(4), 15–26. doi:10.1145/964723.383061

Patange, D. V., & Butey, P. K. (2015). Analyze Cluster Techniques for Web Crime Patterns of Web Users. *International Journal of Advanced Research in Computer Science and Software Engineering*, *5*(4), 128–131.

Patil, G. P., & Taillie, C. (2004). Upper level set scan statistic for detecting arbitrarily shaped hotspots. *Environmental and Ecological Statistics*, *11*(2), 183–197. doi:10.1023/B:EEST.0000027208.48919.7e

Patond, K., & Deshmukh, P. (2014, April). Survey on Data Mining Techniques for Intrusion Detection System. *International Journal of Research Studies in Science Engineering and Technology*, *1*(1), 93–97.

Pendar, N. (2007). *Toward spotting the pedophile telling victim from predator in text chats*. Washington, DC: IEEE. doi:10.1109/ICSC.2007.32

Peng, T., Leckie, C., & Ramamohanarao, K. (2003). *Protection from distributed denial of service attacks using history-based IP filtering*. Paper presented at the Communications.

Peng, T., Leckie, C., & Ramamohanarao, K. (2007). Survey of network-based defense mechanisms countering the DoS and DDoS problems. *ACM Computing Surveys*, *39*(1), 3, es. doi:10.1145/1216370.1216373

Perera, C., Zaslavsky, A., Christen, P., & Georgakopoulos, D. (2014). Context aware computing for the internet of things: A survey. *IEEE Communications Surveys and Tutorials*, *16*(1), 414–454. doi:10.1109/SURV.2013.042313.00197

Perols, J. (2011). Financial statement fraud detection: An analysis of statistical and machine learning algorithms. *Auditing: A Journal of Practice & Theory, 30*(2), 19-50.

Pfister, T., Li, X., Zhao, G., & Pietikainen, M. (2011). Recognising spontaneous facial micro-expressions. *Computer Vision (ICCV), 2011 IEEE International Conference on*, (pp. 1449-1456).

Phillips, P., & Lee, I. (2012). Mining Co-distribution Patterns for Large Crime Datasets. *International Journal of Expert Systems with Applications.*, *39*(14), 11556–11563. doi:10.1016/j.eswa.2012.03.071

Polikovsky, S., Kameda, Y., & Ohta, Y. (2009, Dec). Facial micro-expressions recognition using high speed camera and 3D-gradient descriptor. *Crime Detection and Prevention (ICDP 2009), 3rd International Conference on*, (pp. 1-6).

Polikovsky, S., Kameda, Y., & Ohta, Y. (2013). Facial Micro-Expression Detection in Hi-Speed Video Based on Facial Action Coding System (FACS). *IEICE Transactions on Information and Systems*, *96*(1), 81–92. doi:10.1587/transinf.E96.D.81

Ponniah, P. (2004). *Data warehousing fundamentals: a comprehensive guide for IT professionals*. John Wiley & Sons.

Poor, H. V., & Hadjiliadis, O. (2009). *Quickest detection*. Cambridge University Press.

Portnoy, L., Eskin, E., & Stolfo, S. (2001). *Intrusion detection with unlabeled data using clustering*. Paper presented at the ACM CSS Workshop on Data Mining Applied to Security (DMSA-2001).

Prates, M. O., Assunção, R. M., & Costa, M. (2012). Flexible scan statistic test to detect disease clusters in hierarchical trees. *Computational Statistics*, *27*(4), 715–737. doi:10.1007/s00180-011-0286-9

Prathibha, R. (2014). A comparative study of defense mechanisms against SYN flooding attack. *International Journal of Computers and Applications*, *98*(18).

Predpol. (2013). *PredPol Predicts Gun Violence*. Retrieved from http://cortecs.org/wp-content/uploads/2014/10/predpol_gun-violence.pdf

PredPol. (2013). *PredPol Predicts Gun Violence*. Retrieved from http://cortecs.org/wp-content/uploads/2014/10/predpol_gun-violence.pdf

Prolexic Technologies, I. (2012). *Prolexic quarterly global DDoS attack report (Q4 2012)*. doi:knowledge-center-ddos-attack-report-2012-q4.html

Protovis. (n.d.). Retrieved from http://mbostock.github.io/protovis/

Purchase, H. C., Andrienko, N., Jankun-Kelly, T. J., & Ward, M. (2008). Information Visualization. In A. Kerren, J. T. Stasko, J.-D. Fekete, & C. North (Eds.), *Theoretical Foundations of Information Visualization* (Vol. 1, pp. 46–64). Berlin, Heidelberg: Springer-Verlag. doi:10.1007/978-3-540-70956-5_3

Qin, X., Lee, W., Lewis, L., & Cabrera, J. B. (2002). *Integrating intrusion detection and network management*. Paper presented at the Network Operations and Management Symposium.

Quantum GIS Development Team. (2012). Quantum GIS Geographic Information System. *Open Source Geospatial Foundation Project*. Retrieved from http://qgis.osgeo.org

Quick, D., & Choo, K.-K. R. (2014). Impacts of increasing volume of digital forensic data: A survey and future research challenges. *Digital Investigation*, *11*(4), 273–294. doi:10.1016/j.diin.2014.09.002

R Development Core Team. (2011). R Language Definition. *Web*, *0*, 62. doi:10.1016/0164-1212(87)90019-7

Raghuram, S., Xia, Y., Palakal, M., Jones, J., Pecenka, D., Tinsley, E., & Geesaman, J. et al. (2009). Bridging Text Mining and Bayesian Networks. In *Proceedings of the IEEE International Conference on Network-Based Information Systems.*

RAIDSONLINE. (n.d.). Retrieved from https://www.raidsonline.com

Ramanathan, A. (2002). *WADeS: A tool for distributed denial of service attack detection.* (Doctoral Thesis).

Ramanathan, V., & Wechsler, H. (2012). Phishing Website Detection Using Latent Dirichlet Allocation and AdaBoost. In *Proceedings of IEEE International Conference on Intelligence and Security Informatics (ISI).* doi:10.1109/ISI.2012.6284100

Ranjan, P., & Vaish, A. (2014). Apriori Viterbi Model for Prior Detection of Socio-Technical Attacks in a Social Network. *In Engineering and Telecommunication (EnT), International Conference on.*

Rasheed, A., & Wiil, U. K. (2014). *PEVNET: A Framework for Visualization of Criminal Networks.* Paper presented at the 2014 IEEE/ACM International Conference on Advances in Social Networks Analysis and Mining (ASONAM). doi:10.1109/ASONAM.2014.6921689

Ratcliffe, J. H., & McCullagh, M. J. (1999). Hotbeds of crime and the search for spatial accuracy. *Journal of Geographical Systems, 1*(4), 385–398. doi:10.1007/s101090050020

Ravisankar, P., Ravi, V., Rao, G. R., & Bose, I. (2011). Detection of financial statement fraud and feature selection using data mining techniques. *Decision Support Systems, 50*(2), 491–500. doi:10.1016/j.dss.2010.11.006

Read, P., & Meyer, M.-P. (2000). *Restoration of motion picture film.* Butterworth-Heinemann.

Rekhis, S., & Boudriga, N. (2011). Formal reconstruction of attack scenarios in mobile ad hoc and sensor networks. *EURASIP Journal on Wireless Communications and Networking*, (1): 1–17.

Rekhis, S., & Boudriga, N. (2012). A Hierarchical Visibility theory for formal digital investigation of anti-forensic attacks. *Computers & Security, 31*(8), 967–982. doi:10.1016/j.cose.2012.06.009

Renushe, H. N., Rasal, P. R., & Desai, A. S. (2012, May-June). Data Mining Practices for Effective Investigation of Crime. *Int.J. Computer Technology & Applications, 3*(3), 865–870.

Republic of South Africa. Department of Safety and Security CSIR Pretoria, National Crime Prevention Centre. (2013). *A Manual for Community Based Crime Prevention - Making South Africa Safe*. Retrieved from http://www.causes.com/causes/

Republic of South Africa. South African Police Service. (2011). *SAPS Together Squeezing Crime to Zero: Annual Report 2010/2011.* Retrieved from www.saps.gov.za

Republic of South Africa. South African Police Service. (2013). *Crime Statistics Overview:RSA 2011/2012.* Retrieved from http://www.saps.gov.za/statistics/reports/crimestats/2012/downloads

Republic of South Africa. Statistics SA. (2014). *Victims of Crime Survey: P0341*. Statistics South Africa. Private Bag X44, Pretoria 0001. Retrieved from http://beta2.statssa.gov.za/publications/P0341/P03412013.pdf

Republic of South Africa. Trading Economics Report. (2013). *Urban population growth (annual %) in South Africa*. Retrieved from http://www.tradingeconomics.com/south-africa

Republic of South Africa. Western Cape Government Report. (2013). Retrieved from http://www.westerncape.gov.za/eng/pubs/

Riesen, M., & Serpen, G. (2009). A Bayesian Belief Network Classifier for Predicting Victimization in National Crime Victimization Survey. In *Proceedings of the IEEE International Conference on Artificial Intelligence*.

Riesen, M., & Serpen, G. (2009). A Bayesian Belief Network Classifier for Predicting Victimization in National Crime Victimization Survey. In *Proceedings of the International Conference on Artificial Intelligence*.

Roberts, S. (1959). Control chart tests based on geometric moving averages. *Technometrics*, *1*(3), 239–250. doi:10.1080/00401706.1959.10489860

Rossmo, D. K. (1995). *Geographic profiling: Target patterns of serial murderers. ProQuest Dissertations and Theses. Theses (School of Criminology)*. Simon Fraser University.

Roth, R. E., Ross, K. S., Finch, B. G., Luo, W., & MacEachren, A. M. (2013). Spatiotemporal Crime Analysis in U.S. Law Enforcement Agencies: Current Practices and Unmet Needs. *Government Information Quarterly*, *30*(3), 226–240. doi:10.1016/j.giq.2013.02.001

Russell, T. A., Chu, E., & Phillips, M. L. (2006). A pilot study to investigate the effectiveness of emotion recognition remediation in schizophrenia using the micro-expression training tool. *The British Journal of Clinical Psychology*, *45*(4), 579–583. doi:10.1348/014466505X90866 PMID:17076965

Ruth, D., & Lovelin Ponn Felciah, M. (2014, May). A Survey on Intrusion Detection System with Data Mining Techniques. *International Journal of Innovative Science. Engineering & Technology*, *1*(3), 271–275.

Samatova, N. F., Ostrouchov, G., Geist, A., & Melechko, A. V. (2002). RACHET: An Efficient CoverBased Merging of Clustering Hierarchies from Distributed Datasets. *Distributed and Parallel Databases*, *11*(2), 157–180.

Sandig, J. D. E., Somoba, R. M., Concepcion, M. B., & Gerardo, B. D. (2013). Mining Online GIS for Crime Rate and Models based on Frequent Pattern Analysis. In *Proceedings of the World Congress on Engineering and Computer Science*.

Santos, R. B. (2012). Crime Analysis With Crime Mapping (3rd ed.). Thousand Oaks, CA: SAGE Publications, Inc.

Sarmah, S., Das, R., & Bhattacharyya, D. K. (2007). Intrinsic Cluster Detection Using Adaptive Grids. *15th International Conference on Advanced Computing and Communications (ADCOM 2007)*. http://doi.org/ doi:10.1109/ADCOM.2007.18

Sathyadevan, S., Devan, M. S., & Surya Gangadharan, S. (2014). Crime analysis and prediction using data mining. *In Networks & Soft Computing (ICNSC), First International Conference on.*

Savage, S., Wetherall, D., Karlin, A., & Anderson, T. (2001). Network support for IP traceback. *IEEE/ACM Transactions on Networking, 9*(3), 226-237.

Savage, S., Wetherall, D., Karlin, A., & Anderson, T. (2000). Practical network support for IP traceback. *Computer Communication Review*, *30*(4), 295–306. doi:10.1145/347057.347560

Savci, H. S., Sula, A., Wang, Z., Dogan, N. S., & Arvas, E. (2005, April). MICS transceivers: regulatory standards and applications [medical implant communications service]. In *Proceedings of the IEEE SoutheastCon* (pp. 179-182).

Schindler, L. W. (1991). *Understanding the immune system*. DIANE Publishing.

Schmidhuber, J. (2015). Deep learning in neural networks: An overview. *Neural Networks*, *61*, 85–117. doi:10.1016/j.neunet.2014.09.003 PMID:25462637

Scott, L., & Warmerdam, N. (2005). Extend Crime Analysis with ArcGIS Spatial Statistics Tools. *ArcUser, 8*.

Shafiq, M. Z., & Farooq, M. (2007). *Defense against 802.11 dos attacks using artificial immune system. In Artificial immune systems* (pp. 95–106). Springer.

Sharef, N. M., & Martin, T. (2015). Evolving fuzzy grammar for crime texts categorization. *Applied Soft Computing*, *28*, 175–187. doi:10.1016/j.asoc.2014.11.038

Sharma, A., & Panigrahi, P. K. (2013). *A review of financial accounting fraud detection based on data mining techniques.* arXiv preprint arXiv:1309.3944

Sharma, M. (2014). Z-CRIME: A data mining tool for the detection of suspicious criminal activities based on decision tree. In *Data Mining and Intelligent Computing (ICDMIC), International Conference on* (pp. 1-6). doi:doi:10.1109/ICDMIC.2014.6954268 doi:10.1109/ICDMIC.2014.6954268

Shi, L., & Janeja, V. P. (2011). Anomalous window discovery for linear intersecting paths. *IEEE Transactions on Knowledge and Data Engineering*, *23*(12), 1857–1871. doi:10.1109/TKDE.2010.212

Shneiderman, B., & Plaisant, C. (2009). *Designing the User Interface: Strategies for Effective Human-Computer Interaction* (5th ed.). Addison Wesley.

Shreve, M., Godavarthy, S., Goldgof, D., & Sarkar, S. (2011). Macro-and micro-expression spotting in long videos using spatio-temporal strain. *Automatic Face & Gesture Recognition and Workshops (FG 2011), 2011 IEEE International Conference on*, (pp. 51-56).

Siaterlis, C., & Maglaris, V. (2005). *Detecting incoming and outgoing DDoS attacks at the edge using a single set of network characteristics*. Paper presented at the Computers and Communications. doi:doi:10.1109/ISCC.2005.50 doi:10.1109/ISCC.2005.50

Sindhu, K. K., & Meshram, B. B. (2013). Digital Forensics and Cyber Crime Data mining. *Journal of Information Security*, *3*(3), 196–201. doi:10.4236/jis.2012.33024

Singh, N. & Khare, N. (2014, July-August). Efficient Data Mining Techniques to Enhance Intrusion Detection System. *International Journal of Latest Research in Science and Technology, 3*(4), 122-125.

Singhal, A., & Jajodia, S. (2006, September). Data warehousing and data mining techniques for intrusion detection systems. *Journal Distributed and Parallel Databases*, *20*(2), 149–166. doi:10.1007/s10619-006-9496-5

Singh, K., Guntuku, S. C., Thakur, A., & Hota, C. (2014, September). Big Data Analytics framework for Peer-to-Peer Botnet detection using Random Forests. *Information Sciences*, *278*, 488–497. doi:10.1016/j.ins.2014.03.066

Siris, V. A., & Papagalou, F. (2006). Application of anomaly detection algorithms for detecting SYN flooding attacks. *Computer Communications*, *29*(9), 1433–1442. doi:10.1016/j.comcom.2005.09.008

Sitaram, D., Sharma, M., Zain, M., Sastry, A., & Todi, R. (2013, October). Intrusion Detection System for High Volume and High Velocity Packet Streams: A Clustering Approach. *International Journal of Innovation. Management and Technology*, *4*(5), 480–485.

Sjoerd, T., Hendrik, P., Charles, M., Silja, R., & Bart, V. (2014) Extracting Legal Arguments from Forensic Bayesian Networks. In *Legal Knowledge and Information Systems.JURIX 2014: The Twenty-seventh Annual Conference*.

Sjoerd, T., Charles, M., Hendrik, P., Silja, R., & Bart, V. (2015) A Structure-guided Approach to Capturing Bayesian Reasoning about Legal Evidence in Argumentation. In *Proceedings of the ICAIL international conference.*ACM.

Somal, I. K., & Virk, S. (2014). *Classification of distributed denial of service Attacks–Architecture, taxonomy and tools*. Academic Press.

Song, D. X., & Perrig, A. (2001). Advanced and authenticated marking schemes for IP traceback. *Proceedings of the IEEE*, *2*, 878–886.

Soro, S., & Heinzelman, W. (2009). A survey of visual sensor networks. *Advances in Multimedia*, *2009*, 640386. doi:10.1155/2009/640386

SpotCrime. (n.d.). Retrieved from http://www.spotcrime.com/

Srinivasan, V., Stankovic, J., & Whitehouse, K. (2008). Protecting your daily in-home activity information from a wireless snooping attack. In *Proceedings of the 10th international conference on Ubiquitous computing* (pp. 202-211). doi:10.1145/1409635.1409663

Stahlschmidt, S., Tausendteufel, H., & Härdle, W. K. (2013). Bayesian Networks for Sex-related homicides: Structure Learning and Prediction. *Journal of Applied Statistics*, *40*(6), 1155–1171. doi:10.1080/02664763.2013.780235

Stasko, J., Görg, C., & Liu, Z. (2008). Jigsaw: Supporting Investigative Analysis Through Interactive Visualization. *Information Visualization*, *7*(2), 118–132. doi:10.1057/palgrave.ivs.9500180

Steinfeld, R., Bull, L., Wang, H., & Pieprzyk, J. (2003). Universal designated-verifier signatures. Advances in Cryptology-Asiacrypt, 2894(2003), 523-542. doi:doi:10.1007/978-3-540-40061-5_33 doi:10.1007/978-3-540-40061-5_33

Stone, M. (2009). *Information Visualization: Challenge for the Humanities*. Paper presented at the Promoting Digital Scholarship: Formulating Research Challenges in the Humanities, Social Sciences and Computation, Washington, DC.

Stone, R. (2000). *CenterTrack: An IP overlay network for tracking DoS floods*. Paper presented at the USENIX Security Symposium.

Strategy, I., & Unit, P. (2005). ITU internet reports 2005: The internet of things. Geneva: International Telecommunication Union (ITU).

Streilein, W. W., Fried, D. J., & Cunningham, R. K. (2003). *Detecting flood-based denial-of-service attacks with snmp/rmon*. Paper presented at the Workshop on Statistical and Machine Learning Techniques in Computer Intrusion Detection, Fairfax, VA.

Sujatha, R., & Ezhilmaran, D. (2013). A Proposal for Analysis of Crime Based on Socio–Economic Impact using Data Mining Techniques. *International Journal of Societal Applications of Computer Science*, *2*(2), 229–231.

Sundmaeker, H., Guillemin, P., Friess, P., & Woelfflé, S. (2010). *Vision and challenges for realising the internet of things*. Academic Press.

Sung, M., & Xu, J. (2003). IP traceback-based intelligent packet filtering: A novel technique for defending against internet DDoS attacks. *Parallel and Distributed Systems. IEEE Transactions On*, *14*(9), 861–872.

Surette, R. (2010). *Media, Crime, and Criminal Justice*. Retrieved from http://books.google.com/books?id=geK4L1Q7fqAC&pgis=1

Suthaharan, S. (2014, March-April). Big Data Classification: Problems and Challenges in Network Intrusion Prediction with Machine Learning. SIGMETRICS Perform. Eval. Rev., 41(4), 70-73.

Tan, H., Hu, W., & Jha, S. (2011). A TPM-enabled remote attestation protocol (TRAP) in wireless sensor networks. In *Proceedings of the sixth ACM workshop on Performance monitoring and measurement of heterogeneous wireless and wired networks* (pp. 9-16). doi:10.1145/2069087.2069090

Tartakovsky, A. G., Polunchenko, A. S., & Sokolov, G. (2013). Efficient computer network anomaly detection by changepoint detection methods. *Selected Topics in Signal Processing. IEEE Journal Of*, *7*(1), 4–11.

Tartakovsky, A. G., Rozovskii, B. L., Blazek, R. B., & Kim, H. (2006). A novel approach to detection of intrusions in computer networks via adaptive sequential and batch-sequential change-point detection methods. *Signal Processing. IEEE Transactions On*, *54*(9), 3372–3382. doi:10.1109/TSP.2006.879308

Tavli, B., Bicakci, K., Zilan, R., & Barcelo-Ordinas, J. M. (2011). A survey of visual sensor network platforms. *Springer Multimedia Tools and Applications*, *60*(3), 689–726. doi:10.1007/s11042-011-0840-z

Tayal, D., & Jain, A. (2014). Crime Detection and Criminal Identification in India using Data Mining Techniques. *AI & Society: International Journal of Knowledge, Culture and Communication.*

Tayal, D. K., Jain, A., Arora, S., Agarwal, S., Gupta, T., & Tyagi, N. (2015). Crime detection and criminal identification in India using data mining techniques. *AI & Society*, *30*(1), 117–127. doi:10.1007/s00146-014-0539-6

Toews, V. (2013). *Royal Canadian Mounted Police Report on Plans and Priorities 2013-2014.* Canada: RCMP. Retrieved from http://www.rcmp-grc.gc.ca/rpp/2013-2014/rpp-eng.htm

Tomar, D., & Agarwal, S. (2013). A survey on Data Mining approaches for Healthcare. *International Journal of Bio-Science and Bio-Technology*, *5*(5), 241–266. doi:10.14257/ijbsbt.2013.5.5.25

Tonkin, M., Woodhams, J., Bull, R., & Bond, J. W. (2012). Behavioural Case Linkage with Solved and Unsolved Crime Crimes. *Forensic Science International*, *222*(1-3), 146–153. doi:10.1016/j.forsciint.2012.05.017 PMID:22704669

Tsai, C., Chang, A. Y., & Ming-Szu, H. (2010). *Early warning system for DDoS attacking based on multilayer deployment of time delay neural network.* Paper presented at the Intelligent Information Hiding and Multimedia Signal Processing (IIH-MSP). doi:doi:10.1109/IIHMSP.2010.178 doi:10.1109/IIHMSP.2010.178

Tseng, Y.-H., Ho, Z.-P., Yang, K.-S., & Chen, C.-C. (2012, September). Mining term networks from text collections for crime investigation. *Expert Systems with Applications*, *39*(11), 10082–10090. doi:10.1016/j.eswa.2012.02.052

Uddin, O. O., & Uddin, P. S. O. (2014, March). Data Mining: An Active Solution for Crime Investigation. *International Journal of Computer Science and Technology*, *5*(1), 28–32.

Vapnik, V. N. (1995). *The Nature of Statistical Learning Theory.* New York, NY: Springer-Verlag New York, Inc. doi:10.1007/978-1-4757-2440-0

Varghese, B. M., Unnikrishnan, A., Jacob, P., & Jacob, J. (2010, December). Correlation Clustering Model for Crime Pattern Detection. *International Journal of Advancements in Computing Technology*, *2*(5), 125–128. doi:10.4156/ijact.vol2.issue5.14

Vermesan, O., Friess, P., Guillemin, P., Gusmeroli, S., Sundmaeker, H., Bassi, A., & Eisenhauer, M. et al. (2011). Internet of things strategic research roadmap. *Global Technological and Societal Trends*, *1*, 9-52.

Villatoro-Tello, E., Juárez-González, A., Escalante, H. J., Montes-y-Gómez, M., & Villaseñor-Pineda, L. (2012). *A Two-step Approach for Effective detection of Misbehaving Users in Chats*. Presented at the Notebook for PAN at CLEF'12, Rome, Italy.

Vincent, N., Stephen, C., Derek, L., & Cheung, Y. (2007). Incremental Mining for Temporal Association Rules for Crime Pattern Discoveries. In *Proceedings of the ACM eighteenth conference on Australasian database*.

Vishwakarma, R. K., & Shankar, R. (2013). Modeling brain and behavior of a terrorist through fuzzy logic and ontology. In *Industrial Engineering and Engineering Management (IEEM), IEEE International Conference on* (pp. 857-861). doi:doi:10.1109/IEEM.2013.6962533 doi:10.1109/IEEM.2013.6962533

Vladimir, E., & Ickjai, L. (2001). Data Mining Techniques for Autonomous Exploration of Large Volumes of Geo-referenced Crime Data. In *Proceedings of the 6th International Conference on Geocomputation*.

Vlek, C. S., Prakken, H., Renooij, S., & Verheij, B. (2013c). Unfolding Crime Scenarios with Variations: A method for building a Bayesian network for legal narratives. In Legal Knowledge and Information Systems - JURIX.

Vlek, C., Prakken, H., Renooij, S., & Verheij, B. (2013a). Modeling Crime Scenarios in a Bayesian Network. *The 14th International Conference on Artificial Intelligence and Law (ICAIL 2013). Proceedings of the Conference*, (pp. 150-159). New York: ACM.

Vlek, C., Prakken, H., Renooij, S., & Verheij, B. (2014). Building Bayesian networks for legal evidence with narratives: a case study evaluation. Journal of Artificial Intelligence and Law, 22(4), 375-421. doi:10.1007/s10506-014-9161-7

Vlek, C., Prakken, H., Renooij, S., & Verheij, B. (2013). Modeling crime scenarios in a Bayesian network. In *Proceedings of the Fourteenth International Conference on Artificial Intelligence and Law* (pp. 150-159). doi:10.1145/2514601.2514618

Vlek, C., Prakken, H., Renooij, S., & Verheij, B. (2013b). Representing and Evaluating Legal Narratives with Sub-scenarios in a Bayesian Network.*Workshop on Computational Models of Narrative*. OASICS Schloss Dagstuhl Publishing.

Walther, G. (2010). Optimal and fast detection of spatial clusters with scan statistics. *Annals of Statistics*, *38*(2), 1010–1033. doi:10.1214/09-AOS732

Wang, B., Dong, H., Boedihardjo, A. P., Lu, C.-T., Yu, H., Chen, I.-R., & Dai, J. (2012). *An Integrated Framework for Spatio-Temporal-Textual Search and Mining*. Academic Press.

Wang, B., Dong, H., Boedihardjo, A., Lu, C., Yu, H., Chen, I., & Dai, J. (2012). An Integrated Framewrok for Spatio-Temporal-Textual Search and Mining. In *Proceedings of the ACM International Conference on Advances in Geographic Information Systems (SIGSPATIAL GIS)*.

Wang, H., Jin, C., & Shin, K. G. (2007). Defense against spoofed IP traffic using hop-count filtering. *IEEE/ACM Transactions on Networking, 15*(1), 40-53.

Wang, S.-J., Yan, W.-J., Li, X., Zhao, G., & Fu, X. (2014). Micro-expression Recognition Using Dynamic Textures on Tensor Independent Color Space. *Pattern Recognition (ICPR), 2014 22nd International Conference on*, (pp. 4678-4683).

Wang, T., Rudin, C., Wagner, D., & Sevieri, R. (2013b). Learning to Detect Patterns of Crime. In Machine Learning and Knowledge Discovery in Databases (LNCS), (vol. 8190, pp. 515–530). Springer-Verlag Berlin Heidelberg. doi:10.1007/978-3-642-40994-3_33

Wang, D., Ding, W., Lo, H., Stepinski, T., Salazar, J., & Morabito, M. (2013a). Crime Hotspot Mapping using the Crime Related Factors- a spatial data mining approach. *Journal of Applied Intelligence*, *39*(4), 772–781. doi:10.1007/s10489-012-0400-x

Wang, T., Rudin, C., Wagner, D., & Sevieri, R. (2013c). *Detecting Patterns of Crime with Series Finder*. AAAI Late Breaking Track.

Wang, , & Zhang, , & Shin. (2002). Detecting SYN flooding attacks. Paper presented at the INFOCOM 2002. Twenty-First Annual Joint Conference of the IEEE Computer and Communications Societies. *Proceedings of the IEEE*, *3*, 1530–1539. doi:10.1109/INFCOM.2002.1019404

Warren, G., Schertler, E., & Bull, P. (2009). Detecting deception from emotional and unemotional cues. *Journal of Nonverbal Behavior*, *33*(1), 59–69. doi:10.1007/s10919-008-0057-7

Wheeler, A. P. (2015). *Tables and Graphs for Monitoring Temporal Crime Patterns (ID 2551472)*. Retrieved from Rochester; http://papers.ssrn.com/abstract=2551472

White, J., & Roth, R. (2010). *TwitterHitter: Geovisual Analytics for Harvesting Insight from Volunteered Geographic Information.* Paper presented at the GIScience 2010, Zurich, Switzerland.

White, T. (2012). *Hadoop - The Definitive Guide* (3rd ed.). O'Reilly Media / Yahoo Press.

Woodberry, O., & Mascaro, S. (2015). Programming Bayesian Network Solutions with Netica. Bayesian Intelligence. Retrieved from http://bayesian-intelligence.com/programming-bns/

Wu, X., Kumar, V., Ross Quinlan, J., Ghosh, J., Yang, Q., Motoda, H., … Steinberg, D. (2008). Top 10 algorithms in data mining. *Knowledge and Information Systems* (Vol. 14). http://doi.org/<ALIGNMENT qj></ALIGNMENT>10.1007/s10115-007-0114-2

Wu, Q., Shen, X., & Fu, X. (2011). The machine knows what you are hiding: an automatic micro-expression recognition system. In *Affective Computing and Intelligent Interaction* (pp. 152–162). Springer. doi:10.1007/978-3-642-24571-8_16

Wu, S.-Y., & Yen, E. (2009, April). Data mining-based intrusion detectors. *Expert Systems with Applications*, *36*(3), 5605–5612. doi:10.1016/j.eswa.2008.06.138

Yaar, A., Perrig, A., & Song, D. (2003). *Pi: A path identification mechanism to defend against DDoS attacks*. Paper presented at the Security and Privacy. doi:doi:10.1109/SECPRI.2003.1199330 doi:10.1109/SECPRI.2003.1199330

Yahia, M., & El-taher, M. (2010). A New Approach for Evaluation of Data Mining Techniques. *International Journal of Computer Science Issues, 7*(5), 181-186.

Yamuna, S., & Bhuvaneswari, N. S. (2012). Datamining Techniques to Analyze and Predict Crimes.[IJES]. *International Journal of Engineering Science*, *1*(2), 243–247.

Yang, Y., & Pedersen, J. O. (1997). A Comparative Study on Feature Selection in Text Categorization. In *Proceedings of the Fourteenth International Conference on Machine Learning* (pp. 412–420). San Francisco, CA: Morgan Kaufmann Publishers Inc.

Yau, D. K., Lui, J., Liang, F., & Yam, Y. (2005). Defending against distributed denial-of-service attacks with max-min fair server-centric router throttles. *IEEE/ACM Transactions on Networking, 13*(1), 29-42.

Yeh, I.-C., & Lien, C.-H. (2009, March). The comparisons of data mining techniques for the predictive accuracy of probability of default of credit card clients. *An International Journal Expert Systems with Applications*, *36*(2), 2473–2480. doi:10.1016/j.eswa.2007.12.020

Ye, N., Borror, C., & Zhang, Y. (2002). EWMA techniques for computer intrusion detection through anomalous changes in event intensity. *Quality and Reliability Engineering International*, *18*(6), 443–451. doi:10.1002/qre.493

Ye, N., Vilbert, S., & Chen, Q. (2003). Computer intrusion detection through EWMA for autocorrelated and uncorrelated data. *Reliability. IEEE Transactions On*, *52*(1), 75–82.

Youssef, A., & Emam, A. (2011, December). Network Intrusion Detection Using Data Mining and Network Behaviour Analysis.[IJCSIT]. *International Journal of Computer Science & Information Technology*, *3*(6), 87–98. doi:10.5121/ijcsit.2011.3607

Yu, C.-H., Ward, M. W., Morabito, M., & Ding, W. (2011). Crime Forecasting Using Data Mining Techniques. *2011 IEEE 11th International Conference on Data Mining Workshops*, (pp. 779–786). http://doi.org/ doi:<ALIGNMENT.qj></ALIGNMENT>10.1109/ICDMW.2011.56

Yu, J., Lee, H., Kim, M., & Park, D. (2008). Traffic flooding attack detection with SNMP MIB using SVM. *Computer Communications*, *31*(17), 4212–4219. doi:10.1016/j.comcom.2008.09.018

Yun, M., & Yuxin, B. (2010). *Research on the architecture and key technology of internet of things (IoT) applied on smart grid.* Paper presented at the Advances in Energy Engineering (ICAEE).

Zargar, S. T., Joshi, J., & Tipper, D. (2013). A survey of defense mechanisms against distributed denial of service (DDoS) flooding attacks. *IEEE Communications Surveys and Tutorials*, *15*(4), 2046–2069. doi:10.1109/SURV.2013.031413.00127

Zhang, Y. (2010). *Hotspot Analysis of Highway Accident Spatial Pattern Based on Network Spatial Weights*. Academic Press.

Zhang, C., & Fang, Z. (2013). An Improved K-means Clustering Algorithm. *Journal of Information & Computational Science.*, *10*(1), 193–199.

Zhang, G., & Parashar, M. (2006). Cooperative defense against ddos attacks. *Journal of Research and Practice in Information Technology*, *38*(1), 69–84.

Zhang, J., Li, H., Gao, Q., Wang, H., & Luo, Y. (2014, October). Detecting anomalies from big network traffic data using an adaptive detection approach. *Information Sciences*, *318*, 91–110. doi:10.1016/j.ins.2014.07.044

Zhang, T., Ramakrishnan, R., & Livny, M. (1996). BIRCH: an efficient data clustering method for very large databases. In *Proceedings of the 1996 ACM SIGMOD international conference on Management of data SIGMOD'96*. doi:10.1145/233269.233324

Zhao, J. L., Bi, H. H., Chen, H., Zeng, D. D., Lin, C., & Chau, M. (2006). Process-Driven Collaboration Support for Intra-Agency Crime Analysis. *Decision Support Systems*, *41*(3), 616–633. doi:10.1016/j.dss.2004.06.014

Zhong, X. (2013). The Application Of Apriori Algorithm For Network Forensics Analysis. *Journal of Theoretical and Applied Information Technology*, *50*(2), 430–434.

Zhou, C. V., Leckie, C., & Karunasekera, S. (2010). A survey of coordinated attacks and collaborative intrusion detection. *Computers & Security*, *29*(1), 124–140. doi:10.1016/j.cose.2009.06.008

Zhou, W., & Kapoor, G. (2011). Detecting evolutionary financial statement fraud. *Decision Support Systems*, *50*(3), 570–575. doi:10.1016/j.dss.2010.08.007

Ziauddin, Kammal, S., Khan, K., & Khan, M. (2012). Research on Association Rule Mining. *Journal of Advances in Computational Mathematics and its Applications*, *2*(1), 226-236.

Zoete, J. D., Sjerps, M., Lagnado, D., & Fenton, N. (2014). Modelling Crime Linkage with Bayesian networks. *Journal of Science and Justice, Elsevier, Ireland*, *7*(5), 1–9. PMID:25934374

About the Contributors

Omowunmi Isafiade is currently a senior teaching assistant and a doctoral researcher at the University of Cape Town (UCT), South Africa. She obtained an M.Sc. degree in Computer Science from her current affiliation (UCT), in December 2012. Past affiliations were with the African Institute for Mathematical Sciences (AIMS) and the University of the Western Cape, Cape Town, South Africa, where she obtained a post-graduate diploma (PGDs) degree in Mathematical Sciences in June 2010, and a Bachelor (BSc.) honors degree in computer science from Federal University of Agriculture Abeokuta (FUNAAB), Nigeria. Omowunmi's area of research includes Machine learning, data mining & knowledge management, ubiquitous intelligence and pattern recognition. Omowunmi has quality journal publications, technical reports and refereed conference publications in the aforementioned research areas.

Antoine Bagula obtained his doctoral degree from the KTH-Royal Institute of Technology in Sweden. He held lecturing positions at Stellenbosch University (SUN) and the University of Cape Town (UCT) before joining the Computer Science department of the University of the Western Cape (UWC) in January 2014. Since 20016, Professor Bagula has consulted for the UNESCO, the World Bank and other international organizations on different telecommunication projects. Professor Bagula has been on the technical programme committees of more than 50 international conferences and on the editorial board of international journals. He has also co-chaired international conferences in the field of telecommunications and ICT. Professor Bagula has authored/co-authored more than 100 papers in peer-reviewed conferences, journals and book chapters. Professor Bagula's research interest is communication networking with a specific focus on the Internet-of-Things, Cloud Computing, Network security and Network protocols for wireless, wired, and hybrid networks integrating wireless and wired technologies and protocols.

* * *

Sonia Berman has a PhD from the University of Cape Town and is currently Head of the Computer Science Department there. In addition to Chairing two Software Engineering conferences in Cape Town, she has served on several international conference committees in her primary field of interest, database research. Sonia has undertaken Computer Science Department reviews at 5 South African Universities, and regularly serves on South African Research Funding Panels.

Vishal Bhatnagar holds BTech, MTech and PhD in the engineering field. He has more than 13 years of teaching experience in various technical institutions. He is currently working as an Associate Professor in Computer Science in Engineering Department at Ambedkar Institute of Advanced Communication Technologies and Research(Government of Delhi), GGSIPU, Delhi, India. His research interests include database, advance database, data warehouse, data-mining, social network analysis and big data analytics. He has to his credit more than 50 research papers in various international/national journals and conferences.

Noureddine Boudriga received the Ph.D. degree in algebraic topology from University Paris XI, France, and the Ph.D. in computer science from University of Tunis, Tunisia. He is currently a full Professor of Telecommunications at the University of Carthage, Tunisia, and the Director of the Communication Networks and Security Research Laboratory (CNAS), University of Carthage. He has served as the General Director and founder of the Tunisian National Digital Certification Agency (2000–2004). He was involved in very active research in communication networks and system security. He authored and coauthored many chapters and books on information security, security of mobile networks, and communication networks. He published over 350 refereed journal and conference papers. Prof. Boudriga is the recipient of the Tunisian Presidential award in Science and Research (2004). He is currently the President of the Tunisia Scientific Telecommunications Society.

James Connan heads up the South African Sign Language research group at the University of the Western Cape. His research interests include computer vision and machine learning.

Nathan De La Cruz is currently studying towards his MSc in Computer Science at the University of the Western Cape. His research focuses on the recognition of facial action units in the context of sign language recognition.

Yacine Djemaiel received the engineering degree (in 2002) from the Tunisian National Institute of Applied Science and Technology (INSAT, Tunisia), and the master diploma in Telecommunications from the Engineering School of Communications (SUP'COM, Tunisia) in 2004. He is member of the Communication Networks and Security (CN&S) research Laboratory (University of Carthage, Tunisia), where he's conducting research activities in the area of intrusion detection, intrusion tolerance, digital investigation of security incidents and network, host, storage level traceback, and management and security of big data. From 2002 to 2006, he has worked for the National Digital Certification Agency (NDCA, Tunisia) where he was member of the networks security Team. Dr. Yacine was involved in the security administration of the NDCA networks and served as a security auditor of different national IT companies. From September 2006 to August 2010, he has worked for the Higher Institute of Informatics and Management (ISIGK, TUNISIA) as a teacher assistant in Telecommunications. Since September 2010, he was an assistant professor in Telecommunications, Institute of Technology in Communications at Tunis (ISET'Com).

Mohammadreza Ebrahimi is a graduate researcher at CEntre of PAtern Reognition and Machine Intelligence (CENPARMI) at university of Concordia. He has been involved in several text/web mining research projects during the last 5 years. He is the holder of Power Corporation of Canada Graduate Award and also Concordia University 25th Anniversary Award which are granted based on academic excellence.

Emre Eftelioglu is a Ph.D. candidate at the Univer- sity of Minnesota - Twin Cities, MN in Computer Sci- ence. He received his Bachelor's degree in Turkey (2004) in Systems Engineering and his Master's de- gree at the University of Minnesota (2014) in Com- puter Engineering. His research interests include spatial data mining, spatial databases.

Boutheina A. Fessi received his analyst diploma (in 2002) from the Higher Institute of Management (ISG) and the master's diploma and PhD in Computing Applied to the Management from Higher Institute of Management (ISG) in 2004 and 2012. She is a member of the Communication Networks and Security (CN&S) research Laboratory (University of Carthage, Tunisia), where she is conducting research activities in the area of intrusion detection, strategic intelligence and digital security, big data, and security project management. From September 2008 to August 2013, she has worked for the Faculty of Economic Sciences and Management of Nabeul (FSEGN) as a teacher assistant in Computing Applied to the Management, after three years as a contractual assistant at the Higher Institute of Computer Science (ISI), Ariana, Tunisia. Since September 2013, she was an assistant professor teacher in Computing Applied to the Management in the Faculty of Economic Sciences and Management of Nabeul (FSEGN), Tunisia.

Mehrdad Ghaziasgar is the project manager of the South African Sign Language research group at the University of the Western Cape. His research interests include image processing, computer vision and machine learning, with applications to facial and body gesture recognition in the context of sign language recognition.

Mahima Goyal is pursuing her MTech in Information Security at GGSIPU, Delhi, India. Her research interests include database, data warehouse, data mining, business analysis and big data analysis.

Alicia Iriberri is Assistant Professor in Computer Information Systems at California State University, Fresno since August 2013. She was Assistant Professor in Management Information Systems at University Illinois, Springfield (August 2011-July 2013) and Visiting Professor at Instituto Tecnológico Autónomo de México, Mexico City (August 2009-July 2011). Dr. Iriberri's research on virtual communities, crime reporting and information extraction, data visualization, and data mining is published in the International Journal of Electronic Government Research, Electronic Government: An International Journal, Decision Support Systems, and ACM Computing Surveys. She also published a book chapter and has 13 refereed proceedings. She serves as editorial reviewer for Hawaii International Conference on Systems Sciences (HICSS), European Conference on Information Systems (ECIS), Americas Conference on Information Systems (AMCIS), and International Conference on Information Systems (ICIS), Decision Support Systems and Journal of Information Technology for Development (ITD).

Arushi Jain is doing her M.tech in Information Security at Ambedkar Institute of Advanced Communication Technologies and Research,New Delhi,India. Her research interest include database, data warehouse, data mining, big data, virtual reality.

Goutam Jena is a graduate in Information Technology with a concentration in business analytics from Lawrence Technological University, Southfield, Michigan. He has done his bachelors in Mechanical Engineering in 2007 from Biju Patnaik University of Technology,India. He has almost 7 years of full time experience in Business Analysis, Product, Application & Infrastructure Support in a publicly traded multinational IT services company. He graduated in July 2015. He is currently working with a publicly traded IT consulting firm, Perficient Inc., as a senior business consultant, mostly on data related projects.

Mohammadreza Keyvanpour is an Assistant Professor at Alzahra University, Tehran, Iran. He received his B.S. in Software Engineering from Iran University of Science &Technology, Tehran, Iran. He received his M.S. and Ph.D. in Software

Engineering from Tarbiat Modares University, Tehran, Iran. His research interests include Data mining, Machine Learning and Database.

Chih-Hao Ku is an Assistant Professor in the College of Management (IT) at the Lawrence Technological University. He received his M.S. and Ph.D. in Information Systems and Technology at Claremont Graduate University. He received his B.S. and M.S. degree in Information Management in Taiwan. He is an active ACM, IEEE, ISSA, and AIS Member. His research currently focuses on natural language processing, decision support systems, and information visualization. He has published his work in the Journal of the American Society for Information Science and Technology (JASIST), Government Information Quarterly (GIQ), and in conferences among others.

Necmiye Genc Nayebi obtained her Bachelor Degree in Electrical Engineering in Sabanci University with honor and continued her study in the same field at Bogazici University in Turkey. She is also publisher of 2 European Patent Office and 1 Turkish Patent Office accepted patents. In addition to academic life, she has worked on various fields such as Software Development, Software Measurement and Analysis, Application, Network and Database security in last 9 years and holds PMP (Project Management Professional), CISA (Certified Information Systems Auditor), CEH (Certified Ethical Hacker), ISO 27001 Lead Auditor and ITIL (IT Infrastructure Library) V3 Certificates.

Olga Ormandjieva is Associate Professor in the Computer Science and Software Engineering (CSE) Department at Concordia University, Montreal, Quebec (Canada) and a member of the Ordre des Ingénieurs du Québec (OIQ). She holds a Ph.D. in Computer Science (2002) and Master's Degree in Computer Science and Mathematics (1987). Dr. Ormandjieva research interests are in the areas of Measurement in Software Engineering and its extension to the development of formal methods for modelling and monitoring functional and non-functional requirements. She has published 15 journal articles and over 90 conference and workshop papers to her name, as well as five book chapters. Dr. Ormandjieva has received grant funding from the Natural Sciences and Engineering Research Council (NSERC) since 2002. She has supervised over 25 graduate students. Currently she is teaching software engineering undergraduate and graduate courses at Concordia University.

Slim Rekhis received the University Habilitation and the Ph.D. degrees in Information and Communication Technologies from the Engineering School of Communications (SUP'Com, Tunisia) in 2007, and 2013, respectively. He is currently an Assistant Professor in the School of Communication engineering (SUP'Com,

University of Carthage, Tunisia) and member of the Communication Networks and Security (CN&S) research Laboratory at the same University. Dr. Rekhis is conducting his research activities in the area of digital investigation of security incidents, formal modeling, intrusion detection and tolerance, traceback of host and network attacks, wireless security and QoS, and security of implantable medical devices.

Shashi Shekhar, a McKnight Distinguished University Professor at the University of Minnesota, is a leading scholar in Geographic Information Systems (GIS). He co-edited an Encyclopedia of GIS and co-authored a Spatial Databases textbook. He received the IEEE-CS Technical Achievement Award, the UCGIS Education Award and was elected a Fellow of the IEEE and the AAAS. Shashi is a co-Editor-in-Chief of Geo-Informatica journal (Springer) and has served on the Computing Community Consortium Council, National Academies' committees (Mapping Sciences, GEOINT Workforce). He co-organized the "From GPS and Virtual Globes to Spatial Computing 2020" workshop to catalyze community research visions.

Ching Y. Suen is the Director of CENPARMI and the Honorary Concordia Chair on AI & Pattern Recognition. He received his Ph.D. degree from UBC (Vancouver) and his Master's degree from the University of Hong Kong. He has served as the Chairman of the Department of Computer Science and as the Associate Dean (Research) of the Faculty of Engineering and Computer Science of Concordia University. Prof. Suen has served at numerous national and international professional societies as President, Vice-President, Governor, and Director. He has given 45 invited/keynote papers at conferences and over 200 invited talks at various industries and academic institutions around the world. He has been the Principal Investigator or Consultant of 30 industrial projects. His research projects have been funded by the ENCS Faculty and the Distinguished Chair Programs at Concordia University, FCAR (Quebec), NSERC (Canada), the National Networks of Centres of Excellence (Canada), the Canadian Foundation for Innovation, and the industrial sectors in various countries, including Canada, France, Japan, Italy, and the United States. Dr. Suen has published 5 conference proceedings, 12 books and more than 500 papers, and many of them have been widely cited while the ideas in others have been applied in practical environments involving handwriting recognition, thinning methodologies, and multiple classifiers. Dr. Suen is the recipient of numerous awards, including the Gold Medal from the University of Bari (Italy 2012), the IAPR ICDAR Award (2005), the ITAC/NSERC national award (1992), and the "Concordia Lifetime Research Achievement" and "Concordia Fellow" awards (2008 and 1998 respectively). Prof. Suen has supervised 87 doctoral and master's students to completion, and guided/hosted 89 long-term visiting scientists and professors. He is a fellow of the IEEE (since 1986), IAPR (1994), and the Academy of Sciences of the

Royal Society of Canada (1995). Currently, he is the Editor-in-Chief of the journal of Pattern Recognition and an Adviser or Associate Editor of 5 journals. Actually he has held previous positions as Editor-in-Chief, or Associate Editor or Adviser of 5 other journals. He is not only the founder of three conferences: ICDAR, IWFHR/ICFHR, and VI, but has also organized numerous international conferences including ICPR, ICDAR, ICFHR, ICCPOL, and others. In 1997, he created the IAPR ICDAR Awards, to honour both young and established outstanding researchers in the field of Document Analysis and Recognition. He has always been fascinated by letters and characters, ever since he started his doctoral research on teaching the computer to read multifont documents with a voice output for the blind.

Xun Tang is a Ph.D. student at the University of Minnesota – Twin Cities in Computer Science. He received his Bachelor's and Master's degrees from Harbin Institute of Technology, Harbin, China in 2011 and 2013, respectively. His research interests include spatial data mining and spatial databases.

Index

J

L

M

N

O

P

R

S

www.ingramcontent.com/pod-product-compliance
Lightning Source LLC
LaVergne TN
LVHW080907300926
849162LV00003B/589
* 9 7 8 1 5 2 2 5 0 4 6 3 4 *